THE GREENWOOD ENCYCLOPEDIA OF
Women's Issues
WORLDWIDE

THE GREENWOOD ENCYCLOPEDIA OF
Women's Issues
WORLDWIDE

NORTH AMERICA AND THE CARIBBEAN

Editor-in-Chief
Lynn Walter
Volume Editor
Cheryl Toronto Kalny

GREENWOOD PRESS
Westport, Connecticut • London

Library of Congress Cataloging-in-Publication Data

The Greenwood encyclopedia of women's issues worldwide : North America and the
  Caribbean / Lynn Walter, editor-in-chief, Cheryl Toronto Kalny, volume editor.
    p. cm.
    Includes bibliographical references and index.
    ISBN 0–313–32787–4 (set : alk. paper)—ISBN 0–313–31852–2 (alk. paper)
    1. Women—North America—Social conditions. 2. Women's rights—North Amer-
ica. 3. Women—Caribbean Area—Social conditions 4. Women's rights—Caribbean
Area. I. Title: Encyclopedia of women's issues worldwide. II. Walter, Lynn, 1945–
III. Kalny, Cheryl Toronto.
  HQ1400.G74 2003
  305.42'097—dc21   2003048524

British Library Cataloguing in Publication Data is available.

Library of Congress Catalog Card Number: 2003048524
ISBN: 0–313–32787–4 (set)
      0–313–32087–X (Asia and Oceania)
      0–313–32129–9 (Central and South America)
      0–313–31855–7 (Europe)
      0–313–31888–3 (The Middle East and North Africa)
      0–313–31852–2 (North America and the Caribbean)
      0–313–32145–0 (Sub-Saharan Africa)

First published in 2003

Greenwood Press, 88 Post Road West, Westport, CT 06881
An imprint of Greenwood Publishing Group, Inc.
www.greenwood.com

Printed in the United States of America

∞

The paper used in this book complies with the
Permanent Paper Standard issued by the National
Information Standards Organization (Z39.48–1984).

10 9 8 7 6 5 4 3 2 1

Volume map cartography by Mapcraft.com. Country map cartography by Bookcomp, Inc.

CONTENTS

CONTENTS

*The Six-Volume Comprehensive Index begins on
page 569 of the final volume, Sub-Saharan Africa*

SET FOREWORD

The Greenwood Encyclopedia of Women's Issues Worldwide is a six-volume set presenting authoritative, comprehensive, and current data on a broad range of contemporary women's issues in more than 130 countries around the world. Each volume covers a major populated world region: Asia and Oceania, Central and South America, Europe, the Middle East and North Africa, North America and the Caribbean, and Sub-Saharan Africa. Volumes are organized by chapters, with each focusing on a specific country or group of countries or islands, following a broad outline of topics—education, employment and the economy, family and sexuality, health, politics and law, religion and spirituality, and violence. Under these topics, contributors were asked to consider a range of contemporary issues from illiteracy and wage discrepancies to unequal familial roles and political participation and to highlight issues of special concern to women in the country. In this way, the set provides a global perspective on women's issues, ensures breadth and depth of issue coverage, and facilitates cross-national comparison.

Along with locating women's agenda in specific national and historical contexts, each chapter looks at the cultural differences among women as well as the significance of class, religion, sexuality, and race on their lives. And, as women's movements and their non-governmental organizations (NGOs) are among the most worldwide forms of civic participation, their effectiveness in addressing women's issues is also examined. In addition to focusing on national and local organizations, many authors also highlight the major role the United Nations has played in addressing women's issues nationally and in supporting women's networks globally and point to the importance of its 1979 Convention on the Elimination of All Forms of Discrimination Against Women (CEDAW), which is still the most comprehensive international agreement on the rights of women.

Contributors were chosen for their expertise on women's issues in the country or area about which they write. Each contributor provides an authoritative resource guide with suggested reading, web sites, films/videos, and organizations as well as a selected bibliography and extensive references. The chapters and resource guides are designed for students, scholars, and engaged citizens to study contemporary women's issues in depth in specific countries and from a global perspective.

This ambitious project has been made possible by the work of many scholars who contributed their knowledge and commitment. I want to thank all of them and especially the other volume editors, Manisha Desai, Cheryl Toronto Kalny, Amy Lind, Bahira Sherif-Trask, and Aili Mari Tripp. Thanks also to Christine Marra of Marrathon Productions and Wendi Schnaufer of Greenwood Publishing Group for their editorial assistance.

As I read the many chapters of this series what struck me most was the sheer force and determination of the many women and men who are seeking solutions to the problems of inequality and poverty, discrimination, and injustice that lie at the root of women's experiences worldwide. I hope this series will further their vision.

Lynn Walter, Editor-in-Chief

USER'S GUIDE

The Greenwood Encyclopedia of Women's Issues Worldwide is a six-volume set covering the world's most populated regions:

Asia and Oceania

Central and South America

Europe

The Middle East and North Africa

North America and the Caribbean

Sub-Saharan Africa

All volumes contain an introduction from the editor-in-chief that overviews women's issues around the world today and introduces the set. Each volume editor broadly characterizes contemporary women's issues in the particular region(s). The volumes are divided into chapters ordered alphabetically by country name. A few chapters treat several countries (e.g., Tajikistan, Kazakhstan, Turkmenistan, and Kyrgyzstan, which are grouped together as Central Asia) or a group of islands (e.g., the Netherlands Antilles).

The comprehensive coverage facilitates comparisons between nations and among regions. The following is an outline showing the sections of each chapter. In rare instances where information was not available or applicable for a particular country, sections were omitted.

Profile of [the Nation]

A paragraph on the land, people(s), form of government, economy, and demographic statistics on female/male population, infant mortality, maternal mortality, total fertility, and life expectancy.

Overview of Women's Issues

A brief introduction to the major issues to be covered, giving the reader a sense of the state of women's lives in the country.

Education

Opportunities

Literacy

Employment and Economics

Job/Career Opportunities

Pay

Working Conditions

    Sexual Harassment

Support for Mothers/Caretakers

    Maternal Leave

    Daycare

    Family and Medical Leave

Inheritance and Property Rights

Migration

Social/Government Programs

    Sustainable Development

    Welfare [and Welfare Reform]

Family and Sexuality

Gender Roles

Marriage

Reproduction

    Sex Education

    Contraception and Abortion

    Teen Pregnancy

Health

Health Care Access

Diseases and Disorders

    AIDS [and Sexually Transmitted Diseases]

    Eating Disorders

    Cancer

    Heart Disease

    Depression

Politics and Law
Suffrage
Political Participation
Women's Rights
>   Feminist Movements
>   Lesbian Rights
>>   Marriage
>>   Parenthood
Military Service

Religion and Spirituality
Women's Roles
Rituals and Religious Practices
Religious Law

Violence
Domestic Violence
Rape/Sexual Assault
Trafficking in Women and Children
War and Military Repression

Outlook for the Twenty-first Century

Notes

Resource Guide
Suggested Reading
Videos/Films
Web Sites
Organizations

Selected Bibliography

A regional map is in the inside cover of each volume. Additionally, each chapter has an accompanying country or mini-region map. Each volume has an index consisting of subject and person entries; a comprehensive set index is included at the end of the Sub-Saharan Africa volume.

INTRODUCTION

Women in North America and the Caribbean, on the surface, might appear to have little in common other than a geographic proximity. What issues would women in urban, highly industrialized, populous northern societies share with women in small, largely agrarian Caribbean island states? Indeed, significant political, economic, and social differences exist not only between the two regions, north and south, but even within the Caribbean community itself. Nevertheless, threads of commonality, such as institutionalized patriarchy, economic marginalization, and domestic and public violence, connect women around the globe and ultimately offer the opportunity for women to recognize and understand each other across potential barriers of language, culture, geography, race, and socioeconomic class.

North America and the Caribbean examines women's issues in fourteen chapters, three on North America—Canada, the United States, and Mexico—and eleven comprehensively covering the Caribbean—the Bahamas, Barbados, Cuba, the Dominican Republic, Haiti, Jamaica, Puerto Rico, Trinidad and Tobago, the Netherlands Antilles (which includes the Leeward Islands of Aruba, Bonaire, and Curaçao, and the Windward Islands of St. Maarten, St. Eustatius, and Saba), the French Caribbean (which includes Guadeloupe and Martinique), and the former British Caribbean holdings of the Organization of Eastern Caribbean States (which consists of seven regular members, Antigua and Barbuda, Dominica, Granada, Montserrat, Saint Kitts and Nevis, Saint Lucia, and Saint Vincent), and the Grenadines (along with the associated member states of Anguilla and the British Virgin Islands). Each chapter is a self-contained study of an individual country or nation and of the specific issues and challenges facing women there today. The outline of the chapters allows for comparative analysis within the volume or across the entire set. Each chapter opens with a brief profile of the country and an overview of women's issues. This introductory material is followed by an analysis of women's issues in seven major areas: education, employment and economics, family and sexuality, health, politics and law, religion and spirituality, and violence. These major topics are further subdivided for a closer look at women's lived experiences from country to country. Each chapter concludes with an outlook for the twenty-first century that sums up the major challenges still confronting women in the respective countries. Resource guides at the end of each chapter provide additional reference resources for students and researchers. Suggested readings, videos/films, web sites, and organizations relevant to women's issues give readers opportunities to pursue their own research quests, seek additional information in any of the topic areas, or make direct contact with groups and organizations involved in women's issues today.

NORTH AMERICA

Canada, the United States, and Mexico share much in common, including geography, culture, and history. They also face common problems of environmental degradation, drug trafficking, and climate changes. In recent years, a number of trilateral agreements have sought to cement the economic and social bonds shared by these North American partners, including the North American Free Trade Agreement, the Memorandum of Understanding signed in September 1999, and the Smart Border Declaration signed by Canada and the United States after the September 11, 2001, terrorist attacks on the United States.

Population figures and demographics are similar for the three nations. All are highly populated, urban-dwelling, ethnically diverse, and industrially based societies with representative forms of government. In addition, each is an overwhelmingly Christian nation that nevertheless endorses religious pluralism and toleration.

The overall quality-of-life standards for women and children are similarly high in each country, although minority and indigenous women in each country often experience discriminatory treatment. In the United States, Native American life expectancy rates are lower than national averages, while infant mortality rates among black communities are significantly higher than the national average. In Mexico, deaths attributed to obstetric causes are highest among indigenous populations where women have little access to prenatal care, and the secondary-school dropout rate among Aboriginal populations in Canada is nearly double the national average.[1]

Not surprisingly, women throughout North America suffer similar health problems stemming, in part, from exposure to the pollutants of highly industrialized societies which often produce higher standards of living at the expense of degraded environments. After heart disease and stroke, lung, breast, and reproductive cancers are leading causes of death for women in Canada, the United States, and Mexico. In addition, malnutrition-related deaths are common among indigenous women in Mexico, while tuberculosis continues to ravage indigenous communities in the United States and Mexico. Women make up almost 25 percent of the HIV/AIDS-infected population in both Canada and the United States, and rates are increasing among women in the poor, rural states of Mexico. In the United States, more than 47 percent of all reported HIV/AIDS cases are among African Americans, and this disease is now the second-leading cause of death among African American women.

THE CARIBBEAN

Since the end of World War II, continuous change has marked the histories and societies of the Caribbean. Politically, a number of former colonies achieved independence in the postwar decades, including Jamaica, Trinidad and Tobago, the Dominican Republic, Barbados, Haiti, and the Bahamas. In each case, a parliamentary democracy was established, and universal suffrage was achieved. Other colonies retained ties with European partners after negotiating new relationships. The islands of the Netherlands Antilles became autonomous members of the Kingdom of the Netherlands in 1954, and residents of Martinique and Guadeloupe were granted French citizenship in 1946. The Organization of Eastern Caribbean States (OECS) was formed shortly after its members achieved independence from Great Britain in the 1970s. Cuba, which had been an American protectorate since 1898, underwent a socialist revolution in 1959. One exception to this timing of political change is Puerto Rico, whose people had been granted U.S. citizenship in 1917.

Throughout most of the region, the quality of life has improved significantly for women and children during these same decades. Life expectancy rates for Caribbean women average about seventy-six years, infant mortality rates range from 7.89 per 1,000 live births in Cuba to 24.5 in Jamaica, and the female literacy percentages have risen into the 90s in most countries. The lone exception to these encouraging numbers today is Haiti, which falls significantly behind in life expectancy (approximately forty-nine years), infant mortality rate (74 percent), and female literacy (46 percent).

Several diverse cultural and racial streams wind through the Caribbean, most notably with African and Spanish roots. Between 90 percent and 100 percent of the peoples in the Bahamas, Barbados, Jamaica, the French Caribbean, and Haiti are of African descent. Spanish history and culture continue to heavily influence Cuba, Puerto Rico, and the Dominican Republic, while Afro-Trinidadian and Indo-Trinidadian populations are almost equally represented in Trinidad and Tobago. Cultural variations, social customs, and religious affiliations are often tied to these diverse roots. A cult of male authority (patriarchy) and machismo and a rigid differentiation of gender roles continue to dominate public and private life in predominantly Roman Catholic Puerto Rico, the Dominican Republic, and Cuba, although Communist rule for more than forty years has lessened the church's hold in Cuba. Similarly, African-based religions such as Santeria and Vodou are more commonly practiced in those parts of the Caribbean having significant African populations.

Women's health issues continue to be a concern throughout the Caribbean community, especially the escalating HIV/AIDS infection rates. The Caribbean Association for Feminist Research and Action (CAFRA) has targeted AIDS reduction as one of its most urgent goals.[2] The Caribbean has the second-worst infection rate in the world after sub-Saharan Africa, and within the region, Jamaica has the highest increase in the rate of HIV/AIDS infections. AIDS is the second-leading cause of death today for Jamaicans in the age group thirty to thirty-four. Almost 10 percent of the population in Haiti is infected with the virus, and in Trinidad and Tobago 45 percent of all new AIDS cases in 1997 were female, with a female-to-male infection rate of five to one. International agencies from the United States, Canada, Great Britain, and Germany are working in conjunction with the Caribbean Epidemiology Center located in Trinidad and Tobago in its efforts to support the prevention strategies and programs of nongovernmental organizations (NGOs) throughout the region.[3] This deadly epidemic threatens the social, economic, and developmental goals of the entire Caribbean region.

WOMEN'S RIGHTS

The impact of international women's rights conventions such as the Universal Declaration of Human Rights in 1948 and the 1979 Convention on the Elimination of All Forms of Discrimination against Women (CEDAW) would be hard to exaggerate. Since CEDAW, most of the countries in the Western Hemisphere have not only ratified the convention, but have worked hard to bring their countries into conformity with its articles. By the mid-1980s, the Netherlands Antilles, Jamaica, Trinidad and Tobago, the OECS, the Bahamas, and most of the Caribbean had signed CEDAW. Mexico, which had hosted the First World Conference on Women in 1975, ratified CEDAW in 1981, as did Canada. The United States has not ratified CEDAW.[4]

Regionally and nationally, women's rights groups continue to work toward a variety of goals and objectives. Throughout the Caribbean community, CAFRA coordinates various feminist objectives, such as female literacy, reproductive rights, and economic and political opportunities being advanced by such organizations as Developing Alternatives for Women Now (DAWN), and Women and Development (WAND). PROFAMILIA (International Planned Parenthood Federation) also operates throughout the region. In Canada, Women's Legal Education and Action Fund (LEAF) is a national organization working to promote women's equality, similar to the National Organization for Women (NOW) in the United States.

Individual countries throughout the Caribbean have seen the emergence of feminist groups in response to specific issues and circumstances directly related to their individual situations. Kay Fanm in Haiti, where the majority of female workers are subsistence farmers, grew out of earlier grassroots, peasant-based women's groups such as Tet Kole (Put Our Heads to Work) and Tet Ansanm (Let's Unite Our Heads). The Movement of Dominico-Haitian Women (MUDHA) is working to organize and unionize Dominican and Haitian women living and working in the sugarcane plantations. The 3.2-million-member Federation of Cuban Women (FMC) has worked for four decades to advance gender equality in all areas of life in Cuba, as has the Association of Women's Organizations of Jamaica (AWOJ) in Jamaica.

GLOBALIZATION

When NAFTA was signed on January 1, 1994, proponents predicted that the creation of the world's second-largest free trade zone would mean jobs and economic prosperity not only in Canada and the United States but in Mexico as well. Critics today point to the proliferation of foreign-owned multinational corporations (*maquiladoras*) along the U.S.-Mexican border as representative of how NAFTA has failed. These corporations take advantage of the cheap labor in Mexico, much of which is female, as well as the lax enforcement of environmental and worker's rights laws. Economic dependency is produced instead of higher standards of living.[5]

Globalization has brought similar ills to parts of the Caribbean. The internationalization of economies has increased poverty, hunger, and inequality while decreasing social services throughout the region. In the Dominican Republic, women who are employed in the free trade zones are often required to produce certificates of sterilization and are paid exploitative wages. In Jamaica, efforts to improve competitiveness in a global marketplace have resulted in downsizing and layoffs that have disproportionately affected women workers, who make up 66.9 percent of these "redundancies." One result of high female unemployment rates in the region is the increase in the numbers of women finding jobs in the informal sectors of the marketplace, such as the street vendors (*ti machann*) in Haiti, along with an increased reliance on extended family and friends for child care. Unemployment rates for females in the OECS, where most women work in the service industry, range from 5 percent in Antigua and Barbuda to more than 20 percent in Dominica and Saint Vincent and the Grenadines.

Another result of high female unemployment rates is out-migration, a growing phenomenon throughout the region. Significant proportions of the populations of Puerto Rico, Trinidad, and the Dominican Republic have migrated to the United States and Canada seeking jobs. Today, one out of every six Haitians lives abroad. Globalization and out-migration have so depleted government revenues in such places as the Dominican Republic, Haiti, and Barbados that social services such as maternal care, child care, and health care are being cut and, in some cases, completely defunded.

The economic situations of women in the British, Dutch, French, and U.S. dependencies vary from country to country. In Guadeloupe and Martinique, where tourism is now the leading industry, women's unemployment rate is 33 percent. In female-headed families, however, which are 25 percent of all families, the unemployment rate is above 50 percent. Women's wages are approximately 85 percent of men's wages. The structural adjustment program in the Netherlands Antilles has made women's lives more difficult in recent years and has contributed to the feminization of poverty. Women are overrepresented in the unemployment and welfare rolls and in 1900 earned approximately 20 percent less pay than men. The economy in the OECS, as in other Caribbean countries that depend on tourism dollars, has been substantially and negatively affected by the decline of tourism following the September 11, 2001, terrorist attacks. Puerto Rican women, whether living and working on the island or on the mainland, earn substantially less than their male counterparts and are thus disproportionately overrepresented in the ranks of the poor.

POLITICAL PARTICIPATION

Most women in North America had won the right to vote and hold public office by 1950. After more than seventy years of ceaseless struggle, women in the United States won the suffrage battle with the passage of a constitutional amendment in 1920, the Susan B. Anthony (or Nineteenth) Amendment. In Canada, female suffrage began in the western provinces in 1916, but Quebec held out until 1940. Universal female suffrage, including Native women, was not realized until 1960. Women in Mexico were accorded full citizenship rights in 1953 when they became eligible to vote in popular elections. Women's full and equal participation in the political process, however, has been gradual and continues to be limited in the three North American nations. In the last forty years, only three women have held cabinet-level posts in Mexico, and women make up only about 11 percent of the U.S. Congress. No woman has reached the presidency in either Mexico or the United States. Canada, however, elected its first female prime minister, Kim Campbell, in 1993.

Cuba and Puerto Rico were the first Caribbean countries to grant women the vote. Both were U.S. protectorates when universal suffrage was granted in 1933 and 1935, respectively. Not until 1992, however, was the first Puerto Rican woman elected to the U.S. House of Representatives (as a congressperson from New York), and the first female governor in the history of Puerto Rico, Sila Calderón, was elected in 2000.

Since the Cuban revolution in 1959, and despite women's active participation in that revolution, women have made up only about 25 percent of the Communist Party. No Cuban woman has ever been a member of the

Communist Party Secretariat. In the Dutch protectorates of the Netherlands Antilles, women won the right to vote in 1948 and shortly after that elected the first female member of Parliament in 1950. Women today continue to work toward a 50 percent representation rate as ministers, commissioners, and cabinet members. In the French protectorates of Martinique and Guadeloupe, women were granted French citizenship rights in 1946. Since then, women have remained underrepresented in political life. Only 5 percent of the members of the General Council in Guadeloupe and Martinique are women. In 1992, a woman was elected president of the Regional Council of Guadeloupe, but the Regional Council of Martinique has no female members today. The political situation for women in the OECS varies from country to country. Women hold 20 percent of ministerial positions in Dominica, but no women have reached ministerial-level positions in Antigua and Barbuda and Saint Kitts and Nevis.

The same pattern of limited female participation in the government, especially at the national level, continues throughout much of the Caribbean. In the Bahamas, the first woman was elected to Parliament in 1982, but women continued to hold fewer than 10 percent of seats in the House of Assembly. Women in Jamaica and Trinidad and Tobago won the right to vote in 1944 and 1946, respectively, but more than fifty years later they continue to be underrepresented in Parliament. Of thirty-six elected representatives in the 2001 general election in Trinidad and Tobago, five were women. Despite the fact that women in the Dominican Republic were granted suffrage in 1942, competing tyrants (*caudillos*) with their death squads have kept tight control over the political system until recent elections. Both Barbados and Haiti are examples of countries with elected female heads of state that nevertheless continue to have limited numbers of women in government posts. In Barbados, the deputy prime minister, the minister of foreign affairs and trade, the minister of education, and the governor of the Central Bank are all women. Despite these achievements, only 20 percent of elected officials are female. Having a female provisional president of Haiti in 1990–1991, Ertha Pascal-Trouillot, has not translated into permanent political power for Haitian women. In 1994, only about 4 percent of legislative seats in Haiti are held by women.

FAMILY AND SEXUALITY

In North America and the Caribbean, as in many other parts of the world, women are the caretakers of the old, the sick, and the young. In addition, in most communities in the Western Hemisphere, men rarely cook, clean, do the marketing, or run the households. A high degree of gender-role differentiation exists, often reinforced by cultural and religious norms. Motherhood is seen as a principal characteristic of women's identities throughout the Caribbean, and the extended family system, with multiple generations of women raising the children, is a common pattern in the region. Ancestral traditions also account for distinctive family patterns. In Trinidad and Tobago, families of African descent tend to be matrilineal and matrilocal—mother centered and female headed. Indo-Trinidadian families, who tend to dominate the middle and upper classes, are more often patrilineal, with formal and legal marriages. However, women's power within the family does not translate into the economic or political realms.

In addition to legally binding civil unions, various patterns of relationships exist throughout the Caribbean. Religious marriages are the ideal in regions dominated by the Catholic Church, but cohabitation is widely practiced in much of the region. In common-law unions, called *plasaj* in Haiti, men and women establish a common household and raise their children together. In visiting unions, however, no joint household is established, and the union is more informal. Whatever the form of union, cultural norms dictate sexual monogamy for females but not for males. So widespread is the phenomenon of philandering husbands and partners that in the Dutch Caribbean there exists a tradition of bringing up someone else's child as one's own (*kria*).

Reproductive issues vary from region to region throughout North America and the Caribbean. In predominantly Roman Catholic Mexico, contraception and abortion are strongly opposed by the church, although sex education programs are taught in government schools. Contraceptive use varies from region to region in Mexico, with only about 30 percent of indigenous populations using contraceptive measures. Legal abortion is restricted to medical emergency and rape cases, with the result that clandestine and botched procedures continue to take the lives of Mexican women every year. Women in the United States have struggled for reproductive rights since the beginning of the twentieth century. It took two landmark Supreme Court decisions to affirm women's constitutional right to birth control (1965) and to an abortion (1973). Efforts to restrict these rights have been mounted since then and, as the United States enters the twenty-first century, these reproductive issues remain among the most controversial topics in women's rights. Similarly, although access to contraception and abortion was liberalized in 1969 in Canada, access to these rights can vary from province to province.

In many parts of the Caribbean, church and culture discourage contraceptive use and abortions. In Haiti, where both Catholicism and Vodou disapprove of contraception and abortion, birth rates are some of the highest in the Western Hemisphere. In Barbados and the French Caribbean, even though the governments support family-planning associations, contraceptive use remains relatively low. Condoms are used primarily with prostitutes to prevent diseases, rather than with spouses and partners to prevent births. Abortion is illegal in the OECS, and in states such as Saint

Vincent and the Grenadines, where more than one-third of the population is under fifteen years of age, teen pregnancy remains a serious problem. In those countries where abortion is illegal, such as the Bahamas and the Dominican Republic, high maternal mortality rates signal the tragic results of underground, unregulated, and unprofessional abortion procedures.[6]

VIOLENCE

Violence against women and children, whether in public places or in the privacy of family life, is a serious and growing problem virtually everywhere in North America and the Caribbean. In the United States, by the end of the twentieth century, the Federal Bureau of Investigation (FBI) had categorized violent assaults against women, both physical and sexual, as being at epidemic levels. The Violence against Women Act passed in 1994 continues to address the growing problem of domestic violence, which today threatens one in four American women. The governments of Mexico and Canada have also created specialized agencies and laws to deal with public and private violence against women. Minority and indigenous women particularly experience mortality rates due to violence nearly three times those of women in the general population.

While gender-based violence is pervasive in the Caribbean, cultural attitudes continue to reinforce the view that domestic violence is a private affair. The stigma associated with rape and incest continues to deter the reporting of these crimes in Jamaica, while in Barbados convicted rapists often receive lighter sentences than petty thieves. While some governments, such as Barbados, the Bahamas, and Trinidad and Tobago, have responded by supporting crisis centers and antiviolence legislation, in other countries, statistics on violence against women are not even compiled. Such is the case in the Dominican Republic, where public prosecutors often reclassify violence complaints and release assailants once the victim's injuries are healed, usually within ten days. Similarly, the Netherlands Antilles does not have specific domestic violence legislation, and there are few shelters for battered women and children other than an informal network of women hiding victims in their homes. In Haiti there is a culture of nonreporting, and no laws against violence exist. In fact, violence against women is often blamed on the victims for disrespecting or disobeying their male partners. In such a case, where human rights violations are accepted as normal social behavior, the phenomenon of roving bands of thugs who regularly break into homes to rape and beat women should not be surprising. Cuba stands alone in the Caribbean with very low rates of reported violence against women, possibly because the actual number of cases is being suppressed, or because the violence itself is being suppressed in a country where 45 percent of judges and 65 percent of district attorneys are women.

OUTLOOK FOR THE TWENTY-FIRST CENTURY

The advance of women's rights in North America and the Caribbean has been a long, hard-fought battle that continues today. Every gain made in the twentieth century in terms of quality-of-life issues and the continuing expansion of basic human rights must be celebrated and protected, but also weighed against the sometimes staggering problems, such as violence, voicelessness, and poverty, that continue to limit and destroy many lives. Nothing has ever been willingly given to women, and hard-won gains for some have not proven to be gains for all. Future advances will not be any easier to accomplish and will remain dependent on the concerted efforts of women working with governmental and nongovernmental groups in their own countries and regions, as well as joining forces throughout the world in support of international agencies, programs, and conventions working for women's rights on many fronts.

NOTES

1. Data in this introduction are taken from the chapters and U.S. Department of State, www.state.gov.
2. CAFRA (Caribbean Association for Feminist Research and Action), www.cafra. org.
3. United States Agency for International Development, www.usaid.gov.
4. United Nations Division for the Advancement of Women, Convention on the Elimination of All Forms of Discrimination against Women, www.un.org/ womenwatch/daw/cedaw.
5. International Forum on Globalization, www.ifg.org.
6. United Nations Development Fund for Women, www.unifem.undp.org.

SELECTED BIBLIOGRAPHY

Barriteau, Eudine. *The Political Economy of Gender in the Twentieth-Century Caribbean.* New York: Palgrave, 2001.

Flexner, Eleanor. *Century of Struggle: The Woman's Rights Movement in the United States.* Rev. ed. Cambridge, MA: Belknap Press of Harvard University Press, 1975.

Freeman, Carla. *High Tech and High Heels in the Global Economy: Women, Work, and Pink-Collar Identities in the Caribbean.* Durham, NC: Duke University Press, 1999.

Hamilton, Roberta. *Gendering the Vertical Mosaic: Feminist Perspectives on Canadian Society.* Toronto: Copp Clark Publishing, 1996.

McGlen, Nancy E., and Karen O'Connor. *Women, Politics, and American Society.* 2nd ed. Upper Saddle River, NJ: Prentice Hall, 1998.

Mohammed, Patricia, ed. *Gendered Realities: Essays in Caribbean Feminist Thought.* Kingston, Jamaica: University of the West Indies Press, 2002.

Prentice, Alison, et al. *Canadian Women: A History.* 2nd ed. Toronto: Harcourt Brace and Co., 1996.

Safa, Helen I. *The Myth of the Male Breadwinner: Women and Industrialization in the Caribbean*. Boulder, CO: Westview Press, 1995.

Senior, Olive. *Working Miracles: Women's Lives in the English-Speaking Caribbean*. Cave Hill, Barbados: Institute of Social and Economic Research, 1991.

Shepherd, Verene, Bridget Brereton, and Barbara Bailey, eds. *Engendering History: Caribbean Women in Historical Perspective*. New York: St. Martin's Press, 1995.

Tiano, Susan. *Patriarchy on the Line: Labor, Gender, and Ideology in the Mexican Maquila Industry*. Philadelphia: Temple University Press, 1994.

I

THE BAHAMAS

Audrey Ingram Roberts

PROFILE OF THE BAHAMAS

The Commonwealth of the Bahamas is an Atlantic Ocean archipelago of approximately 700 islands and 2,500 small limestone islets or cays. This 750-mile-long chain of islands and cays stretches from the northwest island of Bimini, located less than fifty nautical miles south of Florida, to the southeasternmost island of Inagua, located within fifty nautical miles of the Caribbean islands of Cuba and Hispaniola (Haiti and the Dominican Republic). The area of sea over which the islands extend is about 100,000 square miles.

The dry season lasts from December through April, during which time the climate is mild and cool. The rainy season lasts from May through December and is hot and humid, particularly from June through August. Between forty and sixty inches of rain fall annually.

The Bahamas has a land area of approximately 5,352 square miles and a total population of 303,611 (147,715 males, 155,896 females) inhabiting about thirty of the islands.[1] Although the island of Andros is the largest (2,300 square miles), the most populated areas are Nassau, the capital, located on New Providence Island (80 square miles), with a

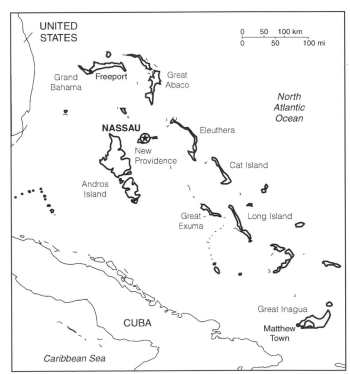

population of 210,842 and density per square mile of 2,635, and Freeport on Grand Bahama (530 square miles), with a population of 46,994 and density per square mile of 89. The other inhabited islets and cays make up the Family Islands or, as they were named in colonial times, the Out Islands. The smallest of these are Harbour Island and Spanish Well, with areas of 12 and 2 square miles, respectively.

The Lucayan Indians of the Taino culture of the Arawak Indians who inhabited the northern Caribbean Islands were the first inhabitants of the Bahamas. By landing in 1492 on the Bahama island he named San Salvador, Christopher Columbus brought the Bahamas and indeed all of the New World under Spanish domination. Shortly thereafter, the Lucayan population was greatly reduced, and the islands were eventually depopulated. In the late 1640s, the Eleutheran Adventurers, a group chartered in England aiming to escape religious persecution, made the first organized attempt to resettle the islands. In 1785, as reported by the lieutenant governor, the population exceeded 7,000.[2]

The population is predominantly of African descent. However, there are small minorities of peoples of European, Greek, Chinese, and Lebanese descent. These minorities dominate the mercantile sector. There is a large illegal immigrant population of Haitians, Jamaicans, and Cubans. The proximity of the northwest and the southeast of the Bahamas to Florida and to Haiti, Jamaica, and Cuba, respectively, is a key factor in this troubling issue of illegal immigrants. Illegal Cuban immigrants, more than Haitians and Jamaicans, tend to be transient in the Bahamas and determined to reach the United States.

The Bahamas has enjoyed a rich constitutional history of free parliamentary elections since 1729, making it one of the oldest assemblies in the British Empire, along with Barbados and Bermuda. Political advancement and activities in the 1950s led to notable constitutional changes in 1963 and later. In 1962, universal suffrage was implemented; 1963 brought ministerial government, and majority rule was instituted in 1967.

Independence from Britain was gained on July 10, 1973. The Bahamas is an independent sovereign state with a political system of parliamentary democracy. The Constitution of the Bahamas provides for a governor general who exercises executive authority on behalf of the queen. It also provides for a cabinet that has the general direction and control of the government and is collectively responsible to Parliament, which is headed by the prime minister. The two-chamber British-style Parliament has a lower chamber, the House of Assembly, an elected body that has a sitting life of five years, and an upper chamber, the Senate, with senators appointed by the Governor General. The judiciary, as provided by the constitution, is an independent body headed by a chief justice and with the Privy Council as the highest court.

The Bahamian economy is predominantly a market economy inextricably linked with that of the United States. The Bahamian dollar has parity with the U.S. dollar. The main engine of the economy is tourism, which employs approximately two-thirds of the population. However, since September 11, 2001, unemployment has risen as tourists from North America have stayed home.

Banking, particularly international financial services, is the second driver of the economy. The Bahamas is one of the world's leading financial centers. Commercial banks, of which there are seven, had total domestic assets of $4,850 million in 2001.[3] Agriculture, light manufacturing, and industry make up a rather small sector of this service-driven economy. Exports from these sectors are significantly lower than imports.

The Bahamas attracts foreign investments because of its economic and political stability coupled with protective legislation and the absence of any direct taxation. Much of this investment is used to finance hotel and resort development as well as related public utilities, communications, and other infrastructure development essential for a modern hospitality industry and efficient international financial services.

Since 2000, the population has grown at an average annual rate of 1.8 percent. The Bahamas has a youthful population; 29.4 percent is under fifteen years of age, 64.9 percent is between the ages of fifteen and sixty-four, and a mere 5.6 percent is 65 or over. Life expectancy for females is 75.3 years and for men is 68.4 years. The total fertility rate is 2.2 percent. The birth rate is 17.4 and the death rate is 5.3. The infant mortality rate is 14.8 and the maternal mortality rate (per 10,000 live births) was 3.8 in 2000.

OVERVIEW OF WOMEN'S ISSUES

The Bureau of Women's Affairs is the national agency for the advancement of women in the Bahamas. Established in 1981, what was then called the Women's Desk was set up in the Ministry of Labour, Youth, Sports, and Community Affairs as a response to recommendations by the International Women's Conference held in Mexico in 1980. In 1987, it was upgraded to the Women's Affairs Unit with the goal of promoting the participation of Bahamian women in national and international development efforts. The unit advised the formulation of a policy on women's affairs at the national level.

A Bahamian policy on women was drafted in 1987 and revised in May 1991. The National Women's Advisory Council, established in 1985, was central to the process of consultation and participation in the formulation of a National Policy Statement on Women. All these initiatives were undertaken pursuant to the mandate of the Decade for Women from 1975 to 1985. The National Policy Statement highlights major areas of concern still relevant in 2002, such as the family and social structure; education; employment; national machinery; implementation of objectives; staffing; discrimination in areas of inheritance, citizenship, employment, divorce, and family support; violence against women; and health and nutrition.

Funding (government expenditure and bilateral/multilateral financial assistance) and minimum objectives to be achieved by the year 2002 were added to the major issues to be addressed by the revised statement of 1991. Factors included among the minimum objectives to be achieved by 2002 were more comprehensive measures for health education, nutrition, family-life education, family planning, and other welfare services. Emphasis was placed on including more women in policy making locally—in the electoral process and legislative, particularly constitutional, changes. Mechanisms to monitor and assess components of the statement were included.

The statement places women in the context of the family rather than as a separate gender with its own issues and rights. It also gives women the vanguard position in the policy's aim of strengthening the Bahamian family and ultimately the nation. The policy takes an efficiency approach to Bahamian women's development on the assumption that women's economic participation will lead to increased equity.[4] Given this neoliberal market-oriented policy framework, women are targeted as beneficiaries and participants. Hence interventions made through, for instance, programs addressing education and employment needs of women are posited as ways of harnessing women's labor to make national development more efficient rather than making development work for women. Since the Beijing World Conference on Women in 1995, the Bureau of Women's Affairs has continued to focus on poverty, violence against women, economic empowerment of women, women in power and decision making, and health.

EDUCATION

Opportunities

Schooling is compulsory for children between the ages of five and fourteen. The focus for elementary students is on "achieving literacy and numeric skills, fostering a sense of cultural identity and developing a positive attitude towards self, learning and country."[5]

In the public secondary schools, students do not compete for places, and the system provides both practical and academic subjects with programs designed to accommodate the range of abilities and aptitudes represented in the wider society. Equal access to secondary education was enhanced in the late 1970s and early 1980s with the provision of central secondary schools in major islands of the Family Islands. The all-age school, found almost exclusively in the Family Islands, provides both primary and secondary instruction.

The total enrollment in educational institutions in 2001 was 66,240. It appears that in the Bahamas, access to education is not gender determined. Both primary and secondary levels of the formal education system show little difference in the rates of participation by females and males. However, it has been observed that in the transition from primary to secondary school, male students are more likely to drop out or take advantage of the school leaving age of fourteen years.[6]

More females than males enroll at the tertiary level. Presently, male students at the College of the Bahamas make up less than one-third of the total student population. Enrollment in programs offered by other postsecondary institutions, private and offshore institutions, also reflects this pattern of significantly more female enrollment and participation than male. Only the Bahamas Technical and Vocational Institute before its upgrade from an industrial training center was an exception to this pattern of enrollment and indicated a reverse trend of more male enrollment. However, since its status was upgraded, the institute has had a fairly balanced pattern of males and females.

The superior performance and achievement of women in education do not seem to be reflected in their overall economic condition. One of the factors responsible for this is gender stereotyping in the school curricula that directs girls toward clerical and secretarial jobs and the care economy and boys to the technological and scientific areas. Such discrimination, although unintentional, has resulted in the deprivation of opportunity to develop intellectually.

Literacy

In the context of open access, literacy becomes a concern of quality. As in the rest of the Caribbean, the Bahamas does not have a problem of equal and open access to education. It is the quality of education that is the problem. Although no scientific evidence exists, experience and national educational attainment statistics suggest that the differential in literacy achievement favors girls. As regards the Bahamas general certificate of secondary education, not only are there more subject entries by female than by male students, but success rates among females are reflected in the discrepancy between males and females in college entrance results. Twice as many females as males tend to qualify for acceptance into college-level programs.[7]

EMPLOYMENT AND ECONOMICS

According to the 2001 Labour Force Survey, women's participation rate was 71.1 percent to men's 81.7 percent. The total labor force was 164,675. The unemployed labor force was 11,365, with rates of 7.1 percent for women and 6.8 percent for men. Unemployment generally was estimated at 6.9 percent in 2001.[8]

Figures for 2002 are not yet available. However, it is instructive to review the figures of a decade ago with a view to trends and comparisons.

In 1992, women made up 57.7 percent of the unemployed labor force, with a staggering 72.5 percent of the unemployed women then in the age group under thirty. Female teenagers made up 29 percent of the total unemployed labor force, and, in addition, 58 percent of all unemployed teens were female.[9]

Job/Career Opportunities

In 2000, 80 percent of women worked as clerical, sales, and service workers, compared to 30 percent of men. A higher percentage of female workers were employed as professional, technical, and related workers (13.7 percent, compared to men's 10.9 percent).[10] However, this higher percentage is due to the fact that most of the teachers, nurses, medical and dental assistants, and social workers are women. In the professional areas of medicine, law, engineering, accounting, and architecture, women are making gains but are still underrepresented.

In 1992, unemployment was least, 5.7 percent, among professional/technical and administrative/managerial females, who made up only 8.5 percent of the female labor force. It was highest, 12.9 percent, among service workers, who made up 47.5 percent of the female workforce.[11]

The early 1990s saw devastating retrenchment in the hospitality industry, where women were the majority of those employed and were the gender most affected. PanAm and Eastern Airlines went out of business in 1991, which added to the hotel industry's backslide. Overall, thousands of jobs were lost throughout the entire country, particularly in New Providence and Grand Bahama.

Pay

Women's work is seldom remunerated equally with that of men even though women are generally better educated than their male counterparts. A key element that compounds this inequality is the geography of the Bahamas. The Family Islands are more rural than urban, and this has prevented women from sharing equally in the gains made in the labor force. In 2001, the labor-force participation rates of women in the two most developed islands, New Providence and Grand Bahama, were 73.8 percent and 67.9 percent, respectively. In the Family Islands, however, female employment averaged 49 percent, which has been the situation for Family Island women for some years.[12]

Poverty levels began to rise in the 1990s in relative and absolute terms despite the strong economic growth enjoyed in the Bahamas between 1980 and 1990. Essentially, the distribution of costs and benefits of economic performance among various population groups has tended to increase the levels of income concentration. This is evident in today's Bahamas, just over a decade after the boom years. Because of their inadequate participation in the labor market, women were more affected than men by the incidence of increased poverty.

In 2000, the Inter-American Development Bank conducted an initial assessment of what would be required for a poverty study in the Bahamas. As a result, an Interdisciplinary Committee including the Department of Statistics and the Ministry of Economic Development has been established to execute and coordinate a thorough poverty survey.

Working Conditions

Much more effort is required to further public education and awareness about equal treatment for working women and men and equal sharing of work and family responsibilities. The Employment Act 2000 addresses equal pay for equal work, parental leave, minimum wages, and minimum standards of work. It targets hours of work and outlaws discrimination on the grounds of gender. Essentially, the act aims to bring existing laws in line with International Labor Organization conventions.

Support for Mothers/Caretakers

In 2000, the former government of the Bahamas introduced a plan of flexible working hours in the public sector, but it is not yet implemented. The intent is to permit parents, especially single parents, most of whom are mothers, to spend quality time with their children. The goal is to reduce the time that children are left unsupervised and are thereby more susceptible to social ills.

Maternal Leave

The Employment Act 2000 increased maternity leave from eight to twelve weeks at full pay.[13]

Inheritance and Property Rights

The Bahamas acceded to the Convention on the Elimination of All Forms of Discrimination against Women (CEDAW) with reservation on several articles, one of them being Article 16h, which is not consistent with existing inheritance laws. Under existing law, a woman cannot inherit from an individual who dies without a will.

Social/Government Programs

Gender cuts across many issues, and approaches to treat inequality must be multifaceted and multisectoral, even in the absence of a strategic policy and in the presence of unsustainable procedures. Although the Bahamas

Technical and Vocational Institute was not upgraded in the context of a strategic gender mainstreaming policy, its new goals nevertheless address some key gender issues. The institute is now more comprehensive, broader based, and hence more responsive to community needs. The government of the Bahamas has made efforts to expand its technical and vocational base by extending the institute's curriculum to the Family Islands. At least three islands now offer a limited but comprehensive curriculum.

The institute provides instruction in more than twenty disciplines, all of which are available to women. Additionally, an on-site daycare facility partially staffed by trained nurses is available. The daycare facility is an added measure to encourage mothers to seek training by offering the assurance that their children are being well cared for. Upon completion of the program, a student can make use of the job-placement service to match skills with available job opportunities.

In 1996, through funding from the Commonwealth Secretariat, the Bahamas conducted an entrepreneurial development workshop specifically for Family Island participants who were involved in the craft industry. Although it included men, the workshop's purpose was to assist women in refining, pricing, and marketing their products. Participants were introduced to project proposal preparation and methods of funding from the Bahamas Development Bank. The Bahamas Agricultural and Industrial Corporation provided technical assistance and information regarding the use of cooperatives and credit unions to begin new ventures. Similar workshops have been held in New Providence utilizing the expertise of successful female entrepreneurs.

The government, in collaboration with nongovernmental organizations and women's groups, conducted general legal literacy workshops for women of New Providence and Freeport. Unfortunately, one of the constraints of an archipelago is the prohibitive cost involved in decentralizing development efforts. As a consequence, the main population centers benefit most from development activities, while the Family Islands are underserved.

Welfare

The social welfare system provides for national insurance benefits, including retirement, maternity, sickness, and death benefits. In addition, there is social assistance for the unemployed, indigent, and aged, as well as pensions for widows. In 2002, the Ministry of Social Services and Community Development, in which the Bureau of Women's Affairs is located, conducted a survey of needs in disadvantaged New Providence communities. Shelter was found to be one of the most pressing issues impacting a range of age groups. Lack of adequate shelter was most severe for women and old people and also exacerbated other social problems, including domestic violence and abuse of old people. A multiministry approach led by the Ministry of Social Services is addressing housing and other problems.

FAMILY AND SEXUALITY

The concept of the family in the contemporary Bahamas is as multifaceted as the society itself, although on the surface it might appear that family forms are homogeneous. Formerly, when fewer Bahamians traveled and lived abroad for schooling and when the inflow of people from other countries was less, the Bahamian family structure could be considered homogeneous. Many family patterns now exist in the society, however. In keeping with its self-concept as a Christian nation, the Bahamas formally acknowledges only the nuclear and the extended family forms. The former hardly exists, and the latter is prevalent and typical.

Gender Roles

Gender roles in the family in the Bahamas are much like those elsewhere in the Caribbean. Responsibility for much of the overt socialization of children in the home rests with women, who further ensure that such socialization is reinforced by exposing children to the teachings of the church through regular attendance of Sunday school. Women are also caretakers of elderly and ill family members, who may or may not reside under the same roof.

Materially, men provide for the family, but are not consistently active in socializing children in the family. Generally, most men do not physically participate in caregiving to elderly or sick family members. Financial contributions to the cost of care may be made on a consistent or irregular basis.

Men and women extend their familial gender roles to the community. Women generally participate actively in community management at church and school levels, for example, in parent/teacher associations. Men, although participants at this same level, tend to be more active in sports associations and community security.

Marriage

In the 1963 census, only persons legally married were recorded as such, and common-law unions were not separately identified. In 1970, the common-law category entered the census with the definition "not legally married although having other rights." The proportion of persons legally married showed a decline between 1963 and 1970, the decrease being larger for males than for females. Between 1970 and 1980, the downward change was very substantial, with the proportions of each sex legally married in

1980 being less than three-fourths of the 1970 percentages. In effect, 22 percent of the adult population was legally married.[14]

The incidences of divorce, separation, and common-law unions increased by about 50 percent between 1980 and 1990 so that by 1990, 64 percent of households were headed by a single parent, 43 percent of that being female-headed. By 1998, legal marriages were 5.7 percent per 1,000.[15]

In Bahamian society, as worldwide, comparatively fewer marriages are taking place, and common-law unions are increasing. This can be attributed, in part, to the age distribution of the population because typically, marital status is closely associated with age.

Common-law unions also include same-sex unions in which one partner may have been married before with children, who then are brought into the union. These family forms that fall outside of the norm are not openly acknowledged or accepted in the society. Visiting heterosexual relationships, however, are the most prevalent of all types of relationships. In many instances, visiting relationships include children sired by the male "visitor" or by one or more previous visitors.

Reproduction

A woman's level of education has been found to be one of the demographic characteristics most closely associated with fertility levels in the Bahamas. Reproductive behavior also differs according to socioeconomic status. The higher fertility rate and the correspondingly larger numbers of children in lower-income households often not only prevent mothers from finding better jobs but also prevent their children from eventually acquiring necessary educational and job skills. Overall, there has been a downward trend in fertility. Peak fertility is among women between the ages of twenty and thirty-four years, with a slight upward trend in fertility of the age group thirty-five to thirty-nine. Since the late 1980s, there has been an increase in the fertility of women forty-five and older.[16] In 1997, the government introduced a National Family Planning Policy that operates within the framework of the primary health-care system to facilitate access to reproductive health care.

Sex Education

Sex education is taught in schools as a matter of policy and has been broadened to human sexuality. Even so, the subject is taught more as a science than as a subject that is directly related to students, their sexuality, and their evolving lifestyles. The bias toward heterosexuality is apparently a policy. Outside of a moralistic approach, the present style of sex education hardly strengthens youth skills in decision making and negotiating.

The CARICOM (Caribbean Community and Common Market established in 1973) Multi-Agency Health and Family Life Education Programme has been introduced in the Bahamas by the Ministries of Education and Health. Sex and human sexuality are components of a comprehensive program of human development including conflict management and decision making.

Contraception and Abortion

Ease of access to contraceptives is a significant factor in women's capacity to control their fertility. In the Bahamas, access to contraceptives is easy for the majority of women of all backgrounds in Nassau, New Providence, and Grand Bahama. This has not been the traditional situation in the Family Islands, however, but ease of access has improved greatly since the 1980s.

Findings show that contraceptive use varies directly with age: it is lowest among adolescents and highest among women thirty-five to forty-four years of age. Approximately six out of every ten adolescents are vulnerable or exposed to an early and most probably unwanted pregnancy.[17]

Statistics on abortion rates are undisclosed. Abortion is still not legally available except in cases where the health of the pregnant mother is at risk.

Teen Pregnancy

Teenage pregnancies continue to be a concern from a public health perspective as well as from a social and economic standpoint. Between 1983 and 1990, the birth rates for teenagers between the ages of ten and nineteen ranged from 35.4 to 24.0 per 1,000. The same mothers still occupied the high-fertility age range when they reached twenty-two to thirty-eight years of age. The birth rate among girls under the age of fifteen can be as high as 4 per 1,000 in any given year.[18]

In 1989, 15.4 percent of all children born were born to unwed, teenage mothers. The average age of teenage mothers dropped from seventeen to fifteen years of age, not only impacting the future demographic profile but swelling the ranks of unskilled, unemployed mothers and absentee fathers.[19] In 2000, the total number of teenage births was 964 (12.7 percent of total live births).[20]

Adolescent fertility continues to be a major challenge for the Bahamas. It constitutes both a consequence and a cause of poverty. Teen pregnancies are largely associated with low levels of education, unemployment, and higher involvement in visiting and transient unions. They are an obstacle to sustainable development due to how seriously educational, economic, and personal development are compromised and how teen pregnancies jeopardize the children's life chances.

Teen pregnancy reinforces intergenerational poverty. These obstacles and threats will not dissipate until institutions and society as a whole create policies for teens' continued education and development and also address male responsibility.

HEALTH

The health policy of the Bahamas aims to promote lifestyles conducive to healthy living, reduce and eliminate preventable health risks, and enable overall development of health services that give appropriate emphasis to health education and preventive and restorative health-care delivery systems. The policy also seeks to ensure equal provisions and opportunities for both sexes.

Health Care Access

Policy implementation incurs high infrastructure costs in the context of an archipelago. A network of polyclinic centers has been created to promote preventive general health, advance inoculation against childhood diseases, and encourage increased attention to oral health care. All fees associated with pre- and postnatal care programs have been eliminated at all government health-care facilities to encourage expectant mothers to seek medical care. Additionally, the central government hospital, the Princess Margaret Hospital, has upgraded its intensive-care unit for sick babies and has introduced a maternity program to the Family Islands. Under this program, all pregnant patients identified as "high-risk" are required to deliver in the capital. This initiative has improved the survival rate and quality of life of low-birth-weight infants.

Diseases and Disorders

Major causes of death are diseases of the heart (358 deaths in 2000), HIV/AIDS (245), cancer (224), and accidents, suicides, and homicides (218). The most dramatic increase in major causes of death between the years 1996 and 2000 was in accidents, suicides, and homicides which increased by 98. Seventy-six of these fatalities were accidents, that is, death by transport. Also noteworthy is the decline of 31 in HIV/AIDS-related deaths between these same years.[21]

AIDS

Although the number of new AIDS cases has declined, this pandemic continues to be a major concern to the Bahamas, which ranks highest in the English-speaking Caribbean. HIV-infected women make up approximately 3 percent of the 6,000 annual pregnancies in the Bahamas. Most of these (85 percent) access prenatal care through public health community clinics.[22]

All pregnant women are counseled and offered HIV testing. More than 95 percent of women agree to be tested. Those who are HIV/AIDS positive are referred to the weekly HIV/AIDS Clinic at the Princess Margaret Hospital, where they are further counseled, offered azidothymidine (AZT), and monitored. At the weekly pediatric HIV/AIDS clinic, which runs concurrently with the prenatal clinic, the babies are followed up on a regular basis if they are found to be HIV positive or until they have been shown not to be infected. The government of the Bahamas funds the total cost of providing AZT treatment to HIV-infected pregnant women. This initiative has resulted in the reduction of mother-to-infant transmission rates from 30 percent to 10 percent, thereby significantly reducing infant mortality rates from HIV/AIDS infection.[23]

Research and extended programs work in collaboration with the National AIDS Secretariat to address the current HIV/AIDS crisis. In 1999, the Bahamas was selected by UNIFEM (United Nations Development Fund for Women) as one of the six countries in the world and the only country in the Caribbean to conduct a project on "Gender Focused Interventions to Address the Challenges of the HIV/AIDS Epidemic." The project, which is executed by the Bureau of Women's Affairs, has three components consisting of sensitization workshops, advocacy workshops, and community-based research on the socioeconomic factors that make women more susceptible to contracting HIV/AIDS. Research from this project is targeted to assist the country in reducing the number of women—particularly young women—who contract this disease.

Eating Disorders

Using standards recommended by the World Health Organization, undernourishment in the Bahamas in 1989 was placed at 6.8 percent in New Providence and 2.7 percent in Grand Bahama, with a collective average of 12.3 percent in the Family Islands.[24] Obesity in the Bahamas in 1997 in persons aged fifteen to sixty-five years was 48.6 percent, indicative of undernutrition and poor diet and eating habits.[25]

Cancer

Breast cancer is the leading cancer in women in the Bahamas. Other major cancers are cancers of the cervix, uterus, and stomach, followed by rectal, tracheal, bronchial, and lung cancers.[26] The Ministry of Health, assisted by a nongovernmental organization (NGO), has introduced a free mammography program with a view to the early detection of breast cancers in women, particularly in the age group over thirty-five.

Depression

Little has been documented about depression in women in the Bahamas. Mental illnesses were highest among women in 1985 but remained higher in only two of the disorders treated in 1990, one of these being depression.[27] In the context of mental and behavioral disorders, depression has gained little attention. Except for postnatal depression, depression in women throughout their life cycles has not been addressed.

POLITICS AND LAW

Suffrage

Full adult suffrage was not achieved in the Bahamas until 1962 with the passage of legislation that gave women the right to vote. A property qualification for adult males had been discarded, and this gave momentum to the effort of the women's movement of the 1950s to attain the vote for women. The women who led the movement struggled for fourteen years for the right to vote, attained it, and pressed on to secure further political improvements for women. In 1968, the first woman cabinet minister was appointed, and in 1982, the first woman was elected to Parliament.

Political Participation

Men have always been the primary participants in parliamentary assemblies. Although this pattern continues, the number of women in the elected House of Assembly has increased noticeably since 1980. In 1980, there were no women in the thirty-eight-member assembly; by 1992, women made up just under 10 percent of the seats in the forty-nine-member assembly. By the 2002 election, the numbers of women running for office increased dramatically to almost 40 percent across some six parties. This increase does not, however, completely reflect the high quality and quantity of female participation in party politics.

Women's Rights

The extent to which women's rights in the Bahamas are measured as human rights is arguable. Further, the constitution discriminates against Bahamian women by making no provision for the acquisition of citizenship by the foreign spouse of a Bahamian woman. A foreign female married to a Bahamian male, however, can be registered as a citizen on making application, subject only to "national security and public policy considerations." In addition, the law makes it easier for men with foreign spouses to confer citizenship on their children than for women with foreign spouses. Since the early 1980s, women have protested the obvious disparity between the eligibility for citizenship of foreign spouses of Bahamian males and females. In 2002, a referendum to vote for or against the repeal of these laws was called by the government. However, this effort to allow the electorate, in the context of constitutional reform, to amend such discrimination failed.

Feminist Movements

Development Alternatives with Women for a New Era (DAWN) is a Bahamas feminist NGO whose focus has been on legal literacy and advocacy of women's reproductive rights and health. Unlike the mainstream women's groups with social welfare orientations, DAWN's work has been to challenge the existing patriarchal development paradigm from an alternative, feminist position. DAWN's alliance with the Caribbean Association for Feminist Research and Action provides a connection to the regional feminist movement.

Lesbian Rights

Lesbian rights have not gained currency in mainstream movements for women's rights. For the most part, only a handful of lesbians advocate the rights of lesbians, more as a fairly new parallel assertion of rights than as an element of women's rights overall. Lesbian women have also been among the main advocates of the rights of gay men.

Military Service

The Royal Bahamas Defense Force (RBDF) is a quasi-military force established in October 1976 to protect and defend the territorial integrity of the Bahamas, maintain law and order, and enforce the law in Bahamian waters. It was not until October 1985 that the first female was recruited to the force.

In 2002, the RBDF had a total of 118 enlisted females, of whom 5 were commissioned officers: 1 lieutenant commander, 1 senior lieutenant, 1 lieutenant, and 2 sublieutenants.[28] Training for qualification at these senior levels is acquired in the United Kingdom. Women now make up 2 percent of the force's total strength of 891, whereas in 1985 they were 6.5 percent of the 850 defense force officers on active duty.[29] More women now occupy senior positions. Women are considered to be better educationally and attitudinally prepared recruits than men.

RELIGION AND SPIRITUALITY

The Bahamas prides itself on being predominantly a Christian nation. There are some Muslims, Hindus, Buddhists, and Rastafarians. Of the

Churchgoers, Bahamas. Photo © TRIP/K. Cardwell.

Christians, Baptists constitute the majority, followed by Anglicans, Roman Catholics, Methodists, and Presbyterians.

Women's Roles

As in politics, women's roles in religious activity are for the most part supportive but not leading. Women are the majority in congregations and play a critical role in the maintenance functions of the church. As recently as 2000, the Anglican Church ordained its first female reverend. Other denominations have as yet not followed suit.

Rituals and Religious Practices

Religions of the Bahamas do not, by and large, have any rituals and practices that could be considered extraordinary by adherents of the given faith worldwide.

Religious Law

Religious laws peculiar to the jurisdiction of the Bahamas do not exist. Some Pentecostal denominations, however, do insist on ultraconservative dress codes and behaviors for women members in particular.

VIOLENCE

Domestic Violence and Rape/Sexual Assault

Women suffer sexual and physical assault as a result of domestic disputes and as part of incidents of community violence. In 1992, more than 12,000 females sought medical help for injuries resulting from some type of violence. Seventy-seven percent of these cases were for physical assault and 23 percent were for sexual assault. Seventy percent of the cases of sexual assault were perpetrated against female children. It was noted as a "disturbing fact" by the Royal Bahamas Police Force Report that females aged two years, five years, and eight years had to be hospitalized after sexual molestation in that year.[30] In all cases, there were indications that parents or guardians had prior knowledge of the danger.

In the 1980s, a pressure group, Women Against Rape (WAR), organized two petitions with the Women's Crisis Centre and other concerned organizations such as DAWN. In 1983 and 1988, they strongly influenced parliamentary action to address violence against women. Ultimately, such advocacy led to the passage of the Sexual Offences and Domestic Violence Act (1991), which mandated the reporting of sexual offenses against children, broadened the definition of rape, criminalized incest, and provided stiffer penalties for domestic violence in the case of a married woman. Legislation is still needed to protect unmarried women who are victims of domestic violence.

Violence against women continues to be a serious problem. Women seek advice, counseling, and shelter at both private and government-supported agencies. The Women's Crisis Centre, founded in 1982 to address the needs of rape victims and women facing other crises, provides services for women suffering from battery, incest, sexual molestation, and sexual, physical, or emotional violence. Renamed the Crisis Centre of the Bahamas to reflect its continued service to women, men, and children, the agency receives a partial subsidy from the government of the Bahamas in the form of an annual financial allocation of $30,000, the provision of two trained social workers, and physical accommodations on the premises of the local hospital.

The Domestic Violence Advocacy Programme run by the Crisis Centre links the police with volunteer advocates and social services. The program aims to ensure that the police response to a domestic violence report promotes the safety of victims. Further, the program aims to encourage and facilitate engagement of the victim(s)/perpetrator(s) in continued intervention via attendance at the Crisis Centre.

The government has constructed two safe houses for battered women. The NGO community with corporate support is addressing the issue of more safe houses for girls and women in the New Providence area.

Trafficking in Women and Children

It can almost certainly be said that the Bahamas has no record of trafficking in women and children into or out of the Bahamas. Since 2001, however, illegal trafficking in Haitian illegal immigrants into the Bahamas by Bahamian traffickers has been uncovered. Data reflecting the numbers of women and children are not available at this time, but it appears that more Haitian men than women and children seek to enter the Bahamas illegally.

War and Military Repression

The Bahamas enjoys peace despite being near the United States, which has been at war off and on since 1950. However, by reason of its geographical location, the Bahamas has long been a transit point for persons fleeing economic deprivation and political unrest, particularly from Haiti and Cuba.

OUTLOOK FOR THE TWENTY-FIRST CENTURY

An enabling environment for women's empowerment in the Bahamas will be strengthened once the legal and institutional framework is successfully addressed. Changes will have to be made to the constitution and local laws, which not only discriminate against women but present barriers to each citizen's ability to recognize her/his civil and political rights. In order to make progress toward gender equality, the Bahamas must pursue women's participation in the structures of power and decision making. For instance, leadership programs must be fostered in the schools so that girls can enhance their self-esteem and gain a broader view of their opportunities. But participation is not enough. There must also be more focus on qualitative changes to political structures and systems to reflect more gender sensitivity.

International and regional organizations have greatly contributed to the programs of the Bahamas in areas that affect women. The corporate sector will continue to be encouraged to implement policies and programs to provide support systems for working women, many of whom are heads of households in the Bahamas, and for working parents generally. It is expected that this will continue as the Bahamas seeks to act on health and development issues, keeping pace with the best practices in the region. The continued development of programs for teenage mothers and young women and men and the control and eradication of sexually transmitted infections such as HIV and AIDS are issues of mutual concern to the Bahamas and the Caribbean region. The intractability of these issues to date constitutes a serious threat to efforts to eradicate poverty at national and regional levels.

NOTES

1. "Bahamas Census 2000," www.caricom.org/archives/26sccs-bs.html.
2. Report on the Census of the Bahama Islands, 1911.
3. "Financial Digest of the Bahamas 2002," www.bfdbfd.com/Digest/digest advertising.html.
4. Carolyn Moser, *Five Policy Approaches to Gender and Development* (1993).
5. "Bahamas National Report on the Status of Women 1995," www.cidh.org/countryrep/mujeres95-en/Chapter%202.html.

6. Ibid.

7. Elsa Leo-Rhynie and Barbara Bailey, *Gender: A Caribbean Multi-disciplinary Perspective* (Kingston: Oxford, Ian Randle Publishers, 1997).

8. "Labor Force Survey 2001," www.ilocarib.org.tt/digest/bahamas/bah01.html.

9. "Labor Force Survey 1992," www.ilocarib.org.tt/digest/bahamas/bah01.html.

10. "Labor Force Survey 2001."

11. "Labor Force Survey 1992."

12. "Labor Force Survey 1999," www.ilocarib.org.tt/digest/bahamas/bah01.html.

13. "Employment Act 2000," www.bahamasemployers.org/documents/employmentact.html.

14. Norma Abdulah, *The Bahamas and Its People: A Demographic Analysis* (Trinidad, WI: Institute of Social and Economic Research, University of the West Indies, 1990).

15. "Bahamas Census 2000."

16. Bahamas Family Planning Association, www.ippf.org/regions/whr.

17. Ibid.

18. Bahamas Ministry of Health, www.gksoft.com/gout/en/bs.html.

19. Ibid.

20. Ibid.

21. Department of Statistics.

22. Ibid.

23. Ibid.

24. Ibid.

25. Ibid.

26. Ibid.

27. "Status of Women."

28. Royal Bahamas Defense Force Public Relations Office, www.lamilitary.com/BS.html.

29. Ibid.

30. Bahamas Crisis Center, www.bahamascrisiscenter.org.

RESOURCE GUIDE

Suggested Reading

Abdulah, Norma. *The Bahamas and Its People: A Demographic Analysis*. Trinidad, WI: Institute of Social and Economic Research, University of the West Indies, 1990.

Albury, Paul. *The Story of the Bahamas*. New York: St. Martin's Press, 1976.

Bostwick, Janet G., Attorney General and Minister of Foreign Affairs of the Commonwealth of the Bahamas. Address to the 23rd United Nations General Assembly Special Session, "Women 2000: Gender Equality, Development, and Peace for the 21st Century." New York, June 2000.

Gomez, Carmen. *Women in Crisis*. 1987.

Mondesire, A., and L. Dunn. *Towards Equity in Development: A Report on the Status of Women in Sixteen Commonwealth Caribbean Countries*. Georgetown, Guyana: Caribbean Community Secretariat, 1995.

Organizations

Caribbean Association for Feminist Research and Action
8 Bates Terrace

St. Augustine
Trinidad and Tobago, West Indies
Web site: http://www.cafra.org

Development Alternatives with Women for a New Era (DAWN)
Caribbean Secretariat
11 Gibbons Terrace
Christchurch
Barbados, West Indies
Phone: 246-420-4474
Web site: http://www.dawn.org.fj/

SELECTED BIBLIOGRAPHY

Caribbean Development Bank. *The Institutional Assessment of the Bahamas Technical and Vocational Institute*. 1998.

Department of Statistics. *Report of Census of Population 2000*.

Hardwick, Cary Kristin. "Women, Economic Development, and Social Change: The Case of Cherokee Sound, The Bahamas." Dissertation Thesis. University of Georgia. 1994.

Health Information and Research Unit, Ministry of Health. *Basic Health Indicators 2000*.

Labour Force and Household Income Reports 1991/2.

Mackey, Karol L. "The Beliefs and Attitudes of Bahamian Women Concerning Detection and Prevention of Breast Cancer." Dissertation Thesis. Barry University. 2001.

The National Report of the Commonwealth of The Bahamas to the XXX Assembly of Delegates of the Inter-American Commission of Women (CIM).

Saunders, Gail. *Bahamian Society After Emancipation*. Kingston; Princeton: M. Wiener Publishers; I. Randle Publishers, 2003.

2

BARBADOS

Miriam Zoll

PROFILE OF BARBADOS

Barbados is a Caribbean island located in the Atlantic Ocean north of the equator, 34 kilometers long by 23 kilometers wide, with an area of approximately 430 square kilometers. It is the most easterly of the Caribbean chain islands, approximately 463 kilometers northeast of the South American mainland.

During most of the twentieth century, Barbados's economy was heavily dependent on sugar, rum, and molasses production. Since the 1980s, tourism and manufacturing have surpassed the sugar industry in economic importance. This tiny island nation recently discovered reserves of petroleum and gas.

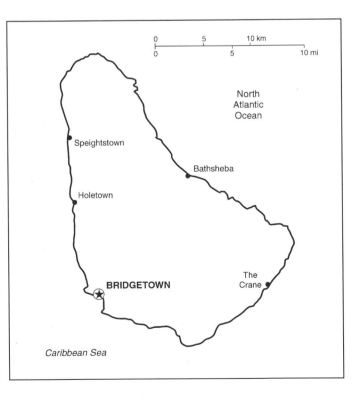

At the end of the last census in 2000, Barbados's resident population was estimated at 268,792, of which 142,493 were women. Government investment in primary and secondary education and preventive health care has shown impressive results in high levels of literacy and a decrease in the infant mortality rate. The average life expectancy is 73.25 years (female, 75.86 years; male, 70.66 years); the infant mortality rate is

12.04 per 1,000 live births; and the maternal mortality rate is 43 out of 100,000 live births.[1]

Ninety-two percent of Barbados's residents are of African descent, and 8 percent are white or of mixed race. A British colony for 441 years, Barbados received its independence from Britain on November 30, 1966. Its Parliament, which dates back to 1639, is the third oldest in the world. Barbados is a parliamentary democracy observing English common law, with Queen Elizabeth II of England serving as chief of state. Sir Clifford Straughn Husbands was appointed governor general by the queen in 1996, and the prime minister, Owen Seymour Arthur, and the deputy prime minister, Billie Miller, a woman, were appointed in 1994 by the former governor general. Barbados's bicameral Parliament consists of twenty-one Senate members appointed by the governor general and 28 House Assembly members who are elected by direct popular vote and serve five-year terms.

OVERVIEW OF WOMEN'S ISSUES

The position and status of women in Barbados are uncommonly different from those of other women in the Caribbean region and most women in the developing world in general. Women's participation in politics and economic decision making ranks higher than in Japan and some of the members of the European Union, according to a global report released by the United Nations in 2000.[2] The United Nations Human Development Report ranks Barbados first among developing countries in human development indicators. These include equal opportunity for all citizens, sustainability of opportunities from one generation to the next, and the ability of citizens to participate in and benefit from development processes.

Despite these strong advances nationally, Bajan (people from Barbados) women's personal lives continue to be limited by traditional and regional gender-role perceptions that prohibit them from fully enjoying new professional and personal opportunities. Though no poverty statistics are available from the government, many Bajan women face severe economic and social hardships, including homelessness, teen pregnancy, underemployment, low wages, and domestic violence.

At the same time, a number of international and domestic women's organizations operate from Barbados, where they actively collaborate with civil society and the government to improve options for women. Feminist organizations such as Development Alternatives with Women for a New Era (DAWN) and Women and Development (WAND) are working to improve women's economic and political opportunities. Other focal points include improving health-care services, creating greater gender awareness among policy makers, electing more women to public office, and encouraging more women to attend secondary educational institutions.

EDUCATION

Opportunities

Education is compulsory for girls and boys from ages five to sixteen. According to the Barbados government's 2000 census, however, only 9.95 percent of Bajan women have attended secondary school, compared to 10.23 percent of men. Statistics from 1999 show that more women (0.35 percent) than men (0.19 percent) graduated from the University of the West Indies. In 2001, there were more female graduates from the Barbados Community College (1.14 percent) than male graduates (0.43 percent). More Bajan men (0.62 percent) than women (0.35 percent) graduated from technical college, reflecting the trend within the Latin American and Caribbean region that women are still underrepresented in scientific and technical disciplines.[3]

Literacy

Barbados boasts a 97 percent literacy rate (female, 96.8 percent; male, 98 percent), one of the highest in the world.[4]

EMPLOYMENT AND ECONOMICS

Job/Career Opportunities

Despite economic and political gains made during the last decades of the twentieth century, not all Bajan women enjoy economic autonomy or access to educational and professional opportunities. As in most of the Latin American and Caribbean region, a large number of Bajan women serve as single heads of households and as the chief family breadwinner. The September 11, 2001, terrorist attacks on the United States damaged Barbados's tourism industry, which has slowly replaced manufacturing as a chief employer of women on the island since 1992. Women's earnings have declined as a result of hotel closings, cruise ship cancellations, and decreases in airline travel.[5]

Approximately 46 percent of the Bajan workforce is female, compared to 54 percent of men. Slightly more than 60 percent of women are employed, and 39.2 percent do not participate in the workforce at all. Statistics on the number of women living below the poverty line and sex-disaggregated data on women's occupations are not available.

Very few women are employers (0.1 percent), and approximately 4.5 percent are self-employed. The largest portion of women (40.7 percent) are privately employed, and 13.1 percent work for the government. An estimated 0.2 percent of women are unpaid family workers or apprentices. When economic recessions hit the Latin American and Caribbean region in the late 1980s, many Bajan women turned to informal-sector work. This alternative income-generating trend continues today and encompasses such work as buying and selling clothing and running cottage industries, such as small-scale garment manufacturing, cosmetics, and hairdressing.[6]

Since the 1980s, globalization has created many new but low-paying jobs for women in Barbados. Research conducted at the University of the West Indies showed that during the 1970s and 1980s, manufacturing established itself as one of the more dynamic sectors of the Barbadian economy. Playtex and Intel were among multinational corporations using Barbados as a manufacturing base. Until the regional economic recession hit the region in the late 1980s, more than 85 percent of workers in the garment industry were women. Female workers made up 55 percent of workers in the electronics industry and more than 75 percent in "miscellaneous" industries. As previously noted, tourism has replaced manufacturing as a principal employer of women on the island.[7]

A number of U.S. and other multinational companies export their data- and text-entry work to developing countries offering low-paid labor, which is usually performed by women. According to the U.S. Congress's Office of Technology Assessment Archives, in some developing countries, wage rates are as little as one-tenth of U.S. rates. International trade-union organizations have outlined detailed wage rates for data-entry work in eight Caribbean countries, comparing them with rates for similar work in the United States. While U.S. workers were typically earning $7 to $8 an hour, staff in Barbados received $2.00 to $2.88.[8]

In the late 1990s, an estimated 3,000 women in Barbados were employed in the information-processing industry. The largest company, Caribbean Data Services, was originally set up by American Airlines to process the data from the airline's used tickets. This company has since diversified and now also undertakes accounting work and the processing of insurance claims. Very low-skilled data-processing work has begun migrating away from Barbados and is being rerouted to countries like China. In the last few years, the Barbados Investment and Development Corporation has employed thousands of Bajan women to conduct payroll accounting, computer-aided design, prepress activities, insurance claims processing, database development, market and consumer surveys, archiving, inbound telemarketing, document indexing and abstracting, basic data entry, and, more recently, software development.[9]

Major publishing houses have used low-paid developing-world labor to do production work on their books. Companies such as netLibrary employ workers in countries such as Barbados, China, Mexico, and India to convert the written word to the cyber word. Most of these workers are women.[10]

Pay

Barbados law sets minimum wages for only two specified categories of workers: household domestics and shop workers. Household domestics, the majority of whom are women, are entitled to a minimum wage of approximately U.S.$.75 per hour.[11]

A recent study by the Inter-American Development Bank showed that within the informal sector in the Latin American and Caribbean region, women earn only a quarter of what men earn. It further showed that current legislation tends to protect prime-age, urban, formal male workers but restricts opportunities for other groups.[12]

Working Conditions

Under Barbados's law, full protection is granted to trade unionists. Bajan women workers are members of two major unions: the National Union of Public Workers, which is independent of any government or political party, and the Barbados Worker's Union, which is associated with the Democratic Labour Party.

Sexual Harassment

In August 2000, Barbados minister of labour Rudolph Greenidge announced the adoption of legislation aimed at preventing sexual harassment in the workplace.[13] This law interprets sexual harassment as rough and commonplace talk, sexual innuendoes, and sexual touching.

Support for Mothers/Caretakers

The government of Barbados has been actively engaged in regional political networks calling for the reform of international financial institution policies that contribute to the feminization of poverty. Policies mandated by the World Bank and the International Monetary Fund, for example, contribute to women's poverty by reducing funding for a variety of social programs usually provided by the state. Denying funding for child and elderly care and for services to people with HIV/AIDS, for example, places an undue burden on women and girls who are expected to leave school or quit jobs outside the home in order to deliver caretaking services. This phenomenon is by no means limited to the Caribbean, and the expectation that females will provide caretaking functions formerly provided by the state apparatus is directly linked to traditional and cultural interpretations of women's and girls' role in the family, community, and state.

Maternal Leave

In 1919, the International Labour Organisation created the first global standard aimed at protecting working women before and after childbirth. The Maternity Protection Convention was created as an essential means of preventing maternity from becoming a source of discrimination against women in employment. That standard currently calls for a minimum twelve-week leave.

Since 1998, the Barbados Social Security System has provided twelve weeks of fully paid maternity leave for pregnant women workers. By law, Bajan women are only eligible for three paid maternal leaves. Despite this important progressive policy, Barbados still lags behind many European countries.

Daycare

Easily accessible care for children through the extended family has broken down, which has placed demands on the formal care sector. The Child Care Board, a governmental agency, provides most daycare services and also licenses private centers. Together, public and private daycare centers cover 80 percent of all three-year-olds. The Child Care Board actively pursues private centers that violate government standards.[14]

Social/Government Programs

The government of Barbados has identified the alleviation of poverty as a priority area for action in advancing the status of women on the island. It has established a poverty-eradication fund and is embarking on a series of measures to boost entrepreneurial and microenterprise activities to increase self-employment and generate greater employment among women and youth.

In the late 1990s, the government of Barbados joined with nineteen other nations to coordinate the implementation of a gender-sensitive budget initiative. Under the auspices of the Commonwealth Secretariat, these projects are designed to increase women's participation in economic decision making and engage more women in the budgetary process. The Barbados initiative assists the government in incorporating a gender analysis at all levels of revenue raising and expenditure allocation, including agriculture, industry, health, education, social services, and public-sector employment. The result has been the identification of areas where gender-based inefficiencies and inequalities exist, as well as efforts to improve the capacity for gender-disaggregated data collection. These initiatives support women's endeavors to hold governments accountable for their commitments to women's rights and link gender equality and women's human rights to the distribution, use, and generation of public resources.[15]

Welfare

According to the International Fund for Agricultural Development, Barbados is ranked the highest of all Latin American and Caribbean countries in satisfaction of basic needs indexes. Although there are committees and programs designed to assist those suffering from poverty, women's groups on the island report that limited efforts are being made to offset root causes of poverty, including gender inequality.

Even with gender-sensitive budget initiatives, gender awareness among predominantly male policy makers remains limited. This makes it difficult but not impossible for female elected officials and women's organizations to insert a gender perspective into new legislation and social and economic programs. For example, in an effort to improve family life and reduce teenage pregnancy and child abuse, the government now provides clinic-based family-life education and school outreach programs for adolescents.

FAMILY AND SEXUALITY

Gender Roles

Although patriarchal social and economic structures continue to dominate Caribbean and Bajan life, male absenteeism has given rise to matriarchal power structures within the family. Women's assertion of power within the family, however, does not necessarily reach into the political and economic realms on the island or in the region as a whole. Out of necessity, many Bajan women function as the chief breadwinners and heads of households. This social circumstance sends mixed messages to boys and girls struggling to integrate traditional Caribbean gender roles with modern economic survival needs and with women's movement toward parity with men.

The International Planned Parenthood Federation examined patterns of socialization in Barbados and found that 25 percent of young Barbadian boys are raised by teenage mothers, with more than three-quarters of those born to unwed parents.[16] As a result of this trend, children's socialization tends to evolve from female norms instituted by matriarchal family households, many of which are characterized by male absenteeism and extra-marital affairs.

Marriage

The Marriage Act of 1979 states that sixteen is the legal age to marry in Barbados. The divorce rate was 1.21 per 1,000 people in 1995, about a quarter of the U.S. rate.[17]

Reproduction

As in most Caribbean cultures, motherhood has been a principal characteristic of Bajan women's identities and the primary indicator of their adult status and wealth in their communities. Regardless of class, a woman's ability to bear and raise children has functioned as a major source of her self-esteem, earning her respect, social approval, and acceptance.

In the 1990s, Bajan women began postponing childbirth or deciding not to have children at all. The birthrate dropped dramatically from 4,235 in 1991 to 3,400 in 1995.[18] According to the Barbados Family Planning Association, rather than spending their most productive years looking after infants, more women between the ages of thirteen and twenty-nine are delaying or sacrificing motherhood altogether in order to devote more time to educational and career challenges. Barbados has no documented population policy, but it has established a task force to address the matter, according to the United Nations Population Information Network.

Sex Education, Contraception, and Abortion

The government fully supports family planning and funds 60 percent of the Barbados Family Planning Association's (BFPA) budget. Free family-planning clinics were established in all public medical facilities between 1993 and 1995. The BFPA was founded in 1954 and works closely with the Ministry of Health, providing counseling, information, and modern contraceptive methods, including voluntary sterilization and abortion. The BFPA has eighty-one community delivery centers.

Contraceptive use among Bajan women is estimated at 55 percent, and efforts are being made to make men more aware of their role in family planning.[19] Studies indicate that condoms are used less as a contraceptive method among married couples and more as a prevention tool against sexually transmitted diseases by unmarried couples and by those engaging in extramarital affairs. Recently, in an effort to encourage more men to use condoms, the public health organization Social Marketing for Change launched a successful advertising campaign specifically oriented toward Bajan men. Effective marketing techniques included using language and visuals appealing to men's masculine sensibilities, a tactic that resulted in an increase of condom use as a contraceptive. Abortion is available under certain medical regulations within the framework of the 1983 Medical Termination of Pregnancy Act.

Teen Pregnancy

The government of Barbados has acknowledged that teen pregnancy is a serious issue contributing to the cycle of poverty on the island. Teen mothers are permitted to return to school after their pregnancies. Despite a law mandating that children must stay in school until age sixteen, many teen mothers refuse to return and are not encouraged by the government or society to do so.

HEALTH

Health Care Access

By the end of the twentieth century, the government of Barbados had begun to perceive women's health as a pivotal factor in the nation's social and economic growth. Health care is seen as a fundamental right, and the government provides free health care for all citizens, including free family-planning services and maternal care.[20]

In the Caribbean, women's health policy has been addressed in terms of reproduction. While important, this medical concern is only a small part of women's overall health needs. In Barbados, as in most of the region, women are working to strengthen the national health-care system and address the root factors that influence the extent and nature of health problems.

Diseases and Disorders

The economic, social, and family stressors of women in the Caribbean, plus little health education, result in prevailing poor health.[21] The results of two national surveys conducted since the 1980s in the Caribbean region indicate that adults have become more obese, and that this condition affects women more than men. The prevalence of obesity in women has created a higher rate of diabetes among women than men.[22] Hypertension and anemia are other serious problems.

AIDS

After Sub-Saharan Africa, the Caribbean region has the second-highest adult prevalence of HIV/AIDS in the world, and 33 percent of these cases are women (World Health Organization).[23] While rates in Barbados are less than in other Caribbean nations, the World Watch Institute in 2000 released information stating that 1.2 percent of the entire population in Barbados was infected with HIV.[24] In 2000, Prime Minister Owen Arthur formed a National AIDS Committee with funding of more than $1 million to manage, treat, and care for people infected with the virus.

Cancer

Reports issued by the Caribbean Epidemiology Center indicate that the most common cancer in Bajan women aged fifteen years and older is breast cancer, followed by cervical cancer.[25] An estimated 10,000 Pap smears are performed every year for cervical cancer prevention purposes. Surveys conducted by the center during the mid-1990s show that 90 percent of the at-risk general population had been screened in preceding years, but that women aged fifty-five to seventy who were at greatest risk were not being adequately screened.[26] The male lung cancer death rate is 0.5; the female rate is zero.[27]

POLITICS AND LAW

Suffrage

Bajan women were granted the legal right to vote in 1950, sixteen years before the nation declared independence from Great Britain.

Political Participation

There are no legal restrictions on Bajan women's right to participate in public and political life on the island. Despite these legal achievements, only 20.4 percent of elected officials are female.[28] Global monitoring by human rights and women's rights organizations has helped to encourage the Barbados government to implement new programs and trainings to offset this low percentage. Barbados deputy prime minister Billie Miller and the minister of foreign affairs and foreign trade are women. The minister of education and the governor of the Central Bank are also women.

The government has also committed itself to increasing the participation of women by creating the Barbados Ministry of Social Transformation. This ministry combines women's affairs with social services, child care, community development, national assistance, care of the elderly, urban development, and the poverty bureau.

Women's Rights

Feminist Movements

The traditional women's organizations of the 1950s were involved in nationalist, anticolonial political parties. With independence and the beginning of a new era of feminism in the 1960s and 1970s around the world, the purposes of these organizations came into question. Women began to understand that political independence enshrined an essentially male sociopolitical system. The Women's Forum was established in 1988, concentrating its efforts mostly on consciousness-raising about women's issues inside and outside the organization. More recently, the traditional women's organizations have concentrated on the issue of sexual violence. The Mothers Union, an Anglican organization, has become involved in the sexual violence issue as well as in advocating for women priests. The Business and Professional Women's Club has been assisting battered women, and the Soroptimists have concerned themselves with women and work.[29]

Lesbian Rights

Lesbians and gay men do not enjoy legal protection in Barbados or in any of the Caribbean nations. From the days of Queen Victoria, Barbados, like other British colonies, viewed homosexuality as possible among men only and unimaginable among women. As a result, homosexuality remains taboo, and anal sex continues to be outlawed.[30]

Lesbian relationships exist privately in Barbados, and public display is repressed by dominant social and cultural norms on the island. Many lesbian women cite loneliness and isolation as conditions of their homosexuality or bisexuality. Culturally, lesbianism is still considered a psychological imbalance that can be remedied with appropriate counseling.[31]

Military Service

Women do not serve in Barbados's military.

RELIGION AND SPIRITUALITY

Barbados is a highly religious community made up predominantly of Anglicans (40 percent), as well as Pentecostals, Methodists, and Roman Catholics. After the abolition of slavery in 1838, many former slaves were drawn to the Anglican Church, which fared far better than other early Christian churches. The Anglican Church currently claims the majority of all churchgoing members.[32]

Churchgoers, Holetown, Barbados. Photo © TRIP/A. Tovy.

Women's Roles

Bajan women continue to play an important role in the religious life of the family, and church attendance is common. Along with other women from the region, some Bajan women are participating in the Caribbean Religions Project, which encourages women to preserve religious customs by collecting local histories and rituals of their communities and families. On a more political note, Bajan religious institutions have participated in international world conferences on religion and peace. A global gathering in Tokyo sponsored by the United Nations Development Programme addressed the role of religious communities in poverty eradication, noting the importance of women's empowerment as an antidote.[33]

VIOLENCE

Domestic Violence

In the 1990s, the Barbados government passed legislation against domestic violence and began providing shelters for battered women and their children. The 1992 Domestic Violence Law specifies the appropriate police response to domestic violence, which protects all members of the family, including men. This law applies equally to marriages and to common-law relationships, and penalties for violent crimes are the same for women and men. Victims of domestic violence have the right to request restraining orders, which are frequently issued by the courts.

Despite these efforts, violence and abuse remain primary health and welfare risks for women and children on the island. The Business and Professional Women's Club, an affiliate of the Caribbean Women's Association, operates a crisis center on the island with thirty staff members who provide legal and medical services. Government-sponsored public education campaigns have been somewhat effective in stemming domestic violence, as have training programs developed to sensitize police officers and personnel in crisis centers.[34]

Rape/Sexual Assault

Human rights monitors have criticized Barbados for an inconsistency in sentencing for rape, incest, and statutory rape. Monitors note that a lack of sentencing guidelines results in longer punishments for persons convicted of petty theft than for incest, and lesser sentences for incest than for rape or sexual assault of nonfamily members. The Sexual Offenses Act of 1992 states that a person under the age of fourteen is deemed incapable of committing an act of rape.[35]

Trafficking in Women and Children

There is no evidence of trafficking of women or children into or out of Barbados.[36]

OUTLOOK FOR THE TWENTY-FIRST CENTURY

Compared to other nations in the Caribbean region, the government of Barbados has done much to elevate the status and living conditions of women on the island. Despite these progressive efforts, gender-specific data on important health, economic, political, and educational concerns are still unavailable. While general population statistics provide an important perspective on a nation's overall progress, the lack of gender-specific data keeps women and many of their concerns invisible. In the economic realm, for example, many women perform work in the informal sector or perform work for no pay, usually for families and family businesses. Though they work long hours, women's informal labor and earnings are not tracked by the government or calculated into national economic indexes.

It is clear from data that do exist that Bajan women fare better than most women in other developing nations and in the Caribbean region in general. As the globalization process evolves, women in Barbados, as in all regions of the world, will continue to bear the brunt of these global economic trends that affect women's and families' health, homelessness, access to health care, and access to educational and professional advancement. Bajan women's ability to maneuver, to influence national and regional policy, and to negotiate for fair wages and working conditions is essential to foster a more democratic globalization system and a more democratic and equitable Bajan society. Electing more women to public office appears to be an important goal for Bajan women in the twenty-first century. This would enable women and women's organizations in Barbados to more directly influence political, social, and economic policy.

NOTES

1. Central Bureau of Statistics: Barbados, www.barbados.gov.bb/stats.htm.

2. Diane Elson, ed., *Progress of the World's Women* (New York: United Nations Development Fund for Women, 2000), 68–77.

3. Latin American and Caribbean Network of Women in Science, www.awis.org/r_interlinks.html.

4. Barbados Ministry of Education, www.usc.edu/dept/education/globaled/wwcu/background/Barbados.htm.

5. *Caribbean Office Annual Report 2001* (United Nations Development Fund for Women).

6. Barbados Bureau of Women's Affairs, www.sdnp.org.gy/hands/crisiscntre.html.

7. Institute of Social and Economic Research, *Weathering the Economic Storm* (Bridgetown, Barbados: University of the West Indies), 12–13.

8. Office of Technology Assessment Archives, www.wws.princeton.edu/~ota.

9. Andrew Bibby, "Offshore Data Processing," *Teleworker Magazine* (United Kingdom) December 1997/January 1998.

10. "Viva la tecnologia: In Case You Missed It," *Boulder Weekly*, 2000.

11. U.S. Department of State, *Human Rights Report* (2000), www.usis.usemb.se/human.

12. Inter-American Development Bank: Barbados, 1998, www.iadb.org/exr/sep/ba981.htm.

13. Terrel Yearwood and Dawn Morgan, "Sex Laws," *Daily Nation*, August 27, 2000, www.hartford-hwp.com/archives/43/192.htm.

14. "Barbados; Statement by Hon. Hamilton Lashley, Minister of Social Transformation at the Twenty-Seventh Special Session of the General Assembly on Children, 8 May 2002, New York," www.un.org; Antoinette Connell, "Day Care Shutdown," *Nation Newspaper Barbados*, April 27, 2002, www.nationnews.com.

15. Elson, 2000.

16. International Planned Parenthood Federation: Barbados, www.ippf.org/regions/countries.

17. Americans for Divorce Reform, "Non-U.S. Divorce Rates," www.divorcereform.org.

18. Barbados Family Planning Association, www.bfpa.net.

19. Ibid.

20. Barbados Ministry of Health, www.uhl.bb/iah/barbados.htm.

21. Patricia Rodney, *The Caribbean State, Health Care, and Women* (Trenton, NJ: Africa World Press, 1998), chapter 6.

22. Caribbean Epidemiology Center, www.carec.org.

23. World Health Organization Report, November 2000, www.cnn.com/2000/HEALTH/AIDS/11/24/un.aids.ap.

24. World Watch Institute, "State of the World 2000," www.worldwatch.org/pubs/sow/2000.

25. Caribbean Epidemiology Center, www.carec.org.

26. Ibid.

27. Ibid.

28. Elson, 2000, 77.

29. Rhoda Reddock, "Women's Organizations in the Caribbean Community from the 19th Century to Today," *Women in Action* 2 (June 30, 1991): 12.

30. Barbados Gays and Lesbians against Discrimination, bglad2000.tripod.com.

31. D. Michelle Cave and Joan French, "Sexual Choice as a Human Right Issue," *LOLA Press, the International Feminist Magazine* 5 (May–October 1996).

32. CIA World Factbook, 2002, www.odci.gov/cia/publications/factbook/goes/bb.html.

33. World Conference on Religion and Peace, www.wcrp.or.jp.

34. Permanent Mission of Barbados to the United Nations, www.un.org/overview/missions.htm.

35. U.S. Department of State, 2000.

36. U.S. Department of State, "Barbados: Country Reports on Human Rights, 2001," www.state.gov.

RESOURCE GUIDE

Suggested Reading

Alexander, Simone A. James. *Mother Imagery in the Novels of Afro-Caribbean Women.* Columbia: University of Missouri Press, 2001.

Barriteau, Eudine. *The Political Economy of Gender in the Twentieth-Century Caribbean.* New York: Palgrave, 2001.

Beckles, Hilary. *Natural Rebels: A Social History of Enslaved Black Women in Barbados.* New Brunswick, NJ: Rutgers University Press, 1989.

Cartey, Wilfred. *Whispers from the Caribbean: I Going Away, I Going Home.* Los Angeles: Center for Afro-American Studies, University of California, 1991.

Freeman, Carla. *High Tech and High Heels in the Global Economy: Women, Work, and Pink-Collar Identities in the Caribbean.* Durham, NC: Duke University Press, 1999.

Gartland, Elizabeth. *Caribbean Women's Drama: An Annotated Bibliography.*

Kincaid, Jamaica. *Lucy.* New York: Plume, 1991.

Marshall, Paule. *Daughters.* New York: Plume, 1992.

Niesen de Abruna, Laura. "Twentieth-Century Women Writers from the English-Speaking Caribbean." In *Caribbean Women Writers: Essays from the First International Conference*, ed. Selwyn R. Cudjoe. Wellesley, MA: Calaloux Publications, 1990.

Waters, Erika J., ed. *The Caribbean Writer.* University of the Virgin Islands, 2001.

Welch, Pedro L.V., and Richard A. Goodridge. *Red and Black over White: Free Coloured Women in Pre-emancipation Barbados.* Bridgetown, Barbados: Carib Research and Publications, 2000.

Videos

I Is a Long-Memoried Woman. 1990. Produced by Ingrid Lewis. Women Make Movies (www.wmm.com). The history of slavery is shown through the eyes of Caribbean women, as is their struggle in the New World.

Web Sites

Barbados Family Planning Association, www.cariblife.com/pub/familyplan/.

Development Alternatives with Women for a New Era, www.dawn.org.fj.

Latin American and Caribbean Women's Health Network, www.reddesalud.web.cl/ingles.html.

LOLA, the International Feminist Magazine, www.lolapress.org/index.htm.

United Nations Development Fund for Women, www.unifem.undp.org/.

Organizations

Barbados Bureau of Women's Affairs
National Insurance Building, Second Floor
Fairchild Street
Bridgetown
Barbados, West Indies
Phone: 246-431-0850
Fax: 246-426-8959

Development Alternatives with Women for a New Era
Caribbean Secretariat
11 Gibbons Terrace
Christchurch
Barbados, West Indies
Phone: 246-420-4474
Email: dawn.org.fj

United Nations Development Fund for Women, Caribbean Regional Office
Room 27, Beckwith Mall
Bridgetown
St. Michael, Barbados, West Indies
Phone: 246-437-3970
Fax: 246-437-7674
Email: unifemcar@unifemcar.org

Women and Development Unit
c/o University of West Indies
Cave Hill Campus
St. Michael
Barbados, West Indies
Phone: 809-436-6312
Fax: 246-436-3006

SELECTED BIBLIOGRAPHY

Bibby, Andrew. "Offshore Data Processing." *Teleworker Magazine* (United Kingdom), December 1997/January 1998.

Cave, D. Michelle, and Joan French. "Sexual Choice as a Human Right Issue." *LOLA Press, the International Feminist Magazine* 5 (May–October 1996).

Elson, Diane, ed. *Progress of the World's Women*. New York: United Nations Development Fund for Women, 2000.

Institute of Social and Economic Research. *Weathering the Economic Storm*. Bridgetown, Barbados: University of the West Indies.

Rodney, Patricia. *The Caribbean State, Health Care, and Women*. Trenton, NJ: Africa World Press, 1998.

"Viva la tecnologia: In Case You Missed It." *Boulder Weekly*. 2000.

3

CANADA

Veronica Strong-Boag and Gillian Creese

PROFILE OF CANADA

Canada is the second-largest nation in the world, with a total area of 9,984,670 square kilometers.[1] Its population of 31,413,990 (2002) is heavily concentrated along its southern border and in larger metropolitan centers such as Toronto, Montreal, Vancouver, and Calgary. In 2002, women made up 50.5 percent of the population, a ratio reflecting the graying of Canadians; only 18.4 percent are under age fourteen, and 12.7 percent are sixty-five or over. Women made up 57.1 percent of Canadians over sixty-five. In 1996, 13,303,625 claimed single ethnic origin, including Aboriginal and Canadian, while 10,224,495 described themselves as of multiple origins, 3,197,480 characterized themselves as visible minorities, and 799,010 as North American Indian, Metis, or Inuit. English was the home language of 19,031,335 and French of 6,359,505; a further 2,556,830 Canadians reported nonofficial home languages, while 580,460 claimed multiple home languages. In 1991, 45.7 percent of the population was at least nominally Catholic, 36.2 percent Protestant, 0.9 percent Muslim, 0.6 percent Buddhist, 0.6

percent Hindu, 0.5 percent Sikh, 1.4 percent Eastern Orthodox, and 1.2 percent Jewish. Another 12.5 percent reported no religious affiliation.[2]

Home from the beginning to a wide range of Aboriginal peoples, or First Nations (the preferred term), Canada began as a colony of France, was conquered by Great Britain in 1760, rejected revolution, resisted American invasions in 1776 and 1812, and confederated as the Dominion of Canada in 1867. Canada is a constitutional monarchy, a bicameral federal state with a Parliament made up of an elected House of Commons and an appointed Senate. It has ten provinces and three territories and is a member of the British Commonwealth of Nations, the Organisation internationale de la francophonie, the United Nations, the North Atlantic Treaty Organization (NATO), and the G8 Summit of major industrialized democracies. It has been officially bilingual and bicultural in French and English since 1969; since 1971, the federal government has also endorsed official multiculturalism.

History and geography have encouraged strong regional identities—Atlantic Canada, Quebec, Ontario, the Prairie West, British Columbia, and the North—and intermittent threats of dissolution, notably from Québécois sovereigntists and, occasionally, from western dissidents. Vocal Native opposition to assimilation and land loss further complicates and enriches discussions of politics and culture. Already ethnically various in its First Nations origins, Canada has been further diversified by immigration, first largely from northern Europe and the United States, then from eastern and southern Europe and the Caribbean, and now increasingly from Asia and South America.

The vitality and debates among the nation's multiple communities prompt Canadians regularly to term themselves a "mosaic." The Charter of Rights and Freedoms, adopted as part of the Constitution Act 1982 that separated the constitution from Great Britain, reflected the uncertain equilibrium between individual and collective rights even as it prohibited discrimination on the basis of color, sex, or creed, confirmed French and English language rights, recognized affirmative-action programs for women and minorities, and acknowledged Aboriginal and treaty rights. Modern Canada is in some ways a microcosm of the world, struggling, as scholars frequently note, to balance unity and diversity and exhibiting tolerance and prejudice in the process.

OVERVIEW OF WOMEN'S ISSUES

As Canada celebrated its first-place ranking among 174 nations according to the United Nations human development index in 1997, its drop to sixth place in the gender-sensitive gender empowerment index was barely noticed. As one observer commented, "Canadians live in the best place in the world; female Canadians live someplace else."[3] Notwithstanding the great diversity among women by class, race/ethnicity, sexuality, age, region, and ability, or the significant increases in gender equality on many fronts during the twentieth century, women continue to be disadvantaged in many ways compared to similarly placed men.

Issues facing Canadian women at the dawn of the twenty-first century resemble those facing their foremothers: political power, economic independence, bodily autonomy, and meaningful choices about how to live. At the root of inequality are the unequal distribution of power—political, economic, and social—and the cultural and institutional histories that shape the perceived value of activities associated with women and men. During the twentieth century, Canadian women gained political rights, yet they remain greatly underrepresented, holding just over 18 percent of seats in the House of Commons in the most recent federal election (2000). Similarly, women reaped educational advances. However, in 1996, university-educated women earned only 76 percent as much as male graduates, only slightly better than the 73 percent recorded for all women employed full time. In spite of entry into nontraditional occupations, most women continue to work in a gender-segregated labor market. Moreover, growth in labor-force participation has not produced a significant redistribution of unpaid domestic and caring labor. Child care and domestic work remain largely female responsibilities, and the double day is still a reality. Uneven domestic obligations contribute to high divorce rates that, combined with lower wages, leave many women and their children in poverty. Not unlike a century ago, poverty rates remain highest among Aboriginal women, those with disabilities, and single mothers and their children. New economic trends, including globalization, the North American Free Trade Agreement (NAFTA), and the ascendancy of neoliberal economic policies, deepen the gulf between women and men and rich and poor. In 2002, a report from the Canadian Centre for Policy Alternatives concluded that the average worth of the richest 50 percent of the population had more than doubled over thirty years, while the poorest Canadians had experienced a significant loss: their debts outpaced their assets.[4] Under the management of the New Right, the pursuit of market-driven globalization at any cost has sharpened social divisions in Canada, as elsewhere in the world.

EDUCATION

Opportunities

Girls and women experience both informal and formal education differently from similarly situated males. From colonial times to the present, class, race/ethnicity, sexuality, age, region, and ability have offered opportunities to some and denied them to others. In the past, poor girls exchanged labor for the three Rs and learned their alphabet in free Sunday schools. With the emergence of public education in the nineteenth century, most girls sat beside boys in primary classes but found paths diverging in secondary education. In Quebec, the slow introduction of compulsory education and clerical power further reduced options. On the other hand, the presence of strong Catholic orders of nuns, notably in education, health care, and social work, offered important opportunities for those with talent and ambition and for those who wished to escape marriage and child-bearing. Black and Native children regularly entered effectively segregated and inferior institutions well into the twentieth century.

In the late nineteenth century, courses aimed at girls were introduced in domestic science and commercial subjects, the latter linked to expanding clerical employment. Gender differences in literacy disappeared early among the Canadian born, but not until after World War II was high-school graduation taken for granted even by European Canadians. As late as 1996, 42 percent of the working-age Aboriginal population and 22 percent of the non-Aboriginal population had not completed secondary schooling.[5]

Despite the success of the tiny minority of women entering universities before World War I, institutions of higher education treated women as interlopers. Only areas that were gendered female, such as nursing, home economics, and general arts, readily welcomed them. Male advantage, visible in the persistence of a masculinist canon in many fields and an overwhelmingly male professorate, especially at the senior ranks, survived into the twenty-first century.

Responsibility for domestic labor remains a critical determinant of educational options. Sexual harassment continues to be commonplace. Bullying among schoolgirls has also recently been identified as a significant problem. Racism and homophobia worsen the situation for many students.[6] At the same time, women's potential as mothers, their quest for knowledge and autonomy, their need to earn a living, and support for equal rights have always opened some doors.

Like its predecessor, the second feminist wave in the latter part of the twentieth century targeted discriminatory education. Girls and young women were encouraged to take science and math, to challenge "males-tream" knowledge, and to plan careers in male preserves. By 1987–1988, women made up 50 percent of undergraduates. Ten years later, their numbers rose to 56 percent, they almost matched men in graduate programs, and they were ahead in part-time graduate and undergraduate enrollment. In 1999, women made up 51.7 percent of students in first-year medicine. Beginning in the 1970s, women's studies and feminist scholarship became widely available, both as separate options and integrated within the main-stream curriculum. Occasional female principals and presidents challenge the glass ceiling that still keeps most senior administration in male hands. Such gains are far from inconsequential. Indeed, their significance is suggested by the jeremiads that greet every step toward narrowing the opportunity gap. Men and boys, whose academic prowess and right to corresponding economic opportunity used to be taken for granted, now have to compete. Some critics of women's recent gains point to a pattern of reverse discrimination, choosing to ignore a long-standing masculine culture that handicaps many boys, especially from the working class, with its dismissal of learning and study.

Despite the appearance of unlimited opportunities, educational choices, albeit improving slowly, remain resolutely gendered and often unequal. In many disciplines, the conventional male canon has remained remarkably resilient. Primary and secondary schools remain resolutely gendered, raced, classed, and heterosexual sites. Homophobia is widely reported, and safety is an issue on all campuses and on school grounds generally. First Nations women are more likely than men in the same community to possess post-secondary credentials, but are underrepresented relative to non-Aboriginal women. In higher education, female students still concentrate heavily in arts, education, social work, and nursing. While primary classrooms rely on female teachers, more than 80 percent of full-time university instructors are male; in both instances, only a tiny minority are other than European in ancestry. Those who test the limits of nontraditional fields encounter an uncertain reception. In 1995, for example, women made up only about 20 percent of undergraduate and master's students and about 10 percent of doctoral students in engineering.

Literacy

Women generally, especially among the native born, have higher literacy rates than men. Older women are more likely than younger women to report literacy difficulties. In 1994, the International Adult Literacy Survey reported that the prose competence of 53 percent of women aged sixty-six and over was at the lowest level, more or less matching that of their male counterparts. In 1998, 49.2 percent of women aged fifteen or over reported daily use of computers, compared to 63.1 percent of men. The highest computing usage by women occurred among the age group twenty-five to thirty-four, 71.1 percent, almost equaling men's usage at 73.7 percent. The difference in Internet usage in the same year was greater: 24.6 percent of all women, compared to 33.8 percent of men. The highest Internet usage occurred among the age group fifteen to nineteen, 47.6 percent of girls, compared to 57.3 percent of boys.

EMPLOYMENT AND ECONOMICS

Job/Career Opportunities

The percentage of women in the Canadian labor force increased steadily in the twentieth century, from 16 percent in 1901 to 55 percent in 1999. Many women made a living in the informal economy, exchanging domestic labor for cash by taking in children, boarders, or piecework. Many were also the family financiers, stretching scant dollars to cover household needs. Until the 1960s, young, single, childless women were most likely to be employed, returning to the informal and domestic economies upon marriage and childbearing. By the 1990s, this pattern had changed; women's labor-force participation is now more similar to men's. Women with children under age sixteen are only slightly less likely than others to be employed in the labor market (69 percent compared to 76 percent). Single-earner families with a male breadwinner are no longer the norm but the exception. In 1995, about one-quarter of Canadian women earned more than their male partners. Women are, however, more likely to work part-time; 28 percent worked less than thirty hours per week in 1999. Forty-one percent of women and 29 percent of men work in nonstandard conditions (part-time, temporary, self-employed, or multiple jobs). For the most part, these jobs have low wages.

As women have increased their formal education, their economic opportunities have expanded. For example, by 1999, women made up 47 percent of doctors and dentists and 35 percent of managers. They continue, however, to be concentrated for the most part at the bottom of these professions. Overall, gender segregation in the labor market remains strong, with 70 percent of all employed women working in traditional female sectors of teaching, nursing, and clerical, sales, and service occupations.

Pay

Canadian women earn significantly lower wages than do men. In 1997, employed women earned only 67 percent of men's incomes, up from 58 percent in 1967; thru 1997 this figure increases to 72 percent among full-time employees. Wage differences exist within as well as among occupations: women employed full time earn significantly less than their male counterparts in management (62 percent), teaching (72 percent), and medicine (50 percent). Among women, recent immigrants, First Nations, and those of visible minority status share lower employment incomes and higher unemployment rates. While traditional economists concentrate on skill differences and rational choice to explain these discrepancies, one observer has noted that "roughly one-half to three-quarters of the gender wage gap cannot be explained" by these factors.[7]

Lower lifetime earnings, less access to private pension plans, and discriminatory laws have compromised old age for many women. Vulnerability is not new. Nineteenth-century poorhouses and shelters were jammed with widowed and elderly women. First Nations citizens and those with disabilities have been especially vulnerable. Until the last quarter of the twentieth century, pension plans were often discriminatory, sometimes, for example, forcing women to take earlier retirement. About half of elderly, unattached women endure poverty at the beginning of the twenty-first century. Nevertheless, women, who are more likely to maintain multiple social roles, have been observed to confront old age more easily than their male counterparts, and today, women's longer stay in the paid labor force is providing better financial preparation.

Working Conditions

Canadian women (31 percent) are almost as likely as men (33 percent) to belong to a union, with unionists concentrated in the public sector. Unionization has clear advantages, such as a smaller gendered wage gap and higher levels of income and job security. Since 1992, women's issues have gained increasing prominence in the labor movement, and provisions dealing with parental leave, pay equity, and sexual harassment have been negotiated in many collective agreements.

The labor movement, along with women's groups and parties on the left, has a long history of pressuring governments to legislate improvements for workers. Legislation in the areas of health and safety, employment standards, employment insurance, pay equity, and employment equity have all been legislated, if somewhat unevenly across provincial and federal labor jurisdictions, since the end of World War II.

Sexual Harassment

The Canada Human Rights Act makes sexual harassment illegal, but it remains a significant problem in the workplace, as elsewhere. The Criminal Code provides penalties for sexual assault and stalking (criminal harassment). Harassment is now considered an abuse of power that makes varying degrees of sexual access a condition of employment and that creates a "chilly climate" for employees.

Support for Mothers/Caretakers

Maternal Leave

In 1971, Canada developed a system of public paid maternity leave, to which parental leave was added in 1990. The period of paid leave following childbirth or adoption is now one year. The Canada Labour Code provides seventeen weeks of maternity leave, fifteen of these with benefits. An additional thirty-five weeks of parental leave may be shared with the father. Parental benefits are now available for adoptive parents. In 1998, 98 percent of all maternity and parental leave benefits were paid to women. Paid maternity leave is tied to the employment insurance system. For all its promise, coverage has in fact fallen because more hours of paid employment are required for eligibility. Thus, despite the ideal of entitlement and recognition, more and more women have found themselves without maternity leave benefits.

The federal contribution-based employment insurance program also provides sickness benefits for up to fifteen weeks. Women's greater likelihood of part-time and interrupted labor-force participation and generally lower wages again undermine the potential of sickness benefits. A significant number of companies, particularly but not only in the service and hospitality sectors, offer part-time employment to avoid paying critical medical and dental benefits.

Daycare

Because most mothers of young children are employed in the labor market, child care is a pressing problem. In 1996, 300,000 daycare spaces were available to preschoolers, but 900,000 families needed at least one space. The Liberal government of Prime Minister Jean Chrétien continues to promise action, most recently in a 2002 Throne Speech. Any federal initiative requires the support of provincial governments, which vary tremendously in their commitment to women's rights. Motivated in part by nationalist pronatalism, in part by the progressive leanings of some administrations, and in part by an active feminist lobby, Quebec has been in the forefront of many initiatives. It quadrupled its regulated daycare spaces in the 1990s. Under Conservative administrations in the 1990s, Ontario, the richest province, emerged as a leading opponent of a national or indeed any universal child-care program. In 2001, regulated child-care spaces were available for the following percentage of children under age twelve: British Columbia, 12.1; Alberta, 9.1; Saskatchewan, 4.2; Manitoba, 12.4; Ontario, 8.9; Quebec, 21.1; New Brunswick, 9.9; Nova Scotia, 8.1; Prince Edward Island, 14.0; Newfoundland, 5.5; and Canada, 12.1.[8] Expense, limited availability, and uneven regulation make many mothers' search for good care a nightmare and condemn many to present and future poverty.

Social/Government Programs

The development of Canada's social security system in the twentieth century held considerable promise. Children and their mothers were early objects of concern. First of all, as is still the case, they made up the majority of those in distress in the nineteenth and early twentieth centuries. Traditions of property holding, domestic violence, and legal inferiority handicapped women and their heirs. Even when it was available, waged employment consistently favored adult males, and businesses, unions, and governments ensured for a long time that this remained largely unchanged. Beginning in the late nineteenth century, feminist middle-class activists and their clerical and other allies responded to the tragedies around them by demanding social and legal recognition of women's primary role as parents and men's responsibilities as breadwinners. Working-class clients of provincial social welfare initiatives, such as Mothers' Pensions/Allowances beginning during World War I, were similarly insistent on winning acknowledgment of their claims to state support for parental duties. This early maternalist interpretation of citizenship, with its demand for official recognition for mothers' work in the creation of moral and responsible adults, floundered, however, during the Great Depression of the 1930s. That decade's particularly harsh times saw mothers' rights increasingly superseded by social security entitlements founded on men's workplace rights. By World War II, wage labor had become the preeminent basis for claims to social security. The result effectively gendered entitlements to social security and thus to full citizenship.

Welfare and Welfare Reform

Today's mothers and children continue to receive state benefits in very large part because individual men are seen to fail in their fundamental role as breadwinners. Women's rights as social citizens are effectively mediated through their relationship to males, whose meaningful citizenship is in turn tied to their success in the economic market. The social entitlement of women and their offspring is compromised when they fail to maintain adult male support. Given the emphasis on individual responsibility, it is no surprise that female social welfare recipients have been commonly expected to demonstrate that the moral failure that brought them to seek aid was not theirs but rather that of a delinquent, whether by accident or by design, male breadwinner. In order to receive secure benefits, Canadian women have historically had to demonstrate moral fitness. This has required their submission to externally imposed standards of conduct with regard to everything from housekeeping to sexuality. Only acquiescence has ultimately confirmed their right to claims against the state. The Canadian child welfare system, with its recurring preference for the investigation of morality over practical support, is one continuing result of women's general disadvantage as citizens.

Widespread prosperity after World War II brought the introduction of Family Allowances (1944), a universal old-age pension system (1951), the Old Age Pension Plan (1965), and the Medical Care Insurance Act and the Canada Assistance Plan (both 1966). In response to the "discovery" of poverty by a Senate Inquiry (1969) and the Royal Commission on the Status of Women (1970), there was even discussion, ultimately fruitless, of a guaranteed annual income. Even in better times, however, stigmatization remained a problem for those receiving social security.

Recently, the gains of the post–World War II years have been undermined. Cuts to the welfare state have reduced social services and assistance to female clients. In the race to the bottom, neoliberal restructuring has eroded employment conditions generally. Even as unemployment rates moved into the double digits in the 1990s, it became harder to qualify for unemployment insurance, and payments were lower. In 1997, women became disproportionately disentitled under the unemployment insurance system, which now favors standard full-time, full-year employment. In addition, the loss of public-sector jobs, which continued to be threatened in 2002, disproportionately affects unionized and higher-paid women workers. At the same time, it forces more unpaid caring work back onto daughters, wives, and mothers. Such developments increase disparities between the sexes and between more advantaged and more disadvantaged groups of women. The suicide of an Ontario woman, eight months pregnant, in 2001 testified to the failings of the system. She had been placed under house arrest and faced a lifetime ban on social assistance because she had collected welfare and received student loans while attending college. The Supreme Court's December 2002 decision, in response to a class-action lawsuit filed by a Quebec woman, that Canadians do not have constitutional guarantees of a minimum income provides another telling indication of neoliberal times.[9]

FAMILY AND SEXUALITY

Gender Roles

As in other countries whose institutional arrangements are rooted in European colonialism, gender relations in Canada have been shaped by patriarchal traditions. The often more egalitarian gender relations experienced by women in Aboriginal communities were undermined by new legal, economic, and religious practices and beliefs that placed men in charge of public life and private households. While women in all communities developed ingenious private strategies to circumvent male power and drew on traditions of female competence, they were repeatedly handicapped by material conditions such as legislative discrimination against female homesteaders and Native women who married non-Natives, both of whom were denied the opportunities of their male counterparts.

Daycare, Toronto, Ontario, Canada. Photo © TRIP/B. Crawshaw.

Gender roles underwent significant changes during the twentieth century as women won formal political and legal equality and asserted economic and sexual independence. While the male breadwinner has been supplanted by new realities, ideas about women's domestic roles have persisted. Despite their dramatic increase in paid labor, women's share of unpaid domestic work, at two-thirds, has remained stable since data were first collected in the 1960s. In 1998, this unpaid work amounted to an average of 4.4 hours per day for women and 2.7 hours per day for men. Women remain primarily responsible for labor involved in running a household and assisting children and elderly relatives. The baby-boom generation born after World War II is now commonly referred to as the "sandwich generation," caught between obligations to offspring who remain longer at home and an increasing population of aging parents. The inequitable division of resulting labor is a key factor in advantaging men and disadvantaging women in the paid labor market.

Marriage

As the household of Anne Shirley, Matthew, and Marilla Cuthbert memorialized in the best-selling Canadian novel *Anne of Green Gables* (1908) made abundantly clear, family forms have always been diverse, but during much of the twentieth century, the heterosexual nuclear family was held to be the norm. Today there is a broader acknowledgment of diverse household arrangements and less pressure to enter into, or stay within, the institution of marriage.

A substantial drop in annual marriage rates has occurred since the 1970s. Women's age of first marriage also jumped from twenty-two in 1971 to twenty-eight in 1997. Still, most Canadian women do wed. In 1996, 71 percent of women and 64 percent of men over the age of fifteen had been married at least once, and 50 percent of women currently lived with their husbands. Alongside declining rates of marriage is a significant increase in common-law unions, including 11.7 percent of families in 1997. Quebec leads the way. In 2001, 70 percent of Québécois, compared to 34 percent of other Canadian women, would start conjugal life as part of a common-law couple. In contrast to the more than 80 percent of women now in their fifties, in both Quebec and the rest of Canada, who chose marriage, those between twenty and twenty-nine now commonly prefer common-law unions to first test intimate household relations.[10] It is unclear how the controversial December 2002 decision of the Supreme Court of Canada that common-law partners, unlike married partners, do not have guaranteed rights to assets if the relationship collapses will shape future choices.

According to constitutional arrangements dating from 1867, marriage law falls under provincial jurisdiction, but divorce is handled by federal legislation. Common law operates in nine provinces and all the territories. The Civil Code applies in Quebec. From the 1960s on, that province's reform of family law gradually overturned decades of legal discrimination, for example, giving married women significant new legal rights with regard to property. In June 2002, the Quebec National Assembly passed Bill 84, which provided same-sex couples with the same rights and obligations, including custody of children, as heterosexual partnerships. In September 2002, Quebec's Supreme Court ruled that the opposite-sex definition of marriage is discriminatory and cannot be justified under the federal Charter of Rights and Freedoms. In the same month, the federal government announced its intention to appeal the provincial decision to the Supreme Court of Canada. The December 2002 decision by that court that common-law couples do not have the same rights and obligations as those who are married suggests that Canadians are going to discuss the meaning and legitimacy of various marital regimes for some time.

Unlike the declining rate of marriage, the incidence of divorce has grown dramatically since laws were liberalized in 1968. In 1997, there were 225 divorces for every 100,000 people, compared to 55 in 1968. Many who divorce later remarry. In 1997, nearly one-quarter of brides had previously been married. Stepfamilies, both married and common law, made up 11.8 percent of all couples with children in 2001.[11] Single-parent families, the great majority headed by women (83 percent in 1996), now make up 19 percent of all families with children, double the 1971 rate. There has been an increase in joint arrangements (27.6 percent), but women still won custody in more than 60 percent of child-custody cases in 1997. In December 2002, the federal Department of Justice announced its intention to amend family law, replacing the terms "custody and access" with the less emotionally charged terminology "parental responsibilities." Supporters claim that this move will better secure the best interests of children, but many feminist observers fear a concession to the fathers' rights lobby and a refusal to acknowledge women's special vulnerability to poverty and violence.

Reproduction

Like marriage rates, birthrates have also dropped dramatically. Access to birth control and, to a significantly more limited degree, to abortion services has significantly improved women's ability to choose whether to become pregnant. In 1997, there were 44 births for every 1,000 women between fifteen and forty-nine years of age, less than half the 1959 rate. Families now have fewer and generally older children living at home than in the past (1.2 children on average in 1996). Aboriginal women have higher fertility rates than other women, with 2.7 children on average, compared to 1.6 for all women. As the report, well titled *Proceed with Care*, of the Royal Commission on New Reproductive Technologies (1989–1993) made clear, sterility was a problem for a significant number of Canadian women.[12] Despite the commission's concerns, surrogate motherhood and in vitro fertilization remain largely unregulated, shaped by the desperation of would-be parents, hopes for corporate profits, and modern society's penchant for scientific quick fixes. The impact of environmental degradation on sterility is well known but little addressed.

Sex Education

In the nineteenth century, Canadians began debating the merits of school sex education, notably the benefits of celibacy and restraint. Since education is constitutionally a provincial responsibility, responses varied, but issues of sexuality were everywhere uneasily, unevenly, and incompletely incorporated into health, domestic science, and physical education classes. While matters have improved, school-based sex education remains a lightning rod, especially if it involves open acknowledgment of homosexual, bisexual, and transgendered sexualities. In response to a lengthy battle in a Vancouver suburb over the introduction of texts about same-sex parents into primary grades, the Supreme Court decreed in December 2002 that school boards must recognize the diversity of household forms and may not ban materials on lesbian and gay families. Volunteer agencies such as Planned Parenthood of Canada, gay and lesbian educators' associations, and the women's health movement in general stand in the forefront of popular sex education for young and old alike.

Gay, lesbian, and bisexual youth are still likely to remain closeted at home and school, despite gay-straight alliances found in some high schools. They have higher suicide rates and substance-abuse problems. Largely because of the educational efforts of gay, lesbian, and bisexual adults, drop-in centers and support programs are becoming available, especially in the larger cities.

Contraception and Abortion

Canadians have regularly practiced contraception, but in 1882 it became a crime to sell or advertise birth control. Exceptions were allowed under section 207 of the Criminal Code that permitted distribution for an undefined "public good." Most doctors, reluctant to test the legislation, protective of male authority, and suspicious of female sexuality, gave little help, especially to the poor. Communities of women, among the First Nations and immigrant groups, for example, exchanged contraceptive information, but until the introduction of sulfa drugs in the 1930s, high maternal mortality rates demonstrated the continuing cost of failures to limit reproduction. A birth-control movement, dominated by the left, emerged in the 1920s. In 1932, the Hamilton, Ontario, Birth Control Society began offering assistance. In British Columbia, the Parents' Information Bureau similarly offered advice, but only to married women, most particularly those who were already mothers. In the 1930s, a Canadian version of the international eugenics movement emerged to argue that certain groups, distinguished by racial, ethnic, or physical and mental characteristics, should not be allowed to reproduce. Eugenics was the inspiration for sterilization legislation in Alberta in 1928 and in British Columbia in 1933.

By the 1950s, some drugstores were discreetly carrying some forms of contraception, often advertised for the prevention of contagious diseases. The 1960s brought a changed climate. Planned Parenthood was established in 1960, and nine years later the federal government legalized birth control and made limited provision for abortion, subject to the approval of hospital committees. Opposition remained, however, especially from religious conservatives who threatened abortion providers and who made it extremely difficult for hospitals to establish the legally required therapeutic abortion committees. In 1988, led by the first woman justice, Bertha Wilson, the Supreme Court struck down legislation that limited access to legal abortion services. Abortion on demand became legally available. In practice, however, access varies widely, limited by provincial funding policies, the politics of local health boards, and pressure from antiabortion activists.

Teen Pregnancy

As elsewhere in the world, the age of menarche for girls (and spermarche for boys) has been decreasing since the nineteenth century. Teenage childbearing has been relatively common in Canadian history, but it is viewed increasingly negatively in light of expectations of labor-force participation, education, and social and health services. Today, despite a brief rise in the late 1980s and early 1990s, teen pregnancies are decreasing. Wider access to contraceptives and abortion services helped halve the birthrate for teens between 1968 and 1997. Despite myths to the contrary, very few girls are sexually active before age sixteen or seventeen. Canadian rates are comparable to those of Australia and Great Britain, greater than those of northern Europe, and lower than those in the United States. As in Australia and the United States, rates among Aboriginal teens are higher than the national average. One researcher has noted that sexually active girls and single mothers are disproportionately "youth who are not in school, are from lower income households and are born in Canada rather than immigrants."[13] In the past, most teen mothers got married or gave up their babies for fostering or adoption. Today they are more likely to choose abortion or face single motherhood.

HEALTH

Health Care Access

Although Canada's modern health-care system is considered one of the best in the world, good health and its determinants have never been distributed equally. Female bodies have traditionally been regarded as inferior and properly subject to male authorities. Poverty and discrimination have regularly worsened the special impact of responsibility for reproductive and domestic life. Despite handicaps, women have endeavored to manage treatment of themselves and their community. Native and settler midwives were common, and nineteenth-century cookbooks show that mothers were expected to provide primary health care from colonial times on. As male doctors asserted a professional monopoly after confederation in 1867, midwives were increasingly banned (only to gain new legal recognition at the end of the twentieth century), and women's traditional knowledge was dismissed. While the medical establishment resisted female doctors, setting informal quotas in medical schools and in internships, professional nurses who knew their place were accepted. Hospitals reinforced class and racial differences in access to good health care; middle-class urbanites remain significant beneficiaries. Infectious diseases, including typhus and tuberculosis, still ravage poor and Native communities; in 1991, First Nations women, while only 4 percent of Canadian women, suffered 20 percent of all female cases of tuberculosis.[14]

The expansion of the welfare state after World War II helped improve health. Public hospital insurance and medicare (1968) joined old-age pensions, unemployment insurance, and family allowances to form the core of social support programs. Women also struggled to gain reproductive control, end violence against women, win admission to medical schools, and insist on gender as a key determinant of health. As a measure of success, a girl born in Canada in 1997 could expect to live into her eighties, compared to age seventy-six for boys. However, in the 1990s, an assault on Canada's social security system threatened the health of women, particularly the one in five who were poor. As access to public health care is undermined in the name of the market, the affluent are able to purchase private services. At the beginning of the twenty-first century, much federal-provincial politics and grassroots activism focus on whether or just how much Canadians in general, the poor in particular, should sacrifice medically in order to satisfy the demands of international drug companies and private medical providers.

Diseases and Disorders

In 1997, 62 percent of women over age twelve reported a chronic health condition. Arthritis and osteoporosis threaten an aging population. In 2002, women made up 69.5 percent of the population over age eighty-five.

The federal Liberal government in power since 1993 has promised the legalization of marijuana for personal use in 2003. Alcohol and tobacco abuse remain more serious for most Canadians than the danger of illegal drugs. In 1995–1996, 1,823 women and 4,681 men died directly, and 29,181 women and 51,765 men were hospitalized, as a result of alcohol.

AIDS and Sexually Transmitted Diseases

By the 1990s, AIDS was closely associated with heterosexual contact and injection drug use. Far fewer women than men have been diagnosed with AIDS. In 2000, women made up 24 percent of positive HIV tests. Community groups like British Columbia's Positive Women lobby for awareness and support, but women's lesser power in many intimate relations continues to make them vulnerable. While rates dropped for a number of years, a recent slow increase in HIV/AIDS presents a particularly serious problem, especially to injection drug users and Native women. Other sexually transmitted diseases are also a significant concern. While syphilis has nearly disappeared, chlamydia, with its threat to later fertility, affects more young women than men.

Eating Disorders

Anorexia and bulimia, involving about one in twenty young women, made Canadian headlines and inspired the first clinics in the 1980s, but diet disorders were visible as early as the mid-nineteenth century. A wide variety of self-help groups can be found on the Internet. The widespread advertising of diet aids, ranging from medications to exercise and self-help groups, suggests many women's preoccupation with meeting socially mandated levels of slimness. On the other side of the coin, Canadians, especially young people, are beginning to exhibit some of the same health difficulties with obesity that increasingly characterize Americans. Lack of exercise in all age groups is a clear contributor to these problems.

Cancer

Canadian women are also experiencing elevated cancer rates as the population ages and the environment degrades. After heart disease and strokes, lung, breast, and reproductive cancers are the third-leading cause of death for women.

Depression

Depression and mental illness correlate strongly with poverty and marginalization. While mood-altering drugs have generally replaced once familiar surgical solutions, the social determinants of mental health are only slowly being addressed.

POLITICS AND LAW

Colonial women, both Native and settler, petitioned authorities and sued opponents to gain rights. They were active alongside men in opposing the British conquest, fighting as United Empire Loyalists, and joining in demands for and against rebellions in the 1830s, responsible government in the 1840s, and confederation in the 1860s. First Nations and black women like the writer E. Pauline Johnson (Tekahionwake) and Mary Ann Shadd Cary championed causes such as land claims and elimination of slavery. Early feminists also slowly won legal reforms in regard to child custody and married women's property rights. The Woman's Christian Temperance Union (WCTU) emerged in the 1870s to articulate mounting resistance to alcohol abuse, violence against women and children, and economic dependence. Until the creation of the National Council of Women of Canada (NCWC) in 1893, the WCTU was the nation's largest women's organization. The WCTU, however, was much quicker to endorse political solutions. The NCWC did not come out in favor of women's suffrage until 1910. In Quebec, the Fédération nationale St. Jean Baptiste, founded as an umbrella organization by feminists in 1907, had to tread still more warily in the face of clerical suspicion.

Suffrage

Colonial women were formally barred from voting in the first decades of the nineteenth century, but they soon lobbied, first for school board and municipal franchises, and increasingly for the provincial and federal ballot. The first local successes came in the 1870s, but feminists did not see provincial victories, beginning in the west, until 1916. Atlantic Canada followed relatively quickly, but Quebec held out until 1940. A partial federal franchise came in 1918, but Japanese and Chinese Canadian women waited until the late 1940s and the Doukhobors until the 1950s. Native women lacked general enfranchisement until 1960.

Political Participation

While women's groups from the nineteenth century to the present have been active lobbyists, women's parties have been rare. Although women have been members of marginal parties, including the Communist Party and the Green Party, most efforts have been concentrated on the mainstream. While not all women holding elected or appointed office have been considered or have considered themselves feminists, many, including many of the firsts mentioned here, have cherished the title. Such feminist politicians have often been important in securing Canadian advances in equality. Agnes Campbell Macphail, first of the United Farmers of Ontario, later of the Cooperative Commonwealth Federation, became the first female member of Parliament in 1921 and had a distinguished career championing peace, prison reform, and women's and workers' rights. The Liberal Mary Ellen Smith, as minister without portfolio in British Columbia, became the first woman in the British Empire to hold ministerial office in 1921. In

1930, Liberal activist Cairine Reay MacKay Wilson took her seat as the first female senator. Conservative member of Parliament Ellen Louks Fairclough was the first federal cabinet minister, secretary of state, in 1957. Jeanne Benoit Sauvé served as Canada's first female governor-general from 1984 to 1990. Adrienne Poy Clarkson was the second woman and the first Chinese Canadian governor-general, serving from 1999 to the present. In 1982, Bertha Wilson became the first female judge of the Supreme Court. In 1999, Beverly McLachlin became the first female chief justice of the Supreme Court.

In 1975, British Columbian Rosemary Brown became the first black Canadian to seek the leadership of a federal party, the New Democratic Party (NDP). Yukon member of Parliament Audrey McLaughlin was the first to lead a federal party, the NDP, in 1989. In 1988, Liberal Ethel Blondin-Andrew took her seat as the first Native woman elected to the House of Commons. In 1993, Conservative Kim Campbell became the first female prime minister but almost immediately faced defeat. In November 1993, federal Liberal Sheila Copps became the first woman to serve as deputy prime minister.

At the provincial level, Louise McKinney of Alberta's Non-Partisan League became the first woman in the British Empire to serve in a legislature in 1917. The first provincial premier was Social Credit member Rita Johnson in British Columbia in 1991. In the same year, Inuvialuit Nellie Cournoyea became the first Aboriginal woman to head a provincial or territorial government as premier of the Northwest Territories. Two years later, Liberal Catherine Callbeck was elected premier of Prince Edward Island. In 1994, provincial Quebec Liberal Fatima Houda-Pepin became the first Muslim woman elected to a Canadian legislature.

While the gender gap in voting is associated with the 1980s, it dates at least to the 1920s, when new female voters helped introduce reforms such as old-age pensions (federally) and mothers' allowances (provincially). At the beginning of the twenty-first century, both the Bloc québécois, the advocate of independence, and the Canadian Alliance, the right-wing representative of western alienation, attract proportionally fewer female supporters than rivals more protective of federal social security initiatives.

Between the suffrage campaigns and the modern feminist movement, women remained active, winning recognition as persons in the constitution (1929), demanding a federal Women's Labour Bureau (1954), and securing equal-pay legislation in a number of provinces in the 1950s. The 1960s saw critical developments with the creation of the Fédération des femmes du Québec (FFQ, 1966), the Association féminine d'éducation et d'action sociale (1966), the Committee on Equality for Women (1966), and the Royal Commission on the Status of Women (1967–1970). In the 1970s, the federal and provincial governments began to set up advisory councils on the status of women. In 1978, the Quebec council produced *Pour les*

Québécoises: Égalité et indépendance, with its deliberately provocative invocation of the sovereigntist principles of equality and independence. A year later, the New Brunswick council published the first Canadian report on family violence. Feminists seemed securely positioned in many state bureaucracies, sparking the neologism "femocrat." Modern constitutional debates created further opportunities. In 1985, women, after a hard-fought campaign, won substantial recognition in the federal Charter of Rights and Freedoms, and Native women, battling since the 1960s, achieved greater equality under revisions to the Indian Act. Since 1984, the Women's Legal Education Action Fund (LEAF) has represented continuing enthusiasm for legal and judicial reform. A volunteer organization including many feminist lawyers, it routinely, if with uncertain success, uses the equality provisions of the charter to advance women's rights.

Women's Rights

Feminist Movements

In the 1960s, women's liberation appeared in Canadian universities. Some recruits, like Judy Rebick, who later became president of the National Action Committee, came from the United States, but Canadians very much drew on their own distinctive progressive traditions. Those known as "red-diaper babies" (the offspring of socialist parents) looked to Canada's long-standing socialist, social democratic, and union traditions to question the sexual status quo. In Quebec and in Native communities, female activists were inspired by their own histories of independent criticism and action. In 1966, le Front de libération des femmes de Québec embraced independence for the province and for women.

Women workers also established powerful caucuses within organized labor. In 1985, Grace Hartman became the head of the Canadian Union of Public Employees, the largest national union. A year later, Shirley Carr became the first female president of the influential Canadian Federation of Labour. Hartman subsequently became the second president of the National Action Committee. In the 1970s and 1980s, women were newsworthy in their leadership of a series of strikes that, if not always successful, dramatically raised the profile of female unionists. Modern unions made major inroads among nurses and teachers who stood on the front lines of some of the bitterly contested labor disputes in the last decades of the twentieth century. In the 1970s, socialists and unionists established International Women's Day committees that made March 8 a major feature of the spring calendar.

In the 1960s, a continuing tradition of peace activism embodied in the Voice of Women/La Voix des femmes (1960) found common cause with younger women involved in such groups as the Student Union for Peace

Action. In the same decade, consciousness-raising groups encouraged questioning of hierarchical organization and insisted that "the personal is political." In the 1970s, restrictions on abortion and birth control rallied many to the new movement. An on-to-Ottawa Abortion Caravan that recruited women nationwide to challenge the Criminal Code in 1970 drew on traditions of street theater that suffragists would have recognized. Challenges to violence against women also became a mainstay of female activism with the creation of Women against Violence against Women (1977) and annual Take-Back-the-Night Marches (beginning in 1981).

The 1967 creation of the Royal Commission on the Status of Women was an offspring of the reenergized Canadian women's movement. Its 1970 report made 167 recommendations aimed at eliminating inequalities in criminal law, education, taxation, poverty, public life, immigration and citizenship, the economy, and the family.[15] In 1972, a conference to consider its implementation prompted the creation of the Ad Hoc Committee that soon emerged as the National Action Committee on the Status of Women (NAC). At the beginning of the twenty-first century, this remains the leading national representative of Canada's organized feminists.

By the 1980s and 1990s, NAC, like the Canadian women's movement in general, was increasingly criticized by Native activists such as Jeannette Armstrong and women of color such as Sunera Thobani as exclusive and overly preoccupied with the concerns of able-bodied, heterosexual, white, and middle-class women. The National Organization of Immigrant and Visible Minority Women of Canada and the Disabled Women's Network represented the new diversity of organized women. Change proved slow and difficult for mainstream feminists. In 1993, Thobani, an Indo-Canadian student activist from British Columbia, became the unanimous choice as president of NAC and the first in a series of nonmainstream leaders who continued the move toward greater inclusiveness. NAC's internal changes, together with its opposition to NAFTA, brought it into increasing conflict with the increasingly conservative federal government that had provided much of its funding since the 1980s. By the late 1990s, it was struggling to survive, far from the robust group that had insisted upon and sponsored the leaders' debate before the 1984 federal election.

If formal political life was often disappointing in its results, women took pleasure and found political meaning and encouragement in their active involvement in cultural production of every sort. This was not new. Women like painter Emily Carr and sculptors and life partners Frances Loring and Florence Wylie had long stood out for their championship of creativity and independence. Music and art festivals, retreats, and poetry and literature enhanced recognition of the joy of female companionship. In their championship of peace, the environment, and women's rights, the Raging Grannies of B.C. challenged conventional notions of the elderly. Writers such as Margaret Atwood, Daphne Marlatt, Dionne Brand, Joy Kogawa, Lee Maracle, and Nicole Brossard, artists such as Joyce Wieland,

Maryon Kantaroff, Rita Letendre, and Mary Pratt, filmmakers such as Anne Wheeler, Anne Poirier, Christine Welsh, Bonnie Klein, and Alanis Obomsawin, and musicians such as Buffy Sainte-Marie, Maureen Forrester, k.d. lang, Susan Aglukark, Sarah McLaughlin, and Pauline Julien drew on contemporary feminism to make significant contributions.

Feminist movements today, as in the past, reflect women's diverse and sometimes conflicting agendas. Pornography and censorship divide activists, as do Quebec independence and free trade. Considerable cooperation nevertheless also occurs through umbrella groups like NAC and the FFQ. Questions of reproductive choice, violence, and daycare generate considerable unanimity. In the 1990s and beyond, the loss of hard-won state support has threatened women's centers and services. Feminists nonetheless continue to rally in opposition to reactionary agendas. Transition houses, like feminist bookstores and self-help health groups, express the local commitment that nourishes many women. Like Maude Barlow, volunteer chair of the nationalist Council of Canadians, many contribute significantly to the antiglobalization and environmental politics that mobilize increasing numbers of Canadians. Elizabeth May, executive director of the Sierra Club, is another such voice, championing Canada's signature to the Kyoto Accord on Environmental Change (2002–2003). In 2001–2002, feminists joined and sometimes led antiwar protests against American adventurism in the Middle East and resisted the rise of racism and intolerance after the September 11, 2001, attacks on New York City's World Trade Towers. While sometimes despaired of by their elders, girls and young women also brought feminist sensibilities and demands to movements, notably protection of the environment and opposition to globalization.

Early feminists drew strengths from membership in international organizations like the International Council of Women and the World Women's Christian Temperance Union. Such links contributed to the continuing international consciousness of many Canadians. Feminist scholars and activists increasingly draw on postcolonial and antiracist theory to question global relations of dominance and subordination. Greater awareness of the significance of difference among women today encourages internationalism. Many feminists argue that NAFTA, like the activities of the General Agreement on Tariffs and Trade, the International Monetary Fund, and the G8, not to mention the increasing power of media empires like those of Canadian Conrad Black and of transnational corporations like Nestlé and the Bank of Montreal, pose threats to democracy worldwide. The United Nations conferences on women, notably at Nairobi in 1985 and Beijing in 1995, have provided important opportunities to compare notes, to support one another, and to organize across national boundaries. Three hundred and sixty-six Canadian groups were counted as supporters of the World March of Women/La Marche mondiale des femmes that met in Montreal in October 2001.

Lesbian Rights

Lesbians have always been active in feminist movements. Critiques of heterosexism and demands for a positive lesbian politics, however, are more recent. Leading feminist organizations such as the NAC and the FFQ now publicly support lesbian rights. Claims of transgendered and bisexual women, however, are much more uncertainly heard. In 1996, the Canadian Human Rights Act prohibited sexual orientation as a basis of discrimination.

Marriage. In 2000, the federal government offered same-sex couples the same social and tax benefits as heterosexual common-law couples.

Parenthood. Some provinces legalized same-sex adoptions in 2000. Lesbians remain, however, far more likely than heterosexual mothers to lose custody of their children.

Military Service

Women have served in the Canadian military since 1885 when they were nurses in the Northwest Rebellions. They also won respect as nursing sisters during World War I (1914–1918). During World War II (1939–1945), Canadian women gained tentative acceptance in the army, navy, and air force, but subsequently permission had to be regained to join the Royal Canadian Air Force in 1951, the Royal Canadian Army in 1954, and the Royal Canadian Navy in 1955. The report of the Royal Commission on the Status of Women drew critical attention to continuing discrimination in the military, but change was slow. With the proclamation of the Human Rights Act of 1979, momentum increased. In 1980, women were permitted to enter Canada's military colleges. In 1989, a human rights tribunal required the termination of all restrictions on employment in the Canadian military with the exception of submarine service. In 1989, Captain Jane Foster and Major Deanna Brasseur became the nation's first female jet fighter pilots. On March 8, 2001, all combat and noncombat roles were opened to women. At the beginning of the twenty-first century, women made up 11.4 percent of the regular forces and 18.6 percent of the reserves. Women have been deployed in a variety of United Nations peacekeeping missions, including actions in Bosnia and Herzegovina and the Congo. In 1993, scientist Roberta Bondar became the first Canadian woman to serve in space as part of the National Aeronautics and Space Administration program.

RELIGION AND SPIRITUALITY

Because religion has traditionally been seen as divisive, God is barely mentioned in Canada's constitution. At the same time, discrimination is prohibited on the basis of religion. While Canada endorses religious pluralism, it remains overwhelmingly Christian. Nevertheless, at the end of the twentieth century, less than a quarter of citizens attended weekly religious services, and even fewer in the most secular regions, Quebec and British Columbia. Not surprisingly, these provinces also show higher tolerance of common-law unions, reproductive choice, and homosexuality. In December 2002, a poll sponsored by the Washington-based Pew Research Center for People and the Press reported that only 30 percent of Canadians agreed that religion was very important in their lives; the figure in Great Britain was 33 percent and in the United States 59 percent. Not unrelated was Canadians' ranking of "religious and ethnic hatred" as their number one concern, followed by pollution and the environment and then the growing gap between rich and poor.

Women's Roles

In the nineteenth century, Christianity represented a progressive force for some feminists as they challenged male sexuality and violence and demanded better fathers and husbands. Catholic and, to a limited degree, Anglican religious sisterhoods provided important alternatives to compulsory heterosexuality. Such spiritual communities also oppressed women, especially unwed mothers. In 1980–1982, feminist Lois Wilson became the first female moderator of the United Church of Canada, the largest Protestant denomination. Today's Christian, Islamic, and Jewish feminists search out liberatory texts and pressure faiths to endorse women-positive policies and values, but religions' close association with patriarchal cultures means that female dissidents are uncertainly tolerated. Fundamentalists of every persuasion join counterparts around the world to reject sexual equality and pluralism. At the beginning of the twenty-first century, an antifeminist religious right engages a few female believers in organizations like the REAL Women, which stands for Realistic, Equal, Active, for life. A handful of women experiment with goddess religions. In short, religion has more public presence in Canada than in western Europe but significantly less than in many other countries, including the United States. For women, as for men, spirituality remains largely a private affair.

VIOLENCE

Canadian women are more likely to be victims than perpetrators of violence. In 1998, women made up 49 percent of all victims, but were only charged with 19 percent of violent crimes. Twenty percent of female victims of violence were under the age of seventeen. Unlike men, who are as likely to be victimized by strangers as by people they know, the vast majority of women recognize their assailants. Aboriginal women and those with disabilities suffer particularly high rates of violence. On December 6, 1989, the "Montreal Massacre" of fourteen young women at the Université de

Montréal's engineering school by a male antifeminist who scapegoated women for his failure to gain admission to engineering provided a brutal wake-up call. Annual marches and memorials across the country, and a federal gun registry program, provide continuing testimony to the influence of December 6. The deaths of Aboriginal women in prisons and on the streets provide an ongoing blot on a nation that claims equality as a basic principle, but these deaths receive less attention. Studies estimate that between one-third and 80 percent of Aboriginal women experience violence; between 1989 and 1993, Status Indian women had a mortality rate due to violence nearly three times that of Canadian women in general.[16]

Women have also immigrated to Canada to escape war, violence, and military repression in their original homelands. In the 1780s, United Empire Loyalists fled brutal American revolutionaries. In the first half of the nineteenth century, Irish and Scots escaped greedy landlords and famine. Jews fled Russian and Polish pogroms at the end of the nineteenth century. In the twentieth century, Canada provided an uncertain welcome to those in flight from state terror. In 1993, however, it led the world when the Immigrant and Refugee Board recognized gender persecution as one basis for claims of refugee status. The Mohawk women who helped lead land-claim resistance against the Canadian military at Oka, Quebec, in 1990 understood full well that repression was a phenomenon found within as well as beyond Canada's borders.

Domestic Violence

Domestic violence remains a serious problem in Canada. Not long ago it was common for family members, neighbors, and police authorities to ignore it as a private matter. When the issue of wife battering was raised by New Democratic member of Parliament Margaret Mitchell in the House of Commons in 1980, the predominantly male assembly dissolved in laughter. Today domestic violence is no longer considered a matter for humor. Significant changes in the ways police and the legal system respond, including mandatory charging policies, mean that offenders are much more likely to be prosecuted. However, less than half of incidents of spousal violence are reported to the police, and there is no indication the rates of domestic violence have lessened.

In 1999, 8 percent of all women living with a male partner had experienced domestic violence in the previous five years. The rate for men was nearly as high (7 percent), but men were more likely to report being slapped or kicked or having something thrown at them, while women were more likely to report beatings, choking, or threats with a gun or a knife, and to report repeated victimization. Women were five times more likely to require medical attention as a result of domestic violence. In 1998, fifty-seven women were killed by their current or former spouse.[17] Children are also victims of domestic battering as well as witnesses to spousal assault.

Rape/Sexual Assault

Sexual assault, which in Canadian law includes the offense of rape, remains significant. Like domestic violence, it is taken more seriously today than in the past. Sexual assault victims are overwhelmingly female (85 percent in 1998). Children make up more than half of all victims of sexual assault. In a survey of crime statistics for 1998, 21 percent of female sexual assault victims were under age twelve, and 32 percent were between twelve and seventeen.[18] An estimated 60 percent to 90 percent of sexual assaults are never reported to the police.

Changes in attitudes toward and policies regarding violence against women have resulted from decades of activism by women's groups. Women have also worked to establish counseling centers and shelters for victims of rape and domestic abuse in cities and towns across the country. In the 1970s and 1980s, such feminist programs began to receive some state assistance. The rise of more reactionary provincial and federal governments jeopardized this funding, leaving many women to remain in brutal situations or to take greater risks in seeking escape.

Trafficking in Women and Children

Prostitution in Canada has a history as long as European settlement and remains visible in major cities. For a variety of reasons, ranging from poverty and lack of job opportunities to abusive homes, the sex trade may be a preferred option for some women. Coercion, however, is also apparent. That prostitution remains illegal poses a significant problem for those involved in the sex trade. In addition to the threat of harassment and criminal charges, prostitutes face a high risk of violence, particularly sexual assault and murder. In 2002, Vancouver, Canada's third-largest city, was just beginning to confront the brutal reality of dozens of missing women, many of them Aboriginal, from the downtown Eastside. Many are dead, and although one man has been arrested, their killer or killers are not yet certainly identified. The thriving business of mail-order brides, mainly from the Philippines or the former Soviet Union, represents yet another version of the trafficking in female bodies that is on the increase.

OUTLOOK FOR THE TWENTY-FIRST CENTURY

The political, economic, and social dimensions of inequality remain intimately connected. Before suffrage, it was almost impossible to get women's issues onto the political agenda in Canada, but the extension of the formal right to vote was insufficient to transform power relations. With few feminist women in powerful and influential positions, their issues get short shrift at elections and typically disappear altogether at other times. Other policy decisions have been wrongly regarded as gender neutral. Recent changes in the welfare state provide a good example. Neoliberal policies, part of the processes of economic globalization exemplified in Canada's partnership in NAFTA, foster a retreat from concerns with substantive equality and widen gaps between rich and poor along the lines of gender, race/ethnicity, class, sexuality, age, region, and ability. Thus at the dawn of the twenty-first century, Canadian women's struggle for equality is neither uniform nor linear, but uneven and contradictory, and still largely uphill.

NOTES

Unless otherwise noted, all statistics come from Statistics Canada or from updated material on the Statistics Canada Web site.

1. One kilometer equals approximately 0.6 miles.

2. Statistics Canada, *Women in Canada 2000: A Gender-Based Statistical Report* (Ottawa: Minister of Industry, 2000).

3. E.D. Nelson and Barrie Robinson, *Gender in Canada* (Scarborough: Prentice Hall, 1999), 519. This book provides a comprehensive survey of the literature on gender in Canada.

4. Steven Kerstetter, *Rags and Riches: Wealth Inequality in Canada* (Ottawa: Canadian Centre for Policy Alternatives, 2003).

5. *Education Indicators in Canada: Report of the Pan-Canadian Education Indicators Program 1999* (Ottawa: Council of the Ministers of Education of Canada, February 2000).

6. On school violence, see Helene Berman and Yasmin Jiwani, *In the Best Interests of the Girl Child: Phase I Report* (London: Alliance of Five Research Centres on Violence and Status of Women Canada, January 2002).

7. Marie Drolet, *The Persistent Gap: New Evidence on the Canadian Gender Wage Gap* (Ottawa: Statistics Canada, January 2001), 17.

8. Margaret Philp, "National Daycare Plan Being Hammered Out," *Globe and Mail*, December 12, 2002.

9. April Lindgren, "Give Welfare Cheats a Break, Jury Recommends," and Janice Tibbetts, "Welfare Is Not a Right, Canada's Top Court Rules," *Globe and Mail*, December 20, 2002.

10. *General Social Survey–Cycle 15: Changing Conjugal Life in Canada* (Ottawa: Statistics Canada, July 2002).

11. Ibid., 9.

12. www.fedpubs.com/subject/health/newrepro.html.

13. Eleanor Matcika-Tyndale, "Sexual Health and Canadian Youth: How Do We Measure Up?" *Canadian Journal of Human Sexuality* 10(1–2) (spring/summer 2001): 11.

14. Madeleine Dion Stout and Gregory D. Kipling, *Aboriginal Women in Canada: Strategic Research Directions for Policy Development* (Ottawa: Status of Women Canada, 1998), 16.

15. www.gov.ns.ca/news/details.asp?id=2002102200I.html.

16. Stout and Kipling, 1998, 16.

17. Statistics Canada, *Canada 2000: A Gender-Based Statistical Report* (Ottawa: Minister of Industry, 2000), 166–68.

18. Ibid., 165.

RESOURCE GUIDE

Suggested Reading

Andres, Lesley. *Policy Research Issues for Canadian Youth: Transition Experiences of Young Women*. Ottawa: Human Resources Development Canada Applied Research Branch, 2001. An assessment of the contemporary education and labor-market situation for young women.

Backhouse, Constance. *Petticoats and Prejudice: Women and Law in Nineteenth-Century Canada*. Toronto: Women's Press, 1991. A consideration of laws and their effects on women's lives in the nineteenth century.

Bashevkin, Sylvia. *Welfare Hot Buttons: Women, Work, and Social Policy Reform*. Toronto: University of Toronto Press, 2002. A comparison of Canada with the United States and Great Britain in the 1980s and 1990s.

Boyd, Susan B. *Child Custody, Law, and Women's Work*. Toronto: Oxford University Press, 2003. An overview of child-custody issues in Canada from the nineteenth century to the present, particularly concerned with developments since the 1980s.

Clio Collective. *Quebec Women: A History*. Trans. Roger Gannon and Rosalind Gill. Toronto: Women's Press, 1987. The standard one-volume history of women in Quebec.

Cook, Sharon Anne, Lorna R. McLean, and Kate O'Rourke, eds. *Framing Our Past: Canadian Women's History in the Twentieth Century*. Montreal: McGill–Queen's University Press, 2001. A popular collection of articles and photographs on women in the twentieth century.

Crow, Barbara, and Lise Gotell. *Open Boundaries: A Canadian Women's Studies Reader*. Toronto: Prentice Hall Canada, 2000. Key issues in Canadian women's studies.

Hamilton, Roberta. *Gendering the Vertical Mosaic: Feminist Perspectives on Canadian Society*. Toronto: Copp Clark, 1996. A feminist perspective on the development of Canadian society.

Nelson, E.D., and Barrie Robinson. *Gender in Canada*. Scarborough: Prentice Hall, 1999. A comprehensive survey of the literature on gender in Canada.

Prentice, Alison, Paula Bourne, Gail Cuthbert-Brandt, Beth Light, Wendy Mitchinson, and Naomi Black. *Canadian Women: A History*. 2nd ed. Toronto: Harcourt Brace and Company, 1996. The standard one-volume history of Canadian women.

Statistics Canada. *Women in Canada 2000: A Gender-Based Statistical Report*. Ottawa: Minister of Industry, 2000. A comprehensive source of statistics on Canadian women.

Stout, Madeleine Dion, and Gregory D. Kipling. *Aboriginal Women in Canada: Strategic Research Directions for Policy Development*. Ottawa: Status of Women Canada, 1998. The standard source on the experience of Aboriginal women.

Strong-Boag, V., Mona Gleason, and Adele Perry, eds. *Rethinking Canada: The Promise of Women's History*. 4th ed. Toronto: Oxford University Press, 2001. The best introduction to the development of Canadian women's history.

Videos/Films

Democracy et la Maude. 1998. Directed by Patricia Kearns. National Film Board of Canada. The political biography of Maude Barlow, the feminist leader of the Council of Canadians, a leading nationalist group.

Keepers of the Fire. 1994. Directed by Christine Welsh. NFB. Examines the resistance of Canadian Native women to colonialism.

Motherland. 1991. Directed by Helene Klodawsky. NFB. Investigates myths, misconceptions, and expectations regarding motherhood and compares them with the actual experiences of Canadian women.

Older, Stronger, Wiser. 1989. NFB. Examines black women in education, church, and family in Canada.

The Other Side of the Picture. 1999. Directed by Teresa MacInnis; NFB. Leading Canadian women artists discuss their careers.

Web Sites

L'Association féminine d'éducation et d'action sociale, www.afeas.qc.ca.
A French-speaking feminist organization dedicated to improving women's living and working conditions and to defending their rights.

Canadian Congress of Learning Opportunities for Women, www.nald.ca/cclow.htm.
A feminist organization dedicated to education and training issues for girls and women.

Canadian Council on Social Development/Conseil canadien de développement social, www.ccsd.ca/.
Focuses on research in areas such as income security, employment, parenting, child welfare, pensions, and government social policies.

Canadian Research Institute for the Advancement of Women/Institut canadien de recherches sur la femme, www.criaw-icref.ca.
A national organization committed to advancing women's equality through research.

Canadian Women's Health Network/Le Réseau canadien pour la santé des femmes, www.cwhn.ca.
Brings together researchers and activists concerned about women's health.

Canadian Women's Studies Association/L'Association canadienne des études sur les femmes, www.brocku.ca/cwsa_acef/.
A feminist association of faculty, students, policy researchers, and community activists.

PAR-L (Policy, Action Research List), a Canadian Electronic Feminist Network/Un Réseau électronique féministe canadien, www.unb.ca/web/PAR-L.
Brings together individuals and organizations interested in woman-centered policy issues.

Room of One's Own, www.islandnet.com/Room/enter/.
Canada's leading feminist literary magazine, publishing short stories, poems, and reviews by women.

Statistics Canada/Statistiques Canada, www.statcan.ca.
The federal government agency responsible for generating statistical information, both contemporary and historical, on Canada.

Status of Women Canada/Condition féminine Canada, www.swc-cfc.gc.ca.
A federal agency promoting gender equality and the full participation of women in the economic, social, cultural, and political life of Canada.

United Nations Division for the Advancement of Women, www.undp.org/fwcw.
The institutional coordinator of many of the United Nations–sponsored activities in which Canadian women are involved.

Organizations

Fédération des femmes de Québec
Web site: www.ffq.qc.ca/ffq.html

The major feminist group in Quebec.

National Action Committee on the Status of Women/Comité canadien d'action sur le status de la femme
Web site: www.nac-cca.ca

A coalition of women's groups, is the largest feminist group in Canada.

National Association of Women and the Law/L'Association nationale de la femme et du droit
Web site: www.nawl.ca

Works to improve the legal status of women.

Native Women's Association of Canada
Web site: www.nwac-hq.org/vision/vision

Addresses the needs and campaigns for the rights of First Nations women.

The Women's Legal Education and Action Fund
Web site: www.leaf.ca

A national organization working to promote equality for women and girls, using the equality provisions of Section 15 of the Canadian Charter of Rights and Freedoms.

SELECTED BIBLIOGRAPHY

Education Indicators in Canada: Report of the Pan-Canadian Education Indicators Program, 1999. Ottawa: Council of the Ministers of Education of Canada, February 2000.

Nelson, E.D., and Barrie Robinson. *Gender in Canada*. Scarborough: Prentice Hall, 1999.

Statistics Canada. *Women in Canada 2000: A Gender-Based Statistical Report*. Ottawa: Minister of Industry, 2000.

Stout, Madeleine Dion, and Gregory D. Kipling. *Aboriginal Women in Canada: Strategic Research Directions for Policy Development*. Ottawa: Status of Women Canada, 1998.

4

CUBA

Sara E. Cooper

PROFILE OF CUBA

The island of Cuba attained independence from Spain in 1898 by means of a population insurgency by the Creole and U.S. intervention (the Spanish-American War); the Platt Amendment gave the United States broad powers and responsibilities in protecting the island from then on. Although Cuba was a protectorate of a democratic state, its string of conservative leaders (including Gerardo Machado and Fulgencio Batista) cultivated a nation divided by class and race in which a small Eurocentric elite controlled the majority of land and goods, while agricultural labor and domestic service were provided by a black and mulatto underclass. For many years, Cuba was a favorite tropical vacation destination, a hotbed of underworld activity, and a thriving sugar and tobacco empire, through which economic ties the Cuban elite maintained strong links to Europe and the United States. The 1959 revolution headed by Fidel Castro radically changed the course of the Caribbean nation, which was declared socialist/Communist in 1961. The unique blend of ethnic and national influences made Cuba develop a sense of national identity distinct from that of other Latin American countries. Its unique flavor is evident in the religious syncretism of Santeria and Catholicism, the Cuban love of American baseball (rather than soccer), and the particular development of feminism in this Caribbean nation.

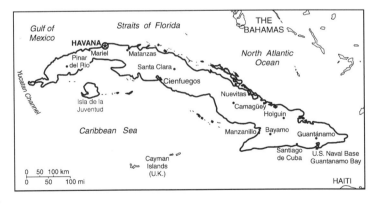

According to the United Nations Statistics Division, the population is approximately 11.27 million, slightly more than half female. Predominant ethnic groups include mulatto (51 percent), white (37 percent), black (11 percent), and Chinese (1 percent). The birth rate is 13.13 births per 1,000 population, with a total fertility rate of 1.57 children born per woman. Maternal and infant mortality rates are lower than anywhere else in Latin America (7.89 infant deaths per 1,000 live births), and life expectancy is very high (73.29 years for men, 78.13 for women).[1]

Cuba has a mostly state-run economy in which the government controls practically all foreign trade. The Cuban economy, long subsidized by the Soviet Union, crashed with the fall of its ally and only rallied slightly in the 1990s. Most Cuban citizens believe that the current "Special Period" of sacrifice is also due in part to the continued U.S. economic blockade of the island. Economic reforms in the mid-1990s legalized agricultural markets and limited private enterprise, both heavily taxed. Legislation allowing Cubans to own and trade with U.S. dollars has effectively created a double economy. A 1997 report by the U.S. Department of Commerce estimates the Cuban gross domestic product (GDP) at $16.9 billion, the real growth rate at 2.5 percent, and the per capita purchasing power at $1,540.[2] To mitigate the low earning power of all Cubans, the socialist/Communist structure provides most basic goods and services such as housing, minimal food, medical care, and education. Nonetheless, the survival and relative comfort of the Cuban family often depend upon the unofficial economy of barter and exchange maintained by networks of women.

OVERVIEW OF WOMEN'S ISSUES

The role and position of women in Cuba have changed drastically since the revolution in 1959. Although strong and exceptional women have been conspicuous throughout Cuba's history, and women's rights groups existed before the changeover, the radical refashioning of society gave women freedoms and responsibilities that they had never before experienced. However, Cuban (and Latin American) women's activism in the late nineteenth and early twentieth centuries generally defended the sanctity of motherhood and the protection afforded to the feminine sex; Cuban feminists found empowerment in politically safeguarding their chosen role. The most accepted symbol for a strong woman remained that of the self-sacrificing mother, like the historical icon Mariana Grajales, who heroically surrendered her sons to die fighting for Cuban independence.[3] This was not seen in any way as antithetical to the feminists' struggle to attain the vote and political power for women in spheres that corresponded to their sex, such as hygiene and the education of children.[4] Some U.S. feminists have questioned the tenets espoused by Cuban women as not sufficiently independent or radical. However, historians of Latin American women's movements are quick to legitimize this and other differences between versions of feminism popular in Latin America and those in the United States.

This demarcation between the private (feminine) and public (masculine) spheres was finally exploded, for good or for ill, as a direct result of the series of rebellions headed by Fidel Castro, who was joined by Argentine revolutionary Ernesto (Che) Guevara. Cognizant of social inequities that included class, gender, and racial oppression, Castro and Guevara visualized a society in which all people would be educated and empowered; these ideals formed a substantial part of the rhetoric employed both before and after the final successful guerrilla campaign. Moreover, according to Guevara, women would constitute a necessary part of the revolutionary corps. His writings on the role of women in revolution give a good sense of the paradoxical position of women in Cuba today. Guevara wrote that women were capable of doing virtually every task that a man could do, including bearing arms and firing upon the enemy if need be, and that, moreover, because of perceptions of female fragility, women could serve especially well in espionage and transmission of messages, supplies, and even arms. Nonetheless, the Argentine guerrilla ended his famous essay by extolling the particularly "feminine" virtues that would also benefit the revolution, including women's ability to sew, cook palatable meals, and compassionately care for the wounded or despairing soldier.[5] In this way, Cuban women were thrust into a role of double duty that resembled the contradictory and difficult expectations of women in any modern and developed nation.

During and since the revolution, fighting women like Celia Sánchez and Haydée Santamaría have been all but canonized, and Cuba's leading actresses have positively portrayed guerrilla fighters in films like *Manuela* (1962). At the same time, with the founding of the Federation of Cuban Women (FMC), a series of programs to educate women and make them productive citizens initially focused equally on general and technical education, women's tasks such as sewing and infant hygiene, and women's place in the emerging revolutionary family. Despite the FMC's support of women's political and socioeconomic development in Cuba, the FMC obstructs any discourse against the governing patriarchy. It seems that progress will be made within the system, rather than by a radical reworking of the system.[6]

Today, women occupy key positions in most industries and professions, take part in the political and religious hierarchies, and enjoy relatively good health care as well as a low rate of sexual discrimination and harassment. They still are expected to fulfill their "womanly" and conjugal duties alongside their social and economic responsibilities. The lengthy period of economic hardships under the Special Period has been especially onerous for women. It is now twice as difficult to meet obligations in the home and in the community, and after decades of little or no prostitution, women are again turning to the sex industry to gain quick access to U.S. dollars and thus the more bountiful black-market goods and services. As Cuban women move into the twenty-first century, many wonder what will happen when the charismatic leader finally must hand over his command. Will they continue to move forward in the struggle toward total liberation, or will they fall prey to neoliberal and regressive politics that characterize other small Latin American nations?

EDUCATION

Opportunities and Literacy

Before the revolution, women and people of color were not expected to exceed or even comply with Cuba's mandatory sixth-grade education. In 1953, less than 1 percent of all women had been to college.[7] Nonetheless, this was part of a general disinterest in education; more than a million people were illiterate at the end of the 1950s, and only 6 percent of students actually completed the sixth grade.[8] In general, the formal education of women was deemed unnecessary for either future middle-class and upper-class housewives or the unskilled women workers of the working class or the poor.[9] Mercedes Riba y Piños was the first woman to graduate from the University of Havana in the late 1880s. María Luisa Dolz soon after graduated in natural sciences and proceeded to fight for women's rights in education, both as a professor of education at the Colegio Isabel la Católica and as an activist.[10] As might be expected, the wealthy and privileged women comprising the early women's movement in Cuba were highly educated. The majority of feminist leaders received their bachelor's degree, and several finished postgraduate work in law, pharmacology, or the humanities.[11] According to one researcher, even "the rank and file of the feminist associations included teachers, nurses, stenographers, and salaried professionals."[12] While early feminists were very concerned with the education of all women, social and political obstacles—even within the women's organizations—stood in the way of their vision.

In 1961, the FMC, in concert with the Communist Party, commenced a series of programs to educate the entire nation, and in particular the women. The Literacy Campaign sponsored a teaching brigade that worked in the fields during the day and taught agricultural workers to read and write at night. The Ana Betancourt Schools gave adult women literacy as well as practical skills.[13] The success of these programs was unprecedented, as the literacy rate quickly climbed to near the current estimated 95.7 percent total and 95.3 percent for women.[14]

Early on, the socialist government nationalized all schools, which not only are free from first grade through the postsecondary level, but also provide free lunches to all students. The national educational requirement was raised to a high-school equivalent for both sexes, and girls are expected to perform well and to prepare themselves for a life of productive citizenship. Both boys and girls take aptitude tests and, on the basis of these and university entrance examinations, are allowed to choose a path of study. They are restricted further both by their own aptitude (for which fields they show promise) and by the market's demand (which fields need more trained professionals). Women were already entering the universities in droves in the first years of the revolution and by the 1980s made up half of the university population, including the school of medicine.[15]

EMPLOYMENT AND ECONOMICS

Job/Career Opportunities

Women made up only slightly more than 10 percent of the official paid workforce for the first half of the twentieth century.[16] However, census data (table 4.1) show that women's placement in the workforce changed over this time. By the mid-1950s, the majority of women (70 percent) were employed in domestic labor, and most of the rest were in the tobacco industry (29 percent); only 1 percent held paying positions in agriculture.[17] When the revolution began to implement employment programs that assumed a shared social responsibility, women began to enter the workplace in ever greater numbers and in sectors formerly prohibited to them. For instance, by 1970, 40 percent of working women were employed in the sugar industry, whether cutting sugarcane or processing sugar.[18] Women joined their husbands and brothers in the volunteer brigades to pick coffee, work in the fields, and bring literacy to the rural areas. Women were offered incentives to enter the workforce, including the privilege of having their grocery shopping done for them. Over the years, and spurred on by multiple training programs sponsored by the FMC, women began to make inroads into sectors requiring refined skills and/or postsecondary education, such as administration, engineering, and the medical professions. Researchers reported that "by 1990, women constituted 66 percent of the teachers, 48 percent of doctors, and 69 percent of dentists."[19]

Table 4.1
Distribution of Women in the Female Labor Force as Percentages, 1899–1943

Work Classification	1899	1907	1919	1943
White-collar jobs	3.6	9.0	13.2	45.3
Blue-collar jobs	61.6	58.0	40.2	32.2
Domestic service	34.6	32.8	46.6	22.4
Other	0.2	0.2	—	—
Total	100.0	100.0	100.0	99.9

Source: K. Lynn Stoner, *From the House to the Streets: The Cuban Woman's Movement for Legal Reform, 1898–1940* (Durham, NC: Duke University Press, 1991), 169.

Despite the obstacles that block their path, Cuban women have become an indispensable and valued part of the workforce. Cubans are urged to enter the most competitive and technical fields without regard to sex. Under the new economic measures, women run small business ventures and negotiate on fairly even terms with their male counterparts. Women hold some high positions in nearly all professions, including the universities, the travel industry, culture and the arts, and government. Women are finally beginning to break into the field of publishing (Basilia Papastamatiu is the assistant director of the prestigious publisher Letras Cubanas), and they finally are being taken seriously as writers of narrative (rather than the more feminine genre of poetry). Nonetheless, it has been asserted that women still do not ascend to the most prestigious or highest levels in most sectors of the economy, but encounter a glass ceiling not unlike that in the United States; the result is that women are caught in a psychological trap of believing that they should strive to excel, but are consistently being held back.[20]

Pay

New legislation in 1979 gave more generous pensions and retirement benefits to women, including a special provision for agricultural workers, who could continue to work past retirement and take home a double salary.[21] Therefore, although women still may earn somewhat less than similarly situated men (pay differentials are small in a socialist system), the costs of these supplemental programs can make women more expensive and thus less attractive to hire.

Working Conditions

In the 1960s and 1970s, women still had to deal with a great deal of discrimination and harassment from their male colleagues. Despite proof to the contrary, men tried to maintain the belief that women were delicate, easily frightened, and in need of protection.[22] Women who fulfilled their new social and political duties at the expense of home and family life were severely criticized. However, the government continued to mount widespread campaigns to change social perceptions, including the backing of popular films such as *Retrato de Teresa* (*Portrait of Teresa* [1979]), in which Teresa's inconsiderate and macho spouse is shown to be hindering the progress of the ongoing socialist revolution.

Sexual Harassment

While antiharassment and affirmative-action legislation tend to be strong in Cuba, as reflects the socialist tenets of gender equality, lack of enforcement means that women have not been fully liberated in this area.

The official government position is that sexual harassment is not a problem.[23]

Support for Mothers/Caretakers

Paradoxically, the very strength of legislated support for mothers and caretakers can interfere with their employment. Resolutions 47 and 48, based on research done in 1965, divided jobs into work that was consistent or inconsistent with women's physical abilities (consistent with labor legislation passed throughout Latin America during this era). The FMC has backed more progressive laws, but until 1992 women were still legally barred from jobs that could jeopardize their childbearing capacities.

Maternal Leave and Daycare

Because the family is considered to be the cornerstone of the revolution, maternal (and now paternal) leave is mandated and generous, up to five months of paid leave.[24] Moreover, pregnant mothers have regularly been exempted from overtime work, night shifts, and other job-related stressors.[25] The *círculos infantiles* provide high-quality and subsidized child care for working mothers, but are unable to accommodate all of the children needing care.

FAMILY AND SEXUALITY

Gender Roles

As a Caribbean island and part of the Hispanic Americas, Cuba has long been influenced by the phenomenon of machismo, a social paradigm rigidly dividing and codifying gender and sex roles in Hispanic society. Women were expected to be the angels of the hearth, maintain a silent and demure demeanor, accede to the wishes of their fathers and husbands, and ultimately care for children and household matters. In the years between independence and the revolution, feminist groups and activists made

Cuban women with child, Havana. Photo © TRIP/K. Cardwell.

many strides in the battle for equality, but for the most part did not advocate for women leaving the domestic sphere.

As in many Latin American countries, Cuban social life revolves around the family. Gasoline shortages and the high cost of eating out and other outside entertainment mean that families often spend more time at home. Extended families tend to reside together, so the socialization of children is shared by multiple generations of women. While the first generation of youth under the revolution was encouraged to break with tradition (and especially with older family members who opposed the move toward socialism), family closeness and intimacy continue to be the norm today. Grandmothers, mothers, daughters, and daughters-in-law share daily life, demystifying the aging process and avoiding the extreme glorification of youth.

Marriage

Women tend to marry or enter a consensual union by the age of eighteen to twenty, but divorce rates—currently more than 51 percent—are high in comparison to other Latin American countries. Despite the 1975 Family Code that holds men to equal responsibility for all work in the home, from child rearing to cleaning, women are often left with the greatest domestic burdens. This is by far the marital problem most commonly cited by Cuban women.[26] Frequent electric blackouts, less access to home appliances, and logistic problems with shopping add time to daily domestic chores. The result is that even women with very successful careers are faced with a particularly onerous double workday. Nonetheless, women's high level of education and participation in the revolution have assured them a voice and a place of respect in Cuban society, which definitely includes the family.

Reproduction

Sex Education

Contemporary Cuba, despite the historical link with Catholicism, sees no conflict between a veneration of the family and a proactive program of reproductive health and sex education. Secondary schools include some degree of education focusing on health and safety issues around sex. The FMC frequently offers workshops that teach women about their bodies. Sex is not a taboo topic; government-sponsored television runs public service announcements about the necessity of safe sex, especially through proper use of condoms. High prioritization of the family and an official commitment to maintaining a sustainable level vof population have assured that women "have free access to high quality prenatal and post-natal services, contraception, and abortion."[27]

Contraception and Abortion

Abortion rates among Cuban women increased by a factor of four between 1968 and 1974, but have substantially decreased since that time, perhaps as a result of strong campaigning by the FMC that has emphasized health risks to women.[28] In general, women in urban areas are more likely to have had an abortion, although statistics vary according to socioeconomic bracket, level of education, and age. However, given the relatively early age of marriage in Cuba, the fairly low levels of abortion do not account for the decreasing fertility rate (1.2 children per woman). According to the Cuban portion of a project called "Demographic Change and the Roles of Women," the widespread knowledge of methods of contraception is a decisive factor. National television runs public service announcements promoting the use of condoms and safe sex. Almost 100 percent of women interviewed in two separate studies knew of at least one form of contraception, and by 1982 most women were at least familiar with intrauterine devices and the pill.[29] Women in rural areas were less educated, but were rated at least as familiar with contraceptive devices as women in the rest of Latin America or other third-world nations.[30] Reported usage of contraception varied between 66.2 percent and 74.2 percent of those interviewed, a higher rate than in most countries studied (exceptions being Costa Rica and Panama).[31]

Teen Pregnancy

Teenage fertility rates are also low; in 1982, urban teenagers averaged .026 children per mother, and rural teenagers between .053 and .156 children per mother.[32] Today, 6 percent of women aged fifteen to nineteen give birth each year, while 70 percent of women between the ages of fifteen and forty-nine use some form of contraception.[33]

HEALTH

Starting in 1960, women entered the health professions in unprecedented numbers, which changed the focus of medical care as well as research. The FMC spearheaded programs to enhance reproductive health and to educate women on all health issues, which are still featured in FMC publications and public debates today. Women volunteered for the immunization programs that raised life expectancy and radically changed the leading causes of mortality to ones similar to those in the United States instead of maladies found in other Latin American countries.[34] Women's health concerns are not as marginalized as in many countries; for instance, one program that existed for twenty years gave mothers intensive training in nutrition and infant health.[35] Along the same lines, even rural areas have access to good pediatric and maternal-infant hospitals.[36] Because medicines and equipment are lacking, alternative health practices have been reintegrated into the medical care system, including the use of medicinal herbs, the employment of midwives, and treatments from Santeria healers, many of whom are women.

Health Care Access

Good-quality health care is available free of charge to all Cubans, including both preventive medicine and treatment of illness or injury. In the forty years since the revolution, and despite the almost wholesale emigration of practicing physicians in 1959–1960, the number of doctors has multiplied by eight and the number of nurses by fifteen.[37] Whereas Havana used to house half of all medical facilities and practitioners, now hospitals and clinics have been built in rural areas, and all medical students are required to spend one year working in nonurban zones. Health care has many levels. The community level includes the Family Doctor Program, in which a doctor and nurse team is assigned for two years to a specific neighborhood or small town so that medical attention is available for all. Polyclinics also provide care to patients on a drop-in basis. On the downside, medicines and other health-related products (including those for "feminine hygiene") continue to be scarce, meaning that sometimes even simple medical conditions, like asthma or arthritis, become a burden.

Diseases and Disorders

Cuba generally faces very distinct health issues in comparison to other tropical and island nations. It has been noted that "by the 1970s the leading causes of death in Cuba were the same as those of the developed world: heart disease, cancer, and stroke."[38] Nevertheless, despite public campaigns to change conduct, Cubans still adhere to risky behaviors such as smoking and eating a diet high in fried food and carbohydrates. For instance, 26.3 percent of Cuban women still smoke (compared to 48 percent of men).[39] Surprisingly few women participate in free Pap smear tests, ultrasound, and mammograms for early detection of cancer; breast cancer and, to a certain degree, cervical or uterine cancer are serious concerns for Cuban women.[40] The medical profession is fully trained in the most modern treatments of these and other illnesses, and all medical attention is free.

AIDS and Sexually Transmitted Diseases

The incidence of sexually transmitted diseases (STD) such as syphilis and gonorrhea rose substantially in Cuba along with the onset of the sexual revolution during the 1970s and 1980s.[41] Perhaps because of the rise of

STDs and the relative difficulty of inculcating safer sex practices within the population, the Cuban government reacted immediately and forcefully when the HIV/AIDS epidemic surfaced in the early 1980s. Individuals who tested positive for HIV and whose infection was confirmed by follow-up exams were given counseling and placed in sanatoriums where they received their regular pay as well as complete room and board in relatively attractive surroundings. They followed an exercise program, ate well, and received specialized medical care, sometimes given by HIV-positive physicians. Their sexual history was traced, and previous partners were tested. Since 1994, residence in sanatoriums has no longer been permanent for HIV-positive individuals, but rather serves as an initial education phase of treatment. Care has deteriorated, partially due to the extreme scarcity of pharmaceuticals and medical equipment in Cuba. The mandated preventive measures taken on the island received intense scrutiny by the global community, and despite the loosening of controls, some sources still point to the governmental programs as a serious human rights violation. Involuntary quarantine, albeit temporary, as well as the obligation to recount one's personal history, can be perceived as in violation of certain United Nations High Commission principles. On the other hand, Cuba has one of the lowest incidences of HIV/AIDS infection in the world, and by the end of 1999 had reported only 120 AIDS-related deaths.[42] As in other countries, the incidence of infection in women is lower than in men.

Eating Disorders

The Cuban diet, based principally on rice, beans, and fried starches like yucca and malanga and augmented as often as possible with meat and sugar, has changed somewhat since the revolution. Farmers' markets operate daily, selling fresh organic fruits and vegetables, which are much less costly and easier to purchase than more traditionally popular products such as white flour, sugar, eggs, condiments, and coffee. However, since the Special Period was instituted in 1989, rations have been cut, and neighborhood stores do not keep all items in stock; Cubans with U.S. dollars fare much better than those without. Because of the favored diet, a reluctance to exercise, and shortages, Cubans, particularly women, tend to be heavier than is recommended by the medical profession. Although this may increase the chance of heart conditions and diabetes, it does not provoke the same social stigma as in other developed nations.

According to one woman in her twenties, Cuban men prefer women with big legs and a nice round behind; she has always been teased for being too skinny and received plenty of positive reinforcement when she gained a few pounds (a phenomenon documented in many sources).[43] Because of the social perception that round is good, eating disorders such as anorexia and bulimia are less prevalent in Cuba.

Depression

According to psychologists, Cuban women suffer from anxiety and depression at least as much as their male counterparts.[44]

POLITICS AND LAW

The political history of women in Cuba begins much earlier than Cuba's independence. In the early 1800s, Creole women of the upper class opposed Spanish rule and protested political repression by cutting their hair short.[45] Author and poet Gertrudis Gómez de Avellaneda, born in 1814 in a region now known as Camagüey, started her career with two highly political novels that denounced gender oppression in Cuba. The romantic novel *Sab* (1841), which also contains a fervent abolitionist message, argues that superior souls, no matter their race or gender, should be freed from unjust oppression and social control. Her work *Dos mugeres* (Two women), released as a serial in 1842–1843, explores the question of whether true love should supersede the marital bond, thus questioning the validity of anti-divorce legislation. Other exceptional women also advocated women's rights in the nineteenth century, such as Ana Betancourt de Mora, who spoke out at a revolutionary convention, and Domitila García, who in the 1880s became the first Cuban woman to both edit and publish a newspaper.[46] *El Correo de las damas* (*The women's circular*) was censured when it ran an article on female sexuality, a very touchy subject in both politics and law.[47] There were abundant issues to spark opposition by proponents of the women's movement; even in the roaring 1920s, when the flapper rage deluged the capital city of Havana, women were still legally regarded as incompetents under the Spanish civil code of 1889.[48]

Suffrage

The early twentieth century saw some legal and political progress for women.[49] Divorce was legalized in 1918, and universal suffrage was instituted in 1933; the current policy is that all citizens sixteen years or older have both the right and the responsibility to vote.

Political Participation

The Club Femenino, founded in 1917, organized Cuba's first National Women's Congress in 1923, where women with higher socioeconomic status debated a wide range of topics, including employment, sexuality, and the vote.[50] In this period, many of women's political concerns were issues centering on family and children, such as equal rights for illegitimate children. The National Feminist Alliance advocated fighting for a better home life based on mutual respect and love. Not all political women were

CUBA

conservatives; in the late 1920s and early 1930s, women attended the university in Havana, became involved in labor unions, and joined the Communist Party. One woman, formerly a domestic worker, joined the party because "the rich folks in our town said that was bad, and I figured if it was bad for them it was good for me!"[51]

Women's Rights

In Fulgencio Batista's elected term as president of Cuba in the 1940s, he sponsored a new constitution that instituted some political changes favorable to women. However, feminist initiatives seemed to plateau by the early 1940s, and Batista's 1952 military coup brought tightening controls and a ubiquitous military presence. At the same time, Havana was inundated by tourists seeking the tropical sensuality and the lively music scene; the already thriving sex industry found new outlets in droves of American and European visitors as well as soldiers from the U.S. naval base in Guantanamo Bay. Class differences expanded and racial tensions intensified with the increasing presence of a Cuban and visiting elite, so that especially black or mulatta women, the great majority of them poor, faced seemingly worsening conditions. Nancy Morejón, a leading Afro-Cuban poet, explains:

I was fourteen years old when the Revolution triumphed. I was just leaving childhood and entering adolescence. I can honestly say that what I witnessed as a result of the Cuban Revolution was an extraordinary change of values! Among the things that most attracted me—apart from agrarian reform, the urban reform, the new health care and educational programs, and so forth—were Fidel's speeches regarding the racial question. It was very moving for me to hear him defend the rights of all Cubans, including blacks, to equal access to Cuba's resources. Fidel spoke about the need to open up all the beaches and clubs to everyone and not to discriminate on the basis of race.[52]

It was this anonymous mass of underprivileged women that made the difference in Fidel Castro's revolutionary drive. Thousands were "selling war bonds and producing rebel uniforms, taking part in propaganda work, participating in action and sabotage units in the cities, transporting arms, and fighting in the mountains."[53] The principal women who maintain political power today were also key players in the insurrection. There is a set of pivotal names that appears in almost any treatise on women and the revolution.[54]

Celia Sánchez was an early rebel soldier close to the Revolutionary General Staff and a former member of the Central Committee of the Cuban Communist Party and Council of Ministers. Vilma Espín, once head of the underground for the entire province of Oriente, is now a member of the Central Committee of the Communist Party, a member of the Council of State, and president of the FMC.[55] Haydée Santamaría and Melba Hernández were the two women involved in the 1953 attack on the Moncada Barracks. Santamaría became a member of the Central Committee of the Party, a member of the Council of State, and director of the Casa de las Américas cultural institution, while Hernández became Cuba's ambassador to Vietnam.[56] Celia Sánchez and Melba Hernández ultimately changed Fidel Castro's opinion about allowing women into the offensive ranks of the guerrillas and later the national military.[57] The fighting women of the Mariana Grajales Platoon also found themselves the subjects of great adulation after the triumph of the revolution; they proved the efficacy of women in battle and have been an influence on Cuba's current armed forces.

Feminist Movements

The principal political organization of and for women since the revolution has been the Federation of Cuban Women (FMC). Female support for Fidel Castro's July 26th Movement was originally culled from the Women's Martí Civic Front, headed by feminist activist Carmen Castro Porta; however, these women did not become the most instrumental in the future government. The Revolutionary Women's Union (UFR), organized in 1959 by Communist activists Elena Gil, Clementina Serra, and Rosario Fernández, began an extensive campaign of door-to-door recruitment and fundraising. A huge contingent from the UFR attended the Congress of Latin American Women in Santiago, Chile, "caus[ing] an uproar."[58] The changes they advocated on and off the island would benefit the working class and poor women at the expense of upper- and middle-class women's agenda. Women in Cuba who protested this focus (along with those in counterrevolutionary groups) were given harsh jail sentences. In 1960, less than a year after Castro's victorious march on the capital, he conflated all existing women's political groups into the FMC. This umbrella organization with a multilevel hierarchy was created to develop laws and programs that worked toward complete equality of women in all levels and sectors of society. The FMC's periodicals, *Mujeres* and *Muchacha* (formerly *Romances*), promote comprehension of and debate of women's issues as well as educate women on their role in the revolution.[59]

The FMC is essential to every sphere of Cuban women's life since the majority are given incentives or otherwise pressured to join. The FMC advocates better domestic conditions, helped set through legislation mandating men's equal participation in household duties and raising children. FMC volunteers went door to door recruiting women for the organization's numerous crusades, including the literacy campaign, the establishment of a daycare system, and job training for housewives and prostitutes. The FMC has also championed women's right to divorce or to take legal action in case of abuse. The efforts of the FMC have radically (if slowly) influenced social and political reality in Cuba since 1960. For instance, the 1976 constitution included wording that ignored the immensity of sexual discrimination; the new document ratified in 1992 made stronger statements supporting gender equality and proscribing discrimination based on "race, skin color, sex, national origin, religious belief, and any other affront to human dignity."[60]

The FMC currently has more than 3.2 million members, including housewives as well as women in virtually every profession.[61] In addition to sponsoring and implementing programs designed to meet women's needs, the FMC collaborates with various governmental bodies such as the Ministry of Education, the Ministry of Health, and the National Commission on Employment and Social Security. Despite the positive changes wrought by the FMC and other activists, women are still underrepresented in the higher echelons of government. Women constitute less than a quarter of the membership in the Communist Party and only 25 percent of the Confederation of Cuban Workers. Few women have ever served on the Council of State, the Politburo, or the Central Committee, and no woman has been a member of the Communist Party's Secretariat.[62] Moreover, debate still exists about the efficacy of the National FMC Congresses, held approximately every five years. One criticism notes the lack of actual dialogue between the FMC and other legislative bodies and observes that the women's resolutions did not always translate into national actions.[63]

Lesbian Rights

While women's rights have been a central focus for the FMC, lesbian rights as such are seldom an issue on any official agenda. Cuba tends to mirror the general Latin American tendency to tolerate relationships between women as long as nobody has to talk about it. For instance, the prominent writer and historian Lydia Cabrera, an author of fiction as well as several books on Afro-Cuban culture, lived most of her life in Cuba with her lifelong companion María Teresa de Rojas.[64] A homophobia intrinsic to Cuban society was exacerbated in the early years of the revolution, when conformity to an ideal was vigorously policed.[65] Lesbian and gay rights have progressed substantially in the last fifteen years of the revolution. Discrimination against and harassment of gays was widespread in the 1960s and 1970s, including mass roundups and incarceration of gays and transvestites (reminiscent of the Stonewall roundups in New York City), and forced internment in rehabilitation or work camps (made infamous by the Cuban writer Reinaldo Arenas's fiction). Today many prominent writers, artists, educators, and other women are known to be lesbians and gays; however, it is only quite recently that any of these individuals have brought the issue of their sexuality into public debate. In 1994, changing attitudes showed when Tomás Gutiérrez Alea's film *Strawberry and Chocolate*, a story about a friendship between a member of the Communist Youth and a gay artist who becomes his intellectual mentor, was entered in the Cannes Film Festival. After the film's debut and during the public debate that lasted for months, the FMC hosted a visit by representatives of the San Francisco–based organization Queers for Cuba. During the same period, the Communist Party and the Institute of Cuban Film commissioned the documentary film *Gay Cuba* by Sonja DeVries (1995), which presents an optimistic view of the current situation of gays and lesbians on the island.

Military Service

The Cuban armed forces contain thousands of women at varying levels of command. Although women do not participate in the draft, both voluntary service and enlistment into any branch of the service are options. Women have been key in numerous campaigns, both on the island and in military training for insurgency forces such as those in Central America and Africa.

RELIGION AND SPIRITUALITY

Because of the ethnic and racial makeup of Cuba, as well as particular tenets of Marxist doctrine, religion and spirituality are complex issues full of apparent paradoxes on the island. The island and its indigenous population were taken over by Spanish conquistadores starting in 1492. The colonizing forces, mostly made up of male soldiers, adventurers, and missionaries, were operating under multiple agendas. Not only were they in search of personal riches and fame, they were helping the newly united Spain construct its identity as an empire and a Catholic nation.

Women's Roles

The Catholic Church traditionally maintained a strict separation of gender roles, trying to relegate women to a supporting and mostly silent part in social and political spheres. Cuba's position as a military fortress guarding Spain's imperial holdings in the Americas mitigated the oppression of women. Society women often had to run households in the absence of their husbands, sometimes joined exploratory and fighting missions, and entered judicial battles over pensions and land grants owed their deceased husbands and sons.[66] One of the foremost objectives of the Spanish colonizers, linked to their self-image as liberators and redeemers rather than oppressors, was the conversion of the indigenous tribes (and subsequently of the slaves) to Catholicism. The indigenous tribes, including the Taínos, the Ciboneys, and the Guanajatabeyes, were decimated by European germs, forced labor, and overvigorous attempts at conversion. The most famous story from that time is the burning at the stake of Cacique Hatuay, who refused to convert to Christianity and successfully fought the Spanish for four months. The Cuban indigenous people were not to influence modern Cuban religion and spirituality to any great degree.

Because of the growing shortage of labor, black slaves were brought to the island in droves to work the sugar plantations, as well as to perform any other hard labor eschewed by the Spanish colonists and Cuban-born Creoles. The slave trade continued to flourish in Cuba well into the nineteenth century, long after the industry had been abolished in other American territories and countries, resulting in both a huge black/mulatto population (50–60 percent) and a sophisticated and entrenched system of racial discrimination. Counting both mulattos and blacks (divided as such in census data), people of African descent currently make up a full 62 percent of the population. These involuntary immigrants brought with them various fully established religious and/or spiritual (and cultural-linguistic) systems, including Congo, Carabalí, and Yoruba. Although tribes from different regions of the African continent had developed quite distinct religions, certain characteristics were often shared: African religions were for the most part based on an oral tradition, included ritual ceremonies incorporating music and dance, and consisted of worship of multiple deities or *orishas* (male and female). Human intermediaries or *babalaos* (male or female) would communicate with the deities, sometimes through trance or temporary possession, thus interpreting natural signs, foretelling future events, and guiding actions of the believers. Particular colors, foods, and spheres of influence were attributed to the *orishas*, much like the Catholic saints. General terms that began to refer to the entirety of African religions practiced in Cuba include Santeria and *La Regla Lucumi* or *Rechla de Ocha*. Closely related is the communication with spirits through mediums (*Espiritismo*). Although women's roles traditionally have been more powerful and flexible in Santeria, perhaps reflecting the existence of powerful goddesses who are worshipped in their own stead, certain rights and responsibilities have been reserved for male practitioners until very recently.

Rituals and Religious Practices

As in other parts of the Americas, especially in Brazil, Catholic missionaries in Cuba began to implement a conversion strategy that capitalized on the similarities between Catholicism and African religions. Whenever possible, even minor Catholic feast days would be celebrated on a large scale when they fell near important sacred days normally kept by the African slaves. Catholic saints were "transposed" onto the African *orishas*, resulting in a complex syncretism in which Catholic icons might grace the altar of an espiritista (a person who believes in spirit mediums) or conversely were believed to have attributes of his/her African counterpart. Examples include Changó (associated with thunder and lightning), who is connected with St. Barbara; Elegua (roads and gates), who is linked with St. Anthony; and Babalu Aye (patron of the sick), whose Catholic counterpart is St.

Lazarus. Despite the interweaving of the systems, Christianity in general and specifically Catholicism were long considered to be the most acceptable religions, especially in the middle and upper classes. Conservative church doctrine influenced law and social mores, a heritage that has been difficult to abandon despite radical changes in legislation and the official stance on women and religion.

Before Fidel Castro assumed power, the officially sanctioned religion was the Roman Catholic Church, whose members included 85 percent of the population, the rest being divided unevenly between Protestants, Jehovah's Witnesses, Jews, and Santeros. Policy changes in 1959 included official intolerance of any religions because Marxist theory prescribed atheism as the preferred practice. One could not be a practicing Catholic and a member of the Communist Party, and even having one's children baptized could affect one's rise through the ranks. Widespread consternation at this drastic transition was counterbalanced by the accompanying positive social changes. Women were urged to enter into community organizing, contribute to the evolving economy, and become involved in politics, rather than going to mass or praying alone. Sanctions on abortion and contraceptives were lifted, as was other church-influenced legislation limiting women's rights.

Although Afro-Cuban dance, music, art, literature, and history were embraced as part of the culture of the masses, these elements were carefully separated from the religious context, at least in theory. Literary and dramatic texts such as *Santa Teresa de la Habana Vieja* encouraged the people to let go of superstition and spirit worship and instead invest their energy in the overhaul of the Cuban society and economy. Nonetheless, many Cubans continued to follow their spiritual practices in the privacy of their own homes; religion and worship became more personal and individual rather than an institution of the state. Perhaps for this reason, and because the revolution strives to erase class differences, Cuba's religious syncretism has spread to communities of all colors, ethnicities, and socioeconomic backgrounds.

In the early 1990s, freedom of religion became a major issue at the Communist Party Congress. Soon afterward, policy on public worship became much more lenient, and Pope John Paul's visit in January 1998 galvanized the Catholic community. Likewise, Santeros became more open. María Antonia Carrillo, an Afro-Cuban dance-troupe director and artist, sees this as a very positive step:

> Now that there's more freedom of religious expression, an increasing number of young people have been initiated into Santería. And since they no longer fear losing their jobs or facing other hassles because of their religion, you can see people on the streets wearing colored, beaded necklaces that correspond to their particular saint. . . . I believe, just as my African ancestors believed, that the gods are everywhere—in nature,

in the air, in the trees, in the sun, and in the moon. Human beings may disappear, but the universe is everlasting. For me, this is my religion; this is my idea of God, and this is everything to me![67]

Others are concerned about the recent trend toward official acceptance of religious worship and are afraid that social progress and women's rights may be retarded or even backslide as a result. What must be recognized, however, is that both Catholicism and Santeria have so permeated the Cuban culture that even government intolerance could not obliterate their impact during the more than four decades of the revolution. Equally as important, the Cuban people already have assimilated the idea that strong, successful women can also embody many of the positive qualities encouraged by both religions, so perhaps this lesson will hold.

VIOLENCE

There is a surprising lack of concrete information on the general topic of women and violence in Cuba. Nevertheless, some issues can be easily addressed. There has been no systematic military oppression of women in Cuba's history. Forces in the battles for independence at the turn of the twentieth century and in the 1950s insurgencies culminating in the revolution did not utilize violence against women as a tool of war. Women participated both in the fight for independence and then on both sides of the revolution, so they were subject to injury, death, torture, and other forms of violence inherent in armed conflict.

Domestic Violence and Rape/Sexual Assault

Domestic violence and rape or sexual assault are assumed to be relics of a capitalist past in Cuba. Very little documentation exists on the issue, but it is unknown whether this is due to an actual low rate of occurrence or a social norm that represses discussion of the matter. On the streets, a woman is likely to hear whistles or compliments, but she rarely if ever will be physically harassed or harmed. Cuban women feel completely safe accepting a ride from a stranger or walking alone, even at night; the official stance on women's rights is supported by the ever-present police force. It is the Cuban home that remains a closed book for investigators. An open letter from the FMC to the Women's Watch of the United Nations affirms that women's freedom from harassment and discrimination is protected not only by the Penal Code and the Family Code, but also by the National Group for the Prevention of and Attention to Domestic Violence, founded in 1997. The letter states that only 1.9 percent of the complaints or requests for assistance received by the FMC are related to acts of violence against women. Moreover, women's employment in the juridical sector is said to be a further assurance of punishment of offenses; statistics from the 1990s show that women constituted 60 percent of the lawyers, 45 percent of the judges, and 65 percent of the district attorneys in Cuba.[68]

Trafficking in Women and Children

Another arena of violence and oppression of women, the sex industry in Cuba flourished until 1959. Rural and poor women were recruited (or bought as girls) to service military men, sugarcane workers, and a general clientele from all socioeconomic levels. For tourists, the island was known as a vacation paradise with a hot music scene and sensual tropical women. Trafficking in women and children was an immediate concern for the revolutionary government, which quickly enacted strict legislation to combat prostitution. Recalcitrant streetwalkers were subjected to severe jail sentences and forced rehabilitation, placing the majority of blame on the women (like legislation in the United States and other countries). On the other hand, the FMC spearheaded a public opinion campaign to woo women away from prostitution and sponsored free education and job training to any who voluntarily left the profession. The Cuban government boasted that it had completely eliminated prostitution in the city of Havana, a claim that was probably close to the truth before the recent economic crisis precipitated by the fall of the Soviet Union and the continued boycott by the United States. Prostitution in Cuba is of a different sort than in other third-world countries: "Here families do not sell their daughters into prostitution rings and young women do not begin to sell their bodies because of extreme poverty and an inability to meet basic needs. Rather, some young women, usually college-educated, decide that they want to expand their wardrobe, save money for luxuries for the family, or enter into the club life frequented most by tourists, all of which require American dollars. They think that the easiest way to accomplish this is part-time prostitution."[69]

War and Military Repression

The military, with Fidel Castro as commander in chief, is fully politicized throughout the ranks by the Communist Party of Cuba. New draftees and lower-ranked members of the armed forces are required, under threat of punishment for insubordination, to attend almost daily political instruction. Admission to officer-training school is controlled by the Communist Party, and those who are not involved in party organizations seldom advance in rank. Just as the party permeates the armed forces, so does the Ministry of Interior's national surveillance system, which is employed to repress dissidence through informants and electronic means. The Ministry of Interior also controls the Revolutionary National Police. The Territorial Troop Militia was created by the party in 1980 as another vehicle to maintain social and political control. Estimated to total 1.5 million people in 1992, the Militia was involved in mobilizing discontents and intensifying political indoctrination.[70]

OUTLOOK FOR THE TWENTY-FIRST CENTURY

The immediate future of Cuba is uncertain. The recent film *Cuba va* makes the point that the island nation is certainly persisting in its evolution, but no one is sure exactly what direction that change will follow. On the positive side, the women of Cuba have a strong history of feminist action and a current legislation that accords them a higher status and level of empowerment than their sisters in many Latin American countries. Women continue to rise in the ranks of professional and governmental hierarchies and to advocate for ever-increasing compliance with the high ideals of the FMC: complete equality of the sexes in all sectors and levels of society. Increasingly, both men and women are committed to achieving this goal. However, Cuban women currently face the multiple stresses that characterize the life of women in developed nations without many of the options and luxuries afforded bourgeois women in western Europe and the United States. Also, the privations stemming from the U.S. economic embargo and the Special Period have a more immediate and devastating impact on women's lives; some women are tiring of carrying the heavy burden imposed by the struggle for social change. Finally, there is the question of what will happen in Cuba when Fidel Castro steps down from his post. Virtually nobody on the island wants to revert to the political and economic system that reigned prior to the revolution, and indeed such a future could prove disastrous to women's rights. Given the level of education in Cuba and the formidable progress made toward equal rights regardless of gender (or other factors), it is unlikely that the Cuban people would allow any major retrogression on these issues. Nevertheless, the women of Cuba need to see evidence of solidarity with women's groups in the rest of the world; this could make the difference between stagnation and further growth in the immediate future.

NOTES

Special thanks to Rosalyn Peck for research assistance.

1. U.S. Department of Commerce, National Trade Data Bank, *Cuba World Factbook*, May 6, 1999, www.tradeport.org/ts/countries/cuba/wofact.html.

2. Ibid.

3. Lois M. Smith and Alfred Padula, *Sex and Revolution: Women in Socialist Cuba* (New York: Oxford University Press, 1996), 11.

4. See K. Lynn Stoner, *From the House to the Streets: The Cuban Woman's Move-*

ment for Legal Reform, 1898–1940 (Durham, NC: Duke University Press, 1991), for a detailed and very subtle exploration of Cuban feminism in the period 1898–1940. Stoner teases out the differences between bands of feminists along the entire continuum of political advocacy, from the radicals who advocated free love and equal rights for natural children to the conservatives who merely wanted to beautify urban areas.

5. Stoner, *From the House to the Streets*, 1991, 131–33.

6. Ibid.

7. Inger Holt-Seeland, *Women of Cuba*, translation of *Con las puertas abiertas* (Westport, CT: Lawrence Hill, 1982), 94–95.

8. Alfonso Farnós, "Cuba," in *Working Women in Socialist Countries: The Fertility Connection*, ed. Valentina Bodrova and Richard Anker (Geneva: International Labour Office, 1985), 201.

9. Margaret E. Leahy, *Development Strategies and the Status of Women* (Boulder, CO: Lynne Rienner, 1986), 94.

10. Stoner, *From the House to the Streets*, 1991, 36–37.

11. Ibid., 82.

12. Stoner, 1991, 79.

13. John Dumoulin and Isabel Larguía, "La mujer en el desarrollo: Estrategia y experiencias de la Revolución Cubana," *Casa de las Américas* 149 (1985): 40.

14. United Nations Statistics Division, 2000, www.unstats.un.org/unsd/databases.html.

15. Susan Eva Eckstein, *Back from the Future: Cuba under Castro* (Princeton, NJ: Princeton University Press, 1994), 56.

16. Dumoulin and Larguía, 1985, 39.

17. Antón L. Allahar, "Women and the Family in Cuba: A Study across Time," *Humboldt Journal of Social Relations* 20(1) (1994): 96.

18. Eckstein, 1994, 34.

19. Smith and Padula, 1996, 110.

20. Norma Vasallo, "Imagining the Unimaginable: Creating Women's Transnational Alliances," International Forum, California State University, August 29, 2000.

21. Smith and Padula, 1996, 106.

22. Octavio Cortázar et al., *Con las mujeres cubanas* (film) (ICAIC, 1975).

23. "Cuba. Thematic Reports," *Mechanisms of the Commission on Human Rights*, http://www.hri.ca/.

24. Valentina Bodrova and Richard Anker, eds., *Working Women in Socialist Countries: The Fertility Connection* (Geneva: International Labour Office, 1985), 228.

25. Smith and Padula, 1996, 123.

26. S. Catasús et al., *Cuban Women: Changing Roles and Population Trends*, Women, Work and Development Series, no. 17 (Geneva: International Labour Office, 1988), 41.

27. Smith and Padula, 1996, 69.

28. Catasús et al., 1988, 83.

29. Ibid., 89.

30. Ibid., 91.

31. Ibid., 94.

32. Ibid., 47.

33. International Planned Parenthood Federation, http://ippfnet.ippf.org/pub/IPPF-Regions/IPPF_CountryProfile.asp?ISOCode=CU.

34. One tropical disease that continues to plague the island, necessitating both

preventive and curative measures, is dengue hemorrhagic fever/dengue shock syndrome, an acute and sometimes fatal disease transmitted by mosquitoes. Having reached epidemic status in the Caribbean, dengue became a problem in Cuba in 1981. Hundreds of thousands of people have been affected (International Development Research Center, 2002, www.idrc.ca/reports/read.html). Drastic measures have been taken, including mandatory fumigation house by house in areas with the worst concentration of mosquitoes, sometimes on a semiweekly basis. Women, children, and elders who are at home during the day are most affected by the fumigation, which requires vacating the home at a moment's notice, often in the heat of the midday sun, and subsequent reentry into the fumigated structure.

35. Smith and Padula, 1996, 60.

36. Holt-Seeland, 1998, 14.

37. Smith and Padula, 1996, 57.

38. Ibid., 63.

39. P. V. Perez, "National Survey in Risk Factors," National Institute for Hygiene, Epidemiology, and Microbiology, Ministry of Health, and National Statistics Office (1995), in U.S. Department of Commerce, National Trade Data Bank, *Cuba World Factbook*, May 6, 1999, http://www.tradeport.org/ts/countries/cuba/wofact.html.

40. Smith and Padula, 1996, 64.

41. Ibid., 66.

42. Anuli Ajene et al., "Cuba Got It Right," Final Project in the Department of International Health Summer Certificate Program, Boston University, August 18, 2000, dcc2.bumc.bu.edu/SCP/MainPages/Course/Sessions/Controversies/Groupswork/cuba/Finalpaper.doc.1.

43. Sara E. Cooper, interview with the Fernandez family, June 2001, unpublished.

44. Norma Vasallo, International Forum titled "Imagining the Unimaginable: Creating Women's Transnational Alliances" held at California State University at Chico and hosted jointly by Latin American Studies, International Programs, and Chicano Studies, August 29, 2000.

45. Stoner, *From the House to the Streets*, 1991, 17.

46. Smith and Padula, 1996, 66.

47. Ibid., 11–12.

48. Ibid., 15.

49. Stoner, *From the House to the Streets*, 1991, gives a thorough treatment of legal and political maneuvering of the women's movement in the first half of the twentieth century, including the dynamics and resolutions of the first and second National Women's Congresses.

50. K. Lynn Stoner, *The Women's Movement in Cuba, 1898–1958: The Stoner Collection on Cuban Feminism* (Wilmington, DE: Scholarly Resources, 1989), 57–60.

51. Margaret Randall, *Gathering Rage: The Failure of Twentieth Century Revolutions to Develop a Feminist Agenda* (New York: Monthly Review Press, 1992), 21.

52. Judy Maloof, ed. and trans., *Voices of Resistance: Testimonies of Cuban and Chilean Women* (Lexington: University Press of Kentucky, 1999), 85.

53. Maloof, 1999, 22.

54. See Smith and Padula, 1996, for a greatly expanded discussion of women's contributions to the revolutionary efforts both before and after 1959.

55. Vilma Espín was married to Raúl Castro, Fidel's brother, for more than twenty years. The fact that her marital or family status is seldom mentioned seems to be an indication of feminist progress.

56. Haydée Santamaría committed suicide in 1980, twenty-seven years to the day after she participated in the assault on Moncada. Melba Hernández died of pulmonary cancer in 1980.

57. Smith and Padula, 1996, 24.

58. Ibid., 34.

59. Ibid., 36.

60. Ibid., 46.

61. Allahar, 1994.

62. Smith and Padula, 1996, 46–47.

63. Randall, 1992, 51.

64. Smith and Padula, 1996, 17.

65. Lourdes Arguelles and B. Ruby Rich, "Homosexuality, Homophobia, and Revolution: Notes toward an Understanding of the Cuban Lesbian and Gay Male Experience," in *Hidden from History: Reclaiming the Gay and Lesbian Past*, ed. Martin Duberman, Martha Vicinus, and George Chauncey, Jr. (New York: Penguin, 1990), 441–55.

66. Sherry E. Johnson, *The Social Transformation of Eighteenth-Century Cuba* (Gainesville: University Press of Florida, 2001).

67. Maloof, 1999, 67.

68. Federación de las Mujeras Cubanas, "Violencia contra la mujer en Cuba, primera parte," Women's Right List Archive, December 2, 1999, www.sdnp.undp.org/ww/women-rights/msg00075.html.

69. Vasallo, 2000.

70. Douglas Payne, "Cuba: Systematic Repression of Dissent," INS Resource Information Center, Perspective Series (PS/CUB/99.001), December 1998, www.worldpolicy.org.

RESOURCE GUIDE

Suggested Reading

Castillo Bueno, María de los Reyes. *Reyita: The Life of a Black Woman in the Twentieth Century*. Trans. Anne McLean. Durham, NC: Duke University Press, 2000. This testimonial, told to Castillo Bueno's daughter, Daisy Rubiera Castillo, is drenched with the richness of an oral text in a movingly written narrative.

Davies, Catherine. *A Place in the Sun? Women Writers in Twentieth-Century Cuba*. New York: St. Martin's Press, 1997.

Espín, Vilma. *Cuban Women Confront the Future: Three Decades after the Revolution*. Ed. Deborah Shnookal. Melbourne: Ocean Press, 1991.

Martínez-Alier, Verena. *Marriage, Class, and Colour in Nineteenth-Century Cuba: A Study of Racial Attitudes and Sexual Values in a Slave Society*. 2nd ed. Ann Arbor: University of Michigan Press, 1989. A scrupulously documented study of racially mixed marriages, conflicts between church and state, the color-based caste system, and the connection between color and honor.

Obejas, Achy. *Memory Mambo*. Pittsburgh, PA: Cleis Press, 1996. This novel by a Cuban woman living in the United States explores the nuances of the Cuban American identity crisis in the life of a young lesbian woman.

Randall, Margaret. *Women in Cuba, Twenty Years Later*. New York: Smyrna Press, 1981. The first feminist sociologist to research an in-depth study of Cuban women after the revolution revisits and renews her topic.

Smith, Lois M., and Alfred Padula. *Sex and Revolution: Women in Socialist Cuba*. New York: Oxford University Press, 1996. Provides a profound and detailed historical contextualization for the topics addressed in this chapter.

Stone, Elizabeth, ed. *Women and the Cuban Revolution*. New York: Pathfinder Press, 1981. Includes speeches by Fidel Castro and Vilma Espín (president of the FMC), as well as documents from the Communist Party of Cuba about women's equality, the Maternity Law, and the Family Code.

Stoner, K. Lynn. *From the House to the Streets: The Cuban Woman's Movement for Legal Reform, 1898–1940*. Durham, NC: Duke University Press, 1991.

Yáñez, Mirta, ed. *Cubana: Contemporary Fiction by Cuban Women*. Trans. Dick Cluster and Cindy Schuster. Boston: Beacon Press, 1998. An impressive and engaging collection of short stories by Cuban women on and off the island.

Videos/Films

Gay Cuba. 1995. Sonja DeVries. Frameline.
Lucia. 1968. Humberto Solás. ICAIC.
Manuela. 1962. Humberto Solás. ICAIC.
Mujer Transparente. 1990. Hector Veitia. ICAIC.
Retrato de Teresa. 1979. Pastor Vega. ICAIC.

Web Sites

Afro Cuba Web, http://www.afrocubaweb.com/.
Maintains discussion groups, a newsletter, and abundant information about conferences, workshops, or events in the United States connected with Afro-Cuban topics and is also a good source of information or contacts on Afro-Cuban artists, writers, and performers.

Buro de Prensa Independiente de Cuba, http://www.bpicuba.org/mujeres/@mujer.htm.
Browser on women's issues with links to political, economic, and cultural information as well as news.

Cuba.cu, http://www.cuba.cu/.
Main Internet portal of Cuba, including a search engine, links to news and cultural events, and multiple categories of interest.

Cubanet, http://www.cubanet.org/.
Nonprofit organization that "fosters free press in Cuba, assists its independent sector develop a civil society and informs the world about Cuba's reality." This site is mostly in English and fairly anti-Castro in stance.

Facultad Latinoamericana de Ciencias Sociales Cuba, http://www.eurosur.org/FLACSO/mujeres/cuba/portada.htm.
Contains information on demographics, health, legislation, politics, socioeconomic profile, work, education, and the FMC as well as other government programs dealing with women's issues in Cuba.

Federación de las Mujeres Cubanas, http://www.cuba.cu/politica/webpcc/fmc.htm.
The official FMC site, which is very simple.

Feminism in Cuba, http://www.cddc.vt.edu/feminism/cub.html.
Maintained by the Center for Digital Discourse and Culture at Virginia Tech University, this site includes a bibliography and links to further bibliographies and selected articles (not all links are current).

Gay Cuba, http://www.gay-cuba.com/.
Eclectic portal site with links to stories, organizations, resources, and history.

Granma Internacional Digital, http://www.granma.cu/.
Main news publication of Cuba, containing a search engine for archived articles as well as daily news and interest stories.

Portal de la Cultura Cubana, http://www.cult.cu/.
Portal of Cuban culture maintained by the Cuban government that includes news stories as well as links to cultural events, publications, and national and local organizations.

Organizations

Central de Trabajadores de Cuba
San Carlos y Peñalver
Centro Habana ó A.A. 10300
Zona # 3
La Habana, Cuba
Phone: 797-420 and 795-014
Fax: 537-335-408

Objectives include contributing to the education of the rural family to achieve women's equal rights, raising skill and education levels of women in rural areas, and creating more stability for women in the country. Works directly with women workers in the field.

Federación de Mujeres Cubanas
Calle Paseo 260 Esq Calle 13, Vedado
La Habana, Cuba
Phone: 537-301-582
Fax: 537-311-259/333-019
Email: fmc.cu@tinored.cu

Founded August 23, 1960. President Vilma Espín Guillois. An official grassroots organization, linked with the Cuban government, whose objectives include developing legislation and programs designed to achieve complete equality of women in all levels and sectors of society.

Queers for Cuba
Phone: 415-995-4678

Works to fight the U.S. blockade of Cuba, build solidarity with the Cuban people, especially homosexuals and people with HIV/AIDS, inform homosexuals about Cuba, and combat homophobia in the solidarity movement.

Unión de Escritores y Artistas Cubanos
Calle 17 #351e/H. Plaza de la Revolución
Ciudad de La Habana, Cuba
Email: informatica@uneac.co.cu
Web site: http://www.uneac.com/

Founded August 22, 1961, the Union of Cuban Writers and Artists guides the great majority of performances and publications on the island and thus has been key in any progress made by women writers and artists in Cuba.

Women's International League for Peace and Freedom
1213 Race Street
Philadelphia, PA 19107-1691
Phone: 215-563-7110
Fax: 215-563-5527
Web site: http://www.wilpf.org/

The league maintains a Committee to Build a U.S. Women's Movement to Normalize Relations with Cuba, whose contact person is Lisa Valanti, 320 Lowenhill St., Pittsburgh, PA 15216.

SELECTED BIBLIOGRAPHY

Ajene, Anuli, et al. "Cuba Got It Right." Final Project in the Department of International Health Summer Certificate Program, Boston University, August 18, 2000, dcc2.bumc.bu.edu/SCP/MainPages/Course/Sessions/Controversies/Groups work/cuba/Finalpaper.doc.

Allahar, Antón L. "Women and the Family in Cuba: A Study across Time." *Humboldt Journal of Social Relations* 20 (1) (1994): 87–120.

Arguelles, Lourdes, and B. Ruby Rich. "Homosexuality, Homophobia, and Revolution: Notes toward an Understanding of the Cuban Lesbian and Gay Male Experience." In *Hidden from History: Reclaiming the Gay and Lesbian Past*, ed. Martin Duberman, Martha Vicinus, and George Chauncey, Jr., 441–55. New York: Penguin, 1990.

Bodrova, Valentina, and Richard Anker, eds. *Working Women in Socialist Countries: The Fertility Connection*. Geneva: International Labour Office, 1985. Explores the interaction between the reproductive and productive roles of women in socialist countries.

Catasús, S. *Cuban Women: Changing Roles and Population Trends*. Women, Work, and Development Series, no. 17. Geneva: International Labour Office, 1988. Investigates fertility rates as connected to the changing situation of women in Cuba.

Dumoulin, John, and Isabel Larguía. "La mujer en el desarrollo: Estrategia y experiencias de la Revolución Cubana." *Casa de las Américas* 149 (1985): 37–53.

Eckstein, Susan Eva. *Back from the Future: Cuba under Castro*. Princeton, NJ: Princeton University Press, 1994.

Farnós, Alfonso, et al. "Cuba." In *Working Women in Socialist Countries: The Fertility*

Connection, ed. Valentina Bodrova and Richard Anker, 197–234. Geneva: International Labour Office, 1985.

Federación de las Mujeres Cubanas. "Violencia contra la mujer en Cuba, primera parte." December 2, 1999. Women's Right List Archive, maintained by WomenWatch, United Nations, http://www.sdnp.undp.org/ww/womenrights/msg00075.html.

Guevara, Ernesto (Che). "El papel de la mujer." In *The Cuba Reader: The Making of a Revolutionary Society*, ed. Philip Brenner et al. New York: Grove Press, 1989.

Holt-Seeland, Inger. *Women of Cuba*. Translation of *Con las puertas abiertas*. Westport, CT: Lawrence Hill, 1982.

International Development Research Center and the Instituto de Medicina Tropical in Havana. http://www.idrc.ca/reports/read_cntryprof.cfm?ovr_id=7.

Johnson, Sherry E. *The Social Transformation of Eighteenth-Century Cuba*. Gainesville: University Press of Florida, 2001.

Leahy, Margaret E. *Development Strategies and the Status of Women*. Boulder, CO: Lynne Rienner, 1986.

Maloof, Judy, ed. and trans. *Voices of Resistance: Testimonies of Cuban and Chilean Women*. Lexington: University Press of Kentucky, 1999.

Perez, P.V., "National survey in risk factors." National Institute for Hygiene, Epidemiology, and Microbiology, Ministry of Health, and National Statistics Office, 1995, in U.S. Department of Commerce, National Trade Data Bank, *Cuba World Factbook*, May 6, 1999, http://www.tradeport.org/ts/countries/cuba/wofact.html.

Randall, Margaret. *Gathering Rage: The Failure of Twentieth Century Revolutions to Develop a Feminist Agenda*. New York: Monthly Review Press, 1992.

Stoner, K. Lynn. *The Women's Movement in Cuba, 1898–1958: The Stoner Collection on Cuban Feminism*. Wilmington, DE: Scholarly Resources, 1989. 13 microfilm reels. The collection, compiled from Cuban archives, covers the period from Cuban independence following the Spanish-American War to the end of the Batista regime, providing information on Cuban women in politics, Cuban feminism, Cuban women's literature, and the legal status of Cuban women, 1898–1940. The documents, which are in Spanish, fall into three general categories: works by feminists about feminists and their causes; works by men about the status of women; and novels, essays, and poetry written by feminist women writers in general as well as literary analysis of these women's works.

Vasallo, Norma. International Forum titled "Imagining the Unimaginable: Creating Women's Transnational Alliances" held at California State University at Chico and hosted jointly by Latin American Studies, International Programs, and Chicano Studies, August 29, 2000.

Yáñez, Mirta. *Cubanas a capítulo: Selección de ensayos sobre mujeres cubanas y literatura*. Santiago de Cuba: Editorial Oriente, 2000.

5

THE DOMINICAN REPUBLIC

Cecilia Ann Winters

PROFILE OF THE DOMINICAN REPUBLIC

The Dominican Republic occupies the eastern two-thirds of the island of Hispaniola, which it shares with Haiti, located in the Caribbean Sea. Colonized by the Spanish in 1492, the Dominican Republic has been occupied by Haiti, by Spain, and twice by the United States. It has moved haltingly toward democracy since 1966. Past governments can be characterized as authoritarian and often brutal. Most of the control is in the hands of the president, who has supreme authority. The legislative branch essentially operates at the behest of the president. The judicial branch of government employs the highly centralized and hierarchical Napoleonic civil code. The population is 8,581,477. The ethnic mix of 16 percent white, 11 percent black, and 73 percent mixed only hints at the diversity of the Dominican population.[1] Over the last several centuries, Spaniards, Sephardic Jews, British, Dutch, Cubans, Puerto Ricans, Koreans, Ukrainians, and Lebanese, Palestinian, and Syrian Arabs have become part of the "mixed" component of Dominican society. Almost all migrants have been thoroughly

assimilated into Dominican society with astonishing speed, usually within a generation or two.[2]

The triple legacies of colonialism, dependency, and authoritarian rule have kept this small country mired in poverty and oppression. Globalization and feminization of the workforce have sealed this fate for women, who are now consigned to a double workday as well as intractable poverty. The World Bank gives the 1998 per capita gross domestic product (GDP) as $1,770, but income is so inequitably distributed that 25 percent of the population, more than two million Dominicans, are living below the poverty line.[3] The wealthiest 20 percent of the population earns almost 50 percent of total income, while the poorest 20 percent earns 7 percent of total income. Average life expectancy is 73.44 years. The infant mortality rate is 34.67 deaths per 1,000 live births,[4] and the 1990 maternal mortality rate is 110 per 100,000 live births.[5] The official unemployment rate of 13.8 percent is unreliable because it fails to take into account those working in the informal sector in which most participants work and live below the poverty line. These statistics point to a poor quality of life for the majority of Dominicans. Given the pervasive culture of patriarchy, these facts do not portend well for Dominican women.

OVERVIEW OF WOMEN'S ISSUES

The subordination of Dominican women was an outgrowth of slavery, colonialism, and the patriarchal tradition of machismo that stemmed from Spanish conquest and domination. Hispanic culture rooted in Roman Catholic tradition has led to antidemocratic and antiprogressive development in much of Latin America and is responsible to some degree for the rigid social codes in the Dominican Republic. Historically, Dominican women have been assigned almost no role in the public sphere and are expected to play a subordinate role in the private sphere. In a time when women are being educated and employed in increasing numbers, they find themselves at odds with both male partners and a paternalistic government as they try to bring awareness to their situation, mediate between their actual and stereotypical roles, and struggle to improve their lives.

Human rights organizations report that women face enormous barriers to participation in public life and decision making. There seems to be no official will to undertake comprehensive and systematic public awareness and information campaigns to change long-standing patriarchal attitudes that deprive Dominican women of equal treatment. Dominican women suffer from segregation in the labor market and discrimination with regard to income and benefits. International agencies report that women suffer from higher unemployment rates than men, making the situation for domestic workers and single mothers especially insecure. Despite the fact that women have higher levels of education than men, they are paid less than men for work of equal value.

The government does not expend the effort it should to enforce compliance with wage, benefits, and workers' safety laws. Dominican law has many provisions that specifically protect women, but employers ignore these because the government does nothing to ensure that women are treated in accordance with their legal rights. Conventions that call for the safety and humane treatment of women working in the free trade zones (FTZs) are ignored. Free trade zones are established by foreign firms within a developing country under special provisions and privileges bestowed by the government. They usually take the form of assembly operations, with apparel manufacturers having particular importance in the Dominican Republic. Companies that establish operations in free trade zone parks receive a fifteen-year renewable period of tax breaks. They are exempt from income taxes as well as taxes on construction, loan contracts and registration or transfer of real estate, taxes on incorporation and increases in capital, municipal taxes, all import taxes, customs duties, customs rights related to raw materials, machinery, construction materials, building parts and office supplies, export and re-export taxes, patent taxes, taxes on the transfer of industrial goods and services, and taxes on consular rights for all imports, among others. The aforementioned agreements apply partially or in full to free trade zones around the world. The intention of establishing these zones is ostensibly to spur economic growth by attracting foreign investment. Foreign firms are attracted, however, by the cheap labor; the lax safety, health, and environmental regulations; and the tax breaks, all of which make for a low overhead. The majority of employees in FTZs are women.[6] Violence against and rape of women by FTZ employers and male partners are tremendous problems for Dominican women.

In the area of social services, major health concerns revolve around pregnancy, childbirth, abortion (which is illegal under any circumstances), the availability of birth control, and diagnosis and treatment of sexually transmitted diseases, especially AIDS. Trafficking in women and children is also a problem that needs to be addressed. All of these issues are outgrowths of a poor, socially stratified, traditionally oppressive nation that still institutionalizes women's subordination.

EDUCATION

Opportunities

Formal education includes primary, secondary, and higher education. The six-year primary cycle is compulsory, but only 17 percent of rural schools offered all six grades as of 1989. A chronic teacher shortage was attributable to low pay, particularly in rural areas, as well as the perception of teaching as a "women-only" profession. Many problems continued after education expanded at all levels after 1961. There were shortages of teaching materials and facilities at every level. Little surplus was left for further investment and growth after salaries and operating expenses were paid.[7]

Sixty-nine percent of women but only 63 percent of men attend school.[8] Female net enrollment in primary school is 83 percent, but drops precipitously to 26 percent in secondary school and declines further to 2.8 percent in higher education.[9] Women's groups agree that more women than men now graduate from professional and higher studies, but many of these women are working in jobs for which they are overqualified. Their superior education has not translated into increased economic or political power.

Education may be a vehicle by which Dominican women can improve their lot, but opportunities have been slow to materialize and disappointing. Without increased public spending on educational services, society's efforts to achieve a more equal distribution of income and women's efforts to improve their situation will be frustrated and delayed. However, since 1996, when free and fair elections were first held in the Dominican Republic, women have begun to achieve a tiny, though greatly hailed, presence in government. The current secretary of state for education and culture is, for the first time, a woman, Milagros Ortiz-Bosch. She concurrently is serving as the vice president and will hopefully raise a strong voice for greater educational opportunities for Dominican women.

Literacy

Despite the Dominican Republic's impoverished commitment to education, the literacy rate grew from 74 percent in 1986 to 82 percent in 1999, and the backlog of illiterate people is slowly shrinking. Men and women are reported to have nearly equal levels of literacy.[10]

EMPLOYMENT AND ECONOMICS

Job/Career Opportunities

The Dominican Republic has changed profoundly since 1961 from a largely rural agrarian to an urban industrial economy. In 1970, 40 percent of the population resided in urban areas, and by 1995, 62 percent of the population had moved from the rural to the urban sector.[11] This has been a consequence of the gender restructuring of the labor force in the Dominican Republic, as well as in other third-world countries, and the new international division of labor, wherein young women are increasingly employed in export manufacturing within designated free trade zones. The increase in employment opportunities for women has been accompanied by deterioration in male employment in the more traditional occupations of the country, such as import-substitution manufacturing and sugar production. Young women provide approximately 60 percent to 80 percent of the labor for export manufacturing in the Dominican Republic.[12] There is little opportunity for Dominican women to enter administration or management. Between 1992 and 1996, women made up only 21 percent of that segment of the workforce.[13] Furthermore, despite the increasing feminization of the labor force, by 1997, the unemployment rate was 28.6 percent for women and 9.5 percent for men.[14] Many of these women actually find poorly paid, unstable employment in the informal sector and are thus counted among the unemployed.

Dominican women are often employed as domestic servants for the wealthy and, in increasing numbers, as prostitutes to work in the burgeoning tourist industry. The latter occupation is outlawed, but socially tolerated and quite public, as it is an old occupation. Observers suggest that the Dominican Republic may have the dubious distinction of being one of the leading suppliers to the international sex industry after Thailand and the Philippines. Few commercial sex workers finish primary school, and about 16 percent are illiterate. Most come from poor rural areas.

Pay

The growth in free trade zones is largely due to the availability of a cheap and docile labor force, consisting mostly of young women working for the lowest wages imaginable. Minimum wages in the Dominican Republic vary by sector. Workers in the tourist industry have a different legally mandated minimum than those in the free trade zones, for example. Women earn less than men for work of equal value. The per capita income of women is one-third that of men.[15] In addition, men holding technical jobs in the free trade zones now outnumber women. They receive preferential pay for these jobs, partially accounting for the male/female wage differential. The workers in the FTZs are reportedly paid higher wages than the legally established minimum, which ranges from a low of RD1,680 per month (U.S.$140) to a high for most workers of between RD2,500 per month (U.S.$208) and RD3,800 per month (U.S.$317).[16] If these amounts are translated to hourly wages, assuming a 42.5-hour workweek, the lowest-paid workers earn about $.82 per hour, while the middle and highly paid workers are earning $1.22 and $1.86 per hour, respectively.

While the minimum wage has increased in the local currency throughout most of the period since 1992, structural adjustment policies that mandated currency devaluations contributed to increases in the cost of living. Thus real wages, that is, workers' purchasing power, has been declining. Many who work in the informal economy earn less than U.S.$100 per month.[17] The decline in purchasing power is occurring at a time when the Dominican government continues to dismantle its public services, and working female heads of households are challenged as never before.

Working Conditions

Low wages, long working hours for which employers ignore legally mandated overtime, too few bathroom breaks, sexual harassment, and abusive treatment characterize working conditions in the free trade zones. A study of about 700 workers in free trade zones found that reproductive disorders are one to three times more common after a woman begins work in an FTZ factory.[18]

The free trade zones would appear to be fertile ground for trade-union organizing, but such a movement has been brutally suppressed by employers with help from the national police. The Dominican constitution and labor code only recently have enshrined the right to freedom of association and collective bargaining, but companies in the free trade zones prevent unionization by intimidating and blacklisting organizers while replacing them with temporary workers. One reason the government remains complacent is that these employers threaten to move and remove jobs from the country.

Working conditions are even more abysmal for rural working women of Haitian descent. These women are confined to the sugarcane fields of the Dominican Republic. Cane cutting is backbreaking labor and miserably paid, and Dominicans want none of it. Thus Haitians are allowed to migrate to the cane fields to perform this work. Legally, these are temporary workers. However, it is cheaper for plantation owners if the Haitian cane cutters live in the fields permanently. Consequently, they remain with their wives, who do not have legal permission to live there and are thus administratively invisible, only to face substandard living conditions such as no sanitation, no education, and no health care. Roughly 5 percent of the cane cutters are women. They receive half of what men receive.[19]

Interestingly, there is a strong trade-union movement for prostitutes, also known as commercial sex workers, called Movimiento de Mujeres, that is proving to be quite successful. One purpose of the union is to provide education about and protection from sexually transmitted diseases and AIDS. Through the trade union, fees, vacation time, and commissions are negotiated. Women employed as commercial sex workers explain that they cannot get other adequately paid jobs that provide enough for their children, thanks to the local culture of machismo and the influence of mass consumerism.

Sexual Harassment

Dominican women are constantly subjected to discrimination because of sexist hiring practices. The offense of sexual harassment was finally included in the Dominican labor code in 1992.[20] This particular section in the labor code is not enforced because workers are afraid to call attention to these conditions, and investors threaten to leave the country if they are sanctioned for them.

Support for Mothers/Caretakers

Maternal Leave

Laws exist in the Dominican legal code that are designed to protect pregnant women and families. Article 232 of the Labor Code prohibits an employer from firing a woman because of pregnancy. However, in the event the woman is fired, the employer must pay her five months' salary. This is not really a prohibition but a condition that the employer must fulfill if he wants to fire a pregnant woman. Most employers can well afford to pay the required compensation and do so, preventing the woman from appealing to the law at all.[21]

Daycare

It would seem nearly impossible for working mothers to support a family on the low wages they earn. There is no effort to provide state-sponsored child-care centers in the Dominican Republic, and employers in the FTZs would never dream of offering this type of support. Consequently, working mothers rely on extended families for support. Extended families made up 40 percent of all households surveyed nationwide in 1991.[22] These extended families include other adult members such as parents, in-laws, or siblings who are either working or looking for work and willing to mind the children for a young woman working in an FTZ. If a parent, partner, sibling, aunt, uncle, or cousin has migrated to another country, such as the United States or Puerto Rico, a young working mother may be able to rely on remittances from abroad for help in supporting the children. In some cases, retired grandparents in the countryside who could not otherwise support themselves will keep children during the working week for a young working mother, who will return home to see the family on weekends.

Essentially, working mothers rely on a system of blood relationships, even more than marital relationships, for family support. The children enjoy the benefit of having an array of loving adults, including adult men, to turn to. When there are several women in the extended household, they often exchange the task of child care and rotate in and out of employment.[23] Nevertheless, these various methods of supporting working mothers and their children are quite ad hoc, and even extended household networks have their limits. The mutual aid among kin described here implies some minimal amount of resources. If there are inadequate basic resources, there will be massive migration to the United States.[24] The net migration rate for the Dominican Republic of −3.81 migrants per 1,000 persons is a testimony to the impoverishment and hardship that globalization has wrought on the Dominican Republic, since globalization does not take support of families and children as one of its imperatives.[25]

Inheritance and Property Rights

According to the Library of Congress, irrigated rice farms, which had been left intact and farmed collectively despite the first land reforms of the 1960s, were slated for division into small, privately owned plots by 1980. All told, by 1980 the Dominican Agrarian had distributed state land to approximately 67,000 families (less than 15 percent of the rural population). The ownership of the plots was naturally remanded to the "heads of families," that is, men. A 1997 amendment to the 1962 Law on Agrarian Reform gave women, whether married or single, the same rights as men regarding land adjudicated by the reform.

Social/Government Programs

Sustainable Development

The general understanding of sustainable development is that a nation's present economic and social choices should not compromise the ability of future generations to meet their own needs. The development path of the Dominican Republic is not sustainable for two reasons. First, the expansion of the free trade zones contributes little to regional or national development because multinational corporations refuse to bear responsibility for the welfare of the communities in which they operate. The free trade zones have contributed to a deterioration of job opportunities for men, shifting the burden of earning income to women. These women earn lower wages than men, thus exacerbating poverty in the Dominican Republic. The second reason is the continued reluctance of the government to alter the dynamic of unequal income distribution and provide the most basic social services to its poorer citizens. The steady stream of outward migration is by no means indicative of sustainable development.

Globalization policies, outward migration, devaluation, and structural adjustment have contributed to a decline in government revenues and a concomitant decline in spending on government programs. In July 1999, the World Bank planned to lend $360 million to the Dominican Republic for new investments in health and education, water and sanitation services, power services, environmental institutions, and telecommunications. With a real economic growth rate of 8 percent in the year 2000, the government's continued neglect of the social services sector does not speak well for its development goals and priorities. Essentially, the Dominican Republic has relied on the presence of international organizations such as the World Bank, the U.S. Agency for International Development, and a plethora of nongovernmental organizations (NGOs) to fill in the gaps in spending on social services. This is yet another manifestation of the Dominican Republic's historical tendency toward dependency.

Welfare

There are no state supports like welfare or unemployment insurance in the Dominican Republic. The government's role in the economy is relatively limited. In the 1970s, government spending (infrastructure development) was 15 percent of GDP. In 1987, it was still low at 20 percent of GDP, and in 1998, it was 16 percent of GDP. Social expenditures (health and education) for 1998 were even lower at about 6–7 percent of GDP, half the Latin American average of about 14 percent.[26]

FAMILY AND SEXUALITY

The traditions of family unity, loyalty, and strong kinship ties run deep in the Dominican Republic. This heritage not only has affected a single mother's ability to work and raise children, but permeates every aspect of Dominican life.

Gender Roles

Sex-role differentiation begins early in the Dominican family: girls are quiet and helpful; boys are given much greater latitude in their behavior. Boys and men are expected to have premarital or extramarital experiences, but fully expect their brides to be virginal and faithful. No shame accrues to the man who fathers many children outside of marriage or maintains relationships with women other than his wife. The man is expected to assume the role of "head of the household" and to support his own children. Despite this cultural mythology, female-headed households have a long history in the Caribbean and the Dominican Republic in particular and should not be seen as pathological, but as a legitimate alternative form of family organization.

The growth in women's employment in the free trade zones and the concurrent decline in men's employment have had a powerful impact on gender roles. The importance of a woman's contribution to the household allows her to resist male domination in the family and affords her the power to negotiate more freely with her husband or partner. Thanks to export manufacturing, women are fast becoming the principal providers in their household. However, this cannot be regarded as a complete victory for women. On the one hand, the patriarchal controls male partners hold over Dominican women's lives may seem to have loosened, thanks to the independence conferred even by women's low wages. On the other hand, the very real displacement of men from traditional employment and from being the head of the household has been disruptive and emasculating. This may fuel a misogynistic backlash against women and lead to greater tension in intimate relationships, the ultimate outcome of which may be domestic violence. These concerns are heightened by the view men hold that women working in the FTZs are irresponsible, loose women who spend their money in bars and beauty salons and contribute little to the household.

Furthermore, thanks to company policies in the FTZs, employers play a controlling role in more than women's working lives. Many employers in the FTZs explicitly express a preference for women with children because they feel that their need to work ensures greater job commitment. However, in an effort to avoid the cost and burden of maternity leave, several employers distribute birth-control pills free of charge to their women workers. Some have been reported to require a pregnancy test or sterilization certificate before women are hired. Employers thus exercise power over a woman's reproductive life as well as her productive life.[27]

Marriage

There are three accepted forms of marriage: civil, religious, and cohabitation. Because the Catholic Church does not allow divorce, couples choose civil marriage over religious marriage. The economic instability introduced by recent neoliberal economic policies makes cohabitation less socially taboo and preferable to legal marriage. Rapid economic transition has introduced great social instability into Dominican life, especially with respect to the traditional bonds of marriage.

The marital bond has been weakened by the economic independence women gain from working. Dominican women in the FTZs are more likely to choose consensual unions and leave the relationship when it becomes unsatisfactory. Paradoxically, when interviewed, most married women refer to the man as the head of the household and always yield to this stratification of power within the family. Perhaps for this reason, only half as many women marry as choose consensual unions. Men rarely, if ever, cook, clean, or take care of children. The extended family and the importance of kinship ties have made it possible for women to gain a degree of actual, if not apparent, independence from men. Even within this hierarchical construct, the kinship relationships of the extended family (sometimes, but not necessarily, including marriage) have traditionally been the rampart of support for people living in a country that has been historically buffeted by political upheavals and economic reversals.

Reproduction

The total fertility rate for 1995 was 3.0, meaning that each woman has an average of three children in her lifetime. The annual population growth rate between 1995 and 2015 is predicted to be 1.4 percent, down somewhat from the period between 1970 and 1995, when it was 2.3 percent. At the current rate of population growth, the population is predicted to double by the year 2037.[28] In a country with a heavily skewed income distribution and no government policies to effectively alleviate poverty, these statistics do not point to a bright future for the Dominican Republic.

Sex Education

Sex education is not officially taught in the Dominican Republic school system. However, Planned Parenthood, PROFAMILIA, and other NGOs offer family planning, information on reproductive health, and sex education, sometimes in the schools.

Contraception and Abortion

Access to contraceptive services is quite good in the Dominican Republic, despite the inaction of the national government, the opposition of the Catholic Church, and the fact that sex education is highly taboo. In fact, the contraceptive prevalence rate using some method of birth control is 64 percent.[29] Many outside agencies, such as NGOs, close the gap in such services. Planned Parenthood is one of the organizations that provides reproductive health and education services for both adolescents and adults. Abortion is illegal, but widely prevalent in the Dominican Republic, accounting for the high rate of maternal mortality, often caused by toxemia and hemorrhaging during abortion.

Some of these NGOs are quite controversial because their goal is to help reduce the fertility rate in the Dominican Republic on the assumption that this will eliminate poverty. The U.S. Agency for International Development funds an NGO, PROFAMILIA, the Dominican Association for the Well-Being of the Family, in Santo Domingo. PROFAMILIA offers sterilization and abortion to Dominican women who request such procedures. There is great resentment in the developing world against the United States for insisting upon population control as a condition of receiving U.S. foreign aid, and the Catholic Church leads the way in expressing this resentment. It emphasizes that the fertility rate is rapidly approaching replacement-rate fertility. Given the high rates of outward migration, the church argues that future economic development would be hindered if population growth were curtailed. Regardless of the wisdom of a population-control policy, women are caught in the middle and face poverty, hardship, and emotional duress regardless of the fertility choices they make.

Teen Pregnancy

Adolescents tend to become sexually active at an early age in the Dominican Republic. Planned Parenthood survey results indicate that the first sexual experience takes place at the average age of 16 for females and 15.3 for males. Almost one-fifth of all fifteen- to nineteen-year-olds in the country are married, but only 17 percent in this cohort use contraception. Only 36 percent of all single, sexually active women use modern contraception; approximately 33 percent of all young women in the Dominican Republic have given birth by the time they reach twenty years of age and are frequently unprepared to provide for the child. Community-based education programs sponsored by Planned Parenthood and PROFAMILIA employ young fieldworkers to offer contraceptives and sex education to their peers under twenty years old. These programs include school-based educational talks, workshops for parents and teachers, community-based educational talks, and promotional campaigns that extend from the workplace to the rural community.[30]

HEALTH

Health Care Access

In 1997, the Secretariat for Public Health and Social Welfare set as its highest priority the reversal of declining expenditures on social services. Reduction in infant and maternal mortality was designated as its primary objective. Indeed, such priorities and objectives must be part of an overall strategy to achieve humane and sustainable development, given the severe social and economic dislocations that foreign investment and export manufacturing have caused in Dominican society.

The number of physicians per 10,000 people is 21.5, and the number of hospital beds is 10 per 1,000 people. The official maternal mortality rate as it was originally reported was 45 per 100,000 live births. This was reestimated later by an outside agency as 110 per 100,000 live births, an underregistration of about 59 percent. Further investigation indicates that the real maternal mortality rate may be even higher in subsequent years at 200 per 100,000 live births.[31] Ninety-five percent of all deliveries take place in an institution but are not always assisted by physicians. The quality of the physicians and midwives attending these births varies greatly, thus helping to account for the high maternal mortality rate.

Some nonprofit private services are provided by clinics and hospitals managed by NGOs. Some of these offer special services for cardiovascular care, diabetes, or cancer. Many of them receive subsidies from the Secretariat for Public Health and may also be directly paid by the users. These programs are located mostly in the two largest cities, Santo Domingo and Santiago, and are accessible to the urban middle class.

In poor, rural districts, health-care access is problematic. Health clinics located in these areas are often not equipped and barely staffed. In order to see a doctor, people have to go into a nearby city or town. Thus survey respondents in one rural district in 1989 reported visiting a health clinic a median number of twice per year.[32] The official overall infant mortality rate is 34.7 per 1,000 births, but the rate is much higher in rural areas, as food and clean water are not abundantly available, with little access to green or yellow fruits and vegetables or high-protein food.[33] The mortality rate for children under five years old is even higher, with a 1996 rate of 56 per 1,000 live births.[34] Poor nutrition, inadequate sanitation and potable water, and lack of access to health-care facilities are the components of the grinding poverty that account for the high mortality rates in young children. If the Secretariat is to achieve its goals, it will have to recognize that the greatest potential for reducing mortality and increasing life expectancy is among children under five years of age.

Diseases and Disorders

Officially generated gender-specific data are not readily available in the Dominican Republic. However, outside organizations, such as the Pan-American Health Organization, do provide a gender-specific profile of women's health. In 1994, diseases of the circulatory system were the leading causes of death among women of all ages, followed by various forms of cancer, communicable diseases, and external causes. Between the ages of thirteen and forty-four, tuberculosis was the leading cause of death in 1990, but had dropped to second place by 1994, followed by cardiovascular diseases. It should be noted that underregistration of deaths was nearly 50 percent in 1994. Thus these statistics are less informative than desired.[35]

AIDS

In 1983, the first case of AIDS was reported in the Dominican Republic. The incidence of the disease has been rising annually and reached a rate of 5 per 100,000 people as of 1995. More than 70 percent of the cumulative total number of cases was among heterosexuals. The male/female ratio in 1996 was 2:1 and continuing to equalize. Homosexuals and bisexuals account or 10 percent of the cases, drug users for 3 percent. Of the total number, 11.3 percent of all cases in women were due to blood transfusions. Only 80 percent of all transfused blood is screened for HIV and hepatitis B. In recent years, there has been an increasing rate of HIV among pregnant women seen at venereal disease clinics and, to a lesser extent, among sex workers. The incidence of HIV among women who cater to sex tourists is cause for concern. Rates of prevalence ranged from 2.9 of pre-natal women in 1994 to 7.9 in 1996. The HIV prevalence rate for sexually active Dominicans is now 2.5 percent. Experts have expressed concern that this rate would increase up to 4.3 percent by the turn of the century.[36] This epidemic hits the young hardest: 55 percent of the cumulative reported AIDS cases are in those between fifteen and thirty-five years of age. The spread of the epidemic can be attributed to a flourishing sex industry, tourism, poverty, social and gender inequity, immigration of Haitians, and alcohol abuse.

From 1993 to 1997, the U.S. Agency for International Development undertook a comprehensive strategy called the AIDS Community Action Program. A prevention strategy targeting young women was developed in close coordination with the recently founded secretary of Women's Affairs. This strategy sought to empower these young women to reduce their vulnerability to and dependency on men. It emphasized and promoted strategies and practical guidelines by which women in this age group could learn to strengthen their bargaining power regarding reproductive and sexual issues. This was the first time that some women were able to talk about their HIV-positive condition. This was a breakthrough, because attitudes toward people who are HIV positive are strongly negative in the Dominican Republic. Thirty-seven percent of youth surveyed consider AIDS to be a punishment from God. Thirty-nine percent of men surveyed believed that touching someone with AIDS could transmit HIV, and 43 percent believed that sharing food with someone with HIV was dangerous. Community education programs attempt to reduce fear and increase social acceptance of individuals with HIV and to counter discrimination against them.

POLITICS AND LAW

The metaphor of family unity and loyalty is no less important in political life than in family life and indicates that powerful families have always exerted a great deal of control over the Dominican Republic. This family tradition of kinship ties has nurtured the ruling clique (*compadrismo*) and the tyranny (*caudillismo*) that to this day have shut out women. Dominican political history is a succession of protracted power struggles between brutal, authoritarian strongmen (*caudillos*) and dependence on larger powers, such as Spain or the United States. There is no deeply rooted commitment to democracy in this small nation. Bloody conflicts for independence and battles for supremacy among competing caudillos have inevitably left the majority of Dominicans desperately struggling in poverty and powerlessness. Political traditions of personality cult, militarism, and socioeconomic elitism, coupled with the tradition in public administration of corruption, nepotism, patronage, and mistrust, have sapped the country's resources and all but ruled out the establishment of a system of governance devoted to public service and sustainable development.

Traditionally, the capital of Santo Domingo served as the seat of government but was oriented toward outside interests and powers (such as economic ties with Spain and later the United States). The power vacuum in the rural provinces was filled by large landowners in the countryside. This relegated the local government to ineffectiveness and helped cultivate the distinctive characteristics of paternalism, authoritarianism, and personality cult in the nation's political system.

By 1989, the Dominican Republic had gone through twenty-nine constitutions in less than 150 years of independence, reflective of a basic lack of consensus on the rules that should govern political life rather than a zealous commitment to them. Successive dictators could not resist the temptation to rewrite the

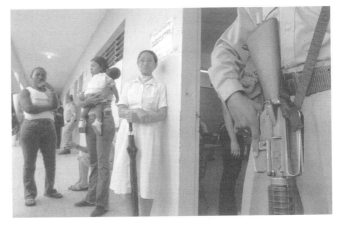

Women wait to cast their ballots at a polling station in Santo Domingo, Dominican Republic, May 2002, with armed security officer in forefront. AP/Wide World Photos.

constitution to afford greater power, wealth, and longevity in office for themselves and their cronies. These various self-styled constitutions allowed the caudillos to send death squads to roam the countryside and wipe out any and all opposition to their brutal regimes.

The stirrings of democracy seemed finally to have taken hold by the end of the twentieth century. Rafael Trujillo's barbaric dictatorship gripped the country from 1930 to 1961. Former Trujillo puppet Joaquín Balaguer, who had ruled for twenty-two out of the thirty-five years since Trujillo's death in 1961, agreed to stay out of the 1996 election only if certain conditions were met. This left the country's authoritarian structure largely intact but opened the way for the election of a politician apparently committed to democracy, Leonel Fernández Reyna. To his credit, Fernández did not seek the presidency past his four-year term, and in May 2000, Rafael Hipólito Mejía Domínguez was elected president. In the same year, for the first time ever, the vice president elected was a woman, Milagros Ortiz-Bosch. Bosch also currently serves as the secretary of education in the president's cabinet.

The three major parties in the Dominican Republic are the Dominican Liberation Party, the Dominican Revolutionary Party, and the Social Christian Reformist Party. The National Congress consists of a 30-member Senate and a 149-member Chamber of Deputies. Members in both legislative houses are elected by popular vote to serve four-year terms. The local government is divided into administrative divisions, consisting of twenty-nine provinces and one district.

Suffrage

Dominican women were given the right to vote and stand for free elections in 1942 after years of struggle by feminist intellectuals and activists, although Trujillo had promised women's suffrage in 1932. The voting age is eighteen, and suffrage is universal and compulsory. All married persons vote regardless of age. The military and police are not allowed to vote.

Political Participation

As women become more activist, their growing political participation becomes a force to be reckoned with. Women's share of votes cast increased by 17 percent in 1996.[37] In 1996, women activists promised to give their vote to the candidate who would give them a ministry. Only Fernández agreed; he was elected and delivered on his promise.

Women are beginning to make a small but notable appearance in the elected offices of government. The United Nations compiles an aggregate measure of women's status in the workplace and political system. Called the gender empowerment measure (GEM), it measures access to economic decision-making power by women's share in professional, technical, administrative, and managerial positions. Political power is measured by women's share of seats in the national legislature. The GEM is calculated by equally weighing three factors: employment status, political status, and women's relative wage income. It is useful if one wants to compare women's progress across countries or just look at the relative ranking of women. In the Dominican Republic, the GEM value for 1998 was a low .424, ranking the country only 58th among more than 300 nations in gender empowerment. In 1994, the percentage of seats held by women in the national legislature was only 10 percent; female administrators and managers made up 21.2 percent; female professional and technical workers made a better showing at 49.5 percent.[38] Comparison of the 1994 data with figures from the 1998 elections shows that progress for women has been slow. In the Senate, women held only 6.7 percent of the seats, or 2 out of 30. This is still the case despite the past commitments made by the 1996–2000 government to have more women in the cabinet during its tenure in office. In the Chamber of Deputies, women show a stronger presence by holding 24 out of 149 seats, or 16.1 percent. Overall, women held 14.5 percent of seats in the national legislature, only a marginal improvement over the 1994 figure of 10 percent. From 1962 to 1994, only 10 women held a seat in the Chamber of Deputies, as compared to 242 men. One positive note is that for two consecutive terms the chairperson has been a woman, Rafaela Albuquerque. Since the late 1970s, there have been 441 female municipal council members, but 4,016 male members.[39] Judges in the country are appointed; as of 1999, 37 percent were women.[40]

Women's groups have pushed an amendment to include a 30 percent quota of women elected to office. Political quota systems can be problematic in a society where gender stratification is institutionalized and women are at a gross disadvantage in every other aspect of their lives. It is clear that women have, to a large extent, internalized the patriarchal social structure in areas from the most intimate family roles and relationships to health care and treatment, employment hiring practices, wages, and work. When women start receiving equal treatment within basic social relationships, perhaps they will be ready to fulfill quotas for elective posts.

Women's Rights

On the surface, the domestic legal policy and constitution seem to protect married women, mothers, and the family and give equal rights to all citizens. This sounds progressive, but there may still be a hidden agenda to marginalize the female-headed household as anomalous to the traditional notion of the nuclear family. Housing and social welfare policies that promote the nuclear family and weaken extended kin ties may enhance the vulnerability of low-income families. Economic and social realities need to be realistically reflected in governance documents.

The labor code protects the rights of pregnant women with provision for punishing those who discriminate against them. Sexual harassment is prohibited. Another recent law, promulgated by the Office for Women's Promotion and supported by the United Nations and PROFAMILIA, is aimed at extending protection for the family by addressing the problem of domestic violence. This progressive law has yet to be enforced by the police or the courts. In 1999, a law created the State Secretariat for Women's Affairs. A ministry of their own opens a range of new possibilities for women in the Dominican Republic.

Feminist Movements

The newly created women's ministry is poised to change the business-as-usual macho politics in the Dominican Republic. Minister Gladys Gutierrez noted that "in previous campaigns, women were the tool of the political parties [sic] but by 1996, we got organized."[41] The ministry is currently working to amend five laws in ways that would end discrimination against women. With help from outside organizations, such as the United Nations Development Program and the United Nations Population Fund, the ministry will see to it that the laws are implemented. The women's ministry has worked to ensure that women who were previously unable to secure loans from the agricultural bank to buy state land can now do so. They have undertaken to train women in the rural areas so that they understand their rights under the law. Since then, 73 percent of the bank's loans have gone to women.[42]

The women's movement is supported by NGOs as well. The Centro de Investigacion para la Accion Femenina, or Research Center for Feminine Action, in partnership with Oxfam, has conducted an international campaign to raise public awareness of the many issues women face. The women's movement is rooted in the popular movement that encompasses union activism and the progressive sectors and is consequently not supported by more conservative outside groups, such as the U.S. Agency for International Development. Furthermore, historically conservative institutions and patriarchal attitudes can render government ministries for women weak and ineffective. This is the case with the "National Plan to Reduce Maternal Mortality." It is not a priority office and does not have a budget to actually pursue the reduction of maternal mortality.

Women's organizations have a fairly strong historical presence. In 1931, feminist teachers, intellectuals, and activists established Accion Feminista Dominicana to advocate for women's suffrage and other rights. They allowed themselves to be co-opted in 1932 by Trujillo's promise to give women the vote. After the fall of Trujillo's dictatorship in 1961, they all but disappeared during the worst political repression the country has ever known. Reappearing in the 1970s, the Dominican women activists were bolstered by the 1975 United Nations declaration of the International Year of the Woman, helping to make the women's movement the most visible social movement in the Dominican Republic today. It has introduced programs, proposals, and plans to advance the cause of women and, by extension, the poor. While not claiming to have mobilized thousands, the movement has raised awareness throughout the country.

The effort to raise public awareness has been successful thanks to the mass media, which have given women activists a spotlight of their own. This has been made possible by the fact that the Dominican Republic has the most advanced telecommunications services in Latin America and the Caribbean. The telecommunications industry is one of the most modern and dynamic sectors of the Dominican economy. This industry has proven fertile ground for grassroots organizing, as the media in the Dominican Republic are considered to be quite open and seem to have no qualms about affording women prime-time television coverage to convey their message.

Women's groups proliferate to help, educate, and serve the poorest and most disadvantaged Dominican women. The Movement of Dominico-Haitian Women is an organization formed by and for Dominican and Haitian women living in the sugarcane plantations to address the problems of illiteracy, social marginalization, racism, and poor living conditions that affect that community. The project involves educational courses on manual skills building, basic financial proficiency, and training to exploit possibilities for entrepreneurial opportunities in local handicrafts.[43]

Feminists and women's rights activists are alive and well in the Dominican Republic. What they lack in mass numbers they make up for in commitment, communication, and political savvy. The progressive women's movement might attract and involve more people if it were not for the pervasive culture of patriarchy and repression, historically bolstered by the Catholic Church.

Lesbian Rights

The law does not distinguish between same-sex and heterosexual relations for adults eighteen years of age or older.[44]

Military Service

Military service is not compulsory. Those eighteen years old or older may enlist. The 1966 constitution as amended requires every able-bodied Dominican to perform the civilian and military services the country may need to defend or preserve itself.[45] In 2000, the government of the Dominican Republic reported 1,455,887 males between the ages of fifteen and forty-nine to be fit for military service. No mention was made of women.[46]

RELIGION AND SPIRITUALITY

The Catholic Church claims 95 percent of the Dominican population as adherents. This does not augur well for Dominican women, as women are not allowed to play a significant role in Catholicism. The church takes an absolutist stand against contraception and abortion and has been known to intervene publicly to pursue its antiprogressive, authoritarian, antidemocratic, patriarchal agenda. The Catholic Church has consistently resisted and publicly attacked the work and purpose of PROFAMILIA, the NGO family planning clinic. Liberation theology, a form of Catholicism oriented toward social justice that swept Latin America in the 1960s and 1970s, never took root in the Dominican Republic. The church condemns African-related religious rituals, which are actively suppressed by the police or within the community itself.[47]

Women's Roles

Since the 1980s, there has been a great expansion of evangelical Protestant churches in Latin America, and the Dominican Republic is no exception. This religious option would seem to portend well for women, as women are allowed and encouraged to play a strong leadership role in the life of the congregation, an ultimately empowering activity. The theoretical argument that Protestantism leads to economic success while Catholicism perpetuates inequality and misery is a controversial one. However, recent evidence from countries that have embraced Protestantism in its various forms shows that women are empowered by the different life view that it has to offer. In Colombia and Guatemala, for example, the research shows that conversion to Protestantism has introduced a different work ethic, strengthened marital bonds, and reduced alcohol consumption among males. Women are usually the first to embrace the new church, sometimes followed by their male partners. Improvement in both material and metaphysical aspects of the lives of the women studied has been documented. Arguably, this kind of participation in church and community life provides a foundation for strong democratic participation.[48]

In the Dominican Republic, the Assembly of God has become the largest Protestant denomination, thanks to participation of laypeople and the young. In the city of Barahona, there are reported to be more than 100 evangelical churches, and 80,000 in outlying areas. It has been estimated that more than 12 percent of the population is evangelical, and half of these are Pentecostal.[49] How this will affect the future of women and the democratic process remains to be seen.

VIOLENCE

The United Nations has stated that statistics and records on domestic violence are not maintained in the Dominican Republic. Thus violence against women has been implicitly institutionalized and allowed to continue at every level of Dominican society.[50]

Domestic Violence

Because of the private nature of most domestic disputes, few cases of domestic violence make it to court. Congress adopted a law against family violence in 1997, but the mere existence of this law should not imply compliance. Police rarely cooperate when a victim tries to register a complaint. If they do receive the complaint and initiate proceedings, the public prosecutor often dismisses the complaint or reclassifies it so that the assailant is released once the injuries heal, usually within ten days. These responses to domestic violence are inadequate and will do nothing to eradicate the problem.

Rape/Sexual Assault

Eighty percent of women who are raped or sexually assaulted are attacked by someone they know or by a family member. These are called "crimes of passion" in more than half the cases.[51]

Trafficking in Women and Children

The trafficking of women is a problem in the Dominican Republic. Young women are promised well-paying jobs and good housing in other countries. Many are not educated past the sixth grade, are just girls, and, once outside the country, are quite vulnerable and easily subjected to exploitation. One recent study found that in 1995 and 1996, most women brought to Europe for the purposes of sexual exploitation came from the Dominican Republic. In another study conducted in Antigua in 1992, half the brothel prostitutes were Dominicans. Dominican women also made up more than half of all prostitutes in the largest cities in the Netherlands.

War and Military Repression

War and military occupation have plagued the Dominican Republic for centuries. Haiti occupied the Dominican Republic between 1822 and 1844. After repelling Haitian forces, the Dominican Republic declared its independence on February 27, 1844. Civil war continued after annexation by Spain from 1851 to 1865. Spain's departure left the country bogged down in conflict and power struggles among authoritarian strongmen who ruled and enriched themselves and their associates at the expense of the Dominican people. The United States occupied the country in 1916 after a series of assassinations, rebellions, and conflicts over leadership and withdrew in 1924 after free and fair elections returned the government to a Dominican named Horacio Vásquez. Vásquez's fatal error was to change the constitution to accommodate his desire to remain in office longer than the election term stipulated. The struggle among competing caudillos resumed, and in 1930, the most brutal strongman of all, Rafael Trujillo, became dictator and ruled the country like a feudal lord for thirty-one years. Systematic terror and repression marked Trujillo's regime, which absolutely controlled the nation's resources by employing the military as his personal police squad. This led to terrible abuses of the civilian population. While elite Dominicans and foreign investors enriched themselves during this period, the majority of the population suffered deprivation, brutal treatment, loss of their human rights, degradation, and increasing poverty.

President Mejía, elected in 2000, decorated five Dominican women at the National Palace for fighting for freedom and democracy during the Trujillo era. The women endured incarceration and torture for their heroic efforts and are just now being recognized for their bravery and service to their country. On November 25, 1981, an International Day against Violence against Women was declared at the Latin American and Caribbean Feminist meeting in Bogota, Colombia, and supported by the United Nations General Assembly. Activists in the Dominican Republic chose this day to commemorate the murder of three Dominican women, the Mirabal sisters, who were assassinated in 1960 for opposing the Trujillo dictatorship. For twenty-one years, this martyrdom had gone unacknowledged. These two stories are representative of the role women played throughout the twentieth century in trying to wrest their country from the seemingly endless historical drama that culminated in Trujillo's cruel and destructive dictatorship.

The election of a left-leaning president in 1962 was followed by a right-wing military coup in 1963 aided by the United States and its fear of Cuba's Communist government. For the second time in the same century, U.S. military occupation directly followed, until the rigged elections of 1966 gave the nation Joaquín Balaguer, a former Trujillo puppet, for president. His regime was characterized by strong military control, repression of opposition by employing national police forces, and death squads that roamed the countryside to kidnap, arrest, or assassinate political dissenters, petty criminals, and purely arbitrary victims. Balaguer managed to maintain his stranglehold for twenty-two of the next thirty years, allowing death squads to continue to operate into the 1970s. He held power until 1996, when fair elections were held and constitutional codes were not violated. The presidency passed democratically from Fernández to Mejía in 2000, but the nation is still haunted by the legacy of the death squads that terrorized and tortured countless of Dominicans in the not-so-distant past.

In early 2000, four participants in Dominican death-squad activity from 1975 were brought to justice. The trial, its inconclusive outcome, and the political reasons for conducting it may be suspect, but it also may be a step toward openness and healing that the country needs so that it can continue to move toward democracy.

OUTLOOK FOR THE TWENTY-FIRST CENTURY

The history of colonialism, slavery, conflict, dependency, and repression should not distract from the fact that the Dominican Republic has been rendered unmistakably friendly for globalization in the form of foreign investment for export manufacturing, most of which comes from the United States. The same low wages that women earn in the FTZs perpetuate the increasingly feminized poverty in the Dominican Republic and are the main attraction for foreign investors. Decades of state repression have precluded the collectivization of the workforce into strong trade unions. However, these tendencies may one day be reversed with constitutional stability, freedom of speech, the ability to communicate widely, and a large enough political contingent in elected bodies that would eventually overturn authoritarianism and help democracy thrive. These trends so far have given Dominican women greater participation and strength in Dominican politics, society, and personal relations. However, given the past history of foreign intervention, domestic corruption, patriarchy, and women's subordination and the current trend toward globalization and the interests of powerful foreign investors, Dominican women still have a long road before them.

NOTES

Special thanks for the assistance and support of Shajira Nazir Adams, Manhattanville College senior and citizen of the Dominican Republic.

1. Central Intelligence Agency, *The World Factbook: Dominican Republic*, www.cia.gov/cia/publications/factbook/geos/dr.html.

2. Library of Congress, *Dominican Republic: A Country Study*, 1989, http://memory.loc.gov/frd/cs/dotoc.html.

3. World Bank, www.worldbank.org/lC/wbank/wtables.html.

4. Central Intelligence Agency, *The World Factbook: Dominican Republic*, www.cia.gov/cia/publications/factbook/geos/dr.html.

5. *United Nations Human Development Report* (*UNHDR*) (New York: United Nations Development Programme, Oxford University Press, 1998), 156.

6. *Dominican Republican*, 2002, www.internationalreports.net/theamericas/dr/2002/freetrade.html.

7. Library of Congress, 1989.

8. Central Intelligence Agency, *The World Factbook: Dominican Republic*, www.cia.gov/cia/publications/factbook/geos/dr.html.

9. *UNHDR*, 1998, 152

10. Central Intelligence Agency, *The World Factbook: Dominican Republic*, www.cia.gov/cia/publications/factbook/geos/dr.html.

11. *UNHDR*, 1998, 174.

12. Helen I. Safa, *Women Coping with Crisis: Social Consequences of Export-Led Industrialization in the Dominican Republic*," North-South Agenda Papers, no. 36 (Coral Gables, FL: North-South Center, University of Miami, 1999), 1.

13. *UNHDR*, 1998, 154.

14. *United Nations Statistical Yearbook: Indicators on Unemployment*, 2002, www.un.org/Pubs/CyberSchoolBus/infonation.html.

15. Central Intelligence Agency, *The World Factbook: Dominican Republic*, www.cia.gov/cia/publications/factbook/geos/dr.html (search query).

16. Safa, *Women Coping with Crisis*, 1999, 7.

17. Ibid.

18. Library of Congress, Trade Unions, www.memory.loc/gov/cgi-bin/query2/r?/frd/cstdy:@field(DØCID+doo092.

19. International Women's Rights Action Watch (WRAW) Publications, *Country Reports: The Dominican Republic*, www.igc.org/iwraw/publications/countries/dominican_republic.html.

20. Inter-American Commission on Human Rights, Organization of American States, "The Situation of Women in the Dominican Republic," www.cidh.oas.org/countryrep/DominicanRep99/Chapter10.htm.

21. Ibid.

22. Safa, *Women Coping with Crisis*, 1999, 12.

23. Helen I. Safa, *The Myth of the Male Breadwinner* (Boulder, CO: Westview Press, 1995); Safa, *Women Coping with Crisis*, 1999.

24. Safa, *Women Coping with Crisis*, 1999, 16–17.

25. Central Intelligence Agency, *The World Factbook: Dominican Republic*, www.cia.gov/cia/publications/factbook/geos/dr.html.

26. United Nations Development Programme, "Dominican Republic Country Assessment," in *Overcoming Human Poverty: UNDP Poverty Report 2000*, www.undp.org/povertyreport/countryprofiles/domini.html.

27. Safa, *The Myth of the Male Breadwinner*, 1995, 105.

28. *UNHDR*, 1998, 176.

29. Ibid.

30. Planned Parenthood Family Planning International Assistance, *Programs in Dominican Republic*, www.plannedparenthood.org/fpia/dominican.html.

31. Pan-American Health Organization Country Health Data, "Dominican Republic," in *Health in the Americas*, 1998 ed., 2: 231, www.paho.org/english/hia_1998ed.htm.

32. Barbara Finlay, *The Women of Azua* (New York: Praeger, 1989), 94.

33. *UNHDR*, 1998, 176.

34. Ibid.

35. Pan-American Health Organization, 1998, 2: 229–230.

36. AIDS Community Action Program/Dominican Republic, "Dominican Republic Final Report: Country Program Description," www.fhi.org/en/aids/aidscap/aidspubs/special/countryprog/DomRep/domexsum.html. All subsequent data on AIDS come from this source.

37. United Nations Development Programme, *Dominican Women Triumph*.

38. *UNHDR*, 1998, 134.

39. Inter-American Commission on Human Rights, "The Situation of Women in the Dominican Republic."

40. United Nations Development Programme, *Dominican Women Triumph*.

41. Ibid.

42. Ibid.

43. IWRAW Publications, *Country Reports: The Dominican Republic*.

44. International Lesbian and Gay Association, "World Legal Survey: Dominican Republic," www.ilga.org.

45. Coalition to Stop the Use of Child Soldiers, "Child Soldiers Global Report," May 1, 2001, www.child-soldiers.org.

46. CIA Factbook. Dominican Republic, www.odci.gov/cia/publications/factbook/geos/dr.

47. Amy Sherman, *The Soul of Development* (New York: Oxford University Press, 1997).

48. Ibid.

49. "Anachronism and Adventurism: Recent Mission Trends," www.religion-online.org/cgi-bin/relsearchd.dll/showarticle?item_id=144.

50. The information in the sections "Domestic Violence," "Rape/Sexual Assault," and "Trafficking in Women and Children" is taken from Inter-American Commission on Human Rights, "The Situation of Women in the Dominican Republic."

51. OAS Inter-American Commission on Human Rights, Organization of American States, "The Situation of Women in the Dominican Republic," www.cidhoas.org/countryrep/DominicanRep99/Chapter10.hm.

RESOURCE GUIDE

Suggested Reading

Chomsky, Noam, and Edward S. Herman. *The Washington Connection and Third World Fascism*. Boston: South End Press, 1979. Decries the role the U.S. government has played in Central America and the Caribbean, specifically in the oppression of working women.

Cocco de Filippis, Daisy. *Documents of Dissidence: Selected Writings by Dominican Women*. New York: CUNY Dominican Studies Institute, 2000. An anthology of writings of Dominican women that encompasses the past 150 years and seeks to keep alive the contribution of Dominican women to all aspects of the Dominican experience.

Safa, Helen I. *The Myth of the Male Breadwinner*. Boulder, CO: Westview Press, 1995. Documents the role globalization and U.S. influence have played in the lives of women in Puerto Rico and the Dominican Republic and researches the effects of the 1991–1995 Special Period crisis on women in Cuba.

Standing, Guy. "Global Feminization through Flexible Labor." *World Development* 17(7) (1989): 1077–96. Perhaps the seminal work on the role globalization has played in the feminization of worldwide poverty, including in the Dominican Republic.

Video/Film

In the Time of the Butterflies. 2000. Directed by Mariano Barroso. MGM/Phoenix Pictures/Barnstorm Films Production. A Hollywood rendition of the life story of the nationally memorialized Mirabal sisters and their courageous opposition to Trujillo's brutal dictatorship.

Web Sites

"Dominican Republic Social and Structural Policy Review—Executive Summary," http://wbln0018.worldbank.org/external/lac/lac.nsf/ebaf58f382dbaf32852567d6006b028e/9add67362d0825a1852568ea0054ca33?OpenDocument.
A nutshell account of the World Bank Group's assessment of the Dominican Republic.

International Women's Rights Action Watch, www.igc.org/iwraw.
An international resource and communications center that serves activists, scholars, and organizations that focus on the advancement of women's human rights.

Organization of American States, www.oas.org.
Established in 1948 to strengthen democracy in the Western Hemisphere and promote sustainable development. In 1959, it created the *Inter-American Commission on Human Rights*, which went on to become a key player in the struggle against the hemisphere's repressive regimes and continues to provide recourse to citizens who have suffered human rights violations.

Pan-American Health Organization, www.paho.org.
The regional office for the Americas of the World Health Organization. Its mission is to improve the health of the peoples of the Americas.

United Nations Development Programme, www.undp.org.
A trusted source of knowledge-based advice and an advocate of a more inclusive global economy, this agency seeks to address the many causes of poverty and to promote development, including the protection of human rights and the empowerment of women.

Organizations

CEDAW
Minu Hemmati
UNED Forum
3 Whitehall Court
London SW1A 2EL, UK
Phone: 44 20 78391784

Fax: 44 20 79305893
Email minush@aol.com
Web site: http://www.earthsummit2002.org/toolkits/women/intro/intro.htm

The Convention on the Elimination of All Forms of Discrimination Against Women
was ratified in the Dominican Republic on September 2, 1982. CEDAW works with
various feminist coalitions to ensure human rights are respected in the Dominican
Republic and elsewhere.

CIPAF: Centro de Investigacion de la Accion Feminista
Luis F. Thomen #358
Ensanche Quisqueya
Santo Domingo, República Dominicana
Phone: 563-5263
Fax: 563-1159
Email: cipaf@tricom.net
Web site: http://funredes.org/coordmujeres/miembras/cipaf.htm

The Women's Center for Feminist Action and Research is an NGO working with
Oxfam to improve current working conditions for Dominican free trade zone workers. Its goal is to strengthen the basic human rights of workers by raising public
awareness about their living conditions.

MUDHA: Movimiento de Mujeres Dominico-Haitianas
Pedro A. Lluberes #1
Gazcue
Santo Domingo, República Dominicana
Phone: 688-7430 / 688-8834
Fax: 689-3532
Email: mudha@hotmail.com
Web site: http://funredes.org/coordmujeres/miembras/mudha.htm

The Movement of Dominico-Haitian Women is an organization formed by, and for
women, concerned with Dominican and Haitian women living in the poverty-
stricken communities of the sugarcane fields.

SEM: Secretario de Estado de la Mujer
Secretaría de Estado de la Mujer (SEM)
Oficinas Gubernamentales Bloque D.
Avenida México, esquina 30 de marzo,
Santo Domingo, República Dominicana
Phone: 1 (809) 685-3755
Fax: 1 (809) 685-8040
Email: SecretariaDeLaMujer@sem.gov.do
Web site: http://www.sem.gov.do

Women's Ministry establishes norms and coordinates the execution of policies and
programs at sectional and inter-ministerial levels as well as in civil society; directs
the realization of gender equality and women's full exercise of citizenship.

UN INSTRAW
United Nations International Research and Training Institute for the Advancement of
Women (UN INSTRAW)

César Nicolás Penson 102-A
Santo Domingo, República Dominicana
Phone: 1 (809) 685-2111
Fax: 1 (809) 685-2117
Email: comments@un-instraw.org
Web site: www.un-instraw.org

The United Nations International Research and Training Institute for the Advancement of Women was established in 1983 to direct attention to the needs of women in developing countries. At present, the Institute benefits from the Dominican Republic's status as one of the most rapidly developing economies and new technology infrastructures in the world.

SELECTED BIBLIOGRAPHY

AIDS Community Action Program/Dominican Republic. "Dominican Republic Final Report: Country Program Description." www.fhi.org/en/aids/aidscap/aidspubs/special/countryprog/DomRep/domexsum.html.

"Anachronism and Adventurism: Recent Mission Trends." www.religion-online.org/cgi-bin/relsearchd.dll/showarticle?item_id=144.

Central Intelligence Agency. *The World Factbook: Dominican Republic*. www.cia.gov/cia/publications/factbook/geos/dr.html.

"Dominican Republic—Report to Treaty Bodies." www.hri.ca/fortherecord1998/vol4/dominicanreptb.htm.

Finlay, Barbara. *The Women of Azua*. New York: Praeger, 1989.

Inter-American Commission on Human Rights, Organization of American States. "The Situation of Women in the Dominican Republic." www.cidh.oas.org/countryrep/DominicanRep99/Chapter10.htm.

International Women's Rights Action Watch: Publications. *Country Reports: The Dominican Republic*. www.igc.org/iwraw/publications/countries/dominican_republic.html.

Library of Congress. *Dominican Republic: A Country Study*. 1989. http://memory.loc.gov/frd/cs/dotoc.html.

Pan-American Health Organization Country Health Data. "Dominican Republic." In *Health in the Americas*, 1998 ed., vol. 2, www.paho.org/english/hia_1998ed.htm.

Planned Parenthood Family Planning International Assistance. *Programs in Dominican Republic*. www.plannedparenthood.org/fpia/dominican.html.

Safa, Helen I. *The Myth of the Male Breadwinner*. Boulder, CO: Westview Press, 1995.

———. *Women Coping with Crisis: Social Consequences of Export-Led Industrialization in the Dominican Republic*. North-South Agenda Papers, no. 36. Coral Gables, FL: North-South Center, University of Miami, April 1999.

Sherman, Amy. *The Soul of Development*. New York: Oxford University Press, 1997.

United Nations Development Programme. "Dominican Republic Country Assessment." In *Overcoming Human Poverty: UNDP Poverty Report 2000*. www.undp.org/povertyreport/countryprofiles/domin1.html.

———. *Dominican Women Triumph*. http://app.netaid.org/WhatWorks/1.2.html?pillar_id=1+&proj_id=118.

United Nations Human Development Report. New York: United Nations Development Programme, Oxford University Press, 1998.

United Nations Statistical Yearbook. New York: Oxford University Press, 2000.

6

THE FRENCH CARIBBEAN

Irma T. Alonso

PROFILE OF THE FRENCH CARIBBEAN

France, a former colonial power, still maintains a presence in a number of islands scattered around the globe, some of which still provide strategic advantage. These ex-colonies are now classified either as territories or as overseas departments. While the territories are the previous colonies under a new name, the ex-colonies that have become departments now are part of the principal administrative divisions of France.[1] There are six overseas territories and one hundred departments, ninety-six in mainland France and four overseas. Two of France's overseas departments are Guadeloupe and Martinique, located in the Caribbean Sea.[2] The people of these over-

seas departments were made French citizens in 1946 with the approval of the Fourth Constitution. The departments retained this status following the establishment of the Fifth French Republic in 1958.

French is the official language of Guadeloupe and Martinique (although a local dialect, Creole patois, is widely spoken), and legally they are as much a part of France as the department of Paris.

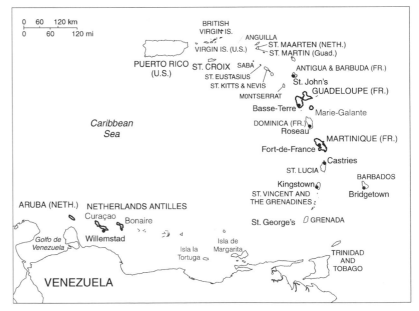

Moreover, with the euro as the national currency, their status as overseas departments of France grants both Guadeloupe and Martinique membership in the European Union. However, they are treated as poor European regions and as such receive special protection designed to assist developing areas. In the case of both islands, there have been separatist attempts to achieve full independence from France, but these endeavors have been unsuccessful. As a result, both Martinique and Guadeloupe continue in the Caribbean as legacies of France's colonial past. However, the identity crisis remains as to whether these islands really belong to Europe or to the Caribbean.

Explorer Christopher Columbus came to Guadeloupe in 1493, and to Martinique in 1493 or 1502.[3] Except for some brief periods of foreign domination, both islands have been ruled by France since 1635. In 1674, Guadeloupe was annexed to France and made a dependency of Martinique until 1775, after which time each island became an independent French colony. For France, the importance of these islands was that they provided the mother country with vast amounts of sugar, produced by slaves brought from Africa after the indigenous populations had been eliminated. Many racial problems were created between the white Europeans and the black African slaves. When slavery was finally abolished in 1848, indentured laborers from India and China were also brought to these islands to work the sugarcane fields.

Guadeloupe has an area of 1,705 square kilometers. It is an archipelago composed of two main islands separated by a river plus several dependencies. The two main islands are Basse-Terre to the east and Grande-Terre to the west, and the smaller dependencies are La Désirade, Isles des Saintes, Marie-Galante, Saint Berthélemy (which France bought from Sweden), Isles de la Petite de la Terre, and the northern half of Saint Martin, an island shared by France and the Netherlands. The capital city is Basse-Terre. Guadeloupe has rugged mountains, with the active La Soufrière volcano occupying the whole central area of Basse-Terre. La Désirade is a rocky, oblong island with an area of 70 square kilometers and a population of 1,600. The Isles des Saintes are eight small islands of which only two are inhabited by a few fishermen and their families. Marie-Galante is a round, flat island with a population of 12,500 where sugarcane and rum are produced. Saint Barthélemy is a small island with few resources. Since no sugarcane was produced on this island and no slaves were imported, in Saint Barthélemy most of the population is white. Isles de la Petite de la Terre are two additional small islands that are nature preserves. The population of the island of Saint Martin is about 30,000 on the French side and 35,000 on the Dutch side. Tourism is the main economic activity of all these islands.

To the south of Guadeloupe is Martinique, a small island with an area of only 1,200 square kilometers. It is of volcanic origin and is mountainous with a rugged coastline. The capital city is Forte-de-France. The Mount

Pelée volcano has been dormant since its eruption in 1902. At that time, 30,000 of Martinique's inhabitants were killed and the original capital city of Saint Pierre was destroyed. Besides the dangers represented by the volcanoes, both departments are plagued by additional natural disasters such as hurricanes and floods, with an average of one major disaster every five years, followed by the need for massive reconstruction.

Guadeloupe's population is estimated at 431,170, of whom 48.9 percent are males and 51.1 percent are females. The average annual rate of population growth is 1.07 percent. By age group, 25 percent of the population is below the age of fourteen, 66 percent is between the ages of fifteen and sixty-four, and the remaining 9 percent is sixty-five years old or above. The median age is 28.4 years. Due to the heavy importation of slaves from Africa, 90 percent of the population is of African descent, 5 percent is white, and the remaining 5 percent is a combination of East Indian and Chinese. The birth rate is 16.91 births per 1,000, while the total fertility rate is 1.93 children born per woman. The infant mortality rate is 9.53 deaths per 1,000 live births, and the death rate is 6.02 per 1,000. The life expectancy at birth is 72.7 years for males and 80.2 years for females.

Martinique's population is estimated at 418,454, of whom 48.5 percent are males and 51.5 percent are females. The average annual rate of population growth is 0.93 percent. The population distribution by age groups is similar to that of Guadeloupe, as 23 percent of the population is below the age of fourteen, 67 percent is between the ages of fifteen and sixty-four, and the remaining 10 percent is sixty-five years old or above. However, the median age is higher and is estimated at 30.6 years. As in Guadeloupe, 90 percent of the population is of African descent, 5 percent is white, and the remaining 5 percent is a combination of East Indian and Chinese. The birth rate is 15.76 births per 1,000. The total fertility rate is 1.8 children born per woman. The infant mortality rate is 7.8 deaths per 1,000 live births, while the death rate is 6.39 per 1,000. Life expectancy at birth is 79.5 years for males and 82.4 years for females.

OVERVIEW OF WOMEN'S ISSUES

Because both Guadeloupe and Martinique are protected by the laws prevailing in France, the constitution guarantees equality for both sexes. Although most of the population in the islands is Roman Catholic, the government supports family planning, sex education, women's development, and abortions as legal rights. However, as in many other places, women are overrepresented in low-skill, low-paying jobs and are underrepresented in the top-level decision-making positions. Moreover, women tend to be concentrated in a few occupations, and they have higher unemployment rates than males. As in other countries of the region, there are a large number of female-headed households, a high prevalence of sex-

Pointe-à-Pitre central market, Guadeloupe. Photo © TRIP/R. Belbin.

ually transmitted diseases, and high rates of illegal abortion. In addition, teenage pregnancy rates continue to be a source of concern in these islands.

EDUCATION

Opportunities

Education is free and compulsory between the ages of six and sixteen years. In 1994–1995, in Guadeloupe there were approximately 61,000 pupils in primary education and 42,000 pupils in secondary education. In 1997–1998, in Martinique there were approximately 56,000 pupils in primary education and 49,000 pupils at the secondary level.[4] Females made up 52 percent of the secondary-education sector in Guadeloupe and 51 percent in Martinique.[5] The curriculum in these schools is culturally and administratively similar to that in schools attended by children in mainland France.

In both Guadeloupe and Martinique, higher education is provided by a branch of the Université Antilles-Guyane. There are also two teacher-training institutes, as well as colleges of agriculture, fisheries, hotel management, nursing, midwifery, and child care. Total enrollment at the university in 1995–1996 was 15,810.[6]

The main problem within the education system is the high rate of pupils needing to repeat the first year of school. For example, in Guadeloupe, only one-third of the students reach the secondary level without having to repeat a grade. Equally significant is that only one-fourth of the students reach the level of *baccalauréat*, and at that level the overall rate of success is just slightly above 50 percent.[7] The main explanation given for these deficiencies in the school system is the difficulty with the French language, as students use it as a second language, while at home and outside school, it is usual to speak Creole.

Literacy

In Guadeloupe, the literacy rate, defined as those fifteen years old or over able to read and write, is estimated at 90 percent for both men and women, while in the case of Martinique it is estimated at 93 percent for women and 92 percent for men.[8]

EMPLOYMENT AND ECONOMICS

When slaves were brought from Africa to cultivate the sugarcane fields, Guadeloupe and Martinique became two of France's most valuable colonies. During the early stages of the colonies, there was a so-called triangular trade: the French colonies exported agricultural products to France and imported manufactured goods from France, while slaves were imported from Africa and brought to the Caribbean. At present, the economies of the French Caribbean islands have been transformed into modern service economies, with tourism being the most important activity.

The estimated gross domestic product (GDP), measured in purchasing power parity (PPP), of Guadeloupe was approximately $3.7 billion in 1997, and $9,000 in per capita terms, while in Martinique the corresponding figures were much higher, $4.4 billion and $11,000, respectively.[9] These levels of per capita income, which place both islands well above Caribbean average, are the results of French aid and subsidies. Of equal importance is that France, as the most important trade partner, finances the enormous trade deficits of both Guadeloupe and Martinique because their exports do not cover more than 15 percent of their imports. The need to import most food products and all other consumer goods, as well as capital goods, far exceeds the capacity of these countries to export. The magnitudes of the islands' trade deficits in 1997 were as follows: Guadeloupe's exports amounted to $140 million, while imports were $1.7 billion. Martinique's exports totaled $250 million, but the value of imported goods and merchandise reached $2 billion.[10] These economies have become transfer economies or consumer colonies that survive mainly on the transfer payments received from France, which may constitute more than one-third of the value of the GDP.[11]

The sectoral composition of GDP in Guadeloupe is as follows: 15 percent from agriculture, 17 percent from industry, and 68 percent from services. In Martinique, the shares are 6 percent, 11 percent, and 83 percent, respectively.[12] The most important agricultural products include sugar, bananas, and other tropical fruits. Most of the industry is based on the production of rum and cement, as well as some oil refining. Services are represented by tourism and a sizable public sector. Most tourists come from France, attracted by advertising campaigns promoting the exoticism of these islands.

Job/Career Opportunities

The participation of women in the paid workforce is one of the highest in the region and, in fact, the world.[13] In Guadeloupe, where the labor force consists of 126,000 workers, women make up 44 percent of the total, while in Martinique, with a labor force of 170,000 workers, women make up 47 percent of the total. In Guadeloupe, during the period 1995–2000, the economic activity rate of adults fifteen years of age or over was 55 percent for females and 72 percent for males. In Martinique, women had a participation rate of 57 percent, while that of men was 70 percent.

Employment surveys conducted in 1986 indicated that nearly 90 percent of working females were employed in the service sector. However, they were employed at the lower end of the sector, with the main occupations being those of servants, followed by clerical workers and then teachers.[14]

The public sector is a very significant employer, employing one-third of the labor force and almost half of all females in the labor force. Females are more likely to be an employee than an employer as well. Men outnumber women three to one as employers. Men also have higher upward mobility in the job market, while female workers have lower upward mobility, given their discontinuous participation in the job market.[15]

The most severe problem found in these islands is that of unemployment as a result of both the collapse of the agricultural sector and the number of young people continuously entering the labor force.[16] In seeking a solution to unemployment, many of the residents of these islands have migrated to France. However, this has not relieved the problem, as many workers from neighboring islands have at the same time emigrated to Guadeloupe and Martinique in search of jobs, while previous emigrants have returned home after being unable to secure jobs in mainland France or after retirement.

The unemployment rate for men is approximately 25 percent, while for women it is estimated at 33 percent. Women not only have a higher rate of unemployment but also have longer unemployment periods than men. Between 15 and 17 percent of the women out of work have been unemployed for one to two years, and half of them for more than two years. The reasons for these higher female unemployment rates as compared to males are related to the limited opportunities for women in the professions and in the productive sectors, as well as the preferences given to men in the workplace. The situation is even more severe in the case of female heads of households, for whom the unemployment rate is above 50 percent.[17] Other groups with unemployment rates above 50 percent are teenagers and young adults (aged fifteen to twenty-four).

Pay

Legislation in the French Caribbean specifies levels of minimum compensation for workers in three classifications: civil servants, who are the highest paid, followed by salaried personnel in the private sector, and last, domestic workers, who are the lowest paid.[18] However, employment surveys reveal that there is inequality in remuneration within these classifications. In the age group fifteen to thirty-nine, women earn only 85 percent of what men earn, and in the age group forty to fifty-nine, women earn only 71 percent of male wages.[19] Women at all levels of education earn much less than men with comparable educational attainments.

Support for Mothers/Caretakers

Maternal Leave

As a result of French laws applicable in both Guadeloupe and Martinique, female workers have access to benefits provided for maternal leave. These benefits entail 100 percent of net earnings payable for six weeks before and ten weeks after confinement for the first and the second child, with other provisions for the third child and beyond.[20]

Social/Government Programs

Since 1978, various laws have set minimum revenues guaranteed for single parents as well as certain allocations for their children. The majority of the recipients of these benefits are women, and compensation is very limited.[21] The allocation of benefits to single mothers has been greatly criticized because it supposedly has increased the number of female-headed households. However, this type of household has constituted a significant proportion of families in the French Caribbean since the era of slavery.

Welfare

France has a social welfare system that was extended to the French Caribbean islands in 1945. At that time, the system was not at the same level as in mainland France, but since then the social protection has reached parity. These programs include measures such as pensions, health insurance, education, benefits for the disabled, family allowances, and single-parent benefits, also called "benefits for single women," given that most single parents are females.[22] Unemployment compensation was not implemented until 1980, and most female workers do not meet the requirements to qualify.

The measure that has been most attacked is the benefits package for single parents. One criticism has been that with this policy, women would evict men from their households in order to receive benefits. The other criticism has been that women would have children in order to receive the allowance and then use the money to support their boyfriends. However, evaluations of this particular policy contradict these criticisms and indicate that only 15 percent of families receive this type of allowance for single parents. At the same time, many men abandoned their families long before the introduction of this policy, so the policy in itself should not be considered a major contributor to the great number of female-headed households. The evaluation of this policy should instead point out the transformation in the lives of these women and their place in society.[23]

FAMILY AND SEXUALITY

Marriage

In the Caribbean, female-headed households have specific historical roots.[24] First, as a result of slavery, marriage was restricted by slave owners, and women assumed the sole responsibility for the upbringing of children. Second, as an outcome of male out-migration, women were also left alone to take care of the children. Currently, single-parent families make up one-fourth of the families in Martinique and one-third of the families in Guadeloupe. These single parents are for the most part underprivileged females. It has been reported that 69 percent of these single mothers did not complete elementary school, half of them are unemployed, and more than half of their homes are extremely small, with at most one or two rooms, and lack basic necessities like running water.[25]

Reproduction

Fertility rates in the French Caribbean have declined from 5.5 children per woman in 1950 to less than 2 children per woman today.[26] Family-planning services did not begin in these islands until the 1970s, and this responsibility was basically in the hands of nongovernmental organizations (NGOs). It was not until 1975 in Guadeloupe, and 1969 in Martinique, that the local governments accepted more responsibility by providing financial support to the Association guadeloupéenne pour le planning familial (AGPF) and to the Association martiniquaise pour l'information et l'orientation familiales (AMIOF).

Sex Education

Local governments in both Guadeloupe and Martinique support family planning and sex education and promote the development of women.[27] Sex education is included in the curriculum of the secondary schools, and the local church has never attacked family planning.

In Guadeloupe, the government offers family-planning services in its maternal and child health centers and hospitals. In Martinique, the government provides extensive maternal and child health services, but, unlike Guadeloupe, does not offer family-planning services. These services are offered instead by AMIOF.

Contraception and Abortion

Contraceptive use on both islands, with the pill as the most popular method, is estimated at between 50 and 55 percent. Moreover, the high rates of abortion suggest a continuous resistance to family planning in certain segments of the population. The French abortion law, which makes abortion a legal right upon request based on social, economic, therapeutic, and medical grounds, applies in both Guadeloupe and Martinique. The abortion rate for both islands has been estimated at 30 per 100 pregnancies.[28] Although abortions are legal, there are monetary costs, and many poor women are unable to afford to end their pregnancies. At the same time, many illegal abortions are performed, with dreadful consequences.

AGPF provides family-planning services in its clinics under medical supervision, but it does not provide sterilization or abortion services. AGPF remains the only organization conducting information and education activities in family planning and coordinates its services with the government in these areas.

AMIOF was the first organization to provide family planning in Martinique. It offers clinical services, including contraceptive methods and counseling. Voluntary sterilization services are also offered to both men and women. However, few men choose vasectomies as the method of family planning.

Teen Pregnancy

One of the major problems is that although many teenagers seek abortions, a large number of children are born to this age group. In the French Caribbean, the birth rate for teenagers is estimated at 50 percent. It has also been found that the birth rate is much higher in the rural areas than in the urban areas, basically as a result of less information available about family planning.[29]

HEALTH

The Secretariat of State for Health in both Guadeloupe and Martinique forms part of the French Ministry of Labor and Social Affairs.[30] A 1992 law provides that all persons residing in France and in the departments have the right to financial assistance for medical treatment costs in case of need. Access to medical attention for low-income residents is organized at the department level. These persons are entitled to receive benefits that cover either the entire cost (as in the case of the homeless) or a portion of the cost of the care provided (depending on the nature of the illness and on the type of medication prescribed). Health insurance is covered by compulsory contributions from salaries. Usually the patient pays to the provider and then is reimbursed by the health insurance. Many persons supplement the state health insurance with private insurance to cover any additional costs. There are three public hospitals and three private clinics in Martinique. In Guadeloupe, there are twenty-five health establishments, of which ten are in the public sector and fifteen are private.

The state has responsibility for general public health, including communitywide disease prevention, sanitation surveillance, and the control of major diseases and drug and alcohol addiction. The state also provides for the training of health personnel, ensures that medical treatment is adequate, and oversees the operation of public hospitals. A prefect, located in Martinique, directs the state's decentralized services in both departments. The training of personnel at the local level is offered in two teaching hospitals located in Fort-de-France and Pointe-à-Pitre and at nursing schools located in each of the departments. Medical personnel receive additional training in France.

Health Care Access

Residents of both Guadeloupe and Martinique have unrestricted access to a wide range of primary and secondary medical services on the islands and also have access to medical services in mainland France. The limitation is that if they receive treatment in France, the cost of the airfare is the responsibility of the patient unless the service is not provided on the islands, in which case it is partially covered.

The French Center for Health Education designs campaigns for a number of health- and hygiene-related topics, and then these campaigns are implemented by the departments. Residents of both Guadeloupe and Martinique have access to regular checkups during the school year and in the workplace. Maternal and child welfare services are also available to pregnant women and to young children, and nearly all birth deliveries are attended by skilled health staff.

Diseases and Disorders

Among the specific health problems affecting these islands are sexually transmitted diseases and serious levels of contagious dengue with epidemic outbreaks.[31] Other health problems include many cases of sickle-cell anemia and a high frequency of diabetes and hypertension. However, there is a low incidence of malignant tumors. The high incidence of traffic accidents is the main contributor to years of potential life lost.

In both Guadeloupe and Martinique, a large proportion of housing units lack basic necessities. It is estimated that 20 percent of houses in Guadeloupe and 14 percent of houses in Martinique do not have access to running water and electricity. Moreover, half of all housing units are not connected to sewer systems.[32]

AIDS

The AIDS epidemic is considered a priority health problem. At the beginning of 1997, there were 731 cases reported in Guadeloupe and 402 cases in Martinique.[33] In addition, a survey conducted in 1994 revealed the significance of constant multiple partners in these two French departments.[34] The majority of those infected with HIV acquired the virus through heterosexual transmission. In Guadeloupe, most persons infected are women within the age group twenty to thirty-nine, who make up 53 percent of the cases, and 59 percent of total cases have died. In Martinique, three-quarters of those infected are males. Mortality rates are high within this group, and 65 percent of persons infected have died.[35]

POLITICS AND LAW

As citizens of French departments, voters from Guadeloupe and Martinique participate in the election of the president of France for a seven-year term. As a result, in both Guadeloupe and Martinique, the chief of state is Jacques Chirac, president of France. He is represented by Prefect Jean Fedini in Guadeloupe and in Martinique by Prefect Jean-François Cordet. The prefects of these departments are appointed by the French president on the advice of the French Ministry of the Interior, whereas the presidents of the General and the Regional Councils are elected by members of these councils. In Guadeloupe, the president of the General Council is Marcellin Lubeth, and the president of the Regional Council is Lucette Michaux-Chevry, while in Martinique they are Clause Lise and Alfred Marie-Jeanne, respectively.[36]

The legislative branch in both Guadeloupe and Martinique is composed of a General Council and a Regional Council. The members of each council are elected by popular vote to serve six-year terms. The main areas in which the General Council is involved include the budget and local matters. The Regional Council has authority in areas of regional planning, transportation, and social and economic development, particularly upper secondary schools. The regional councils have full powers of decision in all these areas, but the state, through the prefect, retains jurisdiction in matters of defense, law, foreign affairs, and higher education.

The parliament in Paris is the ultimate source of legislation. The articles of the constitution establishing the departments created an administrative structure in the departments that is almost identical to that of metropolitan France. France provides subsidies for the infrastructure and bureaucracy of the overseas departments.

Suffrage

The Declaration of the Rights of Man of 1848 proclaimed the equality of French men, but it was not extended to women or to slaves. It was not until nearly a century later that adult suffrage that included women was achieved in 1946 with the Constitution of the Fourth Republic.[37]

Political Participation

With few exceptions, women in the French Caribbean are underrepresented in political life. For example, the election results for 1987 indicate that only 5 percent of the seats in the General Councils in Guadeloupe and in Martinique were filled by women. In the Guadeloupe Regional Council, women made up 7 percent of the membership, but none of the membership in Martinique. Likewise, 2 percent of mayors in Guadeloupe were female, but none in Martinique. In both Guadeloupe and Martinique, the highest representation of women is at the Municipal Council level, where they make up 16 and 17.6 percent of the membership, respectively.[38] Since 1992, the president of the Regional Council of Guadeloupe has been a woman.

RELIGION AND SPIRITUALITY

Although 95 percent of the population in both Guadeloupe and Martinique indicate that their religion is Roman Catholic, there is widespread belief in African rituals and superstitions. It is also very important to note that the Catholic Church has not been opposed to family planning.

VIOLENCE

Domestic Violence and Rape/Sexual Assault

Women in the French Caribbean have been subject to abuse since the time of slavery, both from their partners and from slave owners. At present, cultural perspectives influence the dominance of males in their homes even if they are not present.[39] In particular, women are the victims of male polygamous behavior, expressed in the form of multiple and simultaneous sexual unions. It is reported that if wives show any signs of complaint about the behavior of their partners, men resort to physical punishment in the form of wife beating. Another common type of abuse is that female domestic servants may be expected to be sexually involved with the husband and the sons in the house where they work.[40]

The Union of Women in both Guadeloupe and Martinique has led a movement that attempts to inform women of their rights. The groups have held demonstrations against the killing of women by their partners. These groups have also taken action in cases of rape and other instances of violence against women, have opened information centers, and maintain a legal crisis center to provide some help for battered women.[41]

OUTLOOK FOR THE TWENTY-FIRST CENTURY

The outlook for women in the French Caribbean is promising. With the financial help these islands receive from France, and with the welfare policies implemented by the French government, women in both Guadeloupe and Martinique are better off than women in neighboring Caribbean islands. The women of Guadeloupe and Martinique have been able to attain high levels of life expectancy and literacy rates. In economic terms, by Caribbean standards, the residents of these islands have a high level of GDP per capita, although their GDP is only half of the GDP per capita in mainland France. However, the women from the French Caribbean must become more involved in the political decisions affecting them and their countries. The women of Guadeloupe and Martinique must likewise strive to obtain the best possible education and training so that they may occupy higher decision-making positions in the economy and the government and be able to achieve parity with men in jobs, occupations, and pay.

NOTES

1. Robert Aldrich and John Connell, *France's Overseas Frontier* (New York: Cambridge University Press, 1992), 1–11.

2. In addition to Guadeloupe and Martinique, there are two additional French overseas departments: Reunion in the Indian Ocean and French Guiana in South America. The territories are Mayotte in the Indian Ocean, French Polynesia, New Caledonia, and Wallis and Futuna in the Pacific Ocean, while Saint-Pierre and Miquelon in the Atlantic Ocean and the Austral and Antarctic Territories are called *collectivités territoriales*.

3. Central Intelligence Agency, *2001 World Factbook*, 2002, www.cia.gov/cia/publications/factbook/index.html; Europa Publications, *South America, Central America, and the Caribbean 2001* (London: Europa Publications, 2001); "Guadeloupe," *Encyclopaedia Britannica*, http://search.eb.com/article?eu=127877; "Martinique," *Encyclopaedia Britannica*, http://search.eb.com/article?eu=127880; Pan-American Health Organization and World Health Organization, *Health of the Americas*, 1998, www.paho.org/English/SHA/HIA_1998ed.htm; United Nations, *The World's Women 2000*, 2002, http://unstats.un.org/unsd/demographic/ww2000/index.htm. Unless otherwise indicated, all subsequent statistics in the profile are derived from these sources.

4. Europa Publications, 2001.

5. United Nations, 2002.

6. Europa Publications, 2001.

7. Huguette Dagenais, "Women in Guadeloupe: The Paradoxes of Reality," in *Women and Change in the Caribbean: A Pan-Caribbean Perspective*, ed. Janet Momsen (London: James Currey, 1993), 96–97.

8. CIA, *World Factbook*, 2002.

9. CIA, *World Factbook*, 2002.

10. CIA, *World Factbook*, 2002.

11. In the opinion of Aldrich and Connell, 1992, and Dagenais, 1993.

12. CIA, *World Factbook*, 2002.

13. Janet Momsen, "Development and Gender Divisions of Labour in the Rural

Eastern Caribbean," in *Women and Change in the Caribbean: A Pan-Caribbean Perspective*, ed. Janet Momsen (London: James Currey, 1993), 232–46; United Nations, 2002.

14. Arlette Gautier, "Women from Guadeloupe and Martinique," in *French and West Indian: Martinique, Guadeloupe, and French Guiana Today*, ed. Richard D.E. Burton and Fred Reno (Charlottesville: University Press of Virginia, 1995), 119–36.

15. Ibid.

16. Dagenais, 1993; Gautier, 1995.

17. Dagenais, 1993; Gautier, 1995.

18. Gautier, 1995.

19. Gautier, 1995, 119–36.

20. U.S. Social Security Online, *Social Security Programs throughout the World, 1999: France*, 2002, www.ssa.gov/cgi-bin/cqcgi/@ssa.env.

21. Gautier, 1995.

22. Claudine Attias-Donfut and Nicole Lapierre, "The Welfare Family: Three Generations in Guadeloupean Society," *History of the Family* 5(3) (2000): 329–46.

23. Ibid.

24. Momsen, 1993.

25. Gautier, 1995, 119–36.

26. Dagenais, 1993, 96–97.

27. International Planned Parenthood Federation, *Country Profiles*, 2002, http://ippfnet.ippf.org/.

28. International Planned Parenthood Federation, 2002; Pan-American Health Organization and World Health Organization, 1998.

29. International Planned Parenthood Federation (IPPF), http://ippfnet.ippf.

30. Pan-American Health Organization and World Health Organization, 1998.

31. Ibid.

32. Gautier, 1995.

33. Pan-American Health Organization (PAHO), www.paho.org.

34. Ibid.

35. Pan-American Health Organization and World Health Organization, 1998.

36. CIA, *World Factbook*, 2002.

37. Aldrich and Connell, 1992, 1–11.

38. Gautier, 1995.

39. Dagenais, 1993; Gautier, 1995.

40. Michel S. Laguerre, *Urban Poverty in the Caribbean: French Martinique as a Social Laboratory* (New York: St. Martin's Press, 1990).

41. Gautier, 1995.

RESOURCE GUIDE

Suggested Reading

Burton, Richard D.E., and Fred Reno, eds. *French and West Indian: Martinique, Guadeloupe, and French Guiana Today*. Charlottesville: University Press of Virginia, 1995.

Gautier, Arlette. "Women from Guadeloupe and Martinique." In *French and West Indian: Martinique, Guadeloupe, and French Guiana Today*, ed. Richard D.E. Burton and Fred Reno. Charlottesville: University Press of Virginia, 1995.

MacDonnogh, Giles. "Small, but Perfectly Prosperous." *New Statesman* 128(4432) (1996).

Videos/Films

Portrait of the Caribbean, Program 4: La Grande Illusion. 1992. A Barraclough Carey Production for BBC Television in association with Turner Broadcasting System. Ambrose Video Pub.

Sugarcane Alley. 1983. Director Euzhan Palcy. The story of a high-spirited boy and his forceful grandmother who live in a plantation shantytown, and their struggle to find happiness.

Web Sites

Central Intelligence Agency, *2001 World Factbook*, 2002, www.cia.gov/cia/publications/factbook/index.html.

International Planned Parenthood Federation, *Country Profiles*, 2002, http://ippfnet.ippf.org/.

Island of Guadeloupe, www.antilles-info-business.com/guadeloupe/index-gb.html.

Martinique Regional Council, www.cr-martinique.fr/index.php.html.

Pan-American Health Organization–World Health Organization, *Health of the Americas*, 1998, www.paho.org/English/SHA/HIA_1998ed.htm.

United Nations, *The World's Women 2000*, 2002, http://unstats.un.org/unsd/demographic/ww2000/index.htm.

United Nations Population Information Network, www.un.org/popin.

World Bank, *Gender Statistics*, 2002, http://genderstats.worldbank.org.

Organizations

Association guadeloupéenne pour le planning familial
Mrs. N. Daniere, Executive Director
20, Rue Sadi Carnot
Pointe-à-Pitre, Cedex, 97154
Phone: 590-82-2978 or 590-82-1712
Fax: 590-21-2214

Association founded in 1964, responsible for providing family planning through four clinics and ten information centers.

Association martiniquaise pour l'information et l'orientation familiales
Dr. Roger Boucher, Executive Director
125–127 Rue Moreau de Joanes
Fort-de-France, Martinique

Phone: 596-714-601
Fax: 596-715-682

Association responsible for the provision of family planning and information.

Girls Club Association
Miss Séréna Coralie
Old Borough
97111 Dull with water
97111
Guadeloupe
Phone: 590-242-460
Fax: 590-248-982

CMMF2000 a/s Union des femmes de la Martinique (UFM): Union of the Women
  of Martinique
17 rue Lamartine, Fort de France, 97200, Martinique
Phone: 596-712-626
Fax: 596-771-443
Email: CMMF2000@u.femmesmartinique@wannadoo.fr:UFMque@wanadoo.fr

Union of the Guadeloupéennes Women
Lisette Nirelep
15, Residence of Isles
Not In Pitre
97 110
Guadeloupe

SELECTED BIBLIOGRAPHY

Aldrich, Robert, and John Connell. *France's Overseas Frontier*. New York: Cambridge
    University Press, 1992.
Attias-Donfut, Claudine, and Nicole Lapierre. "The Welfare Family: Three Genera-
    tions in Guadeloupean Society." *History of the Family* 5(3) (2000): 329–46.
Cottias, Myriam, and Annie Fitte-Duval. "Femme, famille, et politique dans les Antilles
    Françaises de 1828 à nos jours." *Caribbean Studies* 28(1) (1995): 76–100.
Dagenais, Huguette. "Women in Guadeloupe: The Paradoxes of Reality." In *Women
    and Change in the Caribbean: A Pan-Caribbean Perspective*, ed. Janet Momsen.
    London: James Currey, 1993: 96–97.
Ducoulombier, Audrey. "Parity Is about Race." *Modern and Contemporary France* 10(1).
    75–87.
Europa Publications. *South America, Central America, and the Caribbean 2001*. London:
    Europa Publications, 2001.
Institut National de la Statistique et des Etudes Economiques. *Guadeloupe: La Région
    en Faits et Chiffres*. 2002. http://www.insee.fr/fr/insee_regions/guadeloupe/
    home/home_page.asp.
———. *Martinique: La Région en Faits et Chiffres*. 2002. http://www.insee.fr/fr/insee_
    regions/martinique/home/home_page.asp.
International Planned Parenthood Federation. *Country Fact Sheets, Family Planning in
    the Western Hemisphere: Guadeloupe*. International Planned Parenthood Feder-
    ation, 1996.

————. *Country Fact Sheets, Family Planning in the Western Hemisphere: Martinique.* International Planned Parenthood Federation, 1996.

Laguerre, Michel S. *Urban Poverty in the Caribbean: French Martinique as a Social Laboratory.* New York: St. Martin's Press, 1990.

Momsen, Janet. "Development and Gender Divisions of Labour in the Rural Eastern Caribbean." In *Women and Change in the Caribbean: A Pan-Caribbean Perspective,* ed. Janet Momsen. London: James Currey, 1993: 232–46.

U.S. Social Security Online. *Social Security Programs throughout the World, 1999: France.* 2002. www.ssa.gov/cgi-bin/cqcgi/@ssa.env.

7

HAITI

Robin B. Devin

PROFILE OF HAITI

The Republic of Haiti occupies the western third of the island of Hispaniola. The island is shared with Haiti's neighbor to the east, the Dominican Republic. The island lies about 600 miles southwest of Florida and is situated southeast of the island of Cuba. The land area of Haiti is 10,600 square miles, an area slightly smaller than the state of Maryland. Haiti is one of the most mountainous countries along the Caribbean archipelago and also one of the world's most densely populated. With a population estimated at 8 million, Haiti has more than 650 people per square mile.

The people are virtually all of African descent and speak Haitian Creole, although French is also an official language. French was the language of the elite and had been the only language taught in schools and used in official government documents, although it was spoken by less than 10 percent of the population. Now, however, Haitian Creole has become a recognized language as well.

The government of Haiti is a constitutional democracy that has been plagued by political violence for most of its history. Originally colonized by the French in the

seventeenth century, Haiti proclaimed itself an independent nation in 1804 following a successful slave revolt. With this victory, Haiti became the world's first black republic. The country then endured an uninterrupted series of dictators and harsh regimes. It has also suffered under foreign intervention. The longest period under foreign occupation began in 1915 when the U.S. Marines invaded Haiti and remained for nineteen years.

The longest-running dictatorship was that of the Duvalier family. François Duvalier (Papa Doc) was elected president in 1957 and in 1964 was named president for life. Upon his death in 1971, he was succeeded by his son Jean-Claude (Baby Doc). Jean-Claude Duvalier was forced to flee Haiti in 1986 following several weeks of unrest, thus ending the twenty-eight-year regime that had been characterized by extreme violence and brutality.

A new democratic constitution was approved by voters in 1987. Following several more years of turmoil and political violence, Father Jean-Bertrand Aristide was elected president in 1990 with overwhelming public support. He was deposed by a military coup less than a year later. The coup regime compiled a record of human rights violations that was among the worst in the Americas. The United Nations imposed an embargo against the dictatorship and finally deployed a multinational force headed by the U.S. military to force the legitimate government's return to power in 1994. Aristide was elected president again in 2000 and succeeded President René Preval, who had served from 1996 to 2000.

Economically, Haiti is the poorest country in the Western Hemisphere. As a colony, it was once the most productive and significant European possession in the Caribbean, but the centuries have taken their toll. Today most areas of the country lack the most basic resources such as electricity, sanitation, and potable water. Nearly 70 percent of the people are subsistence farmers trying to eke out a living in a country where only 20 percent of the land is arable due to extensive deforestation and soil erosion. Once a lush tropical isle, Haiti today retains less than 5 percent of the forests it once had. The principal crops are coffee, sugar, mangoes, corn, and rice. Sugar refining has been the principal industry. Other main industries include flour milling, cement manufacturing, and textiles. Haiti's export business is insignificant. Annual per capita income is difficult to determine, but is currently estimated at approximately $500. The average income of the rural poor is much lower due to the extreme inequality in wealth.

The population is 51 percent female. The infant mortality rate is estimated at 74 deaths per 1,000 live births. The maternal mortality is 457 per 100,000. The total fertility rate is estimated at 4.5 children born per woman.[1] Life expectancy at birth is 54.4 years, the lowest in the Western Hemisphere.[2] For women, life expectancy is 56 years, while life expectancy for men is 52.8 years.

OVERVIEW OF WOMEN'S ISSUES

It has been noted that "although women in Haiti play an important role in society and the economy, the predominant image of women—easily recognizable from Haitian proverbs—is negative."[3] The Haitian woman is viewed as the pillar of society, but is relatively undervalued. Haitian society is highly gender stratified. Women play different roles than men and have different obligations, rights, and privileges.

Women manage the market economy that assures the movement of foodstuffs and other essentials from country to town. They provide the backbone of the rural economy. Yet they bear a double and triple workload as workers, wives, and mothers. Haitian women participate in all aspects of Haitian society and have increased their political participation during the past decade. These actions have not translated into full participation as citizens at all levels.

EDUCATION

Opportunities

Education in Haiti is provided by the government and by religious organizations such as the Roman Catholic Church. Primary education, which normally begins at six years of age and continues for six years, is officially compulsory. Secondary education usually begins at age twelve and lasts for an additional six years. Higher education is available at eighteen vocational training centers, forty-two domestic science schools, and the Université d'Etat d'Haiti. Approximately 20 percent of the total government budget is spent on education.

Haiti's education status reflects the dire struggle with poverty that most of its people face. Although the Haitian constitution guarantees free education to all through the university level, only about 63 percent complete primary school. School attendance is officially compulsory for six elementary years, but the actual enrollment rate is about 73 percent. The rate of attendance is fairly evenly divided between males and females. Primary-school enrollment includes less than 20 percent of both girls and boys in the relevant age groups.[4] This figure highlights the fact that even those children who do attend school are not able to enroll at the appropriate age and continuously attend. Most are enrolled only as family finances permit.

Public education is not widely available. Little more than 10 percent of the schools are free.[5] Even at these tuition-free schools, many families cannot afford the cost of the books and supplies that are needed. The constitution states that materials and books will be provided for free by the state, but the government has not had the resources to make this promise a reality.[6] Private and parochial schools provide three-quarters of all the educational programs offered. Although Haitians place an extremely high value on education, only 20 percent of all children even begin secondary education.[7]

Literacy

Due to these factors, Haiti's overall adult literacy rate is less than 50 percent—50 percent for males and 46 percent for females.[8] Although the difference in literacy rates between men and women is small, there is a lower enrollment of girls at the university level.[9] The 1990 United Nations statistics for the percentage of illiterates over twenty-four years of age included 76 percent of women and 69 percent of men.[10] The percentage of women among university teachers was only 17 percent.[11] Although the percentage of women in higher education may be lower than the percentage of men, this issue is overshadowed by the dismal lack of education for all.

Due to the low level of literacy of the Haitian population, educational messages are often conveyed via a medium other than the printed word. Radio programming is frequently used as a means of informing the people about everything from voters' rights to health issues. But most households, particularly in the rural areas, do not own a radio, and thus many educational messages are delivered by plays, dances, and poems. Women are most often the ones involved in festivities where an original play or song is performed that conveys an important lesson. Rural development and health organizations typically use this method to encourage women to teach others and as a way to exchange information.

EMPLOYMENT AND ECONOMICS

Job/Career Opportunities and Pay

Haiti, as one of the poorest countries in the world, has a population in which 75 percent live in abject poverty. Women make up 43 percent of the total workforce.[12] A glimpse at the streets of urban centers such as Port-au-Prince or the rural markets shows the important contribution of women in creating wealth and in managing poverty, as well as their innovative capacities to resist and survive. The gender division of labor in Haiti results in women creating and reproducing the bulk of the wealth for men.

The agricultural sector employs the majority of the economically active workforce. Nearly two-thirds of all Haitians are small-scale subsistence farmers.[13] They farm their tiny plots by hand without any farm machinery or even animal power. Haitian proverbs joke about falling out of one's field, and in fact, the precipitous terrain of some fields makes this possible. The principal income-producing job for the majority of women is the marketing of the produce from these small plots. A day's marketing typically involves rising before dawn in order to walk for several hours to the local market town, selling in the market, and then walking the same distance home with the day's earnings, which amount to less than a U.S. dollar.

Even this meager income is now threatened because economic structural adjustment policies imposed by the World Bank and the International Monetary Fund have weakened the internal agricultural market by forcing local merchandise to compete with imported goods.

The severe stress of destructive erosion has forced many to move to the cities, particularly Port-au-Prince, the nation's capital, in search of work. The urban migration may be either permanent or temporary. Many

Haitian woman washing fish at traditional market, Acquin. Photo © TRIP/ASK.

rural inhabitants travel to urban areas during particularly difficult economic periods and then return to their rural villages. Many young women typically travel to Port-au-Prince, for example, during their late teens to work as domestics for a few years before returning to their home villages.

Opportunities in the urban areas are limited at best. The unemployment rate is 70–80 percent, and most jobs are menial work for paltry wages.[14] Most urban residents survive on odd jobs or by street hawking. Female vendors are a common sight in Haitian cities, where hundreds of little merchants (*ti machann*) line the congested streets. These women face a precarious existence and are often brutally forced to abandon their curbside stands when armed security guards attempt to clear the clogged roads. In addition to street hawking, there are established open-air market areas, such as Marche Hippolyte in the capital. In this one market, 3,000 to 4,000 people buy and sell all day.[15] But additional areas are needed where women can safely sell their produce and other goods. Construction of market areas in the cities has long been promised, but thus far little has been done.

In Port-au-Prince alone, there are an estimated 700,000 people in the informal sector, and three-quarters of these are women. This number has increased greatly during the last decade as the economy has declined. The markets are full of former nurses, teachers, and maids who are the main breadwinners of their families, often not earning enough to send their children to school. Although nationally 39 percent of heads of households are female,[16] in Port-au-Prince about three-quarters of all households are headed by women or depend on women as the income earner.[17] To get by or to establish their "shops," these vendors live on credit and borrow money from each other or from usurers, paying up to 100 percent interest. The development of women's credit organizations, which could lend women capital to establish these small enterprises, is an issue of central importance.

Women are also the principal workers in the assembly plants in Port-au-Prince. Rawlings baseballs and Walt Disney pajamas are some of the better-known U.S. products that have been sewn by Haitian women workers. These factories are required by law to pay a very small minimum wage, but the devaluation of the Haitian gourde and spiraling inflation have combined to substantially decrease its value. Nevertheless, a woman factory worker's salary typically is used to support a family of six or more. The extreme exploitation of the working class by multinational corporations is an issue of importance here as well as throughout the world. Haitian women have joined others in denouncing widespread violations of workers' rights in the garment and sportswear industry and have fought for the rights of collective bargaining, equal pay for equal work, a living wage, treatment with dignity, and a healthy and safe workplace.[18]

Compounding the problem of low wages and poor conditions for assembly-plant workers is the instability of these jobs. The women's positions depend on the ebb and flow of international capital. These assembly plants come and go with the ups and downs of the precarious Haitian economy. The factories have virtually no investment in the Haitian infrastructure and are able to pull out of the country with a few days' notice at the first sign of political turmoil or to take advantage of opportunities elsewhere.

Working Conditions and Sexual Harassment

Haitian women's organizations such as Kay Fanm have fought for women workers and have participated in demonstrations such as those held on May 1 (the traditional Labor Day). Kay Fanm has raised issues of women's working conditions and pay scales. It has highlighted the fact that female agricultural workers are paid only 60–70 percent of what male workers earn and that a factory worker's salary is not a living wage. It has also denounced sexual harassment by factory supervisors and pointed out that maids are not even recognized as workers in the legal Code de Travail, the Haitian law governing working conditions.[19]

However, changes in the law will not benefit the majority of women who live in the rural areas and make their living by marketing produce grown in subsistence farming. The burden of a market woman who carries a fifty-pound sack of rice to market on her head or who carries ten-gallon buckets of water to her home daily by the same method will not have her working conditions improved without a change in her socioeconomic status.

Support for Mothers/Caretakers

By law, Haitian women are entitled to twelve weeks of maternity leave. Employers are responsible for providing this leave and for paying full wages for six weeks of the covered period.[20] In reality, the law is rarely followed.

Daycare

There is no organized daycare system in Haiti. Children of working mothers are typically cared for by other family members or left home alone. Children and adolescents may also be sent to live with families other than their own to work as domestic servants without compensation. These children, referred to as *restavek*, are mostly between the ages of seven and fourteen and 75 percent of them are girls. The lack of facilities for children has also resulted in a number of children living in the streets, primarily in Port-au-Prince.[21]

Family and Medical Leave

Most workers are beyond the reach of employee protection legislation since they are employed primarily as small farmers or in the informal sector of the economy. The informal sector of the economy, comprised primarily of women, along with the agricultural sector, make up 96 percent of the working class. These workers have no benefits of any kind. Government workers have a poorly organized insurance system and private employees are supposed to receive an indemnity that is paid to beneficiaries in the event of temporary incapacity or permanent disability. The most recent figures showed a decline in enrollment in this program.[22]

Although men are primarily responsible for crop production, the wealth produced through agriculture is considered to be jointly produced by the male and female parnters. If their union is dissolved or terminated, the proceeds are equally divided.[23] The notion of common property does not extend to the wealth produced through female commercial activity. These proceeds, regardless of the source of the original capital, are seen as the sole property of the women and subsequently pass to her heirs only.[24] Since most women hae commercial marketing experience and therefore have the potential for producing their own income, their economic well-being is not totally dependent on male labor. Haitian women thus have a high degree of relative independence.

Both males and females are entitled to own land, and both are given rights of inheritance. Before 1915, a Haitian woman who married a foreigner lost both property rights and citizenship, but that is no longer true.[25] Now property rights are more often lost by both women and men when they are forced off their land into sharecropping or day labor as a result of economic distress.

In Haiti, inheritance is fully divisible and bilateral, as children of either sex can inherit equally from each of their parents. The only restriction is that a legally married man is prohibited by law from recognizing any children born outside of his marriage. That is, a child born to a father who is legally married to a woman other than the child's mother has no inheritance rights.[26] Although the law stipulates that both male and female children inherit equally, in reality, sons often inherit the agricultural land, while daughters inherit the house and only the land on which it stands. This can leave the female offspring without control of land that can be used for subsistence farming.[27]

Although there is no gender discrimination in land tenure or inheritance rights, it should be noted that inheritance is passed from parent to child, not to the surviving spouse. Even if a person dies childless, property is passed to the siblings of the deceased, not to the spouse. This leaves poor peasant women in a particularly vulnerable position. Since inheritance passes to children, not to the spouse, a woman without children can lose all of her property to her spouse's parents and siblings, leaving her destitute. Only by having children can a woman secure her claim to her partner's holdings, and then only through her children's holdings. The situation becomes worse if the man has children by more than one woman, which is frequently the case. In this situation, a female partner, through her children, may inherit only a portion of the land into which she had invested her labor.

Migration

No discussion of the Haitian economy would be complete without touching on the issue of migration. Due to the bleak living conditions and political turmoil within the country, many Haitians have migrated, both legally and illegally, to other parts of the world. The United States, Canada, and other parts of the Caribbean are the destinations that draw the largest number of immigrants. Women make up 55 percent of these immigrants.[28] The exodus is so large that one out of six Haitians lives abroad.[29] The Haitians who have migrated are referred to as the "Tenth Department," nine departments (similar to U.S. states) being the official geographic jurisdictions within Haiti. One of the issues that migration often creates for women is the breakup of the family unit. Male partners migrate in search of better opportunities, leaving their female partners as heads of single-parent households to raise the children by themselves. Mothers also migrate and are often forced to leave children behind in the care of others.

Social/Government Programs

Most social services are provided by nongovernmental organizations and charities. The Haitian government does have a Ministry of Women's Affairs and Rights, but lack of funds has prevented the government from developing needed social programs.

Welfare

The Haitian government provides virtually no essential services to the majority of its population. Public schools are limited in number, and public secondary education is nonexistent in most rural areas. Most areas have no, or only sporadic, electricity and no telephone service.

One of the major problems, which particularly affects women, is the lack of potable water. The state does not provide even this most basic necessity of life, and the situation has been worsening over the past decade. The United Nations Development Program reported that in 1990, 56 percent of Haiti's urban population had access to drinking water. By 1994, that figure had fallen to only 38 percent. In the countryside, the statistics were even worse. In 1994, 23 percent had access to clean water, down from 36 percent in 1990.[30]

As in most other countries, the job of fetching water falls mostly on women, girls, and young children who walk long distances with five-gallon buckets of water on their heads. In rural villages, one round trip carrying water to a household from the nearest water source (which is often polluted) can often consume the better part of an hour. The issue of safe and convenient water is one that has mobilized women to fight for this basic necessity.

FAMILY AND SEXUALITY

Gender Roles

Throughout the rural areas of Haiti, economic survival depends on the joint efforts of men and women. Economic activities are clearly defined by sex roles, and cooperation between a male and female is essential. Men are primarily responsible for agricultural activities, which are seen as a male domain, although women do assist in certain agricultural tasks such as planting, harvesting, and some weeding.

The women are almost exclusively charged with the marketing of produce. All families sell at least a portion of their agricultural crops to purchase necessities for the household. It is women's work to manage the domestic economy on a day-to-day basis. Only a few women are full-time professional market women (known as *madam sara*), but most women have had some experience in commercial marketing of one kind or another. Virtually all women engage in provision marketing by selling their produce to purchase needed items such as matches, laundry soap, and other household items.

In addition to marketing, women are responsible for most domestic tasks, including housekeeping, food preparation, and laundry. Since most rural areas of Haiti have no running water or electricity, these tasks are extremely time consuming. Food is prepared over a wood or charcoal fire, and laundry is taken to the nearest water source to wash. Haitian women labor from long before sunrise to long after dark cooking meals, washing dishes, cleaning the house, doing the laundry, mending clothes, and carrying water.

The one task that is excluded from this gender-linked division of domestic labor is child care. Although the care of children is generally viewed as primarily a female's responsibility, men participate fully in the care of young children. Since women's marketing and other responsibilities often take them away from the household for extended periods, men are often responsible for child-care tasks.[31]

Marriage

In Haiti, gender roles and conjugal mating patterns reinforce women's subordination. Women's place is defined in relation to home and motherhood even in progressive circles. The dominant sexual discourse classifies sexual relations in terms of two extremes—marriage versus prostitution. The ideology of marriage is strong despite the fact that more than 40 percent of conjugal unions are not legally sanctioned.[32] While legal and church-sanctioned marriage in the European tradition is the norm among the Haitian elite, the numerically, historically, and culturally primary form of conjugal relationship in Haiti is not legal marriage, but a form of common-law marriage called *plasaj*.[33] It is a socially accepted conjugal union involving mutual economic and sexual rights. The relationship involves the establishment of a new household by the couple and is essentially equivalent to formal marriage. In the rural areas, legal marriage is less common, largely due to the traditional marriage customs and ceremonies that require costly festivities.

Cultural norms require sexually exclusive monogamy for women but not for men. If a man has the means to support more than one woman and her children, he may do so without social disapproval as long as he does not neglect his present spouse, either economically or in terms of spending time in the household. There is no social stigma implied in a polygynous union unless the man fails to uphold his responsibilities.

In addition to the stable forms of conjugal unions, marriage and *plasaj*, there are also less stable sexual relationships that are often referred to as visiting unions. In these relationships, a joint independent household is not established. These relationships may precede marriage or *plasaj* or may be an alternative to a formal union. If these relationships lead to pregnancy, as they often do, no stigma is attached, and the father typically accepts responsibility for the child as he would if the child had been conceived as a result of a more permanent union.

Because stable unions are based on mutually supportive relationships between a man and a woman, escalating poverty and political turmoil can contribute to the difficulty of establishing long-term conjugal unions, which is particularly great in the urban slums, where economic prospects are better for women than men. An interesting aspect of the male-female dyad in Haiti is that women are seen as more self-sufficient than men. Due to their economic independence, women are viewed, especially in poor, urban areas, as being able to support themselves. A man, on the other hand, is viewed as not being able to get along without a woman.[34] A man must have a woman to care for his domestic needs such as cooking and laundry. A man who is forced to take on these tasks himself is either pitied or viewed as effeminate.

Reproduction

Haitians say, "Pitit se riches pov malere" (children are the wealth of the poor).[35] Children are valued not as an economic asset but more as hope for the future. Children are expected to provide for their parents in old age, as the Haitian government does not provide any old-age benefits.

Children are highly valued and well loved. No preference is given to male over female offspring, and the ideal number of children is left up to "God's will." For a Haitian woman, there is nothing worse than sterility.

Haiti is characterized by a high birth rate, low contraceptive prevalence, and high child mortality. The total fertility rate (births per woman) is 4.4.[36] Surveys have indicated that most women reported having lost children due to preventable disease.[37]

Sex Education

Public health services attempt to educate the public regarding family planning, but progress is limited due to lack of transportation, political turmoil, lack of funds, weak socioeconomic infrastructure, and the low quality of health services delivery.[38] Adding to these problems is the fact that rural health workers (*agents de santé*) are mostly male, and women do not feel comfortable discussing contraceptive methods with them.

Contraception and Abortion

Haiti has the lowest rate of contraceptive use in the Western Hemisphere—less than 10 percent.[39] The contraceptive rate among married women is 18 percent.[40] Access to birth control is a serious issue for Haitian women. Rural men have a low usage rate of condoms since condoms are typically viewed only as protecting men against venereal diseases when they are with prostitutes. The majority of women make their own decisions regarding contraceptive use without the involvement of their male partner, but the lack of availability, cost, and lack of information about contraceptives contribute to their limited use.

Use of contraception is greater in urban areas such as Port-au-Prince, where women do not want to lose their jobs and are therefore eager to avoid pregnancy. In rural areas where fertility is highly valued, women may wish to have a child that would tie them to their partner economically as well as emotionally. Haitians are also deeply religious, practicing Christianity as well as native Vodou, neither of which is supportive of modern contraception. The Catholic Church firmly opposes modern contraception, and Vodou priests (*oungans*) often have a negative attitude toward it as well. Many health facilities are also religiously affiliated and refuse to provide birth control, although some offer counseling on the symptothermal or rhythm methods.

The symptothermal method of birth control relies on a woman's ability to determine her fertile days through awareness of physical signs of fertility such as changes in body temperature or changes in the viscosity of vaginal mucus. It is a method of natural family planning like the rhythm method and, as such, is an acceptable option for those who oppose modern contraceptive methods for religious methods.

Another issue is the quality of care provided at family-planning clinics. The power differential between providers and their poor female clients can result in unsatisfactory medical encounters in which little consideration is given to the problems of the patients. The woman's preferred choice of birth-control method can be ignored, and poor communication may be the norm.[41] Voluntary abortion is not legal in Haiti and data on abortions are not readily available. Haitian advocates for the right to legal abortion participated in the September 28 campaign to decriminalize abortions, along with women from other Latin America countries.[42]

Teen Pregnancy

Teen pregnancy is not an issue in Haiti. Girls are supposed to be modest and are discouraged from becoming intimate with boys at a young age. The average age of first sexual relations is late compared to that in many developing countries. Women generally reported that they had begun having sex at a median age of nineteen, approximately two years before they entered into their first conjugal union.[43] This, combined with a late age of menarche, most likely due to poor nutrition, results in few children being born to teenage mothers.

HEALTH

Health Care Access

In Haiti, access to health care is limited, particularly in rural areas. Only 1.1 percent of the gross domestic product is spent on health.[44] Haiti has the lowest performance of any country in the Western Hemisphere with regard to health surveillance and vaccine coverage indicators. The number of doctors per capita has actually declined over the last ten years. Only 68 percent of pregnant women receive prenatal care, and only 20 percent of childbirth deliveries are attended by skilled health personnel.[45]

The health system suffers from poor planning, lack of adequate supervision, and logistical obstacles. Rural health posts have limited and irregular service hours and suffer from a lack of supplies. National health campaigns have not met their goals, and health-care professionals suffer from a lack of training. Due to the lack of government funding, the vast majority of financial resources come from external sources. Health care in Haiti is generally provided by international organizations, private charities, and religious organizations.

Diseases and Disorders

The health of Haitian women is worse than that of any other national female group in the Western Hemisphere. Besides having a low life expectancy, Haitian women remain vulnerable to food scarcity and the ravages of infectious diseases such as tuberculosis and AIDS.

AIDS

Although health statistics have improved since the 1970s, with a sharp decrease in infant and child mortality, life expectancy in the next five years is expected to decline due to the impact of AIDS.[46] The prevalence rate of AIDS is 6 percent of the population in rural areas and 10 percent in urban settings.[47] As the HIV/AIDS epidemic in Haiti accelerates, the risk to women is increasing. It has been estimated that in 1997 there were 190,000 people in Haiti with AIDS, 34 percent of them adult women.[48] A July 23, 2002, speech by Haitian First Lady Mildred Trouillot Aristide reported the number of infected Haitians at 300,000. The percentage of infected persons who are women has also climbed dramatically, currently reaching 50 percent. This feminization of AIDS parallels the experience in other countries worldwide.

Women report fewer multiple-partner relationships than men and are reasonably well informed on AIDS prevention, but Haitian women's capacity to negotiate safe sex behavior, particularly the use of condoms, is affected by their customary role in the sexual relationship. Gender distinctions in household decision making give women little influence in sexual negotiation once they are in an established relationship. The high value that women attach to the economic importance of a long-term union leads them to condone or overlook a man's sexual activity outside the home. Although women know that they should refrain from sex with a promiscuous partner, they risk the loss of financial support if they take that step. These facts, combined with the prevailing negative image of condoms, make it extremely difficult for women to protect themselves.

With Haiti listed as one of only six countries outside of Africa where AIDS deaths are expected to decrease life expectancy by at least three years by 2005, there is an urgent need to intervene to stop the epidemic. Behavioral norms and expectations that deny most Haitian women the right to protect themselves and their families must be overcome.[49]

The impact of the AIDS epidemic on women is further compounded by their role within the family. As the central caretaker within the family unit, Haitian women carry the heaviest burden in caring for the sick. If the women herself falls sick with AIDS, her illness jeopardizes the health and welfare of her entire family. Since women play a central role in supporting the family economically as well as caring for its members, the entire household is severely affected. Added to this already heavy burden is the care of the thousands of children orphaned by AIDS, who are typically sent to live with grandmothers or other female relatives.

Cancer

Since 1997, the Haitian Ministry of Public Health has been promoting the use of death certificates in an attempt to more adequately establish mortality rates and cause of death within Haiti. A sizable number of deaths still go unregistered, and figures for the causes of death for 1999 reveal that almost half of the certificates have ill-defined diagnoses. An analysis of the deaths by broad categories shows that the number one cause of death is communicable disease, followed by diseases of the circulatory system. External causes of death, such as accidents, ranked third followed by neoplasms. The most frequent neoplasms were tumors of the digestive organs. The leading causes of death among women followed the same pattern as men with the exception that maternal causes were the fourth-leading cause of death among women.[50]

Cancer was not among the twenty leading specific causes of mortality in Haiti in 1999. However, the National Health System does not have adequate means of performing histopathological diagnosis, so malignant neoplasms may be underreported.[51]

Depression

Mental health is not considered a national priority within Haiti. There are only two government institutions for mental health care and both are located in the Port-au-Prince area. There are no public institutions that provide mental health care outside the capital, but there are a growing number of small, private centers in other areas of the country.[52]

POLITICS AND LAW

Suffrage

The women of Haiti have been the backbone of all the political struggles in the country's history from the movement for independence in the late 1700s to the current democratic movement. Despite their active involvement, women only gained suffrage in Haiti in 1950.[53] Even after their recognition as equal voting citizens, women were still legally defined as dependent wives and daughters. Married women were legally minors until 1979.[54] The current constitution of 1987 guarantees equal rights to all women regardless of marital status. Haiti has also ratified the United Nations Convention on the Elimination of All Forms of Discrimination against Women.

Political Participation

Since 1980, the political landscape of Haiti has changed significantly with the intensive participation of women in the political process. Haiti is the only country in all of Latin America and the Caribbean to have a female head of state elected in the 1990s.[55] Ertha Pascal-Trouillot was the first Haitian woman ever to be a Supreme Court judge, and she served as provisional president of Haiti in 1990–1991. Under the Aristide government in 1991, four out of twelve cabinet ministers were women.[56] When Aristide returned to power in 1994, he established a Ministry on the Status and Rights of Women.

Unfortunately, these examples of women participating politically at the highest levels have not been a permanent gain of the women's struggle. In 1994, only 4 percent of the seats within the legislative body were occupied by women, even though Haiti is one of the few countries in Latin America and the Caribbean where more than 25 percent of directors and senior managers are women.[57]

Women's Rights

Even the new ministry, although still in operation, has done little to improve the status of women. In the penal code, there is still a section that allows a man the right to kill a woman if she has committed adultery. Legal procedures regarding rape require that a woman obtain a medical certificate from a state hospital to prove that a rape has occurred.[58]

Overall, women's rights also suffer from the general lack of individual rights within Haiti. Historically, the legal system has been either too corrupt or too weak to protect the rights of the individual. The new constitution of 1987, which guarantees people's rights, is rarely enforced due to the lack of a well-established judicial system. The system suffers from a shortage of trained lawyers and competent judges. Those detained by the police have little hope of a speedy trial, and bribery among local officials remains a problem. Despite Haiti's written protection of human rights, its record in practice remains poor. Haitian women and men lack confidence in the ability of the law-enforcement system to assist them or of the legal system to protect them.

Feminist Movements

The political scene in Haiti has undergone some fundamental changes since 1980 with the emergence of many women's organizations and social groups. Women in grassroots movements organized food riots and school stoppages that led to the overthrow of the Duvalier regime in 1986. By this time, women, particularly in rural areas, had integrated religious, community-based, cultural, and peasant organizations such as Tet Kole (Put Our Heads to Work), Tet Ansanm (Let's Unite Our Heads), and the Papaye Peasant Movement (MPP).[59]

By 1990, there was a proliferation of women's groups in Haiti ranging from traditional philanthropic groups to workers' organizations. These groups, under the leadership of middle-class women, have tended to focus on issues such as health care and education. Other groups, such as Kay Fanm, have focused on survival issues and have worked for economic and social change. In March 1993, women's organizations were even able to organize the first Haitian conference on Violence against Gender in spite of the state of siege that had been imposed at that time by the military regime.[60] Many of these groups had high rates of participation from diaspora women who had resided at one time outside Haiti and had returned with lessons learned from the feminist movements in the United States and Canada.[61]

Military Service

The Haitian armed forces, once used as the henchmen for corrupt dictators, were sharply reduced in size and virtually disbanded following the return of the democratically elected government of Aristide in 1994. In their place, a new police force, the Haitian National Police, was created under the auspices of the United Nations with training by the U.S. Justice Department. Many of the new police are former members of the military. The current size of this civilian police force is 6,000. There is no indication of a female presence in either the armed forces or the police.

RELIGION AND SPIRITUALITY

Haitians are a religious people. The predominant religion is Roman Catholicism. Approximately 80 percent of the population is Catholic. During Haiti's colonization, Roman Catholicism was imposed on all inhabitants of the island. African slaves, who were brought over to replace the indigenous people who had been killed or worked to death, were forcibly baptized into the Catholic Church. Throughout the Spanish and French colonial period, Roman Catholicism continued to be the state religion.

Protestant groups were not allowed into the country until after Haiti's independence in 1804. Today they make up about 10 percent of the religious population. The first Protestant groups in Haiti were the Wesleyan, Anglican, African Methodist Episcopal, and Baptist Churches.[62] Since the 1950s, there has also been an influx of evangelical sects as well as the Jehovah's Witnesses, the Mormons, and the Baha'is. The evangelical Protestant missionaries have converted a small but growing percentage of Haitians to the denominations they represent.

Most Haitians, however, regardless of their church affiliation, are believers in or practitioners of Vodou. Vodou has its origins in African ethnic religion and includes the worship of ancestors. During Haiti's colonial period, French slaveholders tried unsuccessfully to stamp it out. An "anti-superstition" campaign in the 1940s tried again to repress Vodou practitioners, as did a post-Duvalier wave of attacks. But Vodou has continued to thrive and has been seen throughout Haiti's history as a religion of rebellion.

Since Vodou also recognizes a supreme god, Haitians tend to see no conflict in simultaneously practicing Vodou and adhering to a Christian faith. Elements of Christian teachings are frequently mixed with the traditions of the ancestors. Vodou provides everyday strength to the poor, who see its practice as providing them with spiritual assistance.

Women's Roles

Within the Christian churches, women's role is one of subordination. The Roman Catholic Church is run by men, although it is women who fill the pews. This imbalance of power has been carried over from centuries of male domination. Within the Protestant churches in Haiti, a few denominations accept the ordination of women, but most also follow the pattern of having men in the highest positions of leadership.

The practice of Vodou has been much more democratic. A female priestess (*manbo*), practices on an equal basis with any male priest (*oungan*). A person's leadership standing within Vodou is based only on the amount of faith that people have in him or her. The number of women heading Vodou temples has increased in recent years, particularly in urban areas.[63] This is due, in part, to the fact that as more and more Haitians move to urban areas in search of work, women generally fare better than men. Women's small-scale marketing skills and the preference for female labor in assembly factory work have given them more earning power. Thus women in the cities have found themselves as heads of their own houses. This increased autonomy and access to money have made it possible for them to become heads of Vodou "families" or congregations.

Rituals and Religious Practices

Vodou temples run by men tend to mimic a patriarchal family structure. The authority of the priest is absolute, and many *oungan* are notorious for fathering many children.[64] The *oungan* creates a father role that he extends to all those who serve the spirits under his tutelage.

A *manbo* who leads a temple is no more democratic in her relationship with those who serve in her house, but a priestess tends to have more flexibility in her relationships with her followers and is less hierarchical. Women-headed temples have also incorporated social functions, such as serving as daycare centers for working women.

Religious Law

Within the Roman Catholic Church, religious law prohibits the ordination of women as priests. Haitian women thus often turn to Vodou to help them deal with issues, such as domestic problems, that women feel celibate men may not understand. Some feel that Vodou is more closely in touch with the experience of women's lives.

The Roman Catholic Church's prohibition of birth control is also an area where religious belief has a great impact on women. Although women and men may wish to limit family size due to extremely limited economic resources, the prevailing sentiment instilled by the Roman Catholic Church is that the determination of family size should be left to God's will. The use of contraception is strongly discouraged, and access to birth-control methods is severely limited due to the fact that many health clinics are financed in whole or in part by the Roman Catholic Church. These facilities are prohibited from dispensing birth control.

VIOLENCE

Haitian women have long suffered from the effects of domestic, sexual, and political abuse. However, violence against women is not taken seriously by many Haitians, even women. In 1997, an International Tribunal against Violence against Women in Haiti was held. Recommendations from that meeting on how Haiti could work to eliminate violence against women included educating Haitians to consider rape a crime, not an act that brings disrespect to the victims; educating judges on violence against women and emphasizing that these acts require swift judicial remedies; and deploying specialized police units to handle cases of violence against women, as well as providing training to all police on how to handle complaints of sexual and domestic abuse.[65]

Domestic Violence

Domestic violence, both physical and psychological, is a major problem in Haiti. One study of Haitian women living in Cité Soleil, an urban slum area within the capital of Port-au-Prince, reported a 100 percent incidence of battery among the women over a ten-year period. Another study found that 70 percent of Haitian women have suffered physical assault by a domestic partner at some point in their lives.[66] The vast majority of the perpetrators are spouses or male partners. This violence is not "related to level of education, religious beliefs, or economic or marital status, but is prevalent in all strata of Haitian society." Most men consider domestic violence "strictly a family matter and [attempt] to justify such violence in cases where women show disrespect or disobedience to their partners."

There is no special domestic violence legislation in Haiti, and there are inadequate legal guarantees to combat violence against women. Many women never report being battered because they believe that it will only lead to more violence and social censure. Marital rape is not illegal. It is noted that "laws governing divorce and adultery are discriminatory against women, always assigning women the burden of proof."[67]

The legal system also discriminates against women in its view of adultery. A husband is legally allowed to murder his wife if he catches her at home in the act of adultery. The law does not, however, excuse a wife who murders her husband upon discovering him involved in adulterous activity.

Rape/Sexual Assault

Rape in Haiti has become an increasingly frequent phenomenon. A 1995 survey by the Haitian Center for Research and Action for the Promotion of Women reported that 37 percent of women had been raped or otherwise sexually assaulted or knew someone else who had been.[68] Gang members, "zenglendos," will break into houses and rape and beat women. Sexual harassment in the workplace, whether it be of domestic workers, assembly-plant employees, or even state office workers, continues to be a common occurrence. The rape and sexual harassment of female students in schools is also a serious social issue.

Rape is a crime but is considered a crime against morals not serious enough to merit a trial by jury. A virgin who is raped has more of a case than a nonvirgin in the eyes of the court system.

Most rape victims end up settling for money instead of a court case. The settlement may include forcing the victim to marry her attacker. It has been noted that "if a girl is raped by her teacher, it is generally expected that the rapist will marry the victim and no criminal case is brought against the perpetrator."[69] Adding insult to injury, a pregnant girl would be expelled from school.

Trafficking in Women and Children

Due to the subsistence level of agriculture within the country, Haiti does not suffer from the problem of slave labor being forced to work on agricultural plantations, as has been reported in other developing nations. There have been reports, however, of Haitians being forced to work as virtual slaves on sugar plantations in the neighboring Dominican Republic.

The problem within Haiti that most often leads to abuse of children and young women is the practice of rural families sending their young children to work as domestics for wealthier urban families. Rural parents frequently see this as a possibility to provide a better life for their children with the hope that the family who takes their child will provide the child with an education and pay for his or her schooling. These children, called restaveks (from the French *rester avec*, to stay with), are at high risk for abuse. Young female domestic workers are also at risk for violence and sexual abuse from male employers and often are impregnated. Young girls and boys, often far from home in the workplace, are also exploited for their labor in abusive situations.

War and Military Repression

Throughout its history, violence and political repression have gone hand in hand with Haiti's political turmoil. The Duvalier dictatorships resulted in horrendous manifestations of political violence, including political rape. During the period of the military dictatorship from 1991 to 1994 that followed the coup d'état against the democratically elected presidency of Jean-Bertrand Aristide, Haitian women continued to suffer from "structural violence." Under the military coup regime led by General Raoul Cédras, women, for the first time in Haiti's history, became explicit targets of systematic political violence. Opponents of the coup d'état were targets of rape and intimidation. An independent National Commission on Truth and Justice characterized rape as a "politically orchestrated campaign conducted in the context of intimidation and savage repression against opposition to the State."[70]

With the return of the democratically elected government of Jean-Bertrand Aristide, the regime of terror came to an end, although violence against women is still used as a political tactic by the foes of the democratic movement. Efforts in Haiti are currently under way to seek justice for the coup victims and to prosecute the perpetrators of these crimes.

OUTLOOK FOR THE TWENTY-FIRST CENTURY

Although Haitian women face many struggles, few, if any, of their problems are unique to Haiti. Poverty, discrimination, and violence are present in all countries, and their elimination requires a worldwide effort. Haitian women have remained steadfast in their determination to better their lives and that of their families. Without a significant improvement in the dire economic situation facing their country, the prospects for any substantial improvement in the lives of Haitian women remain bleak.

NOTES

1. Central Intelligence Agency, *The World Factbook*, 2000.

2. Pan-American Health Organization, *Country Immunization Profile: Haiti* (Washington, DC: World Health Organization, 2001), 3; Pan-American Health Or-

ganization, *Health in the Americas* (Washington, DC: Pan-American Health Organization), 337.

3. Beate Schmidt. "Expanding the 'Generative Word' Process: Women's Iron Will, Haiti," *Voices Rising* 4(1) (January–February 1990): 20.

4. *The Europa Year Book* (London: Europa Publications, 2002), 1, 985.

5. "Close-up: The Education Situation," *Haiti Info* 5(21) (1997): 3.

6. Ibid., 4.

7. CountryWatch.com, *Haiti*, 2001, www.countrywatch.com.

8. Pan-American Health Organization, 2001, http://www.upinfo.com/country-guide-study/haiti/index.html.

9. "Women's Groups Mark March 8," *Haiti Info* 6(2) (1998): 2.

10. Women in Development Network, *2001 Statistics—Americas*, http://www.focusintl.com/statr4a.htm.

11. Women in Development Network, 2001.

12. United Nations Statistics Division, *The World's Women 2000: Trends and Statistics*, 2001, 5.D, http://www.unstats.un.org/unsd/databases.html.

13. *The Europa Year Book* (London: Europa Publications, 2002), 1, 984.

14. CountryWatch.com, 2001.

15. "Ti Machann 'Pay the Price,'" *Haiti Info* 4(11) (1996): 1.

16. United Nations Statistics Division, *The World's Women 2000: Trends and Statistics*, 2001, 2.B, http://www.unstats.un.org/unsd/databases.html.

17. "Ti Machann," 1996, 1.

18. "World of Labor: People's Tribunal Denounces Multinationals," *Haiti Info* 6(6) (1998): 2.

19. "Commemorations of May 1," *Haiti Info* 6(5) (1998): 1–2.

20. United Nations Statistics Division, *The World's Women 2000: Trends and Statistics*, 2001, 5.C, http://www.unstats.un.org/unsd/databases.html.

21. Pan-American Health Organization, *Health in the Americas* (Washington, DC: Pan-American Health Organization, 2002), 340.

22. Ibid.

23. Ira Paul Lowenthal, "'Marriage Is 20, Children Are 21': The Cultural Construction of Conjugality and the Family in Rural Haiti" (Ph.D. diss., Johns Hopkins University), 1987, 62.

24. Ibid., 63.

25. Beverly Bell, *Walking on Fire: Haitian Women's Stories of Survival and Resistance* (Ithaca, NY: Cornell University Press, 2001), 21.

26. Lowenthal, 1987, 167.

27. Bell, 2001, 22.

28. Carolle Charles, "Gender Politics in Contemporary Haiti: The Duvalierist State, Transnationalism, and the Emergence of a New Feminism (1980–1990)," *Feminist Studies* 21(1) (1995): 149.

29. CountryWatch.com, 2001.

30. "Les Cayes: Mobilization for Water," *Haiti Info* 6(5) (1998): 4.

31. Robin B. Devin and Pamela I. Erickson, "The Influence of Male Care Givers on Child Health in Rural Haiti," *Social Science and Medicine* 43(4) (1996): 479–488.

32. Carolle Charles, "Feminist Action and Research in Haiti," *Caribbean Studies* 28 (1995): 66.

33. Barbara De Zalduondo and Jean Maxius Bernard, "Meanings and Consequences of Sexual-Economic Exchange: Gender, Poverty, and Sexual Risk Behavior," in *Conceiving Sexuality: Approaches to Sex Research in a Postmodern World*, ed. Richard G. Parker and John H. Gagnon (New York: Routledge, 1995), 162.

34. Ibid., 173.

35. Lowenthal, 1987, 302.

36. United Nations Statistics Division, *The World's Women 2000: Trends and Statistics*, 2001, 2.B, http://www.unstats.org/unsd/databases.html.

37. United Nations Statistics Division, *The World's Women 2000: Trends and Statistics*, 2001, http://www.unstats.org/unsd/databases.html.

38. Gisele Maynard-Tucker, "Haiti: Unions, Fertility, and the Quest for Survival," *Social Science and Medicine* 43(9) (1996): 1380.

39. Ibid., 1379.

40. United Nations Statistics Division, *The World's Women 2000: Trends and Statistics*, 2001, 2.B, http://www.unstats.org/unsd/databases.html.

41. M. Catherine Maternowska, "A Clinic in Conflict: A Political Economy Case Study of Family Planning in Haiti," in *Contraception across Cultures: Technologies, Choices, Constraints*, ed. A. Russell, E.J. Sobo, and M.S. Thompson (Oxford: Berg, 2000), 103–26.

42. Pan-American Health Organization, *Health in the Americas* (Washington, DC: Pan-American Health Organization, 2002), 190.

43. Alan Guttmacher Institute, "In Haiti, More Than Half of All Births Are Either Unwanted or Mistimed," *International Family Planning Perspectives* 22(4) (1996): 181–82.

44. Pan-American Health Organization, 2001.

45. United Nations Statistics Division, *The World's Women 2000: Trends and Statistics*, 2001, 3.B, http://www.unstats.org/unsd/databases.html.

46. CountryWatch.com, 2001.

47. United Nations Economic and Social Council, *Integration of the Human Rights of Women and the Gender Perspective: Violence against Women: Report of the Special Rapporteur on Violence against Women, Its Causes and Consequences, Ms. Radhika Coomaraswamy, Submitted in Accordance with Commission on Human Rights Resolution 1997/44: Addendum: Report on the Mission to Haiti* (2000), 22.

48. United Nations Statistics Division, *The World's Women 2000: Trends and Statistics*, 2001, 3.B, http://www.unstats.org/unsd/databases.html.

49. Priscilla R. Ulin, Michel Cayemittes, and Elisabeth Metellus, *Haitian Women's Role in Sexual Decision-Making: The Gap between AIDS Knowledge and Behavior Change*, www.fhi.org/en/fp/fpother/haitiwom/haitiexec.html.

50. Pan-American Health Organization, *Health in the Americas* (Washington, DC: Pan-American Health Organization, 2002), 337–38.

51. Ibid., 343.

52. Ibid., 347.

53. Charles, "Gender Politics," 1995, 146.

54. Ibid., 138.

55. Women in Development Network, 2001.

56. Marie M.B. Racine, *Like the Dew That Waters the Grass: Words from Haitian Women* (Washington, DC: EPICA, 1999), 130.

57. Women in Development Network, 2001.

58. Racine, 1999, 141.

59. Charles, "Gender Politics," 1995, 154.

60. Ibid., 156.

61. Ibid., 152.

62. Racine, 1999, 159.

63. Karen McCarthy Brown, "The Power to Heal: Reflections on Women, Relig-

ion, and Medicine," in *Shaping New Vision: Gender and Values in American Culture*, ed. Clarissa W. Atkinson, Constance H. Buchanan, and Margaret R. Miles (Ann Arbor: UMI Research Press, 1987), 125.

64. Ibid., 126.
65. Ismene Zarifis, "Haitian Women Speak Out against Violence," *Haiti Insight Online* 8(1) (1997), www.nchr.org/insight/speakout.htm.
66. Bell, 2001, 20–21.
67. www.unhchr.ch.
68. Bell, 2001, 21.
69. www.unhchr.ch.
70. Bell, 2001, 21.

RESOURCE GUIDE

Suggested Reading

Adesky, Anne-Chirstine d'. *Under the Bone*. New York: Farrar, Straus and Giroux, 1994. This novel by a journalist of French and Haitian descent explores post-Duvalier Haiti by focusing on a falsely arrested Haitian woman and a female American human rights observer.

Bell, Beverly. *Walking on Fire: Haitian Women's Stories of Survival and Resistance*. Ithaca, NY: Cornell University Press, 2001. Thirty-eight contemporary Haitian women tell their histories in their own words.

Danticat, Edwidge. *Breath, Eyes, Memory*. New York: Random House, 1998. The first novel by a noted Haitian author explores the struggles of three Haitian women.

Farmer, Paul. *The Uses of Haiti*. Monroe, ME: Common Courage Press, 1994. Explores the uses that Haiti has served for the United States and the international community.

Gibbons, Elizabeth D. *Sanctions in Haiti: Human Rights and Democracy under Assault*. Westport, CT: Praeger, 1999. Comprehensive study of the humanitarian impact of the sanctions in Haiti by a former head of UNICEF's office in Port-au-Prince.

North American Congress on Latin America, ed. *Haiti: Dangerous Crossroads*. Boston: South End Press, 1995. A collection of articles covering the political history of Haiti and U.S. political and economic policy toward Haiti.

Racine, Marie M.B. *Like the Dew That Waters the Grass: Words from Haitian Women*. Washington, DC: EPICA, 1999. A collection of interviews that articulates the daily struggle of contemporary Haitian women from all walks of life.

Videos/Films

Bitter Cane. 1983. Haiti Films. Exposé of the Haitian economic system.

Black Dawn. 1978. Icarus Films. An animated film that uses Haitian art to depict the history of Haiti from slavery to independence.

Divine Horsemen. 1951. Mystic Five Video. A classic film on Haitian Vodou and possession adapted from a book by Maya Deren.

Haiti Dreams of Democracy. 1987. Directed by Jonathan Demme. Cinema Guild. Reports on the political fervor in post-Duvalier Haiti.

Web Sites

Washington Office on Haiti, www.igc.apc.org.
Organization that supports the Haitian people's grassroots struggle for democracy, human rights, and self-determined development.

Women in Development Network, Statistics—Americas, www.focusintl.com/statr4a.htm.
Compiles data on health, population, education, labor, family statistics, and statistics related to women in positions of power.

Organizations

Enfofanm
3, bis Rue Sapotille, Pacot
Port-au-Prince, Haiti
Phone: 509-245-1930 or 245-3629

Enfofanm (the National and International Center for Documentation and Information on Women in Haiti) organizes documentation on women and publishes *Ayiti Fanm*.

Kay Fanm
No. 11 rue Armand Holly
Port-au-Prince, Haiti
Phone: 509-245-4221 or 245-5174

A Haitian feminist organization dedicated to fighting systemic discrimination against women.

Lig Pouvwa Fanm
30 Rue Marcelin
Port-au-Prince, Haiti
Phone: 509-245-3035
Fax: 509-245-8200

The League for Women's Empowerment focuses on civic education and encouraging political participation among Haitian women.

Solidarité Fanm Ayisyen
B.P. 1638
Port-au-Prince, Haiti
Phone: 509-249-2242 or 246-3496
Fax: 509-245-8477
Email: marfrantz@hotmail.com

Haitian Women in Solidarity is a feminist group of peasants, grassroots, and professional women interested in consciousness-raising, training, education, and health care.

SELECTED BIBLIOGRAPHY

Alan Guttmacher Institute. "In Haiti, More Than Half of All Births Are Either Unwanted or Mistimed." *International Family Planning Perspectives* 22(4) (1996): 181–82.

Bell, Beverly. *Walking on Fire: Haitian Women's Stories of Survival and Resistance*. Ithaca, NY: Cornell University Press, 2001.

Brown, Karen McCarthy. "The Power to Heal: Reflections on Women, Religion, and Medicine." In *Shaping New Vision: Gender and Values in American Culture*, ed. Clarissa W. Atkinson, Constance H. Buchanan, and Margaret R. Miles, 123–41. Ann Arbor: UMI Research Press, 1987.

Charles, Carolle. "Feminist Action and Research in Haiti." *Caribbean Studies* 28 (1995): 61–75.

———. "Gender Politics in Contemporary Haiti: The Duvalierist State, Transnationalism, and the Emergence of a New Feminism (1980–1990)." *Feminist Studies* 21(1) (1995): 135–64.

"Close-up: The Education Situation." *Haiti Info* 5(21) (1997): 3–4.

"Commemorations of May 1." *Haiti Info* 6(5) (1998): 1–2.

CountryWatch.com. *Haiti*. 2001. www.countrywatch.com.

Devin, Robin B., and Pamela I. Erickson. "The Influence of Male Care Givers on Child Health in Rural Haiti." *Social Science and Medicine* 43(4) (1996): 479–88.

De Zalduondo, Barbara, and Jean Maxius Bernard. "Meanings and Consequences of Sexual-Economic Exchange: Gender, Poverty, and Sexual Risk Behavior." In *Conceiving Sexuality: Approaches to Sex Research in a Postmodern World*, ed. Richard G. Parker and John H. Gagnon, 157–80. New York: Routledge, 1995.

"Les Cayes: Mobilization for Water." *Haiti Info* 6(5) (1998): 4.

Lowenthal, Ira Paul. " 'Marriage Is 20, Children Are 21': The Cultural Construction of Conjugality and the Family in Rural Haiti." Ph.D. diss., Johns Hopkins University, 1987.

Maternowska, M. Catherine. "A Clinic in Conflict: A Political Economy Case Study of Family Planning in Haiti." In *Contraception across Cultures: Technologies, Choices, Constraints*, ed. A. Russell, E.J. Sobo, and M.S. Thompson, 103–26. Oxford: Berg, 2000.

Maynard-Tucker, Gisele. "Haiti: Unions, Fertility, and the Quest for Survival." *Social Science and Medicine* 43(9) (1994): 1379–87.

Pan-American Health Organization. *Country Immunization Profile: Haiti*. Washington, DC: World Health Organization, 2001.

Racine, Marie M.B. *Like the Dew That Waters the Grass: Words from Haitian Women*. Washington, DC: EPICA, 1999.

"Ti Machann 'Pay the Price.' " *Haiti Info* 4(11) (1996): 1, 3.

Ulin, Priscilla R., Michel Cayemittes, and Elisabeth Metellus. *Haitian Women's Role in Sexual Decision-Making: The Gap between AIDS Knowledge and Behavior Change*. 1993. www.fhi.org/en/fp/fpother/haitiwom/haitiexec.html.

United Nations Economic and Social Council. *Integration of the Human Rights of Women and the Gender Perspective: Violence against Women: Report of the Special Rapporteur on Violence against Women, Its Causes and Consequences, Ms. Radhika Coomaraswamy, Submitted in Accordance with Commission on Human Rights Resolution 1997/44: Addendum: Report on the Mission to Haiti*. 2000.

United Nations Statistics Division. *The World's Women 2000: Trends and Statistics.* 2001. www.un.org/Depts/unsd/ww2000.

Women in Development Network. *Statistics: Latin America and Caribbean.* 2001. www.focusintl.com/statr4a.htm.

"Women's Groups Mark March 8." *Haiti Info* 6(2) (1998): 2.

"World of Labor: People's Tribunal Denounces Multinationals." *Haiti Info* 6(6) (1998): 2.

Zarifis, Ismene. "Haitian Women Speak Out against Violence." *Haiti Insight Online* 8(1) (1997). www.nchr.org/insight/speakout.htm.

8

JAMAICA

Barbara Bailey

PROFILE OF JAMAICA

Jamaica, the largest of the English-speaking islands in the Caribbean, is situated just 90 miles south of the Spanish-speaking island of Cuba, 100 miles west of French-speaking Haiti, which forms part of the island originally known as Hispaniola, and 579 miles south of Miami, Florida.[1] Jamaica covers a total area of 4,244 square miles, has a maximum length of 146 miles, and is 51 miles wide at its widest point. Its highest summit, in the Blue Mountains in the east of the island, reaches an elevation of 6,189 feet above sea level.

The earliest colonizers were the Spaniards, who first arrived in 1494 but did not actually occupy the country until 1509. It is estimated that when the Spaniards arrived, there were about 60,000 Arawak Indians inhabiting the island, but according to the Spanish records, this indigenous population was totally exterminated well before the arrival of the British in 1655. Under the British, large sugar estates were established, supported by African slave labor. After the abolition of slavery in 1834, there was a need for laborers to maintain the plantations, and the first migrants arrived from India in 1842. In 1854, Chinese labor was introduced, and in 1869, indentured service was established that attracted many "East Indians" from India.

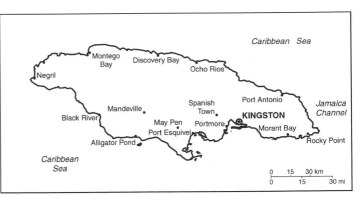

Jamaica remained a British colony until August 1962, when it gained independence within the British Commonwealth with a governor general who represents the queen as head of state. The government is a parliamentary democracy in which the majority party forms the government, and the minority party is the opposition. The term of office for a government is five years, with the majority party having the right to call elections before the expiry of its term of office. The Parliament consists of the House of Representatives and the Senate. The members of the former are elected, while the members of the latter are appointed by the governor general on the recommendation of the prime minister and the leader of the opposition.

In December 2001, the population was estimated at 2,621,100, with females accounting for 50.1 percent.[2] Women of reproductive age (fifteen to forty-nine years) totaled 626,300, and the crude birth rate was 21.2 per 1,000 population. The general fertility rate, which relates births to the actual number of women in the reproductive age group of fifteen to forty-nine years, was 79.4 per 1,000 women in this age group in 2001. The total fertility rate, or the average number of children born alive to a woman during her lifetime, was estimated at approximately 2.8 in 1997.

The infant mortality rate was estimated at 24.5 per 1,000 live births in 1993, and in 1998, the maternal mortality rate was estimated at 111 per 100,000. Life expectancy is estimated to be approximately seventy-two years for both sexes.

OVERVIEW OF WOMEN'S ISSUES

In spite of advancement on many social indicators, women in Jamaica generally continue to be in a subordinate position compared to men in the social, economic, and political spheres. Although females predominate at the higher levels of the education system, most work at the lowest-level jobs, earn less money than men, are unemployed more, are poorer, and are underrepresented in decision-making positions of social and political institutions. Gender-based violence is a persistent problem, and increasing numbers of incidents of domestic violence, rape, and incest, which may be due to improved rates of reporting, suggest that women's right to a life free of violence is constantly under threat.

EDUCATION

Opportunities

Women in Jamaica have, on average, more education than men. In 1997, a Jamaican woman had, on average, 9.1 years of education, compared to 8.5 years of schooling for a Jamaican man. Similarly, on average, a Jamaican male worker had 8.4 years of education, compared to 8.9 years for a Jamaican woman.[3]

Sex differentials in overall performance in favor of females are evident at all levels of the education system. In the 2001 Grade Six Achievement Test, administered to students eleven or more years old at the end of the primary cycle, girls outperformed boys in all five areas: mathematics, science, social studies, language arts, and communication tasks.[4] At the secondary level, sex segregation of the curriculum is still evident, with girls predominantly obtaining better

Local school girls in Ocho Rios. Photo © TRIP/H. Sayer.

grades in the humanities and domestic and business crafts, and boys in science-based and technical crafts.

Data for the June sitting of the 2000 Caribbean Examinations Council examinations, the most sought-after secondary-level school-leaving certificate, indicate that a higher percentage of girls than boys obtained Grades 1, 2, and 3 passes in ten of seventeen academic subjects offered by the council. A larger percentage of boys, however, obtained passes at this level in five of the nine science-based subjects, including mathematics, and girls in six of the eight humanities subjects.[5] At the Mona Campus of the University of the West Indies, the foremost tertiary institution in the island, for the academic year 2000/2001, 74.8 percent of all degrees were awarded to women.[6]

The numerical dominance of women compared to men, both in terms of participation and overall performance at the higher levels of the education system in Jamaica, has gained wide popular attention and has been used to fuel a "male marginalization" thesis. The quantitative gains that women have made in the educational arena have been argued to only obfuscate more essential issues of quality and the ways in which cultural biases and stereotypes and a sexual division of labor, which reinforce women's subordinate sociocultural position, are reproduced through the educational process through both explicit and implicit practices.[7]

Beyond school, females have less of a competitive advantage than their male counterparts. Women's better education and their positioning in certain fields of study can be seen as only serving to ensure that accepted gender codes and stereotypes are well assimilated and accommodated in their mental schema and psyche. This in turn governs attitudes and behaviors and ensures that the cycle of male domination and female subordination is perpetuated and remains unchallenged.

Literacy

According to the *Jamaica Human Development Report 2000*, 81 percent of women were literate, compared to 69 percent of men.[8]

EMPLOYMENT AND ECONOMICS

Job/Career Opportunities

Since the 1970s, the number of women in the Jamaican labor force has steadily increased. However, since 1995, the participation rate, that is, the percentage of the female working-age population aged fourteen years or older who are currently working, unemployed, or looking for work, has fallen from 41.8 percent to 37.2 percent in 2000. In that same year, the employment rate was 77.6 percent for women and 89.9 percent for men, while women had a higher unemployment rate (22.4 percent) than men (10.2 percent). As a result, the job-seeking rate for women was higher (11.7 percent) than for men (5.6 percent).[9]

Occupational segregation still persists, and although Jamaica is unique compared to other developing countries in having more women than men in the top occupational category, the majority are positioned in the low-paying, low-status sectors of the market. In the last quarter of 2000, women made up 57.7 percent of all persons in the "professionals, senior officials, and technicians" category, mainly because of the influence exerted on this sex distribution by traditionally female-dominated professions such as teaching and nursing, a pattern in keeping with tertiary-level educational output. Although women constituted the larger share in this top category, the glass ceiling obstructs the path of upwardly mobile women, breaking to admit only some.[10]

This observation is confirmed by data supplied in the *Jamaica Human Development Report 2000* that show that for thirty-one companies listed on the Jamaica Stock Exchange, all the chairpersons were male, and in only one case was there a female managing director. Of the 316 persons serving on these boards, 92 percent were male. The same was true for special-interest groups such as the Private Sector Organization of Jamaica and the Jamaica Employers Federation, where, for the five groups for which data were available, in no instance did women make up more than 15 percent of the membership of boards. The situation was no better in statutory organizations (organizations that are state-owned but with a fair degree of autonomy in management and operations); in six such organizations, women made up only 28 percent of the total board membership.[11]

Not only at the managerial level, however, do women face discrimination. They are generally at a greater disadvantage than their male counterparts in all areas of the labor market. Statistics for 2000 show that as a result of entrenched occupational sex segregation, the majority of females were positioned in "elementary occupations" (22.0 percent) and in the categories of service workers and shop and market sales (23.8 percent). Thus almost half (45.8 percent) of all females in the employed labor force were concentrated in the low-wage sectors.[12] The sectors in which women are concentrated are paid, for the most part, the minimum wage legislated by the government. As a result, there is a disparity in wage levels, with women's mean income being lower than that of men. Job segregation therefore translates into lower earnings for women.

In recent years, the precarious position of women in the labor market has been further exacerbated by the impact of globalization on small state economies. Perhaps the most visible impact in Jamaica has been the displacement of workers in both the private and public sectors as a result of retrenchments aimed at cutting costs and increasing efficiency to improve competitiveness in the global marketplace. Several mergers in the debt-riddled financial sector and extensive privatization and outsourcing of services in the public sector have resulted in downsizing and layoff of workers.

Data from quarterly labor-force surveys for Jamaica indicate that in 1998, on average, approximately 20,000 persons were made redundant. In 1999, the figure increased to 24,100, a 20.5 percent increase, while in 2000 there was a slight decrease to 22,325 persons, a 7.4 percent decline. Not surprisingly, in all instances, females were the worst hit and made up 68 percent of all redundancies in 1998, 62 percent in 1999, and 66.9 percent in 2000.[13]

The total employed labor force therefore declined in each of these three years due not only to redundancies but also to resignations, dismissals, retirements, completions of jobs, and failed businesses, and females were more affected than males. In fact, in 2000, although there was an overall decline, the number of employed males actually increased in three of the four quarters, whereas the number of females declined in all four quarters.

As a result of the contraction of the employed labor force, "own-account" businesses, operated by a single self-employed individual, have been increasing. A new trend, however, is the entry of professionals into this sector, setting up consultancies and home-based businesses. The percentage of professionals, senior officials, and technicians in self-employment more than tripled between 1991 and 1998, from 10.8 percent in 1991 to 37.1 percent in 1998. However, in spite of the potential of the informal sector to absorb excess labor, it remains a volatile area, particularly in the current financial climate. In 1998, just under 10,000 persons, of whom 74 percent were female, were unemployed because of a failed business. In 1999, the figure was just over 10,000 persons, of whom 76 percent were women. In 2000, the figure had risen to 12,900, of whom 8,400 (65.1 percent) were women.[14]

In addition to disparities in the control and ownership of economic resources, women in Jamaica have historically shouldered a disproportionately large share of the economic and social burden of caring for children, the elderly, and the community. These roles, however, are not market oriented and do not appear in national income statistics but make an important contribution to national development.[15] These unpaid activities were seen to be more numerous in low-income households where the focus of women's activities is on meeting the basic needs of the family.[16] Caribbean feminist economists have therefore agitated for counting unwaged work in national accounts, and this has been agreed on at several levels of the Caribbean Community.

Higher education has therefore not translated into income equality or economic independence for Jamaican women. Sex-disaggregated unemployment figures also suggest that women have had difficulties translating education into labor-market opportunities. For example, unemployment for women with a secondary education is just under 16 percent, compared to 8 percent for men with a secondary education.[17] In 2000, 7.3 percent of women in Jamaica's employed labor force had professional training with degrees or diplomas, whereas this was the case for only 5.6 percent of the men. Similarly, 7.6 percent of women had vocational training with certificates, whereas this was the case for only 3.3 percent of the men.[18] In view of these differences and given that females experience higher levels of unemployment, it can be concluded that men with lower levels of education obtain jobs more easily than their female counterparts. For this reason, it has been noted that "females require higher education to break the pattern that exists in the labour market whereby males with lower levels of education and qualifications can attract relatively good quality employment. For females, the labour market is not as generous."[19]

Pay

In 1997, the gender wage gap was estimated to be 17 percent in favor of males.[20] In 2002, the national minimum wage was increased by 50 percent from JA$1,200 to JA$1,800 per week, or U.S.$25.53 to U.S.$38.30 per week at the exchange rate of JA$47 to U.S.$1. In a study of minimum-wage earners, 27 percent of domestic workers were found to live below the poverty line, and 70 percent of these workers, the majority of whom are female, stated that their income was inadequate to meet their living needs.[21] As a result, women have had to employ a range of survival strategies. According to the *Jamaica Human Development Report 2000*, "Women primarily use informal networks of friends and family from which reciprocal aid and mutual assistance can be obtained; transactional male-female relationships in which women depend on male partners for money and material things in exchange for sex, domestic chores and child bearing; traditional occupations such as working as domestics and garment factory workers, higglering and sidewalk vending."[22]

Working Conditions

Jamaica has a long history of organized labor, and there are a number of trade unions and staff associations that lobby for workers' rights. Organizations associated with professions dominated by women include the Nurses Association of Jamaica, the Jamaica Teachers Association, the Jamaica Household Workers Association, and the United Vendors Association.

Although the Ministry of Labour and Social Security conducts inspections of factories to ensure industrial safety (1,865 inspections in 2000), studies show that working conditions are not always in keeping with international standards. For example, a 1999 study of offshore data-service enterprises in Jamaica indicated that women, twenty-four years old on average, many of whom were new entrants to the labor force, made up about 90 percent of the workforce.[23] They therefore lacked awareness of their rights as workers, were ignorant of International Labor Organization safety standards, and did not understand the long-term effects on their health of working under poor conditions and the need for good posture and ergonomic equipment such as adjustable chairs, antiglare screens, and footrests.

Workers, however, have recourse to the Ministry of Labour and Social Security, which monitors labor relations and maintains a facility where workers may lodge complaints of breaches of legislation and regulations. In 2001, the complaints, in order of frequency, were in relation to termination and redundancy payments (Employment Act), the Holidays with Pay Act, the Minimum Wage Act, and the Maternity Leave Act. Female workers (59 percent) lodged more complaints than male workers.[24] An issue that has generated much discussion recently is the intention of the government to introduce flextime, which could benefit women. The Ministry of Labour and Social Security, the Jamaica Employers Federation, and several trade unions have considered this issue and its implications for the labor force.

Sexual Harassment

Legislation on sexual harassment has not yet been formulated. The Association of Women's Organisations of Jamaica (AWOJA) has called for a statute to be drafted and passed that would be without prejudice to criminal and/or civil actions and that would cover harassment in educational and health institutions, nursing and senior citizens' homes, the workplace, and any other institution or place of employment. The Bureau of Women's Affairs has supported this call and is lobbying for such a bill. In the interim, some workplaces have developed policies on sexual harassment, including the Mona Campus of the University of the West Indies.

AWOJA has also recommended that the practice of punishing a woman who chooses to leave her job rather than be subjected to sexual harassment by writing a vindictive or untruthful reference letter be dealt with legislatively to ensure that all such documents be given to the employee. In this way, a person's right to be given the opportunity to question and/or counter adverse statements would be protected.

Support for Mothers/Caretakers

Maternal Leave

Under the Maternity Leave Act, passed in 1976, women became eligible for twelve weeks of leave, eight of which are paid. Workplaces may, however, institute their own policies with additional leave. Under the 1952 Maternity Protection Convention, signed by the government of Jamaica in 2000, the minimum maternity leave would be extended from twelve to fourteen weeks, six weeks of which would be considered compulsory leave. This proposal is not yet in place, and there is no legislation with regard to paternity leave.

Daycare

At present, a draft Childcare and Protection Act that addresses issues of care and protection of children is currently being debated in Parliament, and a draft Policy and Standards Document to regulate the operations of early childhood institutions has been developed and is to be presented to the government for approval. Although some private-sector companies provide a daycare service at a nominal charge for their employees, daycare is offered primarily through privately operated institutions. These facilities cater to persons from the middle- and upper-income strata, while women from the lower socioeconomic groups depend on social capital networks and more informal arrangements with friends or family either for a small fee or for some mutual benefit. In extreme cases, older siblings may be kept out of school to supervise younger siblings.

Family and Medical Leave

Jamaican law allows for ten days of paid sick leave. Unions and staff associations, however, may negotiate additional leave for those workers who are formally organized, and some workplaces have their own policies with regard to leave. Most workers are allowed up to three sick days without a medical certificate. Once a doctor's certificate is submitted, most employers offer paid sick leave for a period of up to two weeks. Workers also have access to occasional days that can be taken to cover time needed for personal business or sudden illness of a child.

Inheritance and Property Rights

The Family Property (Rights of Spouses) Act 1999 has been submitted to Parliament. This act seeks to ensure the equitable distribution of property between spouses upon the dissolution of a marriage. It includes the recognition of common-law unions, that is, persons who are unmarried and cohabiting for not less than five years. Several interest groups have held discussions on this and submissions have been made to the Joint Select Committee of Parliament, but to date no final decision has been made.

Social/Government Programs

Sustainable Development

The Jamaica Sustainable Development Networking Programme was established in 1997 and launched in 1998 to facilitate sustainable-development information sharing among all sectors of society. The program is hosted by the University of the West Indies. Its focus is placed "primarily on the needs of community-based organizations (CBOs) in rural areas as well as farmers, women's groups, small businesses and entrepreneurs."[25] Among the issues covered are biodiversity, sustainable livelihood, community development, and development projects and assistance.

Welfare

The incidence of poverty decreased from 18.7 percent in 2000 to 16.8 percent in 2001. Poverty was most marked in rural areas. It is estimated that approximately 440,300 persons live below the poverty line and were unable to meet basic needs, estimated at JA$167,083 or U.S.$3,555 annually for a family of five.[26] Sex-disaggregated data on the incidence of poverty show that in 1997 males made up 50.3 percent and females 49.7 percent of the poor, but more female-headed households lived in poverty—15.0 percent, compared to 12.5 percent of male-headed households.[27]

In 1997, the male/female ratio of Jamaica's human poverty index (JHPI), a recalculated United Nations Development Programme HPI, was 1.7:1. The JHPI takes into account longevity, illiteracy, lack of access to safe water and health services, lack of security, the housing-quality index, and malnutrition. The difference between the index for males and females, however, is largely due to a higher illiteracy rate for males than for females.[28]

During 2001, the government of Jamaica continued to focus on improving the relevance and effectiveness of social services and welfare programs for vulnerable groups including women and children. Programs that would be of direct benefit to women included the following:

Expansion of wealth-creating opportunities for microentrepreneurs under a Micro Investment Development Agency, which financed a number of projects, 54.0 percent of which were owned by women. Beneficiaries were primarily in the age range eighteen to thirty-five.

A program for adolescent mothers' education and to improve employment potential among young women operated by the Women's Centre of Jamaica Foundation, which received approximately 70.0 percent of the allocation for women's welfare.

The Food Stamp Programme, which targets pregnant and lactating women, children less than six years old, single-member households, and elderly poor and incapacitated individuals.[29]

FAMILY AND SEXUALITY

Gender Roles

The sharp distinction between the female role of nurturer and the male role of provider is not evident in Jamaican society. In most families, women are engaged in waged work and also carry out the expected nurturing roles. In fact, a growing phenomenon is the number of households headed by a single female where women carry out both productive and social reproductive roles. In 2001, women headed 44.7 percent of all households surveyed.[30]

Along with the responsibility of being head of the household, many of these women also bear the burden of caring for the elderly and the sick as well as identifying additional resources for their children's education in light of decreased government spending on both health and education.[31] This involvement in waged and unwaged work has serious implications for women's physical and mental health, especially as their responsibility for social reproduction is intensified by the continuing contraction of vital social services. In instances where a domestic worker is employed to carry out some of the household work, a woman is hired. Domestic responsibility, in these instances, is simply shifted from one woman to another, for pay, and not to men.

Men's traditional gender role is that of breadwinner, provider, and protector of women and children, but these roles are often challenged and contested. In the Caribbean, masculinity is premised on sexual prowess with many female sexual partners and the fathering of several children. These gender beliefs have been seen to be often based on biblical assumptions that placed males as the head of the home, who are responsible for the care of women and children.[32] Increased economic instability, however, sometimes makes it impossible for men to fulfill these gender roles and results in increased frustration for men and tensions between men and women who both accept these notions of gender. As well, it is increasingly acknowledged that the home is often a site for oppression and resistance where acts of gender-based violence occur.

Marriage

The prevailing family forms in the Caribbean are visiting relationships known as "friending," common-law or consensual unions, and legal marriages. Visiting unions most commonly occur among the African lower class, and one partner, most often the man, visits the other for companionship and sexual intercourse. This may take place in the parental home with parental consent, and the man is expected to contribute to the woman's support and to that of children resulting from the union. Although fidelity is expected of women in these unions, in many cases the male engages in several visiting unions or may even be involved in a marital relationship. These unions often result in female-headed households with a number of children fathered by different men. Common-law unions, on the other hand, are more permanent residential, nonlegal, but stable, unions that involve cohabitation and the pooling of resources to support the family unit.[33]

Before the 1980s, these types of unions lacked any legal protection. Since the 1970s, legislation has been enacted to protect women and children in these relationships. In Jamaica, the Status of Children Act of 1976 removed all social and legal disadvantages from the children of visiting and common-law unions, and the term "illegitimate" was no longer applicable to children. In 1988, the Intestates Estate and Property Charges Act was amended to allow a surviving partner in a common-law union to be a beneficiary as long as both persons were single and had lived together for five years prior to the partner's death.[34]

In Jamaica, legal marriage is viewed as the ideal marital form and is very much a middle-class institution that is endorsed and encouraged by the church. The more common types of relationships are common-law and visiting unions, which can, however, progress from one type to another in succession until the status of a legal marriage is attained. In 2000, there were 23,704 registered marriages, or a mean of 9.1 per 1,000 population, decreasing from 29,155 marriages in 1999. The divorce rate has steadily decreased since 1996. In 2000, it was 4.7 per 100 marriages, or 4.3 per 10,000 mean population.[35]

Reproduction

Sex Education

Sex education is a part of the formal schools' curriculum starting at the primary level. The National Family Planning Board, the Ministry of Health, and a variety of nongovernmental organizations, including Youth NOW and the Women's Centre of Jamaica Foundation, also provide sex education in and out of school settings. The *Jamaica Reproductive Health Survey 1997* found that 73 percent of males and 75 percent of females aged fifteen to seventeen reported receiving sex education in school, 8 percent of males and 11 percent of females reported receiving this information both in and out of school, and 19 percent of males and 14 percent of females reported receiving no sex education.[36]

Contraception and Abortion

Contraception is available islandwide in both public and private institutions. The *Jamaica Reproductive Health Survey 1997* found that two-thirds of females in a union (marriage, common-law union, or visiting relationship) were using contraception. This figure is comparable to that of other advanced developing countries. The pill was the most common method of contraception at 21 percent, followed by the condom at 17 percent, tubal ligation at 12 percent, injectibles at 11 percent, and withdrawal at 3 percent. Abortion is illegal in Jamaica.[37]

The publicly operated National Family Planning Board and the Jamaica Family Planning Association, as well as the privately operated Personal Choice Programme have maintained their efforts to increase contraceptive use. While attendance at family-planning clinics fell in 2001, the number of new users as a percentage of total attendance increased. The number of new users under twenty years of age also increased over the previous year. As a means of protection against HIV/AIDS and other sexually transmitted infections, the dual method is encouraged, that is, the use of condoms with every other method.[38]

Teen Pregnancy

The birth rate of teens aged fifteen to nineteen was 95 per 1,000 teens in 1997, slightly higher than the average of 72 per 1,000 for the Caribbean as a whole.[39]

Attention to adolescent health and the impact of teenage pregnancy, sexually transmitted infections, and particularly HIV/AIDS, substance abuse, injury, and violence, are of paramount importance at this time in Jamaica. Data from the 2000[40] and 2001[41] Economic and Social Surveys support this concern. Information on adolescent health indicates that 25 percent of the total visits to antenatal clinics were within the ten to nineteen age group, an indication of the high level of pregnancies among teens.

This is supported by a survey of girls fourteen to eighteen years old who had dropped out of the formal school system.[42] The number one reason for school drop-out supplied by these girls, many of whom would have been below the legal age of consent at the time, was pregnancy. The prevalence of teenage pregnancy feeds into the cycle of poverty for women, as these young girls become the next generation of low-skilled, low-waged workers responsible for female-headed households, or, at the very worst, become trapped in undesirable relationships in their quest for economic viability.

The Ministry of Education and Culture has introduced a Health and Family Life Education program at the primary level that addresses, among other things, health awareness, interpersonal relationships, human sexuality, drug abuse, and environmental issues. Opportunities for continuing education, counseling, skills training, and daycare facilities are offered by the Women's Centre Foundation of Jamaica (WCFJ) for pregnant teenagers and teenage mothers to minimize the impact of teenage pregnancy which may include interrupted or terminated education, dependency, poor parenting skills, and general underachievement. Services are also offered to teenage fathers and young men at risk.[43]

HEALTH

Health Care Access

The government operates an extensive public system of 364 primary-care centers that deliver free or below-cost services. Primary care has been emphasized in government health-care funding. Forty-six percent of the centers' workload was curative care, and the remaining 54 percent of the workload consisted of family planning, maternal and child health services, and dental services. There is open access to primary care, but private health insurance is a necessity for most people to gain access to higher levels of care. The government also operates twenty-three acute-care hospitals, which account for 95 percent of all inpatient days. The other 5 percent is covered by nine private hospitals. Since 1997, a plan for national health insurance that would provide universal coverage through mandatory insurance has been discussed but not yet passed. Universal coverage is an important women's issue. More than 45.5 percent of households were single-parent families headed by women in 1993, and many of these families were included in the 21.2 percent of households below the poverty level. Complications from abortions performed in unsanitary conditions by untrained people contributed to a maternal death rate of 111 per 100,000 live births in 2000.[44]

Diseases and Disorders

AIDS

In 2001, women made up 54.4 percent of all reported cases of AIDS in Jamaica. The 939 persons who were living with AIDS brought the cumulative total of cases to 6,038 between 1982 and 2001.[45] Men between the ages of thirty and thirty-four are the largest single group of affected persons, and HIV/AIDS is the second-leading cause of death for both men and women aged thirty to thirty-four. The rate of infection, however, is increasing faster among women than among men. Heterosexual sex continues to be the main mode of transmission of HIV, accounting for more than 60.0 percent of cases. Adolescents are reported to have the highest rate of sexually transmitted infections, and the risk to adolescent girls is three times higher than that for boys.[46]

Cancer

Data from the Jamaica Cancer Registry show that 55 percent of all cancer cases are reported by females. The most common sites are related to the reproductive system, with the five most common cancers in women being breast (45 percent), cervical (28 percent), non-Hodgkin's lymphoma (9 percent), colon (8 percent), and lung (5 percent). Unlike men, the incidence of cancer among women is higher for those under sixty years of age, peaking between the ages of forty and forty-nine.[47]

POLITICS AND LAW

Suffrage

In the twentieth century, women in the Caribbean wanted to move from social volunteerism to political activism and electoral politics.[48] An impediment to women's increased political participation in Jamaica, however, was the lack of universal adult suffrage. Women with property secured the right to vote in 1919, but women outside of the elite and business classes remained excluded from voting and running for office until universal adult suffrage was won in 1944.

Political Participation

In 1944, the year all women could vote in Jamaica, four women ran for political office, and Iris Collins became the first woman elected to Jamaica's House of Representatives.

Men continue to dominate political life in Jamaica. In 2000, women made up 13 percent of members of the House of Representatives, 24 percent of the Senate, 12 percent of the cabinet, 24 percent of local government councilors, and 28 percent of justices of the peace.[49] In addition, the two main political parties have traditionally had women's arms that inform the party's position on women and gender issues. At present, women head the two most recently formed parties, the National Democratic Movement and the United People's Party.

In 1992, the Jamaica Women's Political Caucus was formed to increase the number of women in politics and to train and sensitize women about political life. However, although more women are entering political life, women continue to face a number of challenges, including lack of money, low levels of awareness, security issues, and lack of family support.[50]

Women's Rights

Several laws have been enacted to protect women's rights. These include the Maternity Leave Act, the Minimum Wage Act, the Incest Act, the

Offences against the Person Act, and the Domestic Violence Act. An act to amend the Constitution of Jamaica to allow for a Charter of Rights has been tabled in Parliament and referred to the Joint Select Committee of Parliament at present. This charter would guarantee the rights and freedoms of Jamaicans.

The Convention on the Elimination of Discrimination against Women (CEDAW) was ratified by Jamaica in 1981, as was the Convention on the Rights of the Child in 1991. The National Policy Statement on Women was approved by the cabinet in 1987 and is at present under review. The Bureau of Women's Affairs, the government agency with responsibility for women and gender issues, recently completed a review of legislation that affects women and will hold public discussions and generate recommendations for reforms for submission to Parliament.

Feminist Movements

Feminist activists and movements in Jamaica have often straddled other movements. The trade-union movement of the first half of the twentieth century, the Marcus Garvey movement of the 1920s and 1930s, the nationalist movements of the 1950s and 1960s, and the black power and antiwar struggles of the 1970s acted as training grounds for many feminists. The word "feminism" itself is often met with resistance by Caribbean persons who do not wish to be associated with the image of the radical, leftist, "bra-burning sexually liberated North American white woman in the 1960s."[51]

The definition of a distinct Caribbean feminism is therefore an important and ongoing project in the region, one that requires further theorizing and thinking through the subject. The Centre for Gender and Development Studies at the University of the West Indies is playing a critical role in this regard, and its unit at the Mona Campus in Jamaica is spearheading a project titled "The Making of Caribbean Feminism" that examines many of these issues.

Lesbian Rights

Jamaica is generally regarded as a homophobic society with little acceptance of homosexual relationships. In Jamaica, homosexual sex is a criminal act. In 1998, however, a lobby group, the Jamaican Forum for Lesbians, All-Sexuals, and Gays was formed. Its mission is to work "towards a Jamaican society in which the human rights and equality of these persons are guaranteed and to foster the acceptance and enrichment of the lives of same-gender-loving persons who have been, and continue to be, an integral part of society."[52] This lobby group has argued that the constitution should have provisions to protect persons against discrimination on the basis of sexual orientation. According to the group, a person's sexual orientation is outside of his or her control and therefore should not form the basis of discrimination.[53]

Military Service

For some time now, women have been accepted in the two armed forces responsible for national defense and justice in Jamaica: the Jamaica Constabulary Force (JCF) and the Jamaica Defense Force. Women were first enlisted in the JCF in 1949 to work in the areas of child welfare and juvenile delinquency. In 1998, women made up only 15 percent of the JCF, and the highest rank held by women was that of assistant commissioner, where women held two of the thirteen posts. A distinct sexual division of labor exists in the JCF, where women tend to be assigned office and clerical duties. Some women in the force prefer this type of work since it does not include night duty and so allows them time with their families as opposed to being on active duty. Although administrative work is critical to the justice system, it is often overlooked when promotions are made.[54] The Jamaica Defense Force first accepted female recruits in 1977 and in 1998 had its seventh class of female recruits following a five-year hiatus.

RELIGION AND SPIRITUALITY

Jamaica is a religious society with more than 130 registered denominations. Most are Christians. Data from the 1991 census indicate that the majority of the Christian population indicated adherence to the Church of God, followed by the Seventh-Day Adventists, Baptists, Pentecostals, and Anglicans. The Hindu and Muslim religions were introduced when Indians arrived as indentured laborers in the late nineteenth century. A small Jewish congregation meets in the only synagogue, located in Kingston.

The church in Jamaica has always been an organizing center for women, and they have often participated in public and political activities through the church. Although a number of churches, particularly those of European origin, are female dominated in terms of membership, they continue to be male dominated in terms of leadership. It is only since the 1980s that women have been accepted in leadership positions as ordained ministers in these mainstream denominations.

On the other hand, women have always had leading roles in groups that have strong African traditions and influences. In the Revival—or Pukumina—Church, which is more than 200 years old, women have participated from the start and have played leading roles as members, healers, and preachers. Female leaders in the Pukumina and the more recently established Pentecostal and Holiness denominations are commonly referred to as "Mother" or "Queenie," and sacred healing knowledge is passed down from mother to daughter.[55]

The Rastafarian religion is the most recent of the African-derived groups and emerged in 1930 with the coronation of Ras Tafari as emperor of

Ethiopia and as a response of resistance to the prevailing civil and theological order. Rastafarians believe in a supreme creator God, Jah, who is black. There are elders but no priests. The sacramental use of the "weed of wisdom"—marijuana or ganga—and the dreadlocks hairstyle are not articles of faith. Ganga is not universally used, and dreadlocks did not become common until the 1960s.[56]

Rastafarian beliefs regarding females are clearly based on the Bible and fall in line with the view that it is a patriarchal movement. It has been noted that " 'reasonings,' the traditional way of sharing information, cementing views or interpreting the Bible, take place primarily among the males. He takes the responsibility for sharing relevant information with the female. The female however is not restricted from reasoning together particularly at important rituals and/or celebrations. In this way there is intellectual stimulation and the female is, through one way or another, every bit as informed as the male."[57] In 1980, the fiftieth anniversary of the birth of the movement, the issue of women (daughters) and their abilities and place in the movement was raised. Three groups of "daughters" came into being in that year.

VIOLENCE

Domestic Violence

Gender-based violence includes domestic murders, physical and psychological abuse, rape, incest, and violence in domestic-related situations. As in other countries, these forms of violence occur in a significant number of families, not only in the lower classes of society, where it is often more overt, but also within the middle and upper classes. The Jamaica Constabulary Force reports that one-third of all murders in 2001 were caused by domestic violence, and there were 1,649 incidents of sexual offenses, with incidents of rape accounting for the largest number (776).[58]

A report on violence against women and children prepared in 1999 by the Centre for Gender and Development Studies as part of a United Nations Fund for Women campaign against violence against women notes that, based on reported cases, one out of eleven females in Jamaica between the ages of five and sixty would experience an act of violence.[59] A survey of 450 female students aged thirteen to fourteen in the Kingston area found that 13 percent had experienced attempted rape (half of them before they were twelve years old), and one-third of the girls had been molested.[60]

Rape/Sexual Assault

Cultural attitudes in Jamaica reinforce the societal belief that violence in the family is a private matter between a man and a woman and that outsiders should not interfere. The stigma associated with physical violence, rape, incest, and sexual harassment also deters female victims from openly admitting and reporting such incidents. Lack of sensitivity on the part of the various arms of the judicial system has been another deterrent to reporting, but with the creation of the Centre for the Investigation of Sexual Offences and Child Abuse and a Victim Support Unit in 1998, reporting has increased, and there is a more sensitive approach to the handling of offenses against women and children.

Trafficking in Women and Children

Sex as a commercial activity has existed in Jamaica for a long time. It continues, however, to be a stigmatized activity, and the sex worker has been essentially persona non grata in Jamaican society. Prostitution is very much associated with the tourist industry and involves both males and females. A unique feature of prostitution in Jamaica is that pimps do not control female workers, and there is no evidence of trafficking or forced sex work in Jamaica. Commercial sex workers are highly mobile within Jamaica, moving from one resort area to another, depending on the season, to increase their earnings.[61]

A cause for concern is the involvement of children ranging from ten to eighteen years of age in child prostitution. The International Labor Organization carried out a study in 2001 in Jamaica to identify the magnitude, character, causes, and consequences of the involvement of children in prostitution.[62] The study found that most children involved in prostitution and related activities were girls, and there was a gender division of labor in some sexual activities. The most common categories of children engaged in these activities were the following:

Children living and working on the streets, mainly boys, who exchanged sex for the means of meeting basic survival needs

Girls who engaged in formal prostitution and solicited clients on the streets

Girls who were employed as exotic go-go dancers

Girls who were employed as masseuses in massage parlors

Girls and boys in arranged sexual encounters for economic exchange

Factors identified as accounting for child prostitution included, among others, economic poverty, poor parenting, poor family values, peer pressure, limited education, and inadequate monitoring of laws.

Although there is no trafficking of women or girls across borders in organized prostitution, women in Jamaica are engaged in the trafficking of drugs. Like other Caribbean countries, Jamaica is a transshipment point in the movement of hard drugs from the south to the north. In this trade, women are used as couriers or "drug mules." According to a report in one of the daily newspapers, typically these women are "single mothers with three or four children, often with a lot of family responsibilities and who are unemployed. Given their financial circumstances, they are easy prey for the dealers or drug barons who see them as totally expendable."[63] The same article states that the most popular form of transport among these women is to conceal the "wraps" of cocaine about their person or swallow and/or insert the packages into other body orifices, placing themselves at great risk. Reports indicate that 34 percent of all female prisoners in England and Wales are Jamaicans who have been convicted of drug smuggling, and in Jamaica during 2001, at least 10 of some 150 of these arrested women died from the effects of swallowing cocaine.

OUTLOOK FOR THE TWENTY-FIRST CENTURY

In the Caribbean Community, of which Jamaica is a part, the goal of gender equality is being pursued within a broader social justice framework. This is a rights-based approach that is premised on the understanding that all groups and individuals have equal rights to the conditions that will allow them to realize their full human potential to contribute to development in its broadest sense and to benefit from its results. Gender mainstreaming is the strategy that will be used as a means of engendering policies and programs at all levels, and the areas to be addressed up to the year 2005 include, among others, education, with a focus on building human capital; health, with an emphasis on HIV/AIDS; and poverty.[64] The ultimate goal of the framework of social justice and gender equality is "the building of new structures of power-sharing at the household, community, national, regional and global levels, where both men and women can participate fully in developing a system of cooperation in decision-making, as equal partners in the sustainable development of their societies."[65]

NOTES

1. Information for this section, unless otherwise stated, is drawn from *Statistical Yearbook of Jamaica 1999* (Kingston, Jamaica: Statistical Institute of Jamaica, 2000).

2. *Economic and Social Survey Jamaica 2001* (Kingston, Jamaica: Planning Institute of Jamaica, 2002).

3. World Bank Latin America and the Caribbean Gender Database, 2000, www.worldbank.org/data/countrydata/countrydata.html.

4. *Jamaica Education Statistics 2000/2001: Annual Statistical Review of the Education Sector* (Kingston, Jamaica: Statistics Section, Planning and Development Division, Ministry of Education and Culture).

5. Ibid.

6. Ibid.

7. Barbara Bailey, *The Search for Gender Equity and Empowerment of Caribbean*

Women: The Role of Education (Barbados: UNIFEM Caribbean; Georgetown, Guyana: Caribbean Community [CARICOM], forthcoming).

8. *Jamaica Human Development Report 2000* (Kingston, Jamaica: Planning Institute of Jamaica, 2001).

9. *The Labour Force 2000* (Kingston, Jamaica: Statistical Institute of Jamaica).

10. Heather Ricketts and Warren Benfield, "Gender and the Jamaican Labour Market: The Decade of the 90s," in *The Construction of Gender: Development Indicators for Jamaica*, ed. Patricia Mohammed (Kingston, Jamaica: Planning Institute of Jamaica, 2000).

11. *Jamaica Human Development Report 2000*, 2001.

12. *The Labour Force 1999* (Kingston, Jamaica: Statistical Institute of Jamaica); *The Labour Force 2000* (Kingston, Jamaica: Statistical Institute of Jamaica).

13. Ibid.

14. *The Labour Force 1999* and *The Labor Force 2000*.

15. *Jamaica Human Development Report 2000*, 2001.

16. Judith Wedderburn, "Social Reproduction in Jamaica," background paper for the *Jamaica Human Development Report 2000*, 1999.

17. World Bank Latin America and the Caribbean Gender Database, 2000.

18. *The Labour Force 2000*.

19. Ricketts and Benfield, 2000, 55.

20. World Bank Latin America and Caribbean Database, 2000.

21. Aldrie Henry-Lee, Barry Chevannes, Mary Clarke, and Heather Ricketts, *An Assessment of the Standard of Living and Coping Strategies of Workers in Selected Occupations Who Earn a Minimum Wage*, Working Paper no. 4 (Kingston, Jamaica: Planning Institute of Jamaica, 2000).

22. *Jamaica Human Development Report 2000*, 61.

23. Leith Dunn and Hopeton Dunn, *Employment, Working Conditions and Labour Relations in Offshore Data Service Enterprises: Case Studies of Barbados and Jamaica*, Working Paper no. 86. (Geneva, Switzerland: International Labour Office, 1999).

24. *Economic and Social Survey Jamaica 2001*, 2002.

25. Jamaica Sustainable Development Networking Programme, "About Our Programme," www.jdnsp.org.jm.

26. *Economic and Social Survey Jamaica 2001*, 2002.

27. *Jamaica Human Development Report 2000*, 2001.

28. *Jamaica Human Development Report 2000*, 2001.

29. *Economic and Social Survey Jamaica 2001*, 2002.

30. Planning Institute of Jamaica and Statistical Institute of Jamaica, *Jamaica Survey of Living Conditions 2001* (Kingston, Jamaica: Planning Institute of Jamaica and Statistical Institute of Jamaica, 2002).

31. Judith Wedderburn, "Gender and Social Reproduction," in *The Construction of Gender: Development Indicators for Jamaica*, ed. P. Mohammed (Kingston, Jamaica: Planning Institute of Jamaica, 2000), 15–20.

32. Janet Brown and Barry Chevannes, *Why Men Stay So: Tie the Heifer, Loose the Bull. An Examination of Gender Socialization Practices in the Caribbean* (Kingston, Jamaica: University of the West Indies, Mona, 1999).

33. Rhoda Reddock, ed., *Women and Family in the Caribbean: Historical and Contemporary Considerations with Special Reference to Jamaica and Trinidad and Tobago* (St. Augustine, Trinidad: Prepared for the CARICOM Secretariat for International Year of the Family 1994 by Women and Development Studies Group/Centre for Gender and Development Studies, University of the West Indies, 1994).

34. Ibid.

35. *Demographic Statistics* 2000 (Kingston: Statistical Institute of Jamaica).

36. *Jamaica Reproductive Health Survey 1997* (Kingston, Jamaica: National Family Planning Board, 1998).

37. Ibid.

38. *Economic and Social Survey Jamaica 2001*, 2002.

39. Daniel Gatti, "UNFPA Highlights New Trends," InterPress Third World News Agency, September 2, 1998, www.hartford-hwp.com.

40. *Economic and Social Survey Jamaica 2001*, 2002.

41. Ibid.

42. Barbara Bailey and Monica Brown, *Gender Perspectives on the School Experience: What Are the Issues?* (Kingston, Jamaica: The Canada-Caribbean Gender Equality Fund, Canadian International Development Agency [CIDA], 1999).

43. *Economic and Social Survey Jamaica 2001*, 2002.

44. Pan-American Health Organization, "Regional Core Health Data System—Country Health Profile 2001: Jamaica," www.paho.org.

45. *Economic and Social Survey Jamaica 2001*, 2002.

46. Ibid.

47. *Ministry of Health Annual Report*, 1998, www.mohgov.jm.

48. Verene Shepherd, *Women in Caribbean History: The British-Colonised Territories: An Introductory Text for Secondary Schools* (Kingston: Ian Randle Publishers, 1999).

49. *Economic and Social Survey Jamaica 2000*.

50. *Jamaica Human Development Report 2000*, 2001.

51. Patricia Mohammed, "Towards Indigenous Feminist Theorising in the Caribbean," *Feminist Review* 59 (1998): 24.

52. Email from the Jamaican Forum for Lesbians, All-Sexuals, and Gays outlining the history of the group.

53. *Jamaica Gleaner*, "Bishops Oppose Proposals on Homosexuality," December 18, 2001.

54. Gladys Brown-Campbell, *Patriarchy in the Jamaica Constabulary Force: Its Impact on Gender Equality* (Kingston: Canoe Press, University of the West Indies, 1998).

55. Mimi Sheller, "Quasheba, Mother, Queen: Black Women's Public Leadership and Political Protest in Post-Emancipation Jamaica," Online paper, Department of Sociology, Lancaster University, www.comp.lancs.ac.uk/sociology/socD49ms.html.

56. Martin Mordecai and Pamela Mordecai, *Culture and Customs of Jamaica* (Westport, CT: Greenwood Press, 2001).

57. Maureen Rowe, *The Woman in Rastafari*, Caribbean Quarterly Monograph (Mona, Jamaica: University of the West Indies, 1985), 15–16.

58. *Economic and Social Survey Jamaica 2001*, 2002.

59. *National Report on the Situation of Violence against Women and Girls in Jamaica 1999* (Kingston, Jamaica: Prepared for the United Nations Development Programme by the Regional Coordinating Unit, Centre for Gender and Development Studies, University of the West Indies, Mona Campus, 2000).

60. I. Brown, *Resultado de la Violencia Domestica el 45 por Ciento de Los Asesinatos Jamaiquinos*, Indice Informativo de CIMAC, 1999.

61. P. Campbell and A. Campbell, "HIV/AIDS Prevention and Education for Commercial Sex Workers in Jamaica: An Exploratory Study and Need Assessment," National HIV/STI Prevention and Control Programme, Health Promotion and Protection Division, Ministry of Health, Jamaica, 2001.

62. Leith Dunn, *Jamaica, Situation of Children in Prostitution: A Rapid Assessment* (Geneva, Switzerland: International Labour Organisation, International Programme on the Elimination of Child Labour, 2001).

63. "Recruiting the Mules," *Daily Observer*, May 20, 2002: 7.

64. "Gender and Development: A Cross-Cutting Element in Human Resource Development," CARICOM Secretariat, October 2001.

65. "Gender Equality, Social Justice, and Development: The CARICOM Post-Beijing Regional Plan of Action to the Year 2000," CARICOM Secretariat, 1997, 38.

RESOURCE GUIDE

Suggested Reading

Barrow, C., ed. *Caribbean Portraits: Essays on Gender Ideologies and Identities*. Kingston: Ian Randle Publishers in association with the Centre for Gender and Development Studies, University of the West Indies, 1998. This collection of papers looks at gender ideologies and identities, which shape beliefs and attitudes about appropriate identities and behaviors of men and women, and sociocultural realities within the Caribbean. Contributors examine issues of work; hegemony and patriarchy; socialization and schooling; sexuality; and power.

Leo-Rhynie, E., B. Bailey, and C. Barrow, eds. *Gender: A Caribbean Multi-Disciplinary Perspective*. Kingston: Ian Randle Publishers in association with the Centre for Gender and Development Studies, University of the West Indies, 1997. Examines the multifaceted nature of gender issues in the Caribbean from a multidisciplinary perspective. Issues include research and policy; gender and the law; education; language, poetry, and prose; gender and health; and gender and agriculture.

Mohammed, Patricia, ed. *The Construction of Gender Development Indicators for Jamaica*. Kingston: Planning Institute of Jamaica, 2000. A companion to the *Jamaica Human Development Report 2000*, the articles point to the critical need for the development of gender indicators and outline the process for creating gender-responsive data sets in relation to education, health, politics, social production, and the labor market. This is a very useful document that provides sex-disaggregated data for Jamaica.

Mohammed, Patricia, ed. *Gendered Realities: Essays in Caribbean Feminist Thought*. Kingston: University of the West Indies Press and the Centre for Gender and Development Studies, University of the West Indies, Mona, Jamaica, 2002. Explores masculinity and femininity within the Caribbean from a multidisciplinary perspective. Reexamined are feminist theory and methodology; gender and history; gender and academia; women's roles in the family, economy, and society; gender and literature; women, gender, and the media; and constructing gender.

National Report on the Situation of Violence against Women and Girls in Jamaica. Kingston: Centre for Gender and Development Studies and the United Nations Development Programme, 1999. Looks at the situation of violence against women and girls. National statistics are examined, as are data from the Women's Crisis Centre. Services that are available to victims are explored and laws that address the issue are highlighted. In order to develop the context within which gender-based violence occurs, key informants were interviewed. Provides a good overall view of the issue. It does not, however, include the voices of either victims or abusers.

Planning Institute of Jamaica. *Jamaica Human Development Report 2000*. Kingston: Planning Institute of Jamaica, 2001. Each year the United Nations Development Programme produces a Human Development Report on one country. In the year 2000, the report was on Jamaica. A very comprehensive study of human development issues in Jamaica, including poverty, education, health, and gender indicators, among others. A new Human Development Index was calculated using local statistics.

Shepherd, V., B. Brereton, and B. Bailey, eds. *Engendering History: Caribbean Women in Historical Perspective*. London: James Currey; Kingston: Ian Randle Publishers, 1995. The chapters in this book testify to the remarkable research effort that has gone into the study of Caribbean women's history from slavery to modern times and the ongoing attempts to rewrite history based on ever-emerging new contexts. Geographically, the chapters relate primarily to the English-speaking Caribbean but also include material that represents experiences of women in the Hispanic and French-speaking Caribbean.

Videos/Films

The Bureau of Women's Affairs has produced two videos. *Hope Deferred* (40 minutes) chronicles the story of two families and how they deal with the issue of incest. *Starting Over* (1 hour) looks at the issue of domestic violence and how it affects all members of the family.

Bureau of Women's Affairs
4 Ellesmere Road
Kingston 10
Jamaica, West Indies
Phone: 876-754-8575-8, 929-6660, 908-4888
Fax: 876-929-0549
Email: jbwa@cwjamaica.com

Video for Change carries a number of videos dealing with Jamaican history and heritage, the environment, economy, gender and development, sexuality, media images of women, and community development.

Video for Change
PO Box 14
Kingston 2
Phone: 876-927-7599 or 750-0748
Fax: 876-929-1872
Email: vfc@cwjamaica.com

Web Sites and Organizations

Bureau of Women's Affairs
4 Ellesmere Road
Kingston 10
Jamaica, West Indies
Phone: 876-754-8575-8, 929-6660, 908-4888
Fax: 876-929-0549
Email: jbwa@cwjamaica.com

The Bureau of Women's Affairs, located in the Ministry of Tourism and Sports, has a mission to enable Jamaican women to realize their full potential in the country's social, economic, and cultural development. It is also involved in lobbying and advocating for the rights of women and children.

Centre for Gender and Development Studies
University of the West Indies
Mona Campus
Mona, Kingston 7
Jamaica, West Indies
Phone: 876-927-1913/935-8494
Fax: 876-927-1913
Email: cgdsrcu@uwimona.edu.jm
Web site: www.uwicentre.edu.jm/cgds_centre

The Centre for Gender and Development Studies at the University of the West Indies is involved in a program of teaching, research, and outreach. It has units on each of the three university campuses: Mona, Jamaica; St. Augustine, Trinidad; and Cave Hill, Barbados.

Jamaica Women's Political Caucus
12 Easton Avenue
Kingston 5
Jamaica, West Indies
Phone: 876-946-1859
Email: csbrowne@cwjamaica.com

The Jamaica Women's Political Caucus was established in 1992 to increase the quantity and quality of women in politics and at the decision-making level through training, research, and public education.

Woman Inc.
7 Deanhurst Road
Kingston 10
Jamaica, West Indies
Phone: 876-929-2997, 929-9038

Woman Inc. is a nongovernmental organization that aims to increase public awareness of the issue of violence against women. It operates the Women's Crisis Centre and Jamaica's only shelter for abused women and their children.

Women's Media Watch
14 South Avenue
Kingston 10
Jamaica, West Indies
Phone: 876-926-0882
Fax: 876-926-0862
Email: wmwjam@cwjamaica.com

Women's Media Watch is a nongovernmental, voluntary organization established in 1987 that works to improve the image of women in the Jamaican media as one means of reducing the occurrence of violence against women. It also aims to increase public awareness of gender-based violence and to show how images of violence in the media contribute to acts of violence against women.

SELECTED BIBLIOGRAPHY

Mohammed, Patricia, ed. *The Construction of Gender: Development Indicators for Jamaica.* Kingston: Planning Institute of Jamaica, 2000. This publication is a companion to the *Jamaica Human Development Report 2000.* The chapters point to the critical need for the development of gender indicators and outline the process for creating gender-responsive data sets in relation to education, health, politics, social production, and the labor market. Sex-disaggregated data for Jamaica are provided.

National Report on the Situation of Violence against Women and Girls in Jamaica. Kingston: Centre for Gender and Development Studies and the United Nations Development Programme, 1999. This study, commissioned by the United Nations Development Programme, looks at the situation of violence against women and girls in Jamaica. National statistics are examined, as are data from the Women's Crisis Centre. Services that are available to victims are explored, and laws that address the issue are highlighted. In order to develop the context within which gender-based violence occurs, key informants were interviewed. The report provides a good overall view of the issue but does not include the voices of either victims or abusers.

Planning Institute of Jamaica. *Jamaica Human Development Report 2000.* Kingston: Planning Institute of Jamaica, 2001. Each year the United Nations Development Programme produces a Human Development Report on one country, and in 2000 the report was on Jamaica, providing a very comprehensive study of human development issues in Jamaica, including poverty, education, health, and gender indicators, among others. A new human development index was calculated using local statistics.

9

MEXICO

Luisa Gabayet

PROFILE OF MEXICO

The territory of Mexico has a surface area of 1,972,547 square kilometers. In 2002, the population was 103,400,165.[1] In 1995, the ratio of men to women was 49.6 percent to 50.4 percent. The gross mortality rate per 1,000 inhabitants fell from 9.5 in 1970 to 4.99 in 2002, and the infant death rate per 1,000 live births decreased from 73.9 in 1970 to just 24.52 in 2002. The maternal death rate has fallen significantly since the 1940s, from 53 per 10,000 live births in 1940 to 5.1 in 1990. Life expectancy in general rose from 60.4 years in 1970 to 72.03 years in 2002. The figure for Mexican men rose from 58.2 years in 1970 to 69.8 in 2002, and for women from 62.5 to 76.2 during the same period.[2]

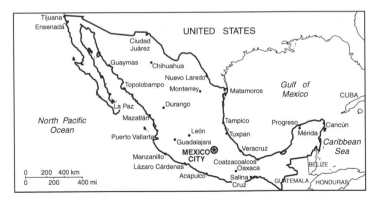

The majority of the population is urban dwellers (defined as those living in localities with more than 2,500 inhabitants). From 1970 to 2000, the proportion of the population residing in urban areas rose from 58.6 percent to 73.5 percent. Of the total urban population, 48.8 percent are men and 51.2 percent are women, which means an average of 105 women for every 100 men. The majority of women now live in urban areas and are principally young adults (not children, as was the case in 1970). In addition, the average number of children born to women during their reproductive years has fallen by more than 50 percent from 7 children per woman in 1970 to 2.57 in 2002.[3]

According to the Constitution of 1917, Mexico, officially the United States of Mexico, is a federal democratic republic divided into thirty-one states and one federal district, where the national capital is located. The Institutional Revolutionary Party (Partido Revolucionario Institucional, or PRI) governed Mexico for seventy-nine years, until it lost the national election in July 2000 to the National Action Party (Partido Acción Nacional, or PAN), which is considered rightist and more conservative than the PRI.

There are tremendous contrasts among the states that make up Mexico. The most marginal states are Oaxaca, Chiapas, Guerrero, Hidalgo, and Puebla; these also have the highest proportions of indigenous people.[4] A comparison of the 2,403 municipalities in Mexico shows that 545 are considered indigenous (that is, 40 percent or more of the people speak an indigenous language). Of these, 71.6 percent suffer severe hardships. Another 15.4 percent have a somewhat higher socioeconomic level, but are not much better off than the former. Thus 87 percent of the indigenous municipalities require immediate attention in all areas of public and social action.[5]

OVERVIEW OF WOMEN'S ISSUES

In the twentieth century, Mexican women made important advances in their social, legal, political, and economic conditions. Nonetheless, much ground remains to be made up, and the female population continues to experience social exclusion and marginalization that derives from social and cultural constructions related to gender in important areas such as education, employment, income, and social status. These social (gender) constructions assign differentiated roles to men and women and thus subject people to distinct risks and conditions that affect various areas of their lives. Although since the 1980s great progress has been made in improving the social situation of Mexican women, gender inequalities are still clearly marked and reinforce the social inequalities arising from class and ethnicity.

Mexican women cannot be cast into a single mold. There are huge differences among them due to class and ethnic affiliations. Women struggle with racism, exclusion, and the grave social, economic, political, and cultural inequality that surrounds them.

Despite their participation in the struggle for independence and the revolution, Mexican women have been largely overlooked by history and politics.[6] Indeed, it was not until 1953 that Mexican women finally obtained the right to vote, after decades of struggle. The traditional values that govern Mexican culture, the highly influential Catholic Church, an exclusive political system, and an authoritarian political culture have combined to make the path of women a difficult one. Their achievements have been partial and sporadic, but there is no doubt that change has accelerated since the 1980s.

EDUCATION

Opportunities

In the twentieth century, the education of Mexicans dramatically improved.[7] In 1900, 78 percent of people above the age of ten were unable to read or write. In 1990, in contrast, only 11 percent were illiterate. Despite these advances, several sectors of the population are victims of inequality and exclusion in the area of education, including women in general and indigenous women in particular. The entire population has seen educational progress slowed by a series of crises in the early 1980s that continue to affect Mexico today.

Data on school attendance, like those on illiteracy, show greater equality between the sexes in the younger generations in access to education. However, continuous attendance in the school system is still higher for boys than girls.

The most important advances in educational levels among the Mexican population occurred in the last years of the twentieth century and have affected both women and men, though important differences according to sex can be detected at all levels. For example, of the total population over the age of twenty-five registered in the country in 2000 as having no schooling, almost 60 percent were women. With respect to the sectors that did finish primary school, the distribution by sex is more balanced (48 percent men, 52 percent women), but large differences between the genders occur at the level of higher education, where 63 percent of all people who have studied are men and only 37 percent are women.[8]

Census data indicate that at the junior-high-school and high-school levels, women make up 54 percent of the total number of students, while men make up 46 percent.[9] This difference can be explained in part by cultural patterns that assign women the responsibility for domestic work and reproductive tasks, and men the responsibility for the economic support of the home. Thus women are more likely to enter programs (nursing, secretarial school, teaching, and the like) that allow them to get a job and at the same time fulfill their assigned social role.

Men receive more schooling than women. The average amount of schooling for men is 6.8 years, while for women it is only 6.2.[10] Differences can be observed between states in the average number of years of schooling by gender that reach a maximum of one year in Chiapas (4.7 years of school for men, but only 3.7 for women) and Mexico City (9.4 and 8.3). These are the states with, respectively, the lowest and highest levels of social well-being in Mexico.

When women enter professional ranks, they tend to study for careers socially identified with their gender status and to enter these occupations. Disciplines like engineering and the hard sciences (physics, mathematics) continue to be dominated by men. At the national level, of 1.9 million professional people identified in the census, 1.3 million are men. This means that only 34 percent of professional people in Mexico are women.

Literacy

According to information from the 1990 census, 12.4 percent of the population above the age of fifteen was illiterate. The gender distribution of illiteracy was unequal: of a total of 6.2 million illiterate people, 2.3 million were men and 3.9 million were women.[11]

Illiteracy is most prevalent in those over the age of thirty, where 80.5 percent of illiterate women and 77.8 percent of illiterate men are found. In all age groups, women have higher illiteracy levels than men, though in lower age groups the gap is narrower. These data show that recent generations have reduced educational inequality, but that the gap between men and women widens with age.

At the national level, female illiteracy is 5.4 percentage points higher than the average for males. In some states, however, this difference surpasses ten points, for example, Chiapas (15.1), Oaxaca (14.9), and Puebla (10.3), states with large indigenous populations. These data reflect great inequality in access to education according to sex. In general, the states with lower indexes of development (indigenous states) also show higher illiteracy rates and the largest differences in this respect according to gender. The more marginal the state, the wider the gap in illiteracy between men and women.

EMPLOYMENT AND ECONOMICS

Job/Career Opportunities

Since the 1980s, one of the most important tendencies in the workforce has been the growing incorporation of women. According to the 1970 census, only one of every five women participated in some economic activity, but the *National Employment Survey* of 2000 found that one of every three Mexican women had entered the labor market.[12]

This growing presence is explained by the country's recent integration, plus the process of modernization and, more concretely, expanding urbanization, a high rate of rural-urban migration, dominated by women, and the expansion and diversification of the tertiary sector (trade, transport, and service enterprises). Other factors include the expansion and restructuring of the industrial sector (especially in industrial assembly plants called maquiladoras) and the increase in education across the entire population. All of these elements foster greater economic participation by women. Reductions in average household incomes, especially because of the recurring economic crises suffered since 1982, have caused greater economic participation by all members of households, particularly women.[13]

Pay and Working Conditions

Women's increasing participation in economic activities since the 1980s has not been accompanied, however, by a similar rise in access to well-paid jobs because stagnation in industrial production has caused a fall in salaried employment.[14] Employment surveys from the 1980s show that much of the increase in women's participation in the workforce can be traced to their entry into independent activities, commerce, services, and industry (principally maquiladoras). Export-oriented maquiladoras have experienced tremendous growth in Mexico since the signing of the North American Free Trade Agreement (NAFTA) and have absorbed large numbers of women. This type of employment, however, is characterized by low pay (less than twice the minimum daily wage), seasonal nature, and working conditions and labor relations that often violate workers' rights by not offering permanent jobs. Women may be subjected to mandatory pregnancy tests and can be fired if they are found to be pregnant. Finally, workers are not allowed to create labor unions at such factories.[15] Another option for women, mainly for mothers who cannot leave their children, is "industrial homework," but these kinds of occupations have even worse conditions than transnational maquiladoras.[16]

Street vendor, Merida, Mexico. Photo © TRIP/G. Howe.

The *National Employment Survey* from 2000 shows that the economically active feminine population was divided approximately as follows: 55 percent wage workers, 25 percent self-employed, and 20 percent family workers who receive no pay.[17] Unlike developed countries, Mexico has no unemployment insurance. This means that despite working conditions that leave much to be desired, women with children continue to enter the workforce, often relying on their social networks for support (women relatives who do not work, such as mothers, daughters, or sisters), instead of daycare services.

Sexual Harassment

Mexico's labor law was originally passed in 1931, when few women worked outside the home, and was last reformed in 1974. A new labor bill under debate in the Chamber in late 2002 would protect women from sexual harassment and abuse, from being fired for becoming pregnant, and would ban pregnancy tests for employment. An agreement was signed by government, business, and labor representatives to change the law. Advocates of the reform claimed that three of every four women were subjected to sexual harassment in the workplace and that 40 percent left their jobs because of it.[18]

Support for Mothers/Caretakers

Maternal Leave

Mexican federal labor law authorizes maternity leave (six weeks before and six weeks after birth) and the creation of daycare centers by companies with more than twenty female employees, among other measures. Few employers respect these laws. Moreover, maquiladoras employing many women demand negative pregnancy tests as a condition of hiring and make women sign a document in which they agree not to become pregnant and to accept their dismissal if they do. In some other types of employment (for example, schools, government offices, and universities), maternity leave is granted.

Daycare

Private daycare centers are scarce and expensive, and free public-sector facilities tend to be overcrowded. For these reasons, women workers are forced to find other daycare resources in order to obtain employment, often with the support of other women in the household or from a woman's extended family.

Inheritance and Property Rights

Mexican legislation stipulates that men and women have the same rights of inheritance and property ownership. This was not the case historically. During colonial rule, women were not allowed to own property. Although changes have occurred and inheritance is now the same for men and women, culture frequently modifies law. For instance, among the indigenous population, the tendency is for men—usually the last born—to inherit land and the house, since he will be taking care of his parents. Among the middle class, women usually inherit some real estate and men inherit businesses.[19]

Social/Government Programs

The Mexican government has implemented social initiatives designed to alleviate the poverty of marginal populations, the most important of which are the Solidarity and Progresa programs. The latter gives monetary grants to children that allow them to improve their nutrition and stay in school.

This program gives priority to girls, who tend to have less opportunity to attend school. The funds are given to mothers, not fathers, because earlier programs found that men were prone to squander the money, mostly on alcohol, and rarely gave the money to their families.

Sustainable Development

The government of Mexico recognizes that "natural resource conservation and the promotion of sustainable development can only be viable within a society in which its citizens participate in the process of decision-making."[20] Women's voices are being heard in the sustainable-development movement, aided by the National Institute for Women, whose mission is in part to "promote the mainstreaming of a gender perspective in national development planning [and] programming."[21] The Native Women's Union of the Simivel Region works in solidarity with the Indigenous Communities of the Simojovel de Allende Region of Chiapas to help Tzotzil and Tzeltal communities organize for sustainable development and environmental protection.[22] Outside agencies are also active in assuring women's involvement. The National Wildlife Federation is educating Mexican undergraduate and graduate students about sustainable development so that they may take that information to their local communities in the hope of creating the next generation of leaders in sustainable development.[23] The United Nations Population Fund has supported the Jocotepec Development Center, which links population and environmental concerns.[24]

Welfare

The social welfare system in Mexico is poorly developed. There is no unemployment insurance or children's benefits like those found in other countries (such as the "baby bonus"). The system of medical care is poor and insufficient. The Mexican Institute of Social Security offers medical services to the working population through a payment system shared by employer and employee. Government employees have a different service, the Institute of Social Security and Health for State Workers. People who do not enjoy access to these agencies can go to the Department of Health and Social Assistance, but its services are precarious at best and clearly inadequate. None of these agencies reaches remote areas of the country, the regions inhabited by the indigenous population.

FAMILY AND SEXUALITY

Gender Roles

In Mexican families, gender roles reflect the saying "women at home and men on the street," which summarizes what is expected of women and men: the former should devote themselves to home and family, while the latter should be outside to earn the family's "daily bread." These roles persist, and despite women's growing participation in education and wage work, changes in gender roles have been almost imperceptible. Men still participate very little in domestic tasks, and women endure the "double workday" of producers and reproducers.

Marriage

The National Survey of Demographic Dynamics for 1997 reveals that in the over-twenty age group, 54.3 percent of men and 52.3 percent of women were married. Single men and women make up 41.75 and 35.6 percent of this population, respectively (reflecting a young population), while the figures for separated or divorced men and women are 4.0 percent and 12.1 percent.[25] This marked difference is explained in part by women's greater longevity and in part because men tend to remarry sooner. In 1997, the average age at marriage was 23.2 years for men and 19.4 for women. The rate of divorce rose from 2.7 per 100 inhabitants in 1940 to 8.7 in 1970 and 6 in 1985.[26]

Over time, the number of women-led households has increased. In 1950, they made up 13.2 of the total number of households, but this figure rose to 15.3 percent in 1970 and to 17.3 percent in 1990, though researchers who study this matter believe that statistics underestimate the number of such families, as this determination is heavily biased by the cultural association between male identity and the status of "head of household" (men as breadwinners and domestic authorities).[27] In 1990, almost 3 million Mexican households were identified as "female led."

Reproduction

In recent decades, the vital statistics of the Mexican population have changed appreciably. The majority now live in urban areas and include primarily young adults. One of the clearest changes has been the fall in fecundity, from an average of seven children per woman during her reproductive years in the 1970s to only 2.57 in 2000. Nonetheless, as with other facets of women's lives (education, medical care), the differences between urban, middle-class women and poor, rural ones (including a high percentage of indigenous women) are dramatic. For example, for women with no schooling, the fertility rate is 6.14, compared to just 2.51 for those who entered or finished high school.[28]

Sex Education

In Mexico, sex education is taught in official (government) schools and in the more progressive private ones. The state sponsors campaigns to promote various contraceptive methods, though the Roman Catholic hierarchy has opposed such initiatives. Textbooks that present sex education in primary and secondary schools have been combated and "satanized" by parents' associations and the authorities of the Catholic Church, who accept only abstinence and so-called natural methods of contraception.

Contraception and Abortion

Through its sex education programs, the government has succeeded in increasing the use of chemical, barrier, and surgical contraceptive methods, thus lowering fertility rates. However, in the southern states of Mexico with large indigenous populations, the frequency of use is much less than elsewhere. For example, in Chiapas, only 32 percent of women of reproductive age use birth control, compared to 53.7 percent in the northern state of Nuevo León.[29]

Abortion in Mexico is permitted only in specific circumstances, such as when the mother's life is in danger or when pregnancy results from rape. Laws vary from state to state, and current PAN governments have attempted to abolish the practice under any and all circumstances. Women who want abortions must procure clandestine operations at a high spiritual and material cost in unsanitary conditions, resulting in many deaths and frequently in sterility of women due to botched procedures.[30] Even so, more than 150,000 abortions are performed each year.

Teen Pregnancy

The lack of sex education causes serious problems, such as the spread of misinformation among adolescents and high indexes of teenage pregnancy and induced abortions. From 1992 to 1997, the percentage of teenagers who had had at least one live birth declined slightly, from 12.3 percent to 11.8 percent, and schooling was one of the most important factors in this reduction. In 1997, the percentage of adolescent women with no education or who had not finished primary school and had had at least one live birth was above 26 percent, while the figure was just 7.5 percent for those who had begun high school or continued their studies beyond that level. There are also differences according to place of residence. In 1992, the percentage of teenage women with a baby was 12.3 at the national level, but in the rural areas it was 16.7 and in urban areas only 10.6. In 1997, the percentage at the national level was 11.8, 15.4 in rural areas and 10.6 in urban areas. Today, one out of every five births, or approximately 450,000 births, are to teen mothers.[31]

HEALTH

Health Care Access

Improvements in health have been notable, though again substantial differences in health and in access to health care are found among women in different regions, distinct ethnic groups, and different socioeconomic levels. The number of deaths related to pregnancy, childbirth, and the postpartum period fell significantly from 1980 to 1992. In 1980, 2,298 deaths of this type were registered, but in 1992, the number fell to just 1,399. Deaths attributed directly to obstetric causes—hemorrhages, toxemia, genitourinary infections, obstructed births, and postpartum complications, among others—occupied first place in both 1980 and 1992. In fact, these indexes increased slightly in relative terms over this twelve-year period, from 89.9 to 92.1 percent of all maternal deaths.[32] In most cases, such deaths are avoidable because most maladies that affect women during pregnancy and childbirth are preventable. Timely, adequate medical care can reduce risks considerably, but the factors affecting timeliness and efficiency are many and complex. A woman's socioeconomic position (including schooling), her cultural patterns, and her status do much to determine her access to medical care both in the prenatal period and during childbirth, though the real availability of accessible health services is also important.

Diseases and Disorders

Other illnesses that claim women's lives include diabetes, cardiovascular disease, and cerebral and hepatic ailments (cirrhosis, hepatitis). Among indigenous women, maladies associated with malnutrition are also important causes of death.

AIDS

The incidence of AIDS has risen greatly, especially in communities that send many migrant workers to the United States. The percentage of AIDS-infected women increased from 1987 to 1992 (8.1 to 15 percent), whereas from 1993 to 1995 it decreased slightly, from 14 to 12.4 percent. In 1996, however, the numbers began to rise again, from 12.8 to 15.1 percent in 1998. In 2000, there were 45,133 new cases of AIDS diagnosed in Mexico. Seventy-seven point three percent of these cases were males, and 33.3 percent were females in the age category of fifteen to forty-four. AIDS is the third-leading cause of death among men of that age group, and the sixth among women. The states with the highest proportions of infected women are Puebla (25.2 percent), Tlaxcala (25 percent), Morelos (23.2 percent), Hidalgo (21 percent), Jalisco (20 percent), and Chiapas (19.9 percent).[33]

Eating Disorders

Among young women from the higher classes, bulimia and anorexia have emerged. This is the sector with the greatest exposure to mass media and, as a result, to fashions imposed in other countries.

Cancer

Cancer, especially breast and cervical-uterine cancer, causes the largest number of deaths among women. In 2000, uterine cancer accounted for 33 percent of women's deaths by cancer, while 16 percent of cancer deaths were from breast cancers. Sixty-four point seven percent of cancer deaths were women, 35.3 percent were men.[34]

Depression

No statistical information exists concerning depression as a health problem in Mexico. The main reported causes that lead people to take their own lives are family problems (42 percent) and "love-related" (8 percent), while in 27 percent of cases no reason is given.[35] The suicide rate is three male suicides to every female suicide, although women attempt suicide four times more than men.

POLITICS AND LAW

Political rights and constitutional guarantees are specifically recognized in the Federal Constitution, which considers men and women as equals in the eyes of the law. Real legal equality is a goal the country has been approaching more quickly in recent years, though it is still far off, due not only to cultural problems that cannot be resolved by decrees, but also to the difficulties that women (especially from low-income families) experience when they attempt to seek justice and have their rights duly respected.

Suffrage

Women's full rights as citizens were recognized in 1953, when they were made eligible to vote in popular elections.

Political Participation

Citizenship essentially confers the right to elect and to be elected. It was not until 1993, however, that political parties began to foster greater participation by women in the country's political life, and only recently has active political participation by women in elected political office increased. Progress has been gradual and continues to be limited. In 1981, a woman occupied a position as secretary of state for the first time (tourism), but no woman has reached the presidency. The first female candidate for president ran in the 1988 elections, and in 1994 there were two women candidates.

Women's participation at the level of national executive power has also been weak. From 1953 (when women obtained full citizenship) to 1992,

169 men held posts in the federal cabinet, compared to only 3 women. At the level of subsecretariats, only 3 percent of officeholders were women during the same period.

In the 2002 legislature, women occupied only 85 of 500 seats, or 17 percent. In April 2002, however, the Chamber of Deputies approved a bill by a vote of 403–7 that forced political parties to ensure that at least 30 percent of their candidates for public office are women. Reforms to the electoral law were also approved that would cap gender participation at 70 percent for male and female candidates.[36] The bill was signed into law in June to be effective for the 2003 elections. The National Women's Institute worked with political leaders for passage of the bill.[37]

Women's Rights

In 1981, Mexico ratified the Convention on the Elimination of All Forms of Discrimination against Women that had been approved by the United Nations in 1979. Family rights are contained in the Civil Code of 1884. Despite the virtual elimination of the legally dictated inferiority of women through a succession of reforms in 1917, 1928, 1954, 1974, and 1983, arbitrary differences due to gender persist as exceptions to these rules.

The Penal Code has also undergone changes. The consideration of a woman's reputation and honor in typifying crimes and calculating penalties has disappeared from several felonies, though it persists in the areas of abortion and infanticide. The treatment of adultery is the same for men as for women, and legislation makes sexual harassment a crime.

Mexican labor law has an important characteristic compared to that of other countries: since 1962, it has contained a separate set of regulations governing the situation of women and minors. The protection it provides to women workers is adequate and is not based on their "condition" as women, but rather on their ability to get pregnant and become mothers.

Mexico has no specific law regulating reproductive rights, which can be explained by the relatively recent emergence of this branch of law. The General Law of Population, established in 1974, contains several provisions concerning family planning, but does not mention all of the facets of reproductive rights that have been defined by doctrine and by international organizations.

Feminist Movements

The history of collective women's movements goes back to the nineteenth century, when they petitioned for access to education. The first Feminist Congress in 1915 led to similar events in which the central themes were education for women and equal pay for equal work. Later, the principal issue became the fight to gain political rights. These struggles continued for years, but a critical moment came with the students' movement of 1968 that culminated in the demand by the citizenry for greater democracy and an opening up of the political system with larger channels of participation. This led to a resurgence of feminism. The celebration in Mexico of the First World Conference on Women, sponsored by the United Nations under the slogan "Equality, Development, and Peace," further strengthened the women's movement. During this era of renewal, several initiatives were undertaken, including the first projected legislation on voluntary motherhood. Many nongovernmental organizations were created to support feminist groups and women in poor neighborhoods, all of which renewed interest in the topic of gender and the creation of exclusive spaces for women.

The Mexican women's movement has linked debates on topics like feminism and democracy. The social weight of the movement has allowed it to influence the state's perspective on women and has yielded concrete results, especially in the area of violence against women, where services such as legal, psychological, and medical support have been established to help victims. However, such services are limited to large urban areas.

Lesbian Rights

Lesbian and homosexual rights are not respected or recognized in Mexico. Same-sex couples can neither marry nor adopt children.

Military Service

Military service is not compulsory for Mexican women, but starting in 2000 they were allowed to volunteer for military service.

RELIGION AND SPIRITUALITY

The system of patriarchal dominion permeates the religious sphere in Mexico and is similar in almost all Christian, para-Christian, and indigenous religious groups with perhaps a few minor differences.[38] It is expressed through the exclusion of women from ecclesiastical and/or ministerial positions, as can be seen in indigenous belief systems, the mainstream Catholic Church (which includes 89 percent of the population that describes itself as "believers"),[39] and even modern religions. The fact that women cannot aspire to positions as ministers, priests, or pastors is not directly related to their participation in rituals and other religious activities. Despite such limitations, women still make up the majority of those who attend daily rituals and devote a considerable part of their time to such activities. A 1996 "Survey of Religious Diversity" in Guadalajara showed that the majority of the 10 percent of all believers who attend church on a daily basis were women over forty-five who on average had attended only primary school.[40] This survey also revealed that those who attend church only once a month or never were mostly male.[41] Together, these data indicate that women are still closer to religious institutions and continue to be the main reproducers of religious values for future generations, especially in the family.

Before December 1992, religious organizations in Mexico were hardly mentioned in the law and the constitution.[42] During the presidency of Carlos Salinas de Gortari (1988–1994), however, the constitution was reformed to give such groups legal recognition as "religious associations." With their legality thus guaranteed, churches may now own goods, real estate, and even educational institutions. It became possible to hold religious acts in public areas, and priests and ministers received the right to participate in popular elections, though not as candidates. During and after these constitutional reforms, Mexico witnessed a series of debates, as part of the Catholic hierarchy did not agree that all religious organizations should be accorded equal treatment. Important personages declared publicly that the Catholic Church should receive preferential treatment and should be distinguished from what it termed "other sects." This new law has caused some problems for Indian communities in Mexico because the majority of indigenous peoples have not registered themselves as religious associations in the new constitutional framework.[43] In practice, the application of the law generates more problems than it resolves. For example, the Huicholes, Yaquis, and Mayos have not registered, as it would be very difficult for the sacred spaces and territories where they practice their rituals to be considered legally as their "property" since they extend across various states of Mexico. The elaboration of the form and nature of the new law of religious associations ignored the special characteristics of the millenary belief systems of the indigenous groups that live in Mexico. In other ways, however, this law has had a positive effect because through it churches can under certain circumstances claim their rights or defend themselves in cases of discrimination.

Women's Roles and Rituals and Religious Practices

National and regional statistics often cannot reflect clearly the subtleties that exist in religious institutions. The limitations imposed by diverse hierarchies to block women's access to positions of authority have not prevented women from intervening in decisions and even usurping spaces of religious authority and power formally reserved for men (priests, ministers). For example, in currents within Catholicism such as the Renovation of the Holy Spirit and the Charismatic Catholic Movement, recent studies speak of groups that often open spaces of power to women, who may reach leadership positions within the lay population that supersede even those of the priests.[44]

Women stand out even more in marginal religions, where they find spaces that allow them to play roles of insubordination, not only with respect to the dominant religion but also to the dominant sex. One observer has noted that it is in "marginal, non-mainstream religions [that] women often have more power and autonomy than in the major religion found in their society."[45] Mexican historians and anthropologists have noted in their studies that since colonial times in Mexico, women have participated more actively in religious and/or spiritual activities, both in terms of numbers and intensity.[46] These scholars confirm that in the Old and New Worlds, women have turned to peripheral religious expressions inside or outside institutions and always well removed from orthodoxy and tradition in order to stand out and play leading roles. It is in such marginal spaces that women—historically and at present—have achieved greater recognition as well as access to otherwise unattainable social spaces.

In popular Catholicism (which is outside the official scope of the church), women have always played a determining role in rituals and devotions practiced throughout the country, such as novenaries, peregrinations, processions, rosaries, funerals, and annual celebrations. Several studies have shown that in Marian Trinity Spiritualism the presence and importance of women is central.[47] The same could be said of their role in Pentecostal-type organizations, though in these groups women are still subject to a series of restrictions based on biblical teachings. In several cases, however, they have prominent roles and attain spaces of freedom both inside their churches and outside of them that allow them to escape from and/or confront male domination.[48]

The topic of the role of women in pre-Hispanic religions has been widely discussed, but no consensus exists. It has been claimed that women occupied a less oppressed position in pre-Hispanic cultures than in the colonial era.[49] This premise, however, has been challenged by historians who hold that in pre-Hispanic societies women were subordinated to male domination, though their position may have worsened in the colonial era.[50] The principal difference between Christianity and pre-Hispanic religions is that the latter had an ample spectrum of goddesses in their sacred pantheons, while Christianity offers only the Virgin Mary to fill the same role. From a strictly theological perspective, the Virgin Mary occupies a subordinate position to God or Christ.

In postcolonial times, however, indigenous women in Catholicism and in indigenous religious traditions (both seen as eminently patriarchal systems) had no opportunity to fill important roles or participate in ways that would have given them spaces for self-affirmation and allowed them to confront the situation of inequality to men that often led to systematic intrafamily violence directed mainly against women and girls.[51] It was only in the 1970s, with the advent of a new social ministry promoted by liberation theologians such as Samuel Ruiz of Chiapas, that indigenous women were able to make their voices heard for the first time. It has been claimed that the new liberal ministries "have encouraged greater participation by women in community development and supported the formation of pastoral agents."[52]

VIOLENCE

Domestic Violence

Domestic violence and other types of violent behavior (sexual harassment, for example) are common in Mexican society. According to studies by various nongovernmental organizations, domestic violence exists in all sectors of the population because it has deep cultural roots and because such actions and attitudes have been positively valued by political and popular leaders, in myth, and in literature.[53] The extent and profound repercussions of violence at the social level have left an imprint on public opinion. In recent years, they have been topics for analysis and debate and have been taken into account in government planning and programs. In 1996 Mexico introduced tough laws aimed at stopping domestic violence, but little progress has been made in enforcing the laws in a culture with the popular belief "If he doesn't beat me he doesn't love me."[54]

Rape/Sexual Assault

Various nongovernmental organizations that support abused and raped women have appeared in recent decades, and since 1989 the government has created specialized agencies for sexual crimes to receive and process accusations and provide help to victims and their families. Though these measures represent significant advances, they are insufficient given the magnitude of the problem, its cultural entrenchment, and the slow pace of their operations. Although more crimes are being reported, the number of sentences shows no increase.

Trafficking in Women and Children

The kidnapping of young boys and girls for purposes of forcing them into prostitution has been reported, as has the white slave trade. A study launched in 2000 found that younger women from rural areas of Mexico, or those who come from poor families, are targeted by members of criminal organizations who mislead them with promises of domestic jobs.[55]

War and Military Repression

In areas such as Chiapas, where armed conflicts occur, there are reports of the rape of indigenous women by members of the army and paramilitary groups, and of massacres (as in Acteal) where the victims were indigenous women and children.

OUTLOOK FOR THE TWENTY-FIRST CENTURY

As the twenty-first century begins, equality for Mexican women is far from being realized because of differences that arise from factors such as class and ethnicity. For Mexico to achieve true equality among its people, it must redistribute resources. To bring about the inclusion of the dispossessed population (indigenous women, men, and children), much work remains.

NOTES

1. *CIA World Factbook: Mexico*, www.cia.gov/cia/publications/factbook/geos/mx.html.

2. Ibid.

3. Ibid.

4. COPLAMAR: National Coordination of the Plan for Marginal Zones, www.cidac.org/libroscidac/vivienda/vivienda-notas.pdf; CONAPO: National Population Council, www.conapo.gob.mx/m_en_cifras/principal.html; INEGI: National Institute of Statistics, Geography and Informatics, www.inegi.gob.mx.

5. Instituto Nacional de Estadística, Geografía, Informática and Sistema Interagencial de las Naciones Unidas (INEGI and SINU), *Perfil estadístico de la población mexicana: Una aproximación a las inequidades socioeconómicas, regionales y de género* (Aguascalientes, México, 2000), 147–263.

6. Carmen Ramos et al., *Presencia y transparencia: La mujer en la historia de México*. (México, D.F.: El Colegio de México, 1987).

7. This section and several of the following ones are based to a large extent on INEGI and SINU, *Perfil estadístico de la población mexicana*, 2000; *Mujeres latinoamericanas en cifras* (México, D.F.: FLACSO/Instituto de la Mujer [Spain]/UNIFEM-UNICEF, 1993); and *Mujeres y hombres en México* (INEGI/Comisión Nacional de la Mujer, 2000).

8. INEGI, *XII Censo General*, 2000, www.inegi.gob.mx/difusion/espanol/poblacion.

9. These levels include technical and commercial studies requiring graduation from junior high school; INEGI, www.inegi.gob.mx.

10. INEGI, *XII Censo General*, 2000.

11. Ibid.

12. National Employment Survey 2000, www.migration.ucdavis.edu/cmpr/feb01/escobar_feb01.html.

13. Orlandina de Oliveira, "La participación femenina y los mercados de trabajo en México: 1970–1980," *Estudios Demográficos y Urbanos* 4(3) (1989).

14. Brígida García, *La fuerza de trabajo en México a principios de los noventa: Problemas de medición, principales características, y tendencias futuras* (Mexico, D.F.: STyPS, 1994); Teresa Rendón and Carlos Salas, eds., "El mercado no agrícola en México: Tendencias y cambios recientes," in *Ajuste estructural, mercados laborales, y tratado de libre comercio* (México, D.F.: El Colegio de México/Fundación Friedrich Ebert/El Colegio de la Frontera Norte, 1992).

15. Luisa Gabayet, *Atrapadas: Las mujeres en la industria electrónica de Guadalajara* (México, D.F.: CIESAS, forthcoming); Susan Tiano, *Patriarchy on the Line: Labor, Gender, and Ideology in the Mexican Maquila Industry* (Philadelphia: Temple University Press, 1994); Kathryn Kopinak, *Desert Capitalism* (Buffalo, NY: Black Rose Books, 1997); María Patricia Fernández-Kelly, *For We Are Sold, I and My People: Women and Industry in Mexico's Frontier* (Albany: State University of New York Press, 1983); Leslie Sklair, *Assembling for Development: The Maquila Industry in Mexico and the United States* (San Diego: Center for U.S.-Mexican Studies, University of California, 1993).

16. Lourdes Benería and Martha Roldán, *The Crossroads of Class and Gender: Industrial Homework, Subcontracting, and Household Dynamics in Mexico City* (Chicago: University of Chicago Press, 1987).

17. National Employment Survey 2000, www.migration.ucdavis.edu/cmpr/feb01/escobar_feb01.html.

18. Laurence Pantin, "Mexico: Seeking to Outlaw Workplace Gender Bias," Inter Press Service, August 9, 2002; "Mexico: Labor, Mexican Government, Unions, and Business Agree to Labor Reforms," EFE News Service, November 27, 2002.

19. Claudio Lomnitz and Perez Lizaur, *Vicios publicos, virtudes privadas: La corrupcion en Mexico*, ed. Claudio Lomnitz (Mexico City: Grupo Editorial Miguel Angel Porrúa SA, 2000).

20. United Nations, "Statement by Mexico in the High Level Segment, 9th Commission on Sustainable Development," 2001, www.un.int/mexico/high_level_9CSD_2001.htm.

21. United Nations, "Statement by Ambassador Jorge Eduardo Navarrete, 45th Session of the Commission on the Status of Women," New York, March 8, 2000, www.un.int/mexico/45CSW_2001_ing.htm.

22. "Mexico: Working with Indigenous Farmers to Support Cultural Survival and Autonomy," www.equalexchange.org/mexico/updateArchive2002.html.

23. National Wildlife Federation, EnviroAction, "NWF Announces a New Program: Women for Sustainable Development," www.nwf.org, 2001.

24. United Nations Population Fund, Working to Empower Women, "Women and the Environment," www.unfpa.org.

25. National Survey of Demographic Dynamics, 1997, www.cicred.ined.fr/pauvrete/actes/tuiran.pdf.

26. Ibid.

27. Ibid.

28. Ibid.

29. Marta Lamas, *Política y reproducción: Aborto: La frontera del derecho a decidir* (México, D.F.: Plaza y Janés, 2001).

30. Ibid.

31. MEXFAM: Mexican Family Planning Association, www.mexfam.org/mx/introducc.htm; UNICEF 2000, www.unicef.org/sowc2000.

32. National Institute of Public Health Mexico, www.insp.mx/cisp/censa/censa.pdf.

33. National Council of AIDS in Mexico, www.ssa.gob.mx/conasida.

34. Mexico Epidemiological Center, www.pitt.edu/~super1/lecture/lec1551.

35. Pilar Franco, *Mexico: Soaring Suicide Rate among Young*, 2000, http://www.oneworld.org/ips2/may00/20_45_077.html.

36. "Mexico—Lower House Passes Reform to Increase Female Candidates," EFE News Service, May 1, 2002, www.globalexchange.org/campaigns/mexico/updateArchive2002.html.

37. Susana Hayward, "Women Answer Mexicans' Cry for Reform; Female Candidates Climbing toward Top of the Ladder," *San Diego Union-Times*, January 5, 2003.

38. I thank Patricia Fortuny for her collaboration in the writing of this section. Christian religious associations are those of Judeo-Christian origin, including Catholicism and evangelical churches (historical, Pentecostal, and neo-Pentecostal). The para-Christian churches are those that emerged in the context of North American Protestantism in the late nineteenth century and that have added Christian dogma to other nonbiblical beliefs, such as the Mormon, the Seventh-Day Adventist, and the Jehovah's Witnesses churches.

39. There are important regional differences in the country; for example, in the northern states of Sinaloa, Tamaulipas, Chihuahua, and Nuevo León and in the southern border states of Chiapas, Campeche, and Tabasco, the percentage of the population that is Catholic is much lower (as little as 70 percent or less in some cases), while those who profess an evangelical affiliation may reach figures as high as 30 percent.

40. Alma Dorantes González, "Sexo, edad, escuela, y religión," in *Creyentes y creencias en Guadalajara*, ed. Patricia Fortuny Loret de Mola (Ciudad de México: INAH, CIESAS, 2000), 75.

41. Ibid.

42. Though the relationship between the Catholic Church and the Mexican government has not always been cordial, it has been characterized by a mutual understanding and a kind of complicity that in most cases has led to the unjust treatment of all other churches (Christian and non-Christian alike), which are disdained and characterized derogatorily as "sects" or "cults."

43. Carlos Garma Navarro, "Las mujeres en las iglesias pentecostales de México," *Religiones y Sociedad* 3 (May/August 1998).

44. Elizabeth Juárez Cerdi, *Mi reino sí es de este mundo* (Zamora: El Colegio de Michoacán, 1997).

45. Rita M. Gross, *Feminism and Religion: An Introduction* (Boston: Beacon Press, 1996), 95.

46. Isabel Lagarriga Attias, "La mujer en la heterodoxia en México," in *Primer Anuario de la Dirección de Etnología y Antropología Social*, ed. Isabel Lagarriga Attias, Colección Obra Diversa (México, D.F.: Instituto Nacional de Antropología e Historia, 1995); Isabel Lagarriga Attias, "Experiencia religiosa y cambios de creencias en algunas mujeres mexicanas," paper presented at the 49th Congreso Internacional de Americanistas, Quito, Ecuador, July 7–12, 1997; Isabel Lagarriga Attias, "Participación religiosa: Viejas y nuevas formas de reivindicación femenina en México," paper presented at the 12th Congreso de Estado, Iglesia, y Grupos Laicos, Jalapa, Veracruz, México, October 28–30, 1998; Silvia Ortíz Echániz, "El poder del trance en la participación femenina en el Espiritualismo Trinitario Mariano," paper presented at the XX Mesa Redonda de la Sociedad Mexicana de Antropología, Mexico, 1987; Silvia Ortíz Echániz, *Una religiosidad popular: El Espiritualismo Trinitario Mariano*, Colección científica (Ciudad de México: INAH, 1990); Noemí Quezada, "Alumbrados del siglo XVII: Análisis de casos," in *Religión en Mesoamérica: XII Mesa Redonda de la Sociedad Mexicana de Antropología* (Ciudad de México: 1972), 581–86; Noemí Quezada, *Enfermedad y maleficio* (Ciudad de México: UNAM, 1989).

47. Ortíz Echániz, *Una religiosidad popular*, 1990; Lagarriga Attias, "La mujer," 1995.

48. Patricia Fortuny Loret de Mola, "Converted Women Redefining Their Family Roles in Mexico," in *Family, Religion, and Social Change in Diverse Societies*, ed. Sharon Houseknecht and Jerry Pankhurst (New York and Oxford: Oxford University Press, 1999).

49. Sylvia Marcos, "Curas, diosas, y erotismo: El catolicismo frente a los indios," in *Mujeres e iglesia: Sexualidad y aborto en América Latina*, ed. Ana María Portugal (México, D.F.: Distribuciones Fontamara, 1989).

50. Carlos Garma Navarro, "La situación legal de las minorías religiosas en México: Balance actual, problemas, y conflictos," *Alteridades* 9(18) (July/December 1999): 134.

51. Concerning this topic, see the novels by Ramón Rubín on ethnic groups in the highlands of Chiapas.

52. Rosalva Aida Hernández Castillo, *La otra frontera: Identidades múltiples en el Chiapas poscolonial* (Ciudad de México: CIESAS, Porrúa, 2001), 235.

53. Marwaan Macan-Markar, *Domestic Violence—No End in Sight*, 2000, www.oneworld.org/ips2/nov00/22_53_078.html.

54. Navarro, 1999.

55. Denise Bonk, *Study Launched on Trafficking of Women and Children in the Americas*, April 12, 2000, http://usinfo.state.gov/topical/global/traffic/00041202.htm.

RESOURCE GUIDE

Suggested Reading

Behar, Ruth. *Translated Woman: Crossing the Border with Esperanza's Story*. Boston: Beacon Press, 1993. Discusses the story of a rural Mexican woman and her struggle for personal power and dignity against the overwhelming currents of male domination and poverty.

Benería, Lourdes, and Martha Roldán. *The Crossroads of Class and Gender: Industrial Homework, Subcontracting, and Household Dynamics in Mexico City*. Chicago: University of Chicago Press, 1987. An anthropological and economic study of women engaged in home production in the capital of Mexico.

Fernández-Kelly, María Patricia. *For We Are Sold, I and My People: Women and Industry in Mexico's Frontier*. Albany: State University of New York Press, 1983. Deals with the lives and working conditions of women in the maquiladoras on the northern Mexican border.

Fowler-Salamini, Heather, and Mary Kay Vaughan, eds. *Women of the Mexican Countryside, 1850–1990*. Tucson: University of Arizona Press, 1994. A picture of Mexican women in the countryside from a historical perspective.

González de la Rocha, Mercedes. *The Resources of Poverty: Women and Survival in a Mexican City*. Oxford: Basil Blackwell, 1994. Tells the lives and strategies of poor Mexican women residing in the second most important Mexican city, Guadalajara, to make ends meet and keep their children alive.

Videos/Films

Hacia el Horizonte. 2002. Directed by Mariano Estrada.
Perfume de Violetas. 2001. Directed by Marisse Sistach. Produced by Quality Films.
A Place Called Chiapas. 1998. Directed by Nettie Wild. Produced by Zeitgeist Films. New York, NY.

Web Sites

CIMAC: Communicación e Información de la Mujer, www.cimac.org.mx/.
Political, social, and cultural aspects of women's lives in Mexico.

CONASIDA: National Council of AIDS in Mexico, www.ssa.gob.mx/conasida.
AIDS and women in Mexico.

GIRE: Grupo de Información en Reproducción Elegida, http://.gire.org.mx/home.
htm/.
Reproductive rights, abortion, and law in Mexico.

Instituto Nacional de Estadística Geografía e Informática, http://.dgcnesyp.inegi.gob.
mx/sisesim.
Statistics on the condition of Mexican women.

Senado: Republic of Mexico, www.senado.gob.mx/mujeres/.
Women and legislation.

Organizations

Centro para Mujeres—Cidhal
Calle las Flores, No. 11
Cuernavaca, 1-579, CP 62001, Mexico, AP
Phone: (01777) 318-20-58
Fax: 314-05-86
Email: cidhal@prodigy.net.mx

Grupo de Información en Reproducción Elegida
Viena 160, Colonia del Carmen
Coyoacán, CP 04100, Mexico, DF
Phone/Fax: 5-658-66-45, 5-658-66-84
Email: Correo@gire.org.mx
Web site: www.laneta.apc.org/cidhal/

Proderechos, Red por la Salud de las Mujeres—Ciudad de México
Bélgica 1007 Depto. 3
Colonia Portales, 03300, Mexico, DF
Phone/Fax: 5-672-18-13
Email: proderechos@laneta.apc.org
Web site: www.laneta.apc.org/proderechos

SELECTED BIBLIOGRAPHY

Fortuny Loret de Mola, Patricia. "Converted Women Redefining Their Family Roles
    in Mexico." In *Family, Religion, and Social Change in Diverse Societies*, ed. Sharon
    Houseknecht and Jerry Pankhurst, 363–86. New York and Oxford: Oxford Uni-
    versity Press, 1999.
Kopinak, Kathryn. *Desert Capitalism*. Buffalo, NY: Black Rose Books, 1997.
Sklair, Leslie. *Assembling for Development: The Maquila Industry in Mexico and the United
    States*. San Diego: Center for U.S.-Mexican Studies, University of California,
    1993.
Tiano, Susan. *Patriarchy on the Line: Labor, Gender, and Ideology in the Mexican Maquila
    Industry*. Philadelphia: Temple University Press, 1994.

SPANISH BIBLIOGRAPHY

2000, *XII Censo General de Población y Vivienda, 2000; Resumen General Ampliado*. México, D.F. 1990.

Dorantes González, Alma. "Sexo, edad, escuela, y religión." In *Creyentes y creencias en Guadalajara*, ed. Patricia Fortuny Loret de Mola, 73–100. Ciudad de México: INAH, CIESAS, 2000.

Fortuny Loret de Mola, Patricia, ed. *Creyentes y creencias en Guadalajara*. Ciudad de México: INAH, CIESAS, 2000.

Gabayet, Luisa. *Atrapadas: Las mujeres en la industria electrónica de Guadalajara*. México, D.F.: CIESAS, forthcoming.

García, Brígida. *La fuerza de trabajo en México a principios de los noventa: Problemas de medición, principales características, y tendencias futuras*. México, D.F.: STyPS, 1994.

Garma Navarro, Carlos. "Las mujeres en las iglesias pentecostales de México." *Religiones y Sociedad* 3 (May/August 1998): 31–48.

———. "La situación legal de las minorías religiosas en México: Balance actual, problemas, y conflictos." *Alteridades* 9(18) (July/December 1999): 134–44.

Hernández Castillo, Rosalva Aída. *La otra frontera: Identidades múltiples en el Chiapas poscolonial*. Ciudad de México: CIESAS, Porrúa, 2001.

Instituto Nacional de Estadística, Geografía, e Informática. *Encuesta nacional de la dinámica demográfica, 1992*. México, D.F., 1994.

Instituto Nacional de Estadística, Geografía, e Informática and Comisión Nacional de la Mujer. *Mujeres y hombres en México*. 4th ed. Aguascalientes, México, 2000.

Instituto Nacional de Estadística, Geografía, e Informática and Secretaria del Trabajo y Previsión Social. *Encuesta Nacional de Empleo, 1993*. México, D.F., 1993.

Instituto Nacional de Estadística, Geografía, e Informática and Sistema Interagencial de las Naciones Unidas. *Perfil estadístico de la población mexicana: Una aproximación a las inequidadas socioeconómicas, regionales y de género*. Aguascalientes, México, 2000.

Juárez Cerdi, Elizabeth. *Mi reino sí es de este mundo*. Zamora: El Colegio de Michoacán, 1997.

Lagarriga Attias, Isabel. "Experiencia religiosa y cambios de creencias en algunas mujeres mexicanas." Paper presented at the 49th Congreso Internacional de Americanistas, Quito, Ecuador, July 7–12, 1997.

———. "La mujer en la heterodoxia en México." In *Primer Anuario de la Dirección de Etnología y Antropología Social*, ed. Isabel Lagarriga Attias, 25–64. Colección Obra Diversa. México, D.F.: Instituto Nacional de Antropología e Historia, 1995.

———. "Participación religiosa: Viejas y nuevas formas de reivindicación femenina en México." Paper presented at the 12th Congreso de Estado, Iglesia, y Grupos Laicos, Jalapa, Veracruz, México, October 28–30, 1998.

Lamas, Marta. *Política y reproducción: Aborto: La frontera del derecho a decidir*. México, D.F.: Plaza y Janés, 2001.

Marcos, Sylvia. "Curas, diosas, y erotismo: El catolicismo frente a los indios." In *Mujeres e iglesia: Sexualidad y aborto en América Latina*, ed. Ana María Portugal, 9–33. México, D.F.: Distribuciones Fontamara, 1989.

Oliveira, Orlandina de. "La participación femenina y los mercados de trabajo en México: 1970–1980." *Estudios Demográficos y Urbanos* 4(3), 1989.

Ortíz Echániz, Silvia. "El poder del trance en la participación femenina en el Espiritualismo Trinitario Mariano." Paper presented at the XX Mesa Redonda de la Sociedad Mexicana de Antropología, Mexico, 1987.

———. *Una religiosidad popular: El Espiritualismo Trinitario Mariano*. Colección ciéntífica. Ciudad de México: INAH, 1990.

Quezada, Noemí. "Alumbrados del siglo XVII: Análisis de casos." In *Religión en Mesoamérica: XII Mesa Redonda de la Sociedad Mexicana de Antropología*, 581–586. Ciudad de México, 1972.

———. *Enfermedad y maleficio*. Ciudad de México: UNAM, 1989.

Ramos, Carmen, et al. *Presencia y transparencia: La mujer en la historia de México*. México, D.F.: El Colegio de México, 1987.

Rendón, Teresa, and Carlos Salas, eds. "El mercado no agrícola en México: Tendencias y cambios recientes." In *Ajuste estructural, mercados laborales, y tratado de libre comercio*. México, D.F.: El Colegio de México/Fundación Friedrich Ebert/El Colegio de la Frontera Norte, 1992.

UNICEF/UNIFEM/FLACSO. *Mujeres latinoamericanas en cifras: México*. Ministerio de Asuntos Sociales. Instituto de la mujer (España), FLACSO, UNICEF y UNIFEM, México. Santiago de Chile. 1995.

10

THE NETHERLANDS ANTILLES

Jacqueline Martis

PROFILE OF THE NETHERLANDS ANTILLES

The Netherlands Antilles is a nonindependent territory within the Kingdom of the Netherlands. It consists of five islands, each with its own unique traits. There is no single Dutch Caribbean identity. Each island has a separate history and development that distinguishes it from the others, but the islands still have enough similarities and common history to tie them together. The most common thread is Dutch colonization over a period of more than three centuries.

The Kingdom of the Netherlands consists of the European Netherlands, the Caribbean Netherlands Antilles, and Aruba. Aruba was part of the Netherlands Antilles until 1986, when it received its separate status in the Kingdom of the Netherlands. The five remaining islands of the Netherlands Antilles are Curaçao and Bonaire (the Leeward Islands) and St. Maarten, St. Eustatius, and Saba (the Windward Islands). Both the Dutch and the French share St. Maarten, which is the second most populous island of the Netherlands Antilles.

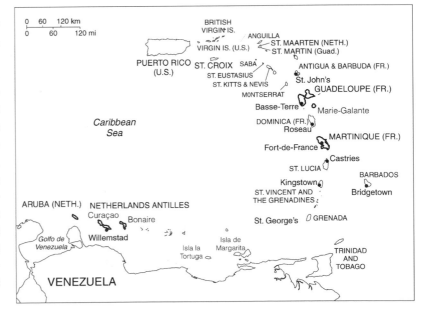

The structure of the Netherlands Antilles is complicated. The Leeward Islands are situated only 60 miles off the coast of Venezuela, whereas the Windward Islands are located about 500 miles away, east of the U.S. Virgin Islands. The Leeward Islands Aruba, Bonaire, and Curaçao were discovered in 1499 by Spaniards and thus became properties of the Spanish king. The original inhabitants of these islands were Indians originally from mainland South America. Since there were no valuable resources found on the islands and they were considered unfit for agriculture, they were declared the useless islands (*Las islas inutiles*).

In 1634, the Dutch were at war with the Spaniards, and the Dutch West India Company (WIC) was in search of salt in the Caribbean. The islands seemed like the perfect solution to their quest. When the Dutch took the islands from Spain, most of the inhabitants—Indians and Spaniards—were carted off to mainland South America.[1] The importance of these islands for the Dutch lay in the great trade possibilities they offered due to their geographic position.

Curaçao became the main African slave depot and slave distribution center of the WIC. The WIC's trade in slaves to the plantations of the mainland became the primary business of the Dutch settlers. Agriculture was left to the Jewish population, the next group of settlers on the island. In 1715, they were given permission by the WIC to develop agriculture, but the natural conditions of these islands made the development of a proper agriculture economy very difficult. Seeing the great opportunities of the geographic position of the island, the Jews turned to the trade of merchandise.[2] Thus the useless island of Curaçao became very useful to the Dutch and the Jews as an important center of the trade market, connecting South American goods with European customers.

Due to the very cheap labor force introduced by the slave trade and the few plantations on the island, a small group of slaves was kept on the island to work for the Dutch and Jews on their plantations and/or in the households. The combination of white Europeans, Jews, and black slaves was the basis for today's multiracial society. The existence of a mixed class consisting of light-colored people who enjoyed a higher status than the black slaves was due to the inevitable contact between slavemasters and (female) slaves. As elsewhere in the Americas, many female slaves were forced to engage in sexual activities or were raped by their owners.

The Curaçao slaves rebelled at various times, fighting for their freedom and/or more humane treatment by the slave owners. The most significant revolt occurred in 1795, but in the end the slaves were overpowered and the rebellion leaders cruelly executed. Slavery was finally abolished in 1863.

The island of Bonaire, on the other hand, was used mainly as a horse-breeding farm and was an important supplier of wood and salt for the WIC. Unlike the situation in Curaçao, native Indians were considered free persons who could live and work on the island but had to adhere to a long list of restrictions. White colonialists were not allowed to settle the island before the nineteenth century. After the WIC ceased operations, Bonaire became a government-owned plantation. In general, the abolition of slavery in 1863 hit the islands hard. The dismal living conditions of the former slaves worsened, and so did the condition of the "mixed" class, which enjoyed a higher status than the blacks.

The Windward Islands were important for the WIC because of their strategic geographic position in the Caribbean. In the seventeenth century, the WIC had so much military and economic power that it dominated trade and shipping in the Caribbean and gave merchants the right to exploit St. Maarten (1632), St. Eustatius (1638), and Saba (1640). As with the Leeward Islands, slaves were brought in to work on plantations. St. Eustatius became a profitable slave depot for the WIC and an important center for illegal trade. St. Maarten also produced tobacco, cotton, indigo, and sugar.

Unlike society on Curaçao and Bonaire, the black and white segments of the population did not mingle. There was a clearer class distinction of whites on top of the societal structure and blacks at the bottom.

After emancipation in 1863, the socioeconomic structure of the islands did not change significantly. The Protestant Dutch and the Jews formed the upper class. A small middle class consisted of the mixed class and some Dutch (mostly members of the military), and the Catholic blacks formed the underclass. The economic dependence of the black ex-slaves and the social distinctions between these groups were maintained by the powerful, white upper class, not only on racial but also on religious grounds.[3]

Some profound changes took place in the economic and social situation and development of the islands with the establishment of the Royal Dutch Shell Company on Curaçao in 1918.[4] Many jobs were created in the refinery and related businesses. The local labor force found better-paying jobs in the refinery and moved in great numbers to the urban areas to work in it.

Eventually, the oil refinery of the Royal Dutch Shell Company needed more workers than the local market could provide, and so immigrants from all over the Caribbean came to Curaçao to work in the refinery. With the influx of these different groups, Curaçao became a more diversified community. Various groups of different ethnic backgrounds had to find a way to live in peace with each other on this very small island. Some of these groups came from the Middle East and India. These became mainly merchants, as did the Ashkenazi Jews who fled from the Nazis. An influx of "new" Dutch upset the socioeconomic balance that existed. The "old" Dutch felt threatened by the European Dutch and started to think of themselves as children of the land (landskinderen, that is, the white Europeans born on the island).

The economic growth of the island was immense. In a few years, Curaçao was transformed from a postemancipation society into a modern industrial society. This economic growth also made Curaçao financially nondependent on the Netherlands, which in turn started a movement toward self-rule of the islands.

The Netherlands Antilles has more than eighty different ethnic groups that have managed to live in harmony for hundreds of years despite their different backgrounds and socioeconomic standing. The colonial heritage is still visible in the social structure. The upper classes still consist mainly of descendants of Jews, Protestants, and Catholics. Other upper-class groups are the Lebanese and Indians who are merchants. The middle class is made up of a large group of "colored" people and darker-skinned blacks. The lower or working class is predominantly dark-skinned blacks and poor immigrants.

Until 1936, the Netherlands Antilles, or "The Colony of Curaçao and dependents," as it was called, was under Dutch colonial rule. Dutch legislation was applied in these Caribbean islands. The Dutch settlers had total political power. In 1936, the Colony of Curaçao received its own constitution, the Staatregeling van de Nederlandse Antillen van 1936 (Constitution of the Netherlands Antilles of 1936). In 1936, the colonial government also agreed to hold a very restricted election in the colonies. Only 3.5 percent of the population (men) was entitled to vote in this election. Universal suffrage was finally granted in 1948, and women could now also vote. Women played an important, albeit hidden, role in the struggle for internal self-rule for Curaçao and dependents.

In 1954, the colonies finally became autonomous members of the Kingdom of the Netherlands with internal self-rule. The Netherlands is still responsible for foreign affairs and defense. The head of state is the queen of the Netherlands, who is represented by the governor general. There are two levels of government: central and island (local). Parliamentary and Island Council elections are held every four years. Curaçao is also the seat of the central government.

The Netherlands Antilles has a total population of about 175,653.[5] Curaçao, the largest of the islands, has a total of 130,627 persons, St. Maarten 30,594, Bonaire 10,791, St. Eustatius 2,292, and Saba 1,349. The female population is 93,132, and the male population is 82,521.

The Netherlands Antilles is a multicultural and multilingual country. Because of the differences in the history of colonial settlement, the Leeward Islands speak Papiamentu, a Portuguese-based Creole, and the Windward Islands speak English. The official language of the Netherlands Antilles is still Dutch. Dutch is mainly used as the language of instruction in schools, in legislation, and in some government business.

The Netherlands Antilles boasts a relatively high level of overall development.

Life expectancy for males in the Netherlands Antilles varies from 71.8 years in Curaçao and 73.9 years in Bonaire to 76.6 years in the Windward Islands. Females have a higher life expectancy than males, 77.5 years in

Curaçao and Bonaire and 79.3 years in the Windward Islands. The infant mortality rate was twice that of the Netherlands in 1993, 12 per 1,000 live births. The maternal death rate for the period 1986–1993 was 54 deaths per 100,000 live births. The fertility rate has been declining steadily throughout the years and currently is 2.09 in Curaçao.[6]

OVERVIEW OF WOMEN'S ISSUES

Although women's roles and contributions in the history of the Netherlands Antilles are yet to be completely documented, women have played and continue to play a pivotal role in its history. Women have always been caretakers. During slavery, the female slaves were also the caretakers of the children of their masters. They were the nannies and had a profound influence on the children. These female slaves also had their own families. They had children with other slaves but also had children with their masters. From all accounts, in many of these so-called relationships, the women were forced to have sex with the masters. A consequence of having children with the master was that these colored children were treated better than black slave children, or so the mothers hoped.

Women's contribution became visible during the struggle for the right to vote and the quest for autonomy from the Netherlands. Before that time, women's place was definitely in the home and taking care of the community. Politics and any kind of public life were solely domains of men. During the struggle for universal suffrage, women began playing an important role. One group of women who called themselves Wednesday Ladies (Damanan di Djarason) started meeting at the headquarters of the People's National Party and made history when they collected more than a thousand signatures for the petition for universal suffrage.[7]

Women did not become equal in the eyes of the law for many decades. Not until the mid-1980s did female civil servants get equal pay for equal work and the right to continue working after they got married. Women and girls now actively participate in public life and in most areas enjoy status equal to that of men. One area where they are still not equal is in relationships with men. Domestic violence and other violent crimes against women seem to be on the rise. Women are well represented in educational institutions, but they are not paid the same as men.

EDUCATION

Opportunities

Historically, the educational system in the Netherlands Antilles has been based on the Dutch educational system. After the abolition of slavery, Catholic missionaries were allowed to take over the education of colored people and "free slaves." The former slave owners were Protestants and did not allow their former slaves to have the same religion as they had for fear that this would affect their status.

Dutch is still imposed as the official language of instruction. School attendance is mandatory up to age fifteen, and the rate of school participation up to that age is 98 percent. However, 26 percent of young people do not finish elementary school, and the dropout rate of those fifteen years old or older is 42 percent.[8]

Since Curaçao is the largest and most populous island, it has more academic facilities than the other islands. Young children living on any of the other islands who want to pursue higher education have to move to Curaçao at a very young age (eleven or twelve) to further their education. Students wanting to pursue a college or university degree have to study abroad in the Netherlands, the United States, or elsewhere.

As is the case in other parts of the Caribbean, girls and women are well represented in schools. Data from the 1999 statistical yearbook show, for example, that a higher number of women enter and graduate from a university. They are overrepresented in all sectors except the technical faculty, where they are underrepresented by a large margin.[9]

Several studies of employment and occupations by the Central Bureau of Statistics show a marked underrepresentation of women in the technical sectors. Even though women are well represented in the educational settings, the picture for less educated women is bleak. A study conducted in 1998 looked at the need for technical/vocational schools for women. This study reported a mismatch between schooling of unemployed women and labor-market needs. Many of the unemployed did not have the right schooling for even the lowest-paying jobs.[10] Many of the job opportunities were in the technical sphere, in which women are underrepresented. They are also underrepresented in legislative and managerial occupations.[11] Women are overrepresented in the sectors of health, education, social work, and financial administration. Since women still carry the bulk of the responsibility of the household and children, this also limits their possibilities in the workforce.

Literacy

The Netherlands Antilles boasts a literacy rate of 98 percent for the total population.[12]

EMPLOYMENT AND ECONOMICS

Job/Career Opportunities

Since 1995, the Netherlands Antilles has been hampered by a serious economic and social crisis. Because of the economic crisis, women's lives have become more difficult, one result of which is the feminization of poverty. Data from a preliminary study indicate that 47 percent of households have an income that is less than 1,000 Netherlands Antilles florins (NAf.) ($555) per month. Of that group, 20 percent has an income that is less than NAf. 700 ($400) per month.[13] Female-headed households are overrepresented within this group at 61 percent. Two-thirds of the heads of the households within the 47 percent are unemployed. With a rate of 74.5 percent in 1998, more women are on welfare than men. Women are overrepresented in the lowest ranks of employment, where the secondary benefits are also very limited. Unemployment rose from 12.8 percent in 1994 to 16.7 percent in 1998. Unemployment among youths was 33.9 percent in 1997 and increased to 37 percent in 1999.[14]

Policewoman, Curaçao, the Netherlands Antilles. Photo © TRIP/A. Tovy.

Women are turning again to the informal sector as a means of providing for their families and themselves. The women in the Netherlands Antilles have always found ways of helping themselves overcome tough times and survive on a daily basis. They have a history of doing informal work as street vendors or household workers or doing household chores like ironing and preparing food for others from their homes.[15] Even during slavery, women were involved in preparing and selling food to make ends meet. After slavery, this tradition continued because black women, especially those with darker skin, were not able to find work in the formal sector.[16]

Pay

Although advances have been made, women are still paid less than men.[17] Overall, statistics show a marked difference in level of income for men and women doing the same kind of work regardless of their level of education. Until 1990, women and unmarried men received 20 percent less pay than married men.[18]

Working Conditions

In 1998, the parliament of the Netherlands Antilles approved an amendment to the Labor Regulation Law whereby a forty-hour workweek was established for all workers in the Netherlands Antilles. This law is beneficial to women, who are massively employed within the service sector and retail trade.[19]

The law regarding civil servants stated that once they got married, women had to leave public service. In 1975, the law discriminating against women was changed, and all women regardless of their civil status could become employees in permanent service with the government. Even so, it was not until 1983 that all female government employees were finally able to obtain permanent employment. Until then, single women could only be employed as contract workers by the government. These advances did not, however, guarantee women equal pay.

Support for Mothers/Caretakers

Maternal Leave

Maternal leave of twelve weeks is mandated by law in the Netherlands Antilles. All pregnant women receive paid leave for six weeks before their delivery due date and six weeks after giving birth. Some companies and agencies give women the choice of working up to two or four weeks before their delivery date.

Daycare

There are many government-subsidized facilities for daycare and after-school care for children, although many women still rely on their mothers and aunts as caretakers of their children when they are not in daycare or instead of daycare. Parents with children in the government-subsidized daycare facilities usually pay a minimal amount for the care of their children. There are also a number of private nonsubsidized daycare facilities. In the private sector, some companies provide after-school care facilities for the children of their employees.

Social/Government Programs

Recent changes regarding the labor law and the sickness insurance law have benefited women. An example is the Old Age Insurance Act, which grants married women an independent right to retirement pensions from the state.

Sustainable Development

The demands of the International Monetary Fund (IMF), the government of the Netherlands, and the government of the Netherlands Antilles have aggravated the already critical social crisis. This has resulted, among other things, in further layoffs of government employees, the breakdown of the market protection of some industries in order to liberalize the market completely, and legislative changes to accommodate IMF conditions.[20]

The structural adjustment program in the Netherlands Antilles includes trade liberalization, tax reform (many exemptions were annulled), and the reduction of public-sector employment. Between 1999 and the first half of 2000, the island government of Curaçao and the central government of the Netherlands Antilles laid off approximately 2,000 employees. The program also introduced special taxes, user fees, an increase in water bills, privatization of government assets like government-owned hotels and industries, and the elimination or reduction of government spending in social services, particularly in the health sector. Budget cuts occurred in social housing, schools, and community centers. The introduction of user fees for medicine, in particular, affected groups at risk like the elderly and female-headed households. Cutbacks in health services and the introduction of user fees shifted the responsibilities of care to the household and in particular onto the shoulders of women.[21]

Welfare

The informal safety nets through the family and the community are crumbling in the Netherlands Antilles. Many low-income women and men who are on welfare and unemployed are black. Many of these women are heads of households and have the financial and social obligations of the family resting solely on their shoulders. Although the Netherlands Antilles has a system of welfare, there is no structured social assistance program. The social assistance programs that do exist have high administrative costs, and the benefits are low and restricted to a small group. The social assistance programs of the government do not have an empowering component to move people out of welfare. There is no structured program for access to credit, technical assistance, and training for small-business development.[22]

FAMILY AND SEXUALITY

Gender Roles

In the Netherlands Antilles, family and family life are important. The extended family is still very much a part of the culture. The woman's role is still that of the matriarch and the caregiver. She not only takes care of her children and husband but also has responsibilities to her parents, nieces, nephews, and other family members. In many cases, women are heads of households, and in many others, the extended family lives together on a piece of land in different houses.

Men and women are socialized to take up their separate spaces in public life. Women's reproductive roles include that of caretaker of the family and household, which also encompasses the extended family. Their productive responsibilities also include earning a living and caring for and contributing to their communities via volunteer work.

Marriage

Marriage is still seen as the ideal, although it would seem that people are not in a hurry to get married. Marriage statistics from the 2001 census show that of the population in the age category twenty to twenty-four, there were 7,520 single people versus 499 who were married. Of those aged twenty-five to twenty-nine, there were 7,624 single versus 2,696 married persons. In the age range thirty-five to thirty-nine, there were more married persons (7,374) than single (7,223). The data on singles also include non-traditional unions like visiting unions and common-law marriages.[23]

Marriage among slaves was forbidden. Slaves could live together and have common-law marriages only if or as long as their owners gave permission. It was common for families to be broken up by the male or female being sold off. The prevalence of common-law unions continued up to the end of the nineteenth century, when the Catholic missionaries began a campaign to convert slaves and former slaves to Catholicism. Although the church emphasized marriage, it was not very successful in promoting it. The Royal Dutch Shell Company's policy of rewarding its workers for being married changed the existing pattern. Only men got pensions, but being married would give a wife and the children protection in case the husband died and also would give the family the possibility of getting credit for the purchase or building of a home.[24]

The civil code in the 1950s granted men authority over their wives as well as the wives' goods and properties. The woman was to obey her husband and was obliged to live wherever he desired. The new civil code of 1985 finally gave women equality under the law.

Women are socialized to become "respectable married women" and are taught to put up with their philandering husbands. Women whose husbands have outside affairs commonly say that it doesn't matter much as long as he comes home at night. The general advice is that men will "grow out of it" and that women must learn to be patient.[25]

A study of relationships, sexuality, and AIDS prevention proposes that there are three types of relationship patterns between men and women: marriages, living together (common-law marriages), and visiting relationships.[26] Marriage gives both men and women respectability and security. When couples live together, although women tend to have less security (financial and emotional), they emphasize that they still have a commitment. The unstable relationship is the visiting union. The men tend to have other relationships and/or are married, yet have the woman as the "byside," that is, the other woman.

Families are very close knit. Grandparents, parents, aunts, uncles, nieces, and nephews keep in close contact and share joys and pains. Married children of all ages continually return to their parents' home for comfort and food. Many wives find themselves competing with their mothers-in-law in cooking and caring for their husbands. Major holidays and special occasions like weddings, baptisms, and funerals are times when families come together. Another important aspect of family life is taking care of or bringing up someone else's child, usually without any legal intervention. These children are accepted as part of the family and are brought up as such.

Although monogamy in marriage and marriage itself are normative ideals, this is not reflected in everyday life. According to available data from the 2001 census, the percentage of single female-headed households had risen to 39.6 percent from 36 percent in 1992.[27] The data clearly show that roughly 40 percent of women on Curaçao are single parents.

Reproduction

The population of the Netherlands Antilles is in the process of graying, and fewer babies are being born. The fertility rate has dropped on all the islands, and the average age of the population has risen well into the thirties since 1992.

Sex Education

Although sex education is not mandatory, most schools provide some form of sex education. Several nongovernmental organizations (NGOs) also teach sex education outside of schools. The debate about sex education centers, not around its importance, but about the most effective way of teaching it. Sexuality as a topic is not openly and candidly discussed. It is widely believed that many parents do not talk to their children about sex. Planned Parenthood gives lectures and classes on sexuality and the proper use of contraceptives.

Contraception and Abortion

Although there is universal health care, contraceptives are not covered in its package. Women need to pay for contraceptives without any subsidies. Although Planned Parenthood used to provide free contraceptives, because of cutbacks in government subsidies, it now asks that the recipient make a "contribution" for the contraceptive.

Abortion is illegal in the Netherlands Antilles and can only be legally authorized by a special committee under certain circumstances such as saving the life of the mother or for very young victims of rape. In reality, though, abortions are commonplace. It is estimated that there are more abortions each year than there are births.[28]

Teen Pregnancy

Until an official change in the age of consent in 2000, teen motherhood had been defined as between thirteen and nineteen years of age. However, in 2000, the age of consent was lowered from twenty-one to eighteen. For this reason, the statistics need to be reevaluated, and the definition of teen pregnancy needs to be changed. The teen pregnancy rate tends to vary between 8 and 10 percent, and regardless—or because—of the change in official age of consent, the number of births increased in the year 2000 to 12 percent among girls twelve to nineteen years old. The services that work with teenage mothers are very concerned about the teen pregnancy rate, are working together to reduce teen pregnancy, and have special programs to assist and guide teen mothers.

HEALTH

The health system in general in the Netherlands Antilles is considered good. Overall health coverage varies from island to island. There are indications now that a relatively high percentage of people do not have any kind of insurance from 5.3 percent in Curaçao to 28.7 percent in St. Maarten.[29] The high rate of uninsured can probably be traced to a high number of immigrants on the islands who have no legal status.

Health Care Access

In the 2001 census, women reported enjoying very good or good health more than 80 percent of the time overall. Compared to the census results for 1992, there was a slight drop in percentages. The Central Bureau of Statistics attributes this to the aging of the population. Between 10 and 20 percent of the female population of the islands report their health as being reasonable. A relatively small percentage—between 1 and 4 percent—report their health as being bad or very bad.[30]

As with other services, it is estimated that women's access to health care will be adversely affected by cuts in government health and social programs. Women can access health care relatively easily once they are insured privately, or if they are government employees or welfare recipients. Some of the services that are available are prenatal care for the mother by a general practitioner, a specialist, or midwives. Midwifery was and to an extent still is a popular alternative for women. All the islands have well-baby clinics where babies go for checkups until the age of four years. Immunizations are available either at these clinics or at a doctor's clinic.

Breast-feeding organizations campaign actively and tirelessly to promote the breast feeding of babies. Since the government is also promoting breast feeding, it has cut down on the number of times and length of time it provides free milk to low-income mothers.

Diseases and Disorders

In Curaçao, the primary killer of women is pulmonary circulatory disease and other heart diseases. The other top killers are cerebrovascular disease, perinatal-related conditions, HIV/AIDS, and breast cancer. The most common chronic diseases are hypertension, followed by dizziness, arthritis and other joint diseases, psychological problems, back pain, diabetes, and headaches.[31]

There are several government-subsidized and privately funded organizations that provide information, help, and guidance to the infirm. Nurse care organizations are housed in neighborhoods and give service to the sick, the elderly, or women who have just given birth.

AIDS

The incidence of HIV infection among women in the Netherlands Antilles is growing. There are roughly 2,133 known cases of HIV/AIDS; of these, 47 percent are in women and 53 percent are in men. Most of the cases are concentrated on the two larger islands, Curaçao and St. Maarten.[32]

Cancer

The primary type of cancer among women in the Netherlands Antilles is breast cancer, followed by cervical cancer.

POLITICS AND LAW

Suffrage

Women won the right to vote in 1948.

Political Participation

The first woman member of Parliament was in office from 1950 to 1954. Since its inception, the Netherlands Antilles has had four cabinets headed by women, but women's participation in active politics has varied over time. Some political parties have active female members who also become members of Parliament, ministers, or commissioners. But the dedication, time, and energy women need to participate in politics directly affects their families. The target rate of 50 percent representation has not yet been reached, but women's groups are dedicated to creating more leadership among women, consciousness about women's role in politics and other areas, and, most important, the conditions that will make it possible for women truly to participate in political life.

Women's Rights

Women's rights are protected by a number of conventions and treaties that the Netherlands Antilles has signed, like the United Nations Convention on the Elimination of Discrimination against Women (CEDAW), International Labor Organization treaties, the Convention on the Rights of the Child, the Covenant on Economic, Social, and Cultural Rights, and several more.

Feminist Movements

The women's movement has been a major force for change in the Netherlands Antilles. The prominent islands of Curaçao and St. Maarten have politically active women's organizations. Most of the women's groups do not call themselves feminist and are afraid of being labeled antimale. The Antilles has one feminist organization, the Caribbean Association for Feminist Research and Action, Netherlands Antilles (CAFRA N.A.), which is part of a larger network of Caribbean feminists and researchers, the Caribbean Association for Feminist Research and Action (CAFRA).

Lesbian Rights

CAFRA's fight for women's rights (and the rights of all oppressed groups) includes lesbian rights. Lesbianism is not an issue that is discussed openly in the Netherlands Antilles and is also not something that any group of women or any individual has taken up as an issue. Although lesbianism is not talked about much, some articles have been written about lesbian relationships. Male homosexuality is more openly talked about, and one can see male homosexual couples, but lesbianism is still not as openly seen or mentioned, although many people "know" about lesbian (*ma-*

choro) women.[33] Women's sexuality in general is not talked about publicly and is rarely mentioned openly in literature.[34]

Military Service

Military service is compulsory for young men eighteen years of age and older, but women are exempt from serving in the military.

RELIGION AND SPIRITUALITY

The overwhelming majority of people in the Netherlands Antilles are Roman Catholics. In Curaçao, for example, 80 percent of the population is Catholic. Bonaire registers similar numbers. The situation for the Windward Islands is a bit different. Catholics make up from one-quarter to about 50 percent of the population.[35] The Methodist Church and other denominations have a strong presence in the Windward Islands.

Most of the data available on religion refer to Curaçao and the Afro-Curaçaoan religion, which is also known as the people's religion. Africans brought with them a diversity of cults and rites from a wide area of western and central Africa.[36] During the seventeenth and eighteenth centuries, an advanced fusion of different ideas, religious expressions of the multicultural Africans, evolved.[37] One must also take into account the influence of other African American religions like Vodou (Haiti) and Santeria and the *palo de monte* (Cuba). Later, when Catholic missionaries were allowed to convert the slaves and "free slaves," Afro-Curaçaoan religions and Catholicism were blended.[38]

Women's Roles

In the people's religion, women, especially older women, still pass on wise advice to young mothers about how to take care of the newborn child and protect it against the "evil eye" and other such threats. Another element of popular belief is medicinal and healing herbs. Many families still rely on the healing properties of certain herbs for all kinds of ailments and problems.

Rituals and Religious Practices

Many Catholic practices are still entwined with Afro-Curaçaoan religious expressions. Families mourning their dead still hold what is called eight days (*Ocho dia*), where in the house of the deceased during eight days the rosary is prayed. The Afro-Curaçaoan belief is that the dead is present in the house and that through prayer and other actions he or she can be ousted from the house. Toward the end of the year, there are special ceremonies and cleansing rituals that one must perform to usher out all the bad spirits and bring good luck for the new year.

VIOLENCE

Domestic Violence

Violence against women seems to be increasing, as more women are reporting cases of violence or rape. In 2001, three women in Curaçao were killed, and beatings by their partners made the front pages of newspapers.

The Netherlands Antilles does not have specific legislation for domestic violence. Domestic violence is still categorized under general violence and assault acts. NGOs have long been lobbying to get a domestic violence bill passed, but without success. In Curaçao, a platform against violence against women was officially launched on November 25, 2000. All major players, including the police, women's organizations, relevant departments of the government, and other NGOs like the Catholic Church are part of this platform.

Generally, women who are battered and want to leave their abusing partners do not have economic resources to do so. The system for assistance is very slow and inefficient, leaving the women with no or very little means for survival. The women's organizations are usually the ones that treat and support these women, financially and otherwise.

Curaçao, the largest island of the Netherlands Antilles, does not have a shelter for battered women, although groundwork has been laid by the women's center. No money or resources have been allocated for this. Women's groups have informal networks, including homes where battered women can hide until they can move elsewhere. Many of the battered women and their children move to Holland to escape violence. St. Maarten has a shelter for battered women that receives government and community support for its operation.

Some effort has been made on the local level to make the support agencies more efficient, but, as with all other social services, this has been severely hampered by the structural adjustment programs. CAFRA is executing a regional project called Domestic Violence Intervention. The aim of this project is to train police officers to get a better understanding of domestic violence and to be able to intervene effectively in cases of domestic violence. The Netherlands Antilles is part of this project.

Rape/Sexual Assault

In 2000, a number of violent rapes shocked the Netherlands Antilles. Although rape and sexual assault are common, it is very difficult to give exact numbers because of faulty registration of cases. Marital rape is now considered rape by the civil code. Previously a married man who raped his wife could be prosecuted for assault or abuse but not for rape.

Trafficking in Women and Children

The government of the Netherlands Antilles has no active policy to combat trafficking in women. There has been an explosive growth in clubs and bars where very young women are brought in under the guise of being "dancers," are put to work as striptease dancers, and are forced to work as prostitutes. The owners of the clubs get permits from the local authorities for a number of women to work as dancers.

These women and girls often borrow money from someone back home (Dominican Republic, Colombia) to come to Curaçao and St. Maarten. Some of the clubs organize recruitment procedures and even have "dancing schools" in the countries where young women are recruited. When the women arrive, they have a large debt to repay to their "employer" (tickets and board) or to a lender at home. Also, it is common practice to take away the girls' and women's passports as a further intimidation and threat.

Women are also recruited to come to work as either bartender/waitresses or domestics and are then forced to work as prostitutes. One such case of forced prostitution went to court in 1997 in Curaçao. In most cases, women are in the Netherlands Antilles with a permit to do another type of work or a tourist visa and suffer threats of deportation by their employer or even by clients if they do not comply with their working conditions.

In the Netherlands Antilles, the act of prostitution itself is not against the law. All the islands have legal, government-controlled brothels, and the government issues permits for non-Antillean women to do sex work. The government-controlled brothels were usually opened at a time when many men, especially sailors, started visiting Curaçao and St. Maarten. The clergy and government were afraid that local women and girls would be attacked in the streets or that they would be willing "victims" and decided to protect Curaçaoan and St. Maarten women. They gave permits to open "hotels" where foreign women, mainly Colombians and Dominicans in Curaçao, and Colombians, Dominicans, and Jamaicans and other black Caribbean nationals in St. Maarten, could work as prostitutes. Although prostitution is permitted in these legal brothels, the law does not allow coercion or pimping. Even so, illegal brothels abound. Women who work in the government-sanctioned brothels have permits for up to three months allowing them to work in these brothels as sex workers. These women have to submit to regular medical checkups.

The brothels employ up to one hundred women (at the largest one in Curaçao) every three months. Most of the prostitution takes place outside of these brothels. The women come from different countries in the Caribbean and Latin America, especially the Dominican Republic, Jamaica, Colombia, and Venezuela, with some Brazilians and Haitians. On all of the islands of the Netherlands Antilles, there are places where illegal prostitution takes place either openly or secretly. In many of the bars, clubs, and brothels, the working and living conditions of the women are deplorable. They get no regular medical checkups and are exposed to many sexually transmitted diseases and AIDS. The island government of Curaçao, in collaboration with an AIDS-prevention NGO, operates a program that tries to give information and condoms to women working illegally as prostitutes. Although prostitution is legal, sex workers with or without permits are not protected by any labor laws and are exposed to diseases, violence, and intimidation by clients and employers alike.[39]

OUTLOOK FOR THE TWENTY-FIRST CENTURY

The women of the Netherlands Antilles are resourceful and creative and have resorted to informal economic activities and other means to supplement their meager incomes. Microenterprises are being encouraged, and several organizations have set up funds to help women become microentrepreneurs. As more girls and women get educated, their numbers will make them a force to be reckoned with. Women will more than ever be called on to hold their families and society in general together during hard times. The mass migration to the Netherlands is tearing families apart, and drug trafficking and use are landing many young people in jail or the morgue, but women prevail, as they did during slavery and other difficult times.

NOTES

1. René A. Romer, *De Curaçaose Samenleving* (Curaçao: Amigoe, N.V., 2000).
2. P. Verton, *Politieke dynamiek en dekolonisatie: De Nederlandse Antillen tusen autonomie en onafhankelijkheid* (Alphen aan de Rijn: Samsom Uitgeverij, 1977).
3. G. Oostindie, *Het Paradijs over zee: De Nederlandse Caraiben en Nederland.* (Amsterdam: Bert Bakker, 1997).
4. Romer, 2000.
5. National Institute of Statistics and Census: Netherland Antilles, *2001 Census*, www.sshub.com/sthamer.html.
6. GGD. *Statisch Overzicht gezondheidszorg 1993–1995.* Willemstad: 1996.
7. Cijntje and Bergen, *Handleiding "Vrouwen in Verandering" Fundashon Material pa Skol* (Willemstad: 1998).
8. Central Intelligence Agency, *World Factbook*, www.odci.gov/cia/publications/factbook/Nt.html.
9. Central Bureau of Statistics, *Statistical Yearbook 1999*.
10. Project Plan Vrouwen vakschool 1997.
11. Central Bureau of Statistics, *Statistical Yearbook 1999*.
12. Central Intelligence Agency, *World Factbook*, http://www.odci.gov/cia/publications/factbook/geos/.
13. Central Bureau of Statistics on poverty.

14. Central Intelligence Agency, *World Factbook*, www.odci.gov/cia/publications/ factbook/Nt.html.

15. Arjanne Uwland, *Handleiding "Vrouwen in Verandering" Fundashon Material pa Skol* (Willemstad: 1998).

16. Ibid.

17. "Inkomensverdeling en armoede in de Nederlandse Antillen," *Modus Magazine* 3(4), (1998).

18. Cijntje and Bergen, 1998.

19. CEDAW (United Nations Committee on the Elimination of Discrimination against Women), *Session Report*, 2001, www.un.org/womenwatch/daw/cedaw/ committ.htm.

20. Ibid.

21. Ibid.

22. Ibid.

23. Central Intelligence Agency, *World Factbook*, www.odci.gov/cia/publications/ factbook/Nt.html.

24. R. Rosalia, *Tanbu* (Zutphen: 1997).

25. Tineke Alberts, *Je Lust en je Leven: Een inventariserend onderzoek naar relatie vorming, sexueel gedrag en AIDS preventie op Curaçao* (Curaçao: National AIDS Committee and the Health Department, 1992).

26. Ibid.

27. Central Intelligence Agency, *World Factbook*, www.odci.gov/cia/publications/ factbook/Nt.html.

28. *September 2001 National Priorities in Health System Document 296*, www.paho. org/english/gov/cd/nea-e.pdf.

29. Central Intelligence Agency, *World Factbook*, www.odci.gov/cia/publications/ factbook/Nt.html.

30. *September 2001 National Priorities in Health System Document 296*, www.paho. org/english/gov/cd/nea-e.pdf.

31. Stat. Overzicht.

32. *AIDS Committee Report 2002*, www.cdc.gov/hiv/pubs/mmwr/children.htm.

33. The word *machoro* is derived from the word *macho* and means "like a man."

34. Alberts, 1992.

35. Central Intelligence Agency, *World Factbook*, www.odci.gov/cia/publications/ factbook/Nt.html.

36. Rosalia, 1997.

37. Ibid.

38. Ibid.

39. CEDAW, 2001.

RESOURCE GUIDE

Suggested Reading

Alberts, Tineke. *Je Lust en je Leven: Een inventariserend onderzoek naar relatie vorming, sexueel gedrag en AIDS preventie op Curaçao*. Curaçao: National AIDS Committee and the Health Department, 1992. A study of relationship forming, sexual behavior, and AIDS prevention in Curaçao.

Ansano, R., J. Clemencia, J. Cook, and E. Martis, eds. *Mundu yama sinta Mira: Wom-*

anhood in Curaçao. Curaçao: Fundashon Publikashon, 1992. Explores and compares women's experiences from both an artistic and a scientific point of view.

Henriquez, Jeanne, ed. *Kòrsou su Muhénan Pionero.* Willemstad: National Archives, 2002. Seventy-five biographies of female pioneers.

Romer, René A. *De Curaçaose Samenleving.* Curaçao: Amigoe, N.V., 2000. Approaches Curaçaoan society from a sociological, economic, and political point of view.

Romer, René A., ed. *Culturele Mozaik van de Nederlandse Antillen: Varianten en constanten.* Zutphen: De Walburg Pers, 1977.

Rosalia, R. *Tanbu.* Zutphen: Instituto Stripan, 1997. A study of the legal and church repression of the local drum music of enslaved Africans and their descendants.

University of the Netherlands Antilles. *Nos Futuro.* Curaçao, N.A.: Zutphen: Walburg, 1986. A compilation of lectures given at the university about the future of the Netherlands Antilles.

Videos/Films

Although no films and videos are available specifically for the Netherlands Antilles, CARINET/Caribbean Interactive Network for Video Producers sponsors the documentary series "Leyenda Familiar," which focuses on films made about countries in the Caribbean: www.carinet.org.

Web Sites

Caribbean Association for Feminist Research and Action, www.cafra.org.

Fundashon Sentro di Dama, www.cafra.org/English_CAFRA/cafra/links.htm.

Organizations

Caribbean Association for Feminist Research and Action
Email: seda@curinfo.an

A regional organization in the Caribbean of individuals and organizations.

Fundashon Sentro di Dama
Seru Fortunaweg 8
Curaçao
Phone: (599) 9-868-4647
Fax: (599) 9-869-3526
Email: seda@curinfo.an

SELECTED BIBLIOGRAPHY

Alberts, Tineke. *Je Lust en je Leven: Een inventariserend onderzoek naar relatie vorming, sexueel gedrag en AIDS preventie op Curaçao.* Curaçao: National AIDS Committee and the Health Department, 1992.

Ansano, R., J. Clemencia, J. Cook, and E. Martis, eds. *Mundu yama sinta Mira: Womanhood in Curaçao.* Curaçao: Fundashon Publikashon, 1992.

Caribbean Association for Feminist Research and Action. *CEDAW Shadow Report for the Netherlands Antilles, 2001*. Willemstad: 2001.

Cijntje, and Bergen. *Handleiding "Vrouwen in Verandering" Fundashon Material pa Skol*. Willemstad: 1998.

GGD. *Statisch Overzicht gezondheidszorg 1993–1995*. Willemstad: 1996.

"Inkomensverdeling en armoede in de Nederlandse Antillen." *Modus Magazine* 3(4), (1998).

Oostindie, G. *Het Paradijs over zee: De Nederlandse Caraiben en Nederland*. Amsterdam: Bert Bakker, 1997.

Project Plan Vrouwen vakschool 1997.

Ramdas, A. *Strijd van de Dansers: Biografissche vertellingen uit Curaçao*. Amsterdam: SUA, 1988.

Romer, René A. *De Curaçaose Samenleving*. Curaçao: Amigoe, N.V., 2000.

———. *Een volk op weg: Een sociologisch historische studie van de Curaçaose saamenleving*. Zutphen: De Walburg Pers, 1979.

Romer, René A., ed. *Culturele Mozaik van de Nederlandse Antillen: Varianten en constanten*. Zutphen: De Walburg Pers, 1977.

Rosalia, René Vicente. *Tanbu*. Zutphen: Instituto Stripan, 1997.

Uwland, A. *Handleiding "Vrouwen in Verandering" Fundashon Material pa Skol*. Willemstad: 1998.

Verton, P. *Politieke dynamiek en dekolonisatie: De Nederlandse Antillen tusen autonomie en onafhankelijkheid*. Alphen aan de Rijn: Samsom Uitgeverij, 1977.

II

THE ORGANIZATION OF EASTERN CARIBBEAN STATES

Irma T. Alonso

PROFILE OF THE ORGANIZATION OF EASTERN CARIBBEAN STATES

The Organization of Eastern Caribbean States (OECS) was created in 1981. The seven regular members are Antigua and Barbuda, Dominica, Grenada, Montserrat, Saint Kitts and Nevis, Saint Lucia, and Saint Vincent and the Grenadines. Anguilla and the British Virgin Islands are associated member states. These nine countries, each one part of the Wind-ward or the Leeward Islands, are located in the Caribbean Sea southeast of Puerto Rico and north of Trinidad and Tobago.

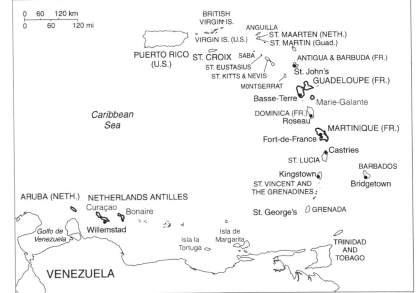

The purpose of the OECS has been to pro-mote unity and soli-darity among its mem-bers. In the 1970s, following their inde-pendence from the

United Kingdom, the regular members entered into this formal arrangement in order to cooperate with each other in achieving economic development and to compensate in part for their small size.

The Headquarters of the Central Secretariat is located in Saint Lucia. OECS's mission of economic development is achieved by working closely with other Caribbean institutions, namely, the Eastern Caribbean Central Bank, the Caribbean Community (CARICOM), the CARICOM Regional Negotiating Machinery, and the Caribbean Development Bank.[1]

The members of the OECS are very small islands, ranging in size from Dominica, the largest, with an area of just 754 square kilometers, to Saint Kitts and Nevis, with an area of only 261 square kilometers.[2] The land areas of the other islands, ordered by size, are Saint Lucia, 616 square kilometers; Antigua and Barbuda, 443 square kilometers; Saint Vincent and the Grenadines, 389 square kilometers; Grenada, 344 square kilometers; and Montserrat, 102 square kilometers.[3]

The total population of the OECS is nearly 550,000. With the exception of Saint Lucia, the rate of growth of the population is significantly less than 1.0 percent; in Saint Lucia, it is 1.24 percent. The low rate of population growth is in part explained by considerable out-migration, particularly of young persons, rather than by low fertility rates.

The total population is divided among the islands as follows: 28 percent in Saint Lucia, 21 percent in Saint Vincent and the Grenadines, 18 percent in Grenada, 13 percent in Dominica, 12 percent in Antigua and Barbuda, and 7 percent in Saint Kitts and Nevis. The population of Montserrat has been very small since more than two-thirds of the people abandoned the island following the eruptions of the Soufriere Hills Volcano, which started in 1995.[4]

The male/female ratio for the total population is close to 1.0, except in the case of the population above sixty-five years of age, where the male/female ratio decreases to approximately 0.71:1. The population below fifteen years of age makes up nearly 30 percent of the population, except in Grenada, where it is even higher at 36 percent. The main population group is between the ages of fifteen and sixty-four with 64 percent of the population, while the population over sixty-five years of age makes up the remaining 6 percent.[5]

The countries of the OECS are parliamentary democracies within the British Commonwealth. The chief of state is the queen of England, represented in each country by a governor general. The governor general appoints a prime minister and a deputy prime minister. The only exception is Dominica, in which a president is elected, and then a prime minister is appointed. Dominica is the first island in the Caribbean to have had a female prime minister, Dame Eugenia Charles, who held this position for fifteen years, from 1980 to 1995.[6]

Nearly 90 percent of the population of these islands is descended from slaves brought from Africa. The rest of the population is a diverse mixture

Table 11.1
Indicators of Human Development in OECS Countries, 2000

Country	Value of HDI	Life Expectancy (years)	Adult Literacy Rate (%)	Combined Primary, Secondary, and Tertiary Enrollment (%)	GDP Per Capita (PPP$)
Antigua & Barbuda	0.800	73.9	86.6	69	$10,541
Dominica	0.779	72.9	96.4	65	5,880
Grenada	0.747	65.3	94.4	65	7,580
Saint Kitts & Nevis	0.814	70.0	97.8	70	12,510
Saint Lucia	0.772	73.4	90.2	70	5,703
Saint Vincent & the Grenadines	0.733	69.6	88.9	58	5,555

Source: United Nations Development Programme, *2002 Human Development Report*, www.undp. org/hdr2002.

of African/Europeans and East Indians. Christianity is the main religion, represented mainly by the Catholic and Anglican Churches.[7]

Because of their accomplishments in terms of health, education, and level of income, the OECS countries are classified as having a relatively good level of human development.[8] In 2000, from a total of 173 countries for which the human development index (HDI) is estimated, the OECS country with the best performance was Saint Kitts and Nevis (which rank 44 among all countries), followed by Antigua and Barbuda (52), Dominica (61), Saint Lucia (66), Grenada (83), and Saint Vincent and the Grenadines (91). Information on the components of the HDI is given in table 11.1.

In terms of human development, values of HDI ranging from 0.814 to 0.733 indicate that OECS countries have achieved, on average, about three-quarters of their capabilities. They have achieved a respectable average life expectancy of 71 years. Equally significant is the literacy rate; on average, 92 percent of the adult population is able to read and write. The enrollment figures, expressed as the percentages of the population groups between the ages of five and twenty-four years enrolled in schools, indicate that only about two-thirds of these groups are registered in school. The average value of gross domestic product (GDP) per capita is nearly $8,000, with Saint Kitts and Nevis and Antigua and Barbuda showing more economic prosperity than the rest.

OVERVIEW OF WOMEN'S ISSUES

The main issues affecting women in the small OECS countries are the large number of female-headed households, the large number of families below the poverty level, the large number of teenage pregnancies, and the large representation of women in low-paying jobs.

EDUCATION

Opportunities

With the exceptions of Dominica and Saint Vincent and the Grenadines, education is compulsory between the ages of five and sixteen. Primary education is for children between the ages of five and ten, and secondary education for children between the ages of eleven and sixteen. The educational system is based on the British system, and most of it is offered free of charge. Private institutions supplement the public offerings. With few exceptions, female students make up at least one-half of all students enrolled at all educational levels. Females perform better than males in passing the Caribbean Examination Council exams, as data from Dominica show.[9]

In Antigua and Barbuda, there are forty-five primary and twelve secondary schools.[10] At the more advanced level, technical and teacher training are provided at the State College. The University of Health Sciences in Antigua was established in 1982. In addition, Antigua participates in the regional University of the West Indies, which offers courses at various campuses in some CARICOM countries. Female pupils constituted 62 percent of the primary enrollment and 72 percent of the secondary enrollment in 2000.

In Dominica, there are seventy-three nursery schools, sixty-six primary schools, nine secondary schools, and a nursing school. Technical and vocational studies are also offered, and a branch of the University of the West Indies is located on the island. There is an offshore medical school, Ross University Medical School, located in Dominica. Female pupils were 48 percent of the primary enrollment and 53 percent at the secondary level in 2000.

In Grenada, there are seventy-four primary schools and nineteen secondary schools. At the higher level, there is a community college and a branch of the University of the West Indies. As in the previous countries, there is an offshore school of medicine, the St. George's University School of Medicine. In the year 2000, female enrollment constituted slightly less than 50 percent of primary enrollment and 59 percent of secondary enrollment.

In Saint Kitts and Nevis, there are sixty-eight schools, with a total enrollment of 21,946, and the St. Kitts Technical College, now a division of the College of Further Education. Female enrollment is close to half of both primary and secondary enrollment. Saint Lucia is home to eighty-five primary schools and sixteen secondary schools. In addition, there are industrial, technical, and teacher-training institutes, as well as a branch of the

University of the West Indies and an Adult Literacy Program. Enrollment of females at the primary level is only 48 percent, while at the secondary level it is 56 percent. In Saint Vincent and the Grenadines, there are sixty-one primary schools, twenty-one secondary schools, a teacher-training college, and a technical college. At the secondary level, there is one high school for girls. Female enrollment is estimated at close to 50 percent.

The OECS has established an Education Reform Unit responsible for coordinating initiatives in education. Its mission is to pay special attention to early childhood education, as well as to all educational efforts contributing to the social and economic development of the member countries.[11]

Literacy

Literacy rates for the OECS countries are shown in table 11.1.

EMPLOYMENT AND ECONOMICS

The members of the OECS coordinate many of their economic activities. In particular, they have a common currency, the Eastern Caribbean dollar, and the rate of exchange in terms of the U.S. dollar is fixed at EC$2.70 to U.S.$1.00. The Eastern Caribbean Central Bank operates as the central bank for all the member countries, and one of its main objectives is that of providing development funds for its members. Its headquarters are located in Saint Kitts. In addition, OECS countries belong to CARICOM.[12]

The members of OECS have relatively small economies (see Table 11.2). In 2001, the GDP of these countries, measured in purchasing power parity (PPI), ranged from a low of $262 million in Dominica to a high of $700 million in Saint Lucia, for a total of $2,738 million for the six countries.

Table 11.2
Economic Indicators in OECS Countries, 2001

Country	GDP (PPP, million $)	Labor Force	Inflation Rate (%)	Economic Sectors (%)		
				Agriculture	Industry	Services
Antigua & Barbuda	$674	30,000	0.4	4	19	77
Dominica	262	25,000	1.0	18	23	59
Grenada	424	42,300	2.8	8	24	68
Saint Kitts & Nevis	339	18,172	1.7	4	26	71
Saint Lucia	700	43,800	3.0	8	20	72
Saint Vincent & the Grenadines	339	67,000	−0.4	10	26	64

Source: Central Intelligence Agency, *2002 Factbook*, www.cia.gov/publications/factbook.

Antiguan woman working in market/post office. Photo © TRIP/ H. Rogers.

The most serious problem these economies are facing is that of unemployment, which official statistics estimate at more than 20 percent in some member countries. However, these statistics do not reflect unemployed persons who have become discouraged and are not looking for jobs, or persons who are underemployed. Statistics also exclude persons who participate in the informal economy, where female participation is significant.[13]

The OECS economies are dominated by the service sector, mainly in tourism. More recently, offshore financial transactions and data entry have been added to activities within the service sector. The second sector in importance is the industrial sector, represented by light manufacturing, consisting of food processing, and textiles and assembly of garments. The most important agricultural crop is bananas, followed by sugar, coffee, and other products, mainly for exports.[14]

Since 2001, the rates of growth of these economies have decreased substantially.[15] The main reason for the decrease has been the significant decline in tourists from the United States following the September 11, 2001, attacks. Another cause is the decrease in exports of bananas as a result of regulations imposed by the World Trade Organization on the banana trade. Further-more, the service sector has been negatively affected by examination of the practices of the off-shore financial sector, which has been accused of money-laundering activities. Because of the complexity of these problems, these small economies face difficult times in the new era of globalization. Additionally, they will be negatively affected as preferential trade arrangements with the United States and the European Union are subjected to further modifications.[16]

Supermarket clerk, Basseterre, St. Kitts. Photo © TRIP/H. Rogers.

Table 11.3

Labor Force Participation by Sector and by Gender in OECS Countries, 2000 (percentage distribution)

Countries	Agriculture		Industry		Services	
	Male	Female	Male	Female	Male	Female
Antigua & Barbuda	5	3	29	7	63	87
Dominica	31	14	24	10	40	72
Grenada	17	10	32	12	46	77
Saint Kitts and Nevis	18	9	34	19	46	70
Saint Lucia	27	16	24	14	49	71
Saint Vincent and the Grenadines	31	14	27	11	42	75

Source: World Bank Group: Gender Statistics, http://genderstats.worldbank.org.

Job/Career Opportunities

Females in the English-speaking Caribbean have high rates of labor-force participation. It has been estimated that this participation rate is as high as 41.0 percent in Saint Kitts and Nevis, 40.1 percent in Antigua and Barbuda, and 39.1 percent in Saint Lucia.[17]

The heavy emphasis on the service sector in these economies increases the opportunities for "female" jobs in areas like tourism, banking, and information technology. Many publications have documented that in the Caribbean, women predominate in jobs related to assembly operations, in data processing, and in secretarial jobs.[18] Earnings in these jobs tend to be low because they are lower-ranking positions.

The gender division of labor by economic sectors in OECS countries is as follows (see Table 11.3): In Antigua and Barbuda, 5 percent of men are employed in agriculture, 29 percent in industry, and 63 percent in services. In comparison, females are concentrated in services (87 percent), while agriculture and industry employ only 3 and 7 percent, respectively. The industrial sector includes small-scale, light industries such as the manufacturing of rum, clothing, and household appliances and assembling electronics. More males (20 percent) tend to be self-employed than females (15 percent). The unemployment rate, not considered a serious issue, is estimated at 6.4 percent for males and 5.6 percent for females.[19]

In Dominica, the agricultural sector provides employment for 31 percent of the males and 14 percent of the females in the labor force. The industrial sector is also more important for males (24 percent) than for females (10 percent). The service sector is more dominated by women (72 percent) than by men (40 percent). Wages and salaries are received by only 62 percent of the males and by 71 percent of the females in the labor force.

The remainder are self-employed. In Dominica, the rate of unemployment is very high, but the problem is more serious for females (27.2 percent) than for males (19.6 percent). The statistics for unemployment by levels of education indicate that 80 percent of the unemployed males had only primary education, while 10 percent had secondary education. Sixty-seven percent of the unemployed women had only primary education, while 24 percent had secondary education.[20]

Grenada shows a more even distribution pattern of males among the three sectors than the other countries—17 percent in agriculture, 32 percent in industry, and 46 percent in services. Female employment in these sectors is 10, 12, and 77 percent, respectively. Self-employment rates are 24 percent for males and 21 percent for females. However, unemployment is twice as serious for females (26.2 percent) as for males (10.5 percent).[21]

Saint Kitts and Nevis show a pattern of employment by sectors similar to that in Grenada: 18 percent of male workers are employed in agriculture, 34 percent in industry, and 46 percent in services. Nine percent of female workers are employed in agriculture, 19 percent in industry, and 70 percent in services. In total, close to half of the workforce is employed in agricultural and industrial activities related to sugar. Self-employment is estimated at 16 percent for males and 13 percent for females.[22]

In Saint Lucia, employment is concentrated in agriculture, tourism, and manufacturing. Agriculture is the direct employer of 27 percent of male workers and 16 percent of female workers. Industry is also significant, employing 24 percent of male workers and 14 percent of female workers. More women (71 percent) than men (49 percent) are employed in services. The problem of unemployment is critical for both, with rates of 16 percent for males and 20.3 percent for females. Half of the unemployed have had only primary education.[23]

Saint Vincent and the Grenadines has a significant agricultural sector employing 31 percent of the male workers and 14 percent of the female workers. Industry employs more men (27 percent) than women (11 percent). However, most women (75 percent) in the labor force are in the service sector, as compared to 42 percent of the men. The unemployment rate is severe for both, estimated at 18.4 percent for males and 22.1 percent for females. More men (27 percent) than women (18 percent) are self-employed.[24]

Pay

In OECS countries, low wages for females in comparison to males prevail. The only data available correspond to 1980, but it is possible that the same ratios still exist. In Dominica the ratio was 68.3 to 32.4; Grenada 69.7 to 36.9; Saint Lucia 71.7 to 36.5; Saint Vincent and the Grenadines 69.0 to 32.0; Antigua and Barbuda 57.1 to 33.2; and Saint Kitts and Nevis 76.4 to 43.2. In 1980, in Dominica, while men earned 68.3, females earned less than half as much at 32.4. In the other countries, the pay ratios were as follows: Grenada, 69.7 to 36.9; Saint Lucia, 71.7 to 36.5; in Saint Vincent and the Grenadines, 69.0 to 32.0; Antigua and Barbuda, 57.1 to 33.2; and Saint Kitts and Nevis, 76.4 to 43.2.[25] It is likely that these differences still prevail.

The differences in pay by sex have also been documented by the Canadian International Development Agency in a proposal prepared by CIDA to help the OECS region. One of the reasons this agency is willing to help OECS countries is the employment situation in these countries. Reference is made to the fact that in OECS countries, women occupy low-status positions, and their salaries are lower than those of men.[26]

Support for Mothers/Caretakers

Maternal Leave

In the OECS countries, the first law establishing sickness and maternity benefits was passed in 1973 in Antigua and Barbuda.[27] This law guarantees that upon qualification, the mother will receive maternity benefits equal to 60 percent of average earnings for a maximum of thirteen weeks, as well as a maternity grant of EC$400. In Dominica, the first and current law dates from 1975. The maternity benefit is 60 percent of average weekly earnings, payable for twelve weeks. The maternity grant is EC$500. In Grenada, the corresponding law dates from 1983 and offers benefits equal to 65 percent of average earnings. The minimum is EC$450. In Saint Kitts and Nevis, the current law was approved in 1977. The maternity benefit is 65 percent of earnings for a maximum of thirteen weeks. The maternity grant is EC$450 per child. In Saint Lucia, the current law, approved in 1978, provides for 65 percent of average salary, payable for three months. The maternity grant is EC$450 plus EC$30 to cover some medical costs. In Saint Vincent and the Grenadines, the current law was passed in 1986 and provides a maternity benefit of 65 percent of earnings, payable for up to thirteen weeks, plus a maternity grant of EC$300.

Social/Government Programs

In Antigua and Barbuda, there is a workers' compensation program funded by both the employee (3 percent of earnings) and the employer (5 percent of payroll).[28] All workers receive medical and social security benefits by making monthly contributions to the plan. In Dominica, workers' compensation is funded completely by the employer. In Grenada, work injuries are covered by a plan to which the employee contributes 4 percent of wages, and the employer contributes 5 percent of wages. In Saint Kitts and Nevis, a social security plan provides benefits to members, with all workers contributing to the scheme, and the fund is financed by a contribution of 1 percent of payroll. In Saint Lucia, the national insurance scheme is funded by employees at 5 percent of earnings and by employers at 5 percent of payroll. In Saint Vincent and the Grenadines, the plan is fully funded from contributions by the employer equal to 0.05 percent of payroll.

Sustainable Development

The Organization of Eastern Caribbean States Environment and Sustainable Development Unit is responsible for overseeing natural resources and environmental management service.[29] It provides technical assistance and manages the natural resources of the members.

Welfare

In most of the OECS countries, the welfare services include free health services, care of the aged, and various pension benefits.[30] Because of difficult economic times, most of these plans are in the process of reform and reevaluation. Because women do benefit most from these welfare plans, they will be most hurt by the restructuring of the system.

FAMILY AND SEXUALITY

In the English-speaking Caribbean countries, definition of the family is difficult.[31] Given the traditions of slavery, heavy mass migration, the conditions of poverty, and even differences of class and race, more and more households are headed by females. In Saint Kitts and Nevis and in Saint Lucia, nearly half of all households are female headed. These households are characterized by poverty, and most of these households have dependent children under the age of fifteen years.[32] In Saint Lucia, the 1995 Poverty Assessment Survey indicated that one-fourth of the population lived in poverty. The same result was found in Saint Vincent and the Grenadines. Furthermore, more than 80 percent of all births occurred outside of marriage.

Gender Roles

Gender roles are a complex factor in Eastern Caribbean countries. Feminine and masculine roles are reinforced by culture. The pattern by which males have multiple partners is learned from childhood. In a study conducted in Saint Kitts and Nevis, it was found that young males growing up at home with brothers and sisters from different fathers learn from a young age that multiple relationships with multiple partners are acceptable.[33]

Additionally, the fact that mothers have the major responsibility of raising their children is reinforced by culture. This concept may be gathered from the very suggestive title of the book by Edith Clarke, *My Mother Who Fathered Me*.[34]

However, by the end of the 1990s, these sex roles began to be altered. Because of the severe problem of sexually transmitted diseases affecting the whole society, and because of high levels of fertility, some modifications have emerged. As more females enter school, join the labor force, and assume political power, and as more modern family-planning methods are implemented, gender roles may evolve into more equitable responsibilities for raising the children. The fear of HIV/AIDS may also reduce the incidence of multiple partners.

Marriage

In the English-speaking Caribbean, marriage is determined to some degree by levels of income. Nonlegal unions are more common in the lower-income classes than in the middle- and upper-income classes.[35] In addition, partners often upgrade the relationship from visiting relationship to common-law union and finally to marriage, a pattern that has prevailed particularly in Eastern Caribbean countries.[36]

Reproduction

Two of the main preoccupations in the OECS are the high rate of illegal abortions and the great number of unintended pregnancies. As a solution, some of the governments of these countries have taken responsibility in offering family-planning services, while others have used the Planned Parenthood Association to provide this service to the community.

Sex Education

Sex education is part of the school curriculum in Saint Kitts and Nevis, Saint Lucia, and Saint Vincent and the Grenadines.[37] In Antigua and Barbuda and in Grenada, sex education is provided by nongovernmental organizations (NGOs) like the Grenada Planned Parenthood Association, or by health personnel at the invitation of school administrators. Since 1984, the government of Dominica has been involved in providing family-planning services. Through its population policies and programs, sex education has been introduced in the school curriculum. Schools in Saint Kitts and Nevis offer contraceptive supplies and family-planning services as well as sex education. At present, a sex education program is being introduced in the school curriculum of Antigua and Barbuda.

Contraception and Abortion

Since 1984, the government of Antigua and Barbuda has been directly involved in providing family-planning services free of charge.[38] However, adolescents are excluded from this service unless they have parental consent. Slightly more than 50 percent of currently married women aged fifteen to forty-four years are using modern contraceptive methods. The Antigua Planned Parenthood Association offers clinical services, like Pap smears, as well as counseling. There has been an increase in the use of contraceptives, with new users indicating a preference for condoms, while active users showed a preference for oral contraceptives and injections. Sterilization is performed at both private and public hospitals. Abortion is illegal except to save the life of the pregnant woman, and if it is approved by a panel of physicians, it should be performed during the first trimester of pregnancy (see Table 11.4).

Even before the Dominican government adopted sex education policies in 1984, the Dominican Planned Parenthood Association started in 1976 to offer family-planning services. Later it added pregnancy tests, counseling, and Pap smears. In Dominica, family planning is used by about 44 percent of women of childbearing age. The most popular methods are oral contraceptives or injections. Abortion is illegal in Dominica except to save the

Table 11.4
Abortion Policies in OECS Countries

Grounds on Which Abortion Is Permitted	Antigua & Barbuda	Dominica	Grenada	Saint Kitts & Nevis	Saint Lucia	Saint Vincent & the Grenadines
To save the life of the woman	Yes	Yes	Yes	Yes	Yes	Yes
To preserve physical health	No	No	Yes	Yes	Yes	Yes
To preserve mental health	No	No	Yes	Yes	Yes	Yes
Rape or incest	No	No	No	No	No	Yes
Fetal impairment	No	No	No	No	No	Yes
Economic or social	No	No	No	No	No	Yes
Available on request	No	No	No	No	No	No

Source: United Nations, Population Policy Data Bank, *Abortion Policies: A Global Review*, www.un.org/isa/population/publications/abortion/.

life of the pregnant woman. If approved, the abortion must be performed by a physician in a hospital.

The Grenada Planned Parenthood Association, founded in 1964, helps the government in implementing the family-planning policy by offering family-planning services and supplies at low cost. Abortion is illegal in Grenada, but the Criminal Code authorizes abortions to preserve the life of the pregnant woman or to preserve physical or mental health.

In Saint Kitts and Nevis, the government has offered family-planning services since 1971. In 1994, the Ministry of Women's Affairs was established. The Saint Kitts Family Life Services Association and the Nevis Family Planning Association work with the government in the provision of services. The range of activities includes educational programs as well as offering contraceptives, counseling, and pregnancy tests, among other services. Contraceptive use is estimated at close to 57 percent of all women of childbearing age. Oral contraceptives are the most popular, followed by injections and intrauterine devices. Abortion is illegal in Saint Kitts and Nevis, but it is allowed to save the life of the pregnant woman.

Since 1985, the government of Saint Lucia has had a population policy to control population growth. There is strong opposition from the Catholic Church to the provision of family-planning services. The Saint Lucia Planned Parenthood Association supplements the government services by providing education through radio and television and by offering family-planning services in local hospitals. In Saint Lucia, the preferred method of contraception is the pill, followed by tubal ligation and contraceptive injections. Abortion is for the most part illegal, but it can be performed for medical reasons.

The government of Saint Vincent and the Grenadines has a national population policy and a national family-planning program. The Saint Vincent Planned Parenthood Association, established in 1965, supports the government programs, in particular by implementing family-life educational programs. The government offers the service to all men and women, including teenagers, regardless of marital status. Abortion is illegal in Saint Vincent and the Grenadines, but in 1977 the law was changed to allow an abortion to be performed if the life of the pregnant woman is at risk. These abortions have to be performed by medical staff in hospitals. In particular, this is the only OECS country to permit abortions in the case of rape or incest. In Saint Kitts and Nevis, abortions are allowed to preserve the physical and mental health of the woman.

Teen Pregnancy

In OECS countries, pregnant teenagers are not allowed to continue in school. This regulation affects negatively the prospects of these girls to become prepared to join the labor force and perpetuates their dependence on government welfare programs.

The high number of teenage pregnancies is a major concern in the organization of Eastern Caribbean States. In 1995 in Dominica, 14.2 percent of all births were to teenagers.[39] These girls are restricted from continuing in school, a policy that compounds the problem for the teenager. The fertility rate among Grenadan adolescents was 82.4 per 1,000, and teenage pregnancies were 17.1 percent of all births in 1995. Since teenage pregnancy is high, the government in Grenada has implemented a population policy to offer family-planning services and low-cost supplies in conjunction with NGOs.

Despite in-school education and contraception and family-planning services, teen pregnancy is high on Saint Kitts and Nevis. In 1995, 16.7 percent of all births were to teenagers.

In Saint Lucia, where nearly half of the population is below the age of twenty, the teenage pregnancy rate is very high, 27 percent of all births on the island. The fertility rate for teenagers is above 80 per 1,000. Around 17 percent of girls use some method of family planning, with contraceptive pills as the most frequent method.

In Saint Vincent and the Grenadines, there are major concerns about teenage pregnancies because more than one-third of the population is below fifteen years of age. The national family-planning program is available to teenagers regardless of marital status.

HEALTH

Health Care Access

Each of the OECS nations is faced with the problem of how to pay for the increasing cost of health-care services, and at the same time with deciding how to improve the quality and availability of services.[40]

In Antigua and Barbuda, the health-care policy offers health services as a human right. Antigua is divided into seven regional districts. Both private and public facilities exist to provide health benefits. Pharmacy services are part of the medical benefits. The country has a general hospital, a private clinic, seven health centers, and seventeen associated clinics. It is estimated that there is one physician per 2,200 inhabitants. Half of the population is between the ages of twenty and fifty-nine, and 52 percent of these are females. Women within this age group have 84 percent of all births.

Dominica's national health plan divides the nation into seven health districts. There are local clinics plus larger health centers in the capital city. It is estimated that there is one physician per 3,000 persons. Pregnant women have universal access to health care, but only about one-third seek prenatal care during the first sixteen weeks of pregnancy.

In Grenada, there is a government policy to provide health services to each person. The strategy has been that of providing primary health care. There are three hospitals, six health centers, and thirty district medical

Table 11.5
Health Indicators in OECS Countries, 2000

Country	Birth Rate per 1,000	Total Fertility per Woman	Infant Mortality per 1,000	Under-Five Mortality Rate per 1,000	Death Rate per 1,000	Access to Safe Water (%)	Life Expectancy (years) M	F
Antigua & Barbuda	18.84	2.29	21.61	21	5.75	92.9	72	78
Dominica	17.30	2.01	15.94	15	7.11	77.5	75	80
Grenada	23.05	2.50	14.63	20	7.63	93.2	62	68
Saint Kitts & Nevis	18.61	2.39	15.83	21	9.04		68	73
Saint Lucia	21.37	2.34	14.80	19	5.30		69	74
Saint Vincent & the Grenadines	17.54	2.01	16.15	20	6.12	93.0	71	74

Sources: Central Intelligence Agency, *2002 Factbook*, www.cia.gov/publications/factbook/; Pan-American Health Organization, *Country Health Profile*, www.paho.org/; World Bank Group, GenderStats, http://genderstats.worldbank.org/.

stations. Services are also provided to handicapped children and geriatric patients. Almost three-fourths of pregnant women attend prenatal clinics, but about 80 percent wait until the sixteenth week of pregnancy or later. The health services provided by the government are free (see Table 11.5 for health indicators). It is estimated that there is one physician per 2,100 inhabitants, one nurse per 1,600, and one hospital bed per 200.

In Saint Kitts and Nevis, there is no national health plan, but government reforms are attempting to recover the cost of provision by modifying the scheme to cover the cost of the health services provided. There are four hospitals in Saint Kitts and one in Nevis. It is estimated that there is one physician per 2,200 inhabitants. Special primary-care services are offered to pregnant women. It is estimated that pregnant women make only three visits to a health facility during pregnancy, when six should be scheduled.

In Saint Lucia, there is a national health policy and a ten-year health-sector plan. The policy combines primary health care with preventive measures. There are thirty-four health centers and two major hospitals. There is one physician per 3,400 persons. Fifty percent of pregnant women make use of public health facilities, but only between 10 and 15 percent do so during the first sixteen weeks of pregnancy. The remaining 50 percent visit private facilities.

In Saint Vincent and the Grenadines, the health plan views access to health care as a basic human right. The government is dedicated to offering comprehensive and affordable health services. The islands are divided into nine districts covered by thirty-eight health centers, plus other facilities. It is estimated that there is one physician per 3,800 persons. Women of childbearing age receive prenatal and postnatal care, together with family-planning services. Only 82 percent of pregnant women visit the health clinic to receive the six prenatal visits recommended. Only about 40 percent of women of childbearing age are using family-planning services.

Diseases and Disorders

In general, life expectancy at birth for females exceeds that of males by as much as six years. In both Antigua and Barbuda and Saint Lucia, more than 56 percent of those sixty years old or older are women. The same pattern may exist in the rest of the islands. The main causes of death in this age group are hypertension, cancer, and strokes.

AIDS

In Antigua and Barbuda, between 1985 and 1995, there were 70 AIDS cases, divided into 64 adults and 6 children.[41] Of these, 56 had died. Of the adults, 55 were men and 9 were women. At the same time, 77 tested positive for HIV, 37 adult males, 36 adult females, and 4 children. Heterosexual contact constituted the main route of infection. In Grenada, by the end of 1996 there were 141 cases of HIV, with twice as many males infected as females. At the same time, there were 96 cases of AIDS, 70 men and 26 women, and 71 had been reported dead. In Saint Kitts and Nevis, only 14 cases of AIDS and only 48 cases of HIV were confirmed in the period 1992–1995. In Saint Lucia, there were 140 cases of HIV reported by 1995, and 81 persons were diagnosed with AIDS. Nearly 90 percent of AIDS patients have died. The transmission of HIV has been mostly by heterosexual contact, with the ratio of males to females estimated at 1.2:1. In Saint Vincent and the Grenadines, by 1995 there were 182 HIV cases, of which 73 had developed into AIDS, and of which 71 had died. Heterosexual contact has been the main method of transmission. In order to combat the spread of HIV, the government channels through the Planned Parenthood Association.

POLITICS AND LAW

Suffrage

In OECS countries, suffrage has been universal since 1951. All persons eighteen years of age or older are allowed to participate in the election process.[42]

Political Participation

In 2000, women in Parliament made up 1 percent of the total in Antigua and Barbuda, 6 percent in Dominica, 4 percent in Grenada, 2 percent in Saint Kitts and Nevis, 2 percent in Saint Lucia, and 5 percent in Saint Vincent and the Grenadines. The percentage of women in ministerial positions in Dominica increased from 9 percent in 1995 to 20 percent in 2000. At the same time, in Grenada, the percentage increased from 10 percent to 14 percent for the same period. In Saint Lucia, women occupied 10 percent of the positions in 2000 as compared to 8 percent in 1995. In Saint Vincent and the Grenadines, women held 10 percent of the ministerial positions, as compared to none just five years earlier. Antigua and Barbuda and Saint Kitts and Nevis are the only OECS countries in which women have not reached ministerial-level positions.[43]

RELIGION AND SPIRITUALITY

Christianity is the main religion in the OECS. The most dominant branches are Anglican and Roman Catholic. As in many other countries in the Caribbean, African religious practices are combined with Christianity, resulting in a unique blend.

VIOLENCE

Domestic Violence

The OECS Family Law and Domestic Legal Reform Project began in January 2001. It is expected that the project will be completed by 2004. The purposes of the project are, first, to harmonize all the provisions of the laws protecting children and women, and second, to make sure that each nation complies with the provisions of the United Nations Convention on the Rights of the Child, the Convention on the Elimination of All Forms of Discrimination against Women (CEDAW), and the Inter-American Convention on the Prevention, Punishment, and Eradication of Violence against Women.[44] All of the members of the OECS signed and ratified CEDAW during the 1980s. Laws protecting women against domestic violence, sexual harassment, and all forms of sexual offenses have been adopted by all CARICOM countries.[45]

OUTLOOK FOR THE TWENTY-FIRST CENTURY

Women in the OECS face difficult problems related to the small size of their countries' economies. High unemployment rates and low government revenues are making it difficult to finance many social programs. Women in these countries are unlikely to continue receiving services needed during their childbearing years and in their old age. The privatization of some of these services will mean hard times for those women not participating in the labor force.

NOTES

1. Further information on OECS is available at www.oecs.org.
2. One kilometer equals approximately 0.6 miles.
3. Central Intelligence Agency, *2002 Factbook*, www.cia.gov/cia/publications/factbook.
4. Ibid.
5. Ibid.
6. Ibid.
7. Ibid.
8. United Nations Development Programme, *2002 Human Development Report*, www.undp.org/hdr2002.
9. Tony Bastick, "Influences on Employment Discrimination in the Caribbean: The Case of the Marginalized Men and Wasted Women in Dominica," paper presented at the (Re)Thinking Caribbean Culture Conference, Cave Hill, Barbados, June 2001.
10. Information on numbers of schools and enrollment figures is from embassies of the Eastern Caribbean States and missions to the European Communities, www.caribisles.org/caribbean/country.htm; World Bank, GenderStats, http://genderstats.worldbank.org/.
11. Additional information on the OECS Education Reform Unit is available from info@oeru.org.
12. Eastern Caribbean Central Bank, www.eccb.org.
13. Mary Johnson Osirin, "We Toil All the Livelong Day," in *Daughters of Caliban: Caribbean Women in the Twentieth Century*, ed. Consuelo López Springfield (Bloomington: Indiana University Press, 1997).
14. Central Intelligence Agency, *2002 Factbook*.
15. Norman Girvan, "Economic Contraction and Fiscal Crisis in the OECS," message of the secretary general of the Association of Caribbean States, August 16, 2000, www.acs-aec.org/column/index48.htm.
16. Irma T. Alonso, *Caribbean Economies in the Twenty-First Century* (Gainesville: University Press of Florida, 2002).
17. Osirin, 1997.
18. Peggy Antrobus, "Gender Implications of the Development Crisis," in *Development in Suspense: Selected Papers and Proceedings of the First Conference of Caribbean Economists*, ed. Norman Girvan and George Beckford (Kingston: Friedrich Ebert Stiftung and Association of Caribbean Economists, 1989).
19. World Bank, GenderStats, http://genderstats.worldbank.org/.
20. Ibid.
21. Ibid.
22. Ibid.
23. Ibid.
24. Ibid.
25. Olive Senior, *Working Miracles: Women's Lives in the English-Speaking Caribbean* (Cave Hill, Barbados: Institute of Social and Economic Research, University of the West Indies, 1991), 111, table 6.1.
26. OECS Sub-Regional Program Plan 2002–2007, www.acdi-cida.gc.ca/cida_ind.

nsf/682f5cd8c017661b8525677d007117d9/619ea72f30d63c8b85256bf00061d575?OpenDocument.

27. U.S. Social Security Online, *Social Security Programs throughout the World, 1999*, www.ssa.gov/statistics/ssptw/1999/English/index.html.

28. Pan-American Health Organization and World Health Organization (PAHO-WHO), www.paho.org; U.S. Social Security Online, *Social Security Programs throughout the World, 1999*. www.ssa.gov/statistics/ssptw/1999/English/index.html.

29. OECS Environment and Sustainable Development Unit, www.oecsnrmu.org/.

30. PAHO-WHO, www.paho.org.

31. Christine Barrow, *Family in the Caribbean: Themes and Perspectives* (Kingston: Ian Randle, 1996).

32. International Planned Parenthood Foundation, *Country Profiles*, http://ippfnet.ippf.org/pub/; Barrow, 1996, xi–xii.

33. International Planned Parenthood Foundation, *Country Profiles*.

34. Kingston, Jamaica: The Press of the University of the West Indies, 1999.

35. Senior, 1991, 111.

36. Ibid.

37. International Planned Parenthood Federation, *Country Profiles*.

38. United Nations, *Abortion Policies: A Global Review*, www.un.org/esa/population/publications/abortion/; International Planned Parenthood Foundation, *Country Profiles*.

39. World Health Organization.

40. All statistics in this section are from PAHO-WHO, www.paho.org.

41. PAHO-WHO, www.paho.org.

42. Central Intelligence Agency, *2002 Factbook*.

43. World Bank, GenderStat.

44. UNICEF–Caribbean Area Office, www.unicef-cao.org/news/OECSFamLaw.html.

45. CARICOM: Model Legislation on Issues Affecting Women, www.caricom.org/womenlegislation.htm.

RESOURCE GUIDE

Suggested Reading

Barrow, Christine. *Family in the Caribbean: Themes and Perspectives*. Kingston: Ian Randle Publishers, 1996.

Bilai, Camara. *20 Years of the HIV/AIDS Epidemic in the Caribbean: A Summary*. This is a report of the Caribbean Epidemology Centre and the Pan-American Health Organization (CARE/PAHO), www.care.org/pdf/20-years-aids-caribbean.pdf.

Leo-Rhynie, Elsa, Barbara Bailey, and Christine Barrow, eds. *Gender: A Caribbean Multi-Disciplinary Perspective*. Kingston: Ian Randle Publishers, 1997.

Mohammed, Patricia, and Catherine Shepherd, eds. *Gender in Caribbean Development*. Cave Hill, Barbados: University of the West Indies, Women and Development Studies Project, 1988.

Momsen, Janet Hensall, ed. *Women and Change in the Caribbean: A Pan-Caribbean Perspective*. Kingston: Ian Randle Publishers, 1993.

Senior, Olive. *Working Miracles: Women's Lives in the English-Speaking Caribbean*. Cave Hill, Barbados: Institute of Social and Economic Research, University of the West Indies, 1991.

Shepherd, Verene, Bridget Brereton, and Barbara Bailey, eds. *Engendering History: Caribbean Women in Historical Perspective*. New York: St. Martin's Press, 1995.

Web Sites

Antigua and Barbuda, www.antigua-barbuda.org.

Dominica, www.dominica.dm.

Grenada, www.grenada.org.

Saint Kitts and Nevis, www.stkitts-nevis.com.

Saint Lucia, www.stlucia.gov.lc.

Saint Vincent and the Grenadines, www.svgtourism.com.

UNICEF Caribbean Area Office, www.unicef-cao.org/news/OECSFamLaw.html.

UNIFEM in Latin America and the Caribbean, www.unifem.undp.org/at_work_worldwide/lac.html.

United Nations Development Programme Regional Office for Barbados and OECS, www.bb.undp.org/.

Organizations

Caribbean Association for Feminist Research and Action (CAFRA).

The national representative in Saint Vincent and the Grenadines is Ancelma Morgan-Rose.
Email: winfa@caribsurf.com
Web site: http://www.cafra.org/English_CAFRA/cafra/about.htm#about.cafa

This organization is a regional network of feminists, individual researchers, activists, and women's organizations.

Caribbean Peoples Development Agency (CARIPEDA)
P.O. Box 1132
Kingstown, Saint Vincent and the Grenadines
Phone: (784) 458-4058
Fax: (784) 458-4658
Email: caripeda@caribsurf.com

Committee for the Development of Women (CDW)
P.O. Box 1343
Kingstown, Saint Vincent and the Grenadines
Phone: (784) 457-7035
Fax: (784) 456-1648

Dominica National Council of Women (DNCW)
P.O. Box 745, Roseau

Phone: (767) 448-3935/7546
Fax: (767) 448-0690

Grenada National Organisation of Women (GNOW)
C/O YWCA, Tyrell Street, St. George's
Phone: (473) 440-2992
Fax: (473) 440-9019
Email: grenco@caribsurf.com

National Council of Voluntary Women's Associations
P.O. Box 1599
Castries, Saint Lucia
Phone: (758) 453-1608; 452-3146
Fax: (758) 451-9279
Email: p.a.s.s@candw.lc

National Council of Women
P.O. Box 1157
Kingstown, Saint Vincent and the Grenadines
Regional Networks

St. Lucia Crisis Centre
P.O. Box 1257, Castries
Phone: (758) 453-1521
Fax: (758) 458-1447

SELECTED BIBLIOGRAPHY

Dann, Graham. "Family Reunification as an Emigration Factor in the Eastern Caribbean." In *Comparative Sociology of Family, Health, and Education: A Volume in Memory of Ferran Valls i Taberner*, 661–78. Málaga, Spain: Cátedra de Historia de Derecho y de las Instituciones, Facultad de Derecho de la Universidad de Málaga, 1991.

Handwerker, W. Penn. "Empowerment and Fertility Transition on Antigua, WI: Education, Employment, and the Moral Economy of Childbearing." *Human Organization* 52(1) (spring 1993): 41–52.

Lazarus-Black, Mindie. "Why Women Take Men to Magistrate's Court: Caribbean Kinship Ideology and Law." *Ethnology: An International Journal of Cultural and Social Anthropology* 30(2) (April 1991): 119–33.

Mondesire, Alicia and Leith Dunn. *Towards Equity in Development: A Report on the Status of Women in Sixteen Commonwealth Caribbean Countries*. Georgetown: Caribbean Community Secretariat, 1995.

Olwig, Karen Fog. "The Migration Experience: Nevisian Women at Home and Abroad." In *Women and Change in the Caribbean: A Pan-Caribbean Perspective*, ed. Janet Hensall Momsen, 150–66. Kingston: Ian Randle Publishers, 1993.

Organization of Eastern Caribbean States Country Session at the 14th Meeting of the Caribbean Group for Cooperation in Economic Development, World Bank Headquarters, June 8, 1998, www.worldbank.org/html/lac/cgced/oecs.htm.

12

PUERTO RICO

Irma T. Alonso

PROFILE OF PUERTO RICO

Puerto Rico is a Caribbean island located between the Caribbean Sea and the North Atlantic Ocean, about 1,000 miles east-southeast of Miami, Florida. Puerto Rico has been linked to the United States since 1898, when Spain ceded both Puerto Rico and Cuba to the United States as a result of the Spanish-American War. Cuba became independent in 1902, while Puerto Rico kept its association with the United States. However, Puerto Rico maintains its deep cultural Spanish roots despite the fact that Puerto Ricans were granted U.S. citizenship in 1917. Although Puerto Ricans are U.S. citizens, they do not participate in U.S. presidential or congressional elections. When the constitution establishing the Commonwealth of Puerto Rico was approved in 1952, the island obtained more control over local issues. Puerto Rico shares national defense responsibilities with the United States, and Puerto Ricans serve in the U.S. armed forces. Puerto Rico's interests are represented in the U.S. Congress via a resident commissioner who has a voice but no vote in the House of Representatives. The United States transfers to the island nearly $10 billion in federal funds every year.

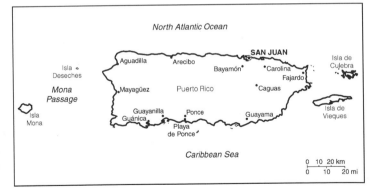

Because of its association with the United States, Puerto Rico's economy has changed from one based on agriculture to one dominated by services (55 percent) and industry (45 percent). In 2000, Puerto Rico's gross domestic product (GDP) was estimated at approximately $40 billion, or $10,000 per capita, with an average annual growth rate of 2.8 percent. In that same year, the estimated inflation rate was 5.7 percent, while the unemployment rate stood at 9.5 percent.[1]

Other transformations in the Puerto Rican way of life have been linked to advances in health and education. A high level of urbanization, with accompanying expansions in roads and other means of communication, has raised environmental concerns because of water and electricity needs. The relationship with the United States has also involved massive migration to the United States to find better job opportunities than those in Puerto Rico. Emigrants have begun to return to the island, and according to the 2000 *U.S. Census of Population*, returning migrants have surpassed those leaving the island.

Puerto Rico's geographic area is only 9,104 square kilometers, but in 2001 its population was estimated at 3.93 million, with an average annual growth rate of 0.54 percent. The island is one of the most densely populated places in the world, with 432 persons per square kilometer. The population consisted of 52 percent females and 48 percent males, with a median age of 33.7 years for women and 30.4 years for men. Twenty-four percent of the population is below the age of fifteen, and 66 percent is between the ages of fifteen and sixty-four. A high proportion (11 percent) of the population is sixty-five years old or older, and this cohort is the fastest-growing population group, increasing at an average annual rate of 3.04 percent, with nearly 60 percent of the total being women. Below the age of fifteen, the number of males exceeds that of females at a ratio of 1.05 to 1. Nevertheless, women exceed men in all higher age groups, particularly within the age group of sixty-five or older, where the ratio of males to females is 0.74 to 1. This is the result of differences in life expectancy, which is 71.28 years for males, but 80.48 years for females. In 2000, the birth rate in Puerto Rico was 15.26 per 1,000, while the infant mortality rate was 9.51 per 1,000. The total fertility rate was 1.9 children born per woman. The death rate was 7.77 per 1,000.[2]

According to the 2000 *U.S. Census of Population*, it is estimated that there are 3.0 million Puerto Ricans residing in the U.S. mainland, 51 percent females and 49 percent males. Sixty-four percent of the total resides in the Northeast of the United States, while 21 percent resides in the South. Forty percent of this population is below twenty-one years of age, 54 percent is in the age group twenty-one to sixty-four, and 6 percent is in the age group sixty-five or older.[3]

OVERVIEW OF WOMEN'S ISSUES

In 2000, Puerto Ricans elected their first female governor, Sila Calderón. The government has been very active in defending women's rights; in particular, in 1973 a commission was created to oversee women's issues at the executive level. In addition, the government has approved laws to protect women's rights and to implement U.S. federal regulations providing equality to women under the law. Despite this progress, many difficulties confront Puerto Rican women, such as the feminization of poverty among both female-headed households and women sixty-five years of age or older, job and pay discrimination in the labor market, the high prevalence of sterilization to control population growth, the epidemic incidence of HIV/ AIDS, which is affecting more women than men (AIDS is the leading cause of death for women in the group aged fifteen to forty-nine),[4] and the serious problem of domestic violence. Because many Puerto Rican women reside on the U.S. mainland, some of the problems affecting these women will be considered as well.

EDUCATION

Opportunities

Puerto Ricans have ample opportunities for education. In addition to the many private schools, the government provides free education, and as in the United States, children are required by law to attend school. Spanish is the language used in schools. English was used before 1949 as a method of "Americanizing" Puerto Ricans, but this program of assimilation was discontinued.[5]

At the primary level, all children in this age group are attending school. However, at the secondary level, only two-thirds of children are attending school. At the tertiary level, nearly one-half of females are enrolled at the university, while only one-third of males are enrolled at this level.[6]

In 2000–2001, enrollment in public schools was 612,725 children, 49.7 percent in elementary schools, 24.0 percent in middle schools, and 26.3 percent in high schools. There are nearly 40,000 full-time teachers. The student/teacher ratio is 15:1 at the elementary level, 16:1 at the middle level, and 18:1 at the high-school level.[7] Three-fourths of the funding for these schools is derived from state sources, and one-fourth from federal sources.

At the university level, the enrollment in 2000 was 210,346 at the undergraduate level, 58 percent female

Graduates gather on the main steps of San Juan University before ceremonies. Photo © Burt Glinn/Magnum Photo.

and 42 percent male. At the graduate and professional level, enrollment was 26,386, 60 percent female and 40 percent male.[8]

It has been calculated that the level of education is higher for women than for men living in Puerto Rico. At least half of females sixteen years old or over have completed high school, and 15 percent have completed a university degree. Nonetheless, 40 percent of this population group has not completed the tenth grade. Women with university-level degrees exceed men at the rate of 60 percent to 40 percent.[9]

For those Puerto Ricans sixteen years of age or older living in the United States, the situation is to some extent different. Slightly more men than women have completed high school (29.7 percent versus 29.3 percent), but significantly more men than women have obtained bachelor's degrees (9.5 percent versus 7.8 percent). However, in advanced degrees, women are slightly ahead of men, 4.5 percent to 4.3 percent.[10]

Literacy

In Puerto Rico, the literacy rate, defined as the percentage of those fifteen years old or over able to read and write, is relatively low, estimated at only 89 percent.[11] However, the youth illiteracy rate, that is, the percentage of people aged fifteen to twenty-four unable to read and write, in 2000 was 3.1 percent for males and only 1.8 percent for females.[12]

EMPLOYMENT AND ECONOMICS

Job/Career Opportunities

The transformation in the Puerto Rican economy began with the implementation of an export-led industrialization strategy called Operation Bootstrap that offered tax incentives and duty-free access to the U.S. market. Many U.S. firms were attracted to set up operations on the island. The original intention of the plan was to offer jobs to males displaced from agricultural jobs. Nevertheless, the industries attracted to the island were labor intensive in the sectors of textiles, garments, and food processing, and these industries attracted a greater number of women than men.[13]

Before this process of industrialization started, the needle industry, between 1920 and 1945, had allowed women to work at home and at the same time take care of the family.[14] The first major change that the new industries brought was that women had to leave the home to work in the factories. The second change was a reversal in the roles played in the household as these women became the major breadwinners. The third major change was that younger women were attracted to the factories because they were preferred over older women for their dexterity and manageability.[15]

The low salaries paid in these factories did not alleviate poverty. Men faced with the heavy burden of unemployment started the massive migration to the United States. Older women with children had to work to maintain the household, while the younger single women worked to supplement the family income. The opportunities in the manufacturing sector with such low-paying jobs did not improve the situation of the family. Many women had few options but to migrate to the United States as well.

As the economy developed, in the 1960s the industrial sector shifted to capital-intensive operations. The pharmaceutical industry became the most important activity, followed by electronics. By then the educational level had risen in Puerto Rico, and these industries were more appealing to the more educated labor force. At the same time, textiles, apparel, and food products lost significant ground because of increased competition from countries with lower labor costs than in Puerto Rico, in particular, countries in East Asia and also other Caribbean countries. Women continued their participation in the manufacturing sector, although at a lower level, but they engaged as well in service activities, and the government sector became their main employer. At the same time, the tourist sector created many jobs for both men and women. It is estimated that by 2000, as a main Caribbean tourist destination, the total number of tourists visiting Puerto Rico exceeded 5 million.[16]

By 2000, the population of those sixteen years old or over had increased to 2.8 million from 1.6 million in 1970. During that time, the participation rate of women in the labor force increased from 28.0 percent to 35.0 percent, whereas the participation rate of men decreased from 69.0 to 58.7 percent.[17]

In 2000, Puerto Rico's labor force stood at 1.3 million persons, with males making up 58.7 percent of the total, while females made up the remaining 41.3 percent. Men in the labor force were slightly older than women, with average ages of thirty-nine and thirty-eight years, respectively. Most of the women in the labor force (75.9 percent) were in the age group twenty-five to fifty-four. The group below twenty-five years of age made up 14.5 percent, while those above fifty-five years of age made up 9.6 percent of the female labor force. In comparison, most of the men (70.1 percent) were also in the age group of twenty-five to fifty-four, but there were more men in both the younger (16.2 percent) and the older (13.3 percent) worker age groups than women.

The problem of unemployment in Puerto Rico has continued to be more serious for males than for females. In 1980, the rate of unemployment for males stood at 19.5 percent, but by 2000 it had decreased to 11.9 percent. The rate for women decreased from 12.3 percent in 1980 to 7.8 percent in 2000.[18]

In general, women in the labor force in Puerto Rico have a higher level of education than men. In 2000, the median level of education of female workers in Puerto Rico was 13.2 years, compared to 12.7 years for males, and 63.0 percent of the female workers in Puerto Rico had received some university-level education, in comparison to 39.4 percent of the males. Some high-school education was the highest level for 28.6 percent of female workers and 41.4 percent of male workers.

The distribution of employment by economic sectors in Puerto Rico is different for females than it is for males. By 2000, women were employed equally in the government (28.8 percent) and the service sectors (28.8 percent). The next sector in importance was trade (20.3 percent), while manufacturing employed only 13.5 percent of working females.

The service sector was the most important employer of males (25.0 percent). Trade and the government followed in importance with shares of 22.0 percent and 16.9 percent, respectively. Manufacturing employed 14.7 percent of the males, while 12.1 percent were employed in construction.

The Puerto Rican Labor Department reports that in 2000 the main occupation for women was in the field of secretarial and office-related jobs, which employed 30.2 percent of the female labor force. Next in importance were service-related occupations, employing 15.5 percent; professional occupations, employing 11.2 percent; and management and administrative positions, held by 11.1 percent of the female workers. Teaching was an important career for females (9.5 percent), but less than 5 percent were health technicians. On the contrary, the main occupations for male workers were in managerial and professional opportunities (24.8 percent). Within these sectors, the most important occupations included managers (13.4 percent) and professionals (7.7 percent), and 8.1 percent were employed as salesmen. Other important occupations were those of craftsmen and foremen (17.7 percent) and operators of machines, assemblers, and inspectors (15.8 percent). Notwithstanding the higher levels of education for females than for males, most females end up performing secretarial and clerical work, while most males are employed in managerial and professional occupations.

Pay

In 1956, 1995, and 1998 new provisions were added to make the minimum wage legislation similar to that of the United States. The Puerto Rican Department of Labor estimated that the median weekly salary for females in 2000 was only $214.80. The two largest employers of women on the island paid weekly salaries above this median. The government sector provided a weekly pay rate of $292.90, while the service sector paid $222.30. On the other hand, the manufacturing sector had a weekly wage slightly below the median at $207.90, and the trade sector paid the lowest salary at only $151.50 per week.[19]

According to the *2001 Statistical Abstract of the United States*, the annual average compensation in Puerto Rico in the year 2000 was $20,069.[20] Hence if it is assumed that the women in the labor force in Puerto Rico worked the maximum of fifty-two weeks in the year, their median weekly salary would have been substantially less than the average compensation paid on the island. The median annual salary paid by the government sector would have been $15,230, while the lowest salary, earned in the trade sector, would have been $7,878.[21] The salaries lower than the median paid to women are probably in great part the result of their being employed mainly in secretarial and clerical occupations.

An additional indicator that female workers earn less than their male counterparts comes from U.S. census data. It was estimated that in 1990 male full-time, year-round workers in Puerto Rico had median earnings of $10,936, compared to median earnings of $10,200 for female full-time, year-round workers. These figures increased in 2000 to $17,097 for males and to $15,698 for females.[22] Although the earnings for both male and female workers increased from 1990 to 2000, the situation for female workers worsened in relative terms. In 1990, the median earnings for women were 93.3 percent of male earnings, a figure that decreased to 91.8 percent in 2000.

Of the 3.0 million Puerto Ricans residing in the United States, 1.3 million (43.3 percent) are in the labor force, 51 percent males and 49 percent females. The most important occupational groups for Puerto Rican women living in the United States are technical, sales, and administrative support positions (46.4 percent), followed by the service sector (20.6 percent) and managers and professionals (19.9 percent). Within these occupational groups, 29.9 percent work as office support personnel, including administrative and clerical, and 19.6 percent work as service providers. Greater male representation is found among occupations such as operators (44.6 percent), technical, sales, and administrative support (23.9 percent), services (15.9 percent), and managers and professionals (14.4 percent). Median yearly earnings for Puerto Rican women living in the United States are slightly less than $22,500, whereas for males the median earnings are $30,000.[23] It has been estimated that the salary difference between the U.S. mainland and Puerto Rico for full-time employees ranged anywhere from $230 for general clerks to $802 for engineers.[24]

The low levels of earnings are reflected in household and family levels of income and are the main cause of the high incidence of poverty. The 1990 U.S. census indicates that the median family income in Puerto Rico was $9,988, a level of income that placed close to 60 percent of persons and 55 percent of all families below the level of poverty.[25] By the year 2000, the median family income had increased to $16,543, but 48.2 percent of persons and 44.6 percent of families were still below the poverty level.

Another relevant figure reflecting earnings is household income. In 1990, the median household income was $8,895, a figure that increased to $14,412 in 2000. According to 2000 U.S. census data, 64.7 percent of the households had earnings, with a mean of $28,462. Income was received in the households from a variety of other sources, not all of them mutually exclusive. An additional 33.8 percent of the households received Social Security income, with a mean of $7,359. Supplemental Security income was received by 1.3 percent of the households, with an average of $5,137. Public assistance income was received by 20.1 percent of the households, with an average income of $2,266. Last, retirement income was received by 10.7 percent of the households, with an average of $12,505.[26]

Families headed by females, with no husband present, were the families most seriously affected by poverty. In Puerto Rico in 1990, there were 142,737 such families, and the number increased to 159,205 in 2000. In 1990, nearly 70 percent of these female-headed households were below the poverty level, compared to 61 percent in 2000. Poverty becomes more serious in households with children, as almost three-fourths of families with children under the age of eighteen were classified as poor in both years. In 1990, 84.3 percent of female-headed families with children below the age of five were classified below the poverty level, a rate that improved somewhat by 2000, but remained extremely high at 76.9 percent.

Of the 3.0 million Puerto Ricans residing in the United States in 2000, one-fourth were classified below the poverty level. Among these, 22 percent were males and 29 percent were females. In the case of females classified as poor, 40 percent were girls below the age of eighteen, and 19 percent were women sixty-five years of age or older. Twenty-three percent of families of Puerto Ricans residing in the United States were classified below the poverty level. In female-headed households, the figure increased to 47.4 percent, compared to 19 percent of male-headed households.

The problem of poverty is serious for older women residing in Puerto Rico, who constitute 11.2 percent of the population. Persons sixty or more years old have a median income of only $8,500, with Social Security payments as their main source of income.[27] Puerto Rican women sixty-five years of age or older make up 6 percent of the Puerto Rican population on the mainland. Of these females, 22.3 percent are below the poverty level, while only 13.7 percent of men aged sixty or over are classified as poor.

Working Conditions

Puerto Rico operates its own Occupational Safety and Health Office (OSHO) under a plan approved by the U.S. Department of Labor. It was implemented in 1978 after the approval in 1975 of the Occupational Safety and Health Act of Puerto Rico. The Act guarantees the safety and healthful working conditions of employees at both the private and public sectors.[28]

Data for 1994–1995 indicates that out of 1,051,000 workers, only 75,823 claims were filed for work-related accidents or illnesses. These cases were divided into 40 percent in the public sector, and 60 percent in the private sector. Only 688 cases resulted in permanent disability.[29]

Sexual Harassment

Since 1959, Puerto Rico's legislature has adopted civil rights and discrimination laws protecting the rights of workers. In particular, Puerto Rico has adopted affirmative-action laws, following laws approved in the United States. These laws prohibit discrimination in the workplace by sex, race, age, and religion or beliefs, among other forms of discrimination. Sexual harassment is considered discrimination based on sex and is punishable on the basis that it prevents the worker from performing the assigned job. Because of the importance of this issue, an executive order was passed in 1988 to develop and implement affirmative-action plans to prevent this kind of gender discrimination in the workplace in Puerto Rico. In 1979, 1988, 1998, and 2000 comparable laws were approved to protect women from sexual harassment in the workplace. These laws not only address the rights of workers but also delineate penalties for offenders. The 1988 law, in particular, places much of the responsibility on the employer who knows that there are instances of sexual harassment but refuses to take action.[30]

Support for Mothers/Caretakers

Maternal Leave

Since 1942, Puerto Rico has required employers to provide eight weeks of paid maternity leave to working mothers. In 2000, the maternity leave was extended to women in the labor force who adopt a preschool-age child.

Daycare

In 1999, legislation was passed creating daycare centers for government employees. Because the government sector is one of the most important employers in Puerto Rico, this provision is of great importance for working mothers.

There is a severe shortage of daycare centers in Puerto Rico if the number of children four years of age or under is compared to the places available to take care of them.[31] In 2000, there were nearly 61,000 of these children. Only 34,400 of these children were registered in the Head Start Program, leaving 26,600 children in need of daycare. There were only 490 licensed/regulated child-care centers and 192 licensed/regulated small family child-care centers in 2000.

The shortage of daycare centers in Puerto Rico has been alleviated by involving grandparents in taking care of grandchildren. Data from the 2000 census indicate that in Puerto Rico, 52.5 percent of grandparents are responsible for their grandchildren.[32]

Family and Medical Leave

The Family and Medical Leave Act is a federal law and, as such, applies to local, state, and federal employees in Puerto Rico. In the private sector, it applies to employers with fifty or more employees. This act requires employers to provide employees up to twelve weeks of unpaid leave in case of serious medical problems of a family member.

Inheritance and Property Rights

The Puerto Rico Civil Code of 1930 established regulations governing private property as well as inheritance. In Puerto Rico, as in the United States, women have the same rights as men to inherit and to own property.

Social/Government Programs

Welfare

In 1943, laws were adopted regulating welfare programs in Puerto Rico, in particular, the eligibility and the responsibility of the participants in these programs. Almost all welfare programs available for citizens in the United States are also extended to those residing in Puerto Rico, including programs such as Medicare, Social Security, food stamps, and supplemental income.

According to the *2000 U.S. Census of Population*, there were 159,205 female householders below poverty level, and 25.7 percent of them received Social Security income and/or public assistance. At the same time, there were 25,451 male householders below poverty level, and 36.2 percent of them received Social Security income and/or public assistance. At or above the level of poverty, there were 103,027 additional female householders and 41.1 percent of them received Social Security income and/or public assistance. In the case of the male householders, of which there were 27,363, 46.3 percent received Social Security and/or public assistance.

FAMILY AND SEXUALITY

Gender Roles

Puerto Rico has a dominant Hispanic culture that has been somewhat modified as a result of modernization of the society and the economy but continues to be influenced by machismo. In this type of culture, the man is considered to be the most dominant figure in the household, and the woman is expected to assume a more passive role. In addition, these traditional gender roles assign the woman the function of housewife and the man the function of breadwinner.[33] The rather strict sexual norms prevailing in Puerto Rico are in agreement with the traditional concepts of gender roles. Men are expected to be interested more in the physiological aspects of sexuality, whereas women are more interested in the emotional aspects related to the relationship.[34]

The concept of machismo has been studied, but studies have been limited to social classes with low levels of income. Machismo has been explained both as a sociobiological theory and as a psychological theory. Some of the research undertaken in different countries, including Puerto Rico, has linked machismo to feelings of inferiority coming from job insecurity and low levels of income. As a result, men attempt to compensate for this sentiment of inferiority by subordinating women. At the same time, women, by permitting this behavior, preserve machismo.[35]

Marriage

In Puerto Rico, marriage is important, as some of the following statistics indicate. In 2000, the population fifteen years of age or over was 2.9 million persons, of whom 52 percent were currently married, 28 percent had never married, 9.6 percent were divorced, 6.8 percent were widowed, and 3.6 percent were separated.[36]

Another source documenting the importance of marriage is a 1995–1996 survey that included almost 6,000 women aged fifteen to forty-nine. Of these women, 58 percent were in a union (45 percent in legal marriage and 13 percent in a consensual union), 16 percent were widowed, separated, or divorced, and 27 percent had never married.[37]

Equally indicative of the importance of marriage is that according to the 2000 U.S. census, there were 1.26 million households in Puerto Rico. Of these households, 80 percent were families. Of these families, 68.0 percent included a married couple (both husband and wife present), while 26.7 percent were female-headed households, with no husband present, and 5.3 percent were male-headed households, with no wife present. That same year, the average household size was 2.98, and the average family size was 3.41.[38]

Notwithstanding the importance of marriage, the substantial number of female-headed households is indicative of the extremely high incidence of divorce. Since 1976, laws have been approved in Puerto Rico allowing the filing of divorce by mutual consent. According to U.S. census data, in 2000, there were 176,549 divorced women in Puerto Rico, two-thirds of all divorced persons. Provisional data for 2000 indicate that in Puerto Rico there were 26,151 marriages, but at the same time there were 13,706 divorces.[39]

Puerto Rico has one of the highest divorce rates in the world, surpassed only by the United States and Bermuda. The elevated divorce rate has been difficult to explain, given the presence of the Hispanic culture and the traditional Catholic opposition to divorce. Some of the studies undertaken to explain the high divorce rate in Puerto Rico have found that divorce is positively related to female participation in the labor force, particularly if this participation starts after marriage. Other studies conducted in Puerto Rico have found a positive correlation between divorce and residence in urban areas. It has also been found that dissolution is higher in the instances in which the couples are cohabitating without being legally married, than in the cases of those couples that are married. The presence of children below the age of six years reduces the possibility of divorce. It was also concluded that the probability of marital dissolution in cases of women participating in and attending church services regularly is higher.[40]

Other studies have been undertaken attempting to find a relationship between divorce and migration to the United States. It has been found that Puerto Rican women who have lived on the U.S. mainland have higher divorce rates than women who have not migrated to the United States.[41] It has also been found that single Puerto Rican women migrating to the U.S. mainland looking for better marriage opportunities are more inclined to get into unions, both formal and informal, than nonmigrants.[42] However, these unions lack the basic social foundation needed to prevent ending in divorce.[43]

Reproduction

Sex Education

The Puerto Rico Department of Education does not have a definitive sex education policy. Instead, the government relies on organizations like PROFAMILIA to help educate the youth. Nevertheless, the government requires students to have parental authorization to obtain the contraceptive supplies offered by these programs.[44]

Contraception and Abortion

In Puerto Rico, the total fertility rate decreased from 2.6 births per woman in 1980 to 1.9 in 2000.[45] The decrease occurred in part due to the prevalence of contraceptive use in women aged fifteen to forty-nine. The number of women using some form of contraception increased from 69 percent in 1980 to almost 80 percent in 2000.[46] The preferred method of contraception is sterilization, which makes up almost 60 percent of all contraceptive use.[47]

The use of sterilization to control population growth in Puerto Rico started in 1937 when sterilization became legal. At that time, the procedure was supported by both the federal and the local governments.[48] In 1965, in a study that was conducted to determine rates of cancer of the uterus, it was discovered that almost one-third of all women in Puerto Rico between the ages of twenty and forty-nine had undergone the procedure.[49] Puerto Rican women are the youngest in the world to undergo sterilization; 92 percent of these women were under the age of thirty-five.[50] This is the highest rate of sterilization in the world.[51] The issue of forced sterilization has been a political dilemma in Puerto Rico. It has been argued that because of its colonial status, the U.S. federal government had forced the sterilization of poor Puerto Rican women as a method of controlling population growth. However, there is no evidence that these women were forced to undergo sterilization.[52]

Puerto Rican women residing on the U.S. mainland have been sterilized in greater percentages than white and African American women, as concluded by surveys undertaken in the Northeast of the United States.[53] Overall, 38 percent of Puerto Rican women residing in the United States have been sterilized. A survey conducted in New York showed that the rate of sterilization of Latinas is seven times higher than that of white women and almost twice that of African American women.[54] Another survey carried out in Hartford, Connecticut, concluded that 50 percent of Puerto Rican women of reproductive age have been sterilized.[55]

From surveys undertaken more recently, it can be concluded that sterilization continues to be the preferred method of contraception. Sterilization is chosen mainly by married women (45 percent), while the pill is used by only 10 percent of women of reproductive age. The prevalence of sterilization has been linked to the level of education and is more prevalent in women with less than an elementary education. Sterilization is influenced also by the number of children and the age of the woman, as it has been found that this is the preferred method by those women between the ages of thirty-five and forty-nine, and in particular after the birth of their third child.[56]

Family planning in Puerto Rico is offered by nongovernmental organizations like PROFAMILIA, an association interested in working with the government to provide this service and to promote sex education in the school curriculum. There is a need to expand family planning, as only 6.56 percent of women of reproductive age receive this service in public health facilities.[57]

Although the provision of family-planning services is low, there are many indicators that a high proportion of expectant mothers in Puerto Rico receive prenatal care. The United Nations reports that in Puerto Rico, 99 percent of pregnant women receive this type of care, and an equal percentage of women have deliveries attended by skilled professionals.[58] The Centers for Disease Control reports that in 1999, 77 percent of the mothers receiving prenatal care received it during the first trimester.[59] Prenatal care is received in private physicians' offices (43 percent), followed by health department clinics (35 percent) and public hospitals (18 percent). The proportion of babies delivered by cesarean section is estimated at one-third. Equally important is the practice of breast feeding, as two-thirds of mothers have nursed their most recent baby.[60]

Federal abortion laws apply in Puerto Rico because of its commonwealth status within the United States. As a result, abortion is legal in

Puerto Rico provided that it is necessary to preserve the woman's health or life. However, after many years, there is still a feeling that abortion remains illegal. The abortion rate in Puerto Rico is only 23 per 1,000 women. This rate is considered low, as most developing countries with legalized abortions tend to have rates of 30 or more abortions per 1,000.[61]

There are many difficulties for women in achieving full abortion rights. Most of the problems are related to the limited information available and the fact that abortions are not performed in public hospitals, so the high cost of the procedure may act as a major deterrent.[62]

Teen Pregnancy

The rate of teen pregnancies in Puerto Rico ranges from 63 per 1,000 women aged fifteen to nineteen, as reported by the United Nations, to 72 per 1,000, as reported by the Centers for Disease Control.[63] In Puerto Rico, teen pregnancy is related to social status. Poverty and nontraditional families were found to be related to teen pregnancy in one 2001 study.[64] Other findings relate teen pregnancies to a high incidence of crime in their place of residence and also to the teenager being an orphan.

In Puerto Rico, adolescents cannot obtain contraceptive supplies through the government programs unless they have written authorization from their parents. Sexual and reproductive health services for youths are mainly provided by nongovernmental organizations like PROFAMILIA, the Puerto Rican association that provides family-planning services.[65]

In a survey conducted by the University of Puerto Rico, it was found that Puerto Rican teens have not effectively used contraception.[66] Although 95 percent of the students knew that condoms could protect them from pregnancies and from contracting sexually transmitted diseases like AIDS, less than 10 percent reported always using them.

In Puerto Rico, sexual activity before marriage increases with age. Seventeen percent of teens aged from fifteen to seventeen engage in sex. In the case of those eighteen to nineteen years old, the rate increases to 38 percent. Sex before marriage was found in only half of those fifteen to twenty-four years old, 35 percent before entering a union and 14 percent afterwards.[67]

HEALTH

The life expectancy of Puerto Ricans is an average of 75.76 years.[68] Ninety-six percent of the population has access to safe water, and at least 50 percent has access to sanitation.[69] There are 17.5 physicians per 10,000 inhabitants, and national health expenditures correspond to 6.0 percent of GDP. The main causes of deaths are diseases of the heart and malignant neoplasms.[70]

Health Care Access

The provision of health care in Puerto Rico has changed dramatically since 1994 when the government started health-care reform. The purpose of the reform was to privatize the public health-care delivery system. Privatizing the service was intended to close the differences between the public and the private health-care systems.

All persons have equal access to health care in Puerto Rico. Under the new reform, there are some health programs intended to have a direct impact on girls and women, including the Adolescent Health Integrated Services Program, the Healthy Start Program, the Folic Acid Campaign, the Puerto Rico Safe Kids Coalition, and Rape Victim Centers.[71] Under the female governor elected in 2000, the reform of the health services has continued.

Diseases and Disorders

AIDS

Puerto Rico has one of the highest incidences of HIV/AIDS cases in the world. HIV/AIDS has become the fifth-leading cause of death in the general population and the third-leading cause of death among women of reproductive age.[72] The Centers for Disease Control reports that Puerto Rico has the highest AIDS rate among women in the United States, 24.9 per 100,000 in 2000. In comparison, in 1999, for the whole population in Puerto Rico, the rate was 32.1 per 100,000.[73] The HIV/AIDS Research and Education Center of the University of Puerto Rico believes that HIV/AIDS infection is caused by a lack of sufficient information about sexuality and gender roles.

Puerto Rican women are heavily affected by HIV/AIDS. This epidemic situation in Puerto Rico is more serious than in other parts of the United States because in Puerto Rico AIDS has been a disease transmitted to women by heterosexual male injection drug users and by bisexual male partners.[74]

Equally important is the lack of skills to adequately negotiate safer sexual practices.[75] Because women are brought up to be submissive, obedient, monogamous, and maternal in order to keep the family as the center of society, they do not have the cultural preparation and skills required to negotiate safe sex with men, who hold all the controlling power.[76]

Clinics and health centers have been created in Puerto Rico to provide basic medical and health care. As well, the U.S. Medicare and Medicaid programs have contributed to improving health quality, as have various other social programs. However, treatment for HIV/AIDS is very expensive, and the public health service in Puerto Rico will not be able to cover all the costs. It has been estimated that one year of treatment may cost as much as $15,000, mainly because of the high cost of drugs.[77]

Cancer

The incidence of cancer among Puerto Rican women was analyzed as part of *Cancer in Women of Color* (2003). This is a comprehensive study undertaken by the U.S. Department of Health and Human Services and the National Cancer Institute.

The study analyzed 930 cases of cancer among Puerto Rican women, from 1992 to 1998, by age groups and by types of cancer. Most of these women were included in the age groups from forty-five to sixty-four years old (40.2 percent) and from sixty-five years old and over (40.8 percent). The age group between thirty-five and forty-four constituted 11.4 percent of the cases, and the remaining 7.5 percent were younger than thirty-four years of age.

The most common types of cancer reported were cancers of the breast (26.1 percent), followed by cancers of the lung (8.4 percent), cancer of the colon and rectum (8.0 percent), and non-Hodgkins lymphoma (6.2 percent). In comparison to non-Hispanic white women, Puerto Rican women have a lower incidence of breast, lung, and colon cancers, but a higher incidence in the case of non-Hodgkins lymphoma. For the non-Hispanic white women, the corresponding rates were: 31.6, 12.7, 9.3, and 3.8 percent, respectively.

The death rate for all types of cancer of Puerto Rican women was 69.6 per 100,000 inhabitants. By type of cancer, breast cancer has the highest death rate, estimated at 13.9. The death rate in the cases of colon cancer was 7.4, and it was 6.6 per 100,000 in the case of lung cancer.

In terms of risk factors, it was found that in 1998, 64 percent of women over the age of forty had had a mammography within the last two years. This represents an improvement over the rate found in the 1980s, which was close to 50 percent. It was also found that 77 percent had had a Papanicolaou test within the last three years. One of the most disturbing findings was that 30.3 percent of the women use tobacco, and this is the highest incidence found among the different groups of Hispanic women studied, but it is lower than the rate found among Puerto Rican women living in the United States.

The data provided for survival rates refer to the time period 1980–1985. The rate for all types of cancer was equal to 72 percent after one year, 53 percent after three years, and 45 percent after five years. For those patients with breast cancer, the rates were 92, 73, and 61 percent, respectively. The survival rates for colon cancer were lower than in the case of breast cancer, estimated at 71, 51, and 42 percent, in that order.[78]

Depression

Studies have found a high rate of symptoms of depression among female heads of households. These women tend to be poorer and less educated than women who are not heads of their households.[79] Furthermore, female householders with young children at home are even more depressed than female heads of households in general.

More than twice as many Puerto Rican women as men suffer from diagnosed depression.[80] Single women who head households have been found to be especially at risk for depression because they tend to be older, less educated, and poorer than other groups.[81] Adolescent girls are less likely to report an absence of depression symptoms than adolescent boys, 41 percent versus 47 percent. While male adolescents reported a higher rate of moderate depression symptoms than their female counterparts (42 percent versus 34 percent), 25 percent of female adolescents reported having severe symptoms of depression, compared to only 11 percent of males.[82]

POLITICS AND LAW

Suffrage

Literate Puerto Rican women have had the opportunity of participating in political elections since 1929, when Puerto Rico became the second Latin American country to allow women to vote.[83] Universal voting rights were extended to all women in 1935.[84]

Political Participation

Women's political participation in Puerto Rico reached the executive level with the election in 2000 of the first female governor in the history of Puerto Rico, Sila Calderón. In 1992, Nydia Velázquez of New York became the first Puerto Rican woman elected to the U.S. House of Representatives. The bicameral Legislative Assembly is composed of a Senate, seven of whose twenty-seven members are women, and a House of Representatives, seven of whose fifty-one members are women. However, there is only one female mayor out of a total of seventy-eight municipalities. In the judiciary, there is only one woman among the seven judges of Puerto Rico's Supreme Court.

Women's Rights

Women's rights in Puerto Rico are protected by the U.S. Constitution and by laws. In particular, there are laws protecting women against discrimination, against domestic violence, and against sexual harassment. However, in reality, women are subjected to many acts of discrimination not only in the labor market, but also in the household as the result of repeated aggression by their partners. The traditional cultural values limit the fair participation of women in both the household and the labor market. Even strict laws do not guarantee women equality with men.

Feminist Movements

Feminist movements began in Puerto Rico before the 1970s with women first fighting for better working conditions and then for issues affecting women such as discrimination in the labor market, lack of representation in decision-making positions, domestic violence, restrictive abortion laws, and health issues, among others. One of their main struggles dealt with the double-workday model. These women promoted laws to help their families as well as to improve working conditions. These initiatives were then imitated in other Latin American countries.[85]

Lesbian Rights

In Puerto Rico, a sodomy law, more than 100 years old, penalizes consensual sexual contact between people of the same sex. The penalty under this law is up to ten years in prison. In 1998, this law was challenged in court based on unequal treatment of gays and lesbians.[86] In 2002, the Supreme Court in Puerto Rico denied the challenge and determined that the sodomy law should be enforced.[87]

Military Service

The national defense of Puerto Rico is the responsibility of the government of the United States. Puerto Rican men and women serve in the U.S. armed forces. In 2002, 6,309 women were serving in the military.[88] There are military bases located in Puerto Rico, and the navy conducts training exercises in Vieques, a small island located to the east of Puerto Rico. Women have been actively involved in asking for these exercises to stop because of concerns about the health of the residents of Vieques. It was believed that health conditions were deteriorating as a result of the noise and vibrations related to the naval exercises. In 2001, a panel was appointed to study the matter, and it was concluded that there was no basis for the allegations.[89] Nevertheless, the protests continued with the active participation of Puerto Rican women, in particular, Governor Sila Calderón. U.S. president George W. Bush ordered the naval exercises to end, which was effective May 2003.

RELIGION AND SPIRITUALITY

Puerto Rico is a religious country.[90] Freedom of religion is guaranteed by both the Constitution of Puerto Rico and the First Amendment to the U.S. Constitution.

Puerto Rico's population is 85 percent Roman Catholic and 15 percent Protestant.[91] In 1898, when the island was ceded to the United States, Protestantism was introduced as a means of acculturation. The heavy influence of Catholicism is due mainly to the cultural ties with Spain, a Catholic country. Puerto Rican women face various religious dilemmas regarding the Catholic doctrines against abortion and divorce, both of which are common in Puerto Rico. The Christian churches in Puerto Rico have opened the possibilities of ministries to women. Programs offered by these churches attempt to strengthen the leadership role of women.

Afro-Christian religious traditions are also found, although in a much smaller percentage than is common in many other Caribbean islands. In Puerto Rico, the Afro-Christian sect takes the name of Spiritualism, which, besides serving as a form of religion, can also be considered a form of psychotherapy and believes in healing powers. Many more women than men suffering from depression seek this kind of spiritual help.[92]

Religion and culture are very important determinants of the sexuality of Puerto Rican women, and together with family and institutions of education they are the sources of sexual messages and guidance.[93] These messages may at times be confusing, setting up a lifelong struggle of cultural values and personal choices.

VIOLENCE

Domestic Violence

As early as the 1970s, the government of Puerto Rico established a Women's Affairs Commission and amended civil and penal codes to offer protection for abused women. Equally important, Puerto Rico approved Law 54 of 1988 against domestic violence as a result of joint efforts of various women's organizations. This law was the first of its kind in a Latin American country, combining Puerto Rican culture with U.S. federal antiviolence legislation.[94] The importance of this law is that it serves as a model for other developing countries to follow because it takes into consideration the abused woman and her children.

Law 54 provides for criminal sanctions, civil remedies, and preventive measures. However, the main focus of the law is on protecting the family structure, and this does not necessarily favor women. In cases in which the children may suffer from domestic violence, the question to be answered is whether the children are better off with or without the abusive father. If the preservation of the family structure takes precedence over the rights of the abused woman, the law has major limitations, given the male-dominated family structure prevalent in Puerto Rico. Although Law 54 requires the legal system to fulfill the spirit of the law, it appears that government officials are not true believers in the merits of the legislation.[95] Some groups in Puerto Rico are even asking for the law to be overturned, considering that instances of domestic abuse are matrimonial disputes and are private family problems. The fear of overcrowding the prisons is another reason why police are reluctant to get involved in this serious issue.[96]

Even with this law, the incidence of domestic violence has been estimated as high as one woman killed by her partner every fifteen days. In addition, 20,000 restraining orders are sought in the courts every year.[97] In 1996, there were in Puerto Rico 19,132 cases of domestic violence, 90 percent of them against women and the remaining 10 percent against men. Most of these assaults (81.3 percent) took place in the home of the victim.[98]

The United Nations reports that in 1991, 48 percent of women in Puerto Rico in any relationship had experienced physical abuse by an intimate partner.[99] This problem is on the rise, and it is estimated that in 2000, at least 60 percent of married women were victims of domestic violence.[100]

Rape/Sexual Assault

Rape cases reported to police rose from 1940 to 1977, when they peaked at 792. Then they began to decline to 569 in 1980, to 426 in 1990, and to 228 in 2000. It is not clear, however, that rape has become less of a problem. It is estimated that only 14 percent of victims report the crime of rape to police. Furthermore, the Rape Victims Aid Center, founded in 1977 by a group of citizens concerned with sexual aggression against women, has treated 600 to 800 victims of sexual aggression each year.[101]

Trafficking in Women and Children

The Victims of Trafficking and Violence Protection Act of 2000 of the United States is intended to alleviate the problem of trafficking in women and children. This law applies to Puerto Rico as well. There are reports that Puerto Rico is being used as a point of transport. For example, pregnant women from the Dominican Republic are used as transporters of children for trafficking purposes. These children are taken to neighboring Puerto Rico and then transferred to other parts of the world.[102] In Puerto Rico there is also a major concentration of women prostitutes from the Dominican Republic.[103]

OUTLOOK FOR THE TWENTY-FIRST CENTURY

The government of Puerto Rico has been very active in promoting women's rights. Local laws have been adopted to implement U.S. federal government regulations protecting women's rights. Despite these regulations, incidents of domestic violence continue to be abundant, and on many occasions women's cultural beliefs dictate their passive response to these acts of violence. Women continue to earn less than the average salary paid in Puerto Rico despite the fact that their levels of education are higher than those of men. The feminization of poverty is extensive both for female-headed households with young children and for older women. The epidemic prevalence of HIV/AIDS, especially among women, is perplexing and will need to be addressed within the global health organizations dealing with the challenges of this epidemic. Although Puerto Rican women may enjoy the same liberties on paper as women on the U.S. mainland, their situation continues to be worse than that of their U.S. counterparts. For a better future, Puerto Rican women must be willing to assume major responsibility for improving their situation. More participation is called for in the economic and political arenas, where their voices can be heard.

NOTES

1. Central Intelligence Agency, *2002 World Factbook*, 2001, www.cia.gov/cia/publications/factbook/index.html.

2. U.S. Census Bureau, *2001 U.S. Census of Population*, 2001, www.census.gov/main/www/cen2002.html; Central Intelligence Agency, 2001.

3. U.S. Census Bureau, *2000 U.S. Census of Population*, 2001.

4. Pan-American Health Organization, "Puerto Rico," *Health in the Americas, 1998*, www.paho.org/english/HIA1998/PuertoRico.pdf.

5. Amilcar Antonio Barreto, "Statehood, the English Language, and the Politics of Education in Puerto Rico," *Polity*, 34(1): (fall 2001): 89–105.

6. World Bank Group, Gender Stats. http://genderstats.worldbank.org/.

7. Council of Chief State School Officers, www.ccsso.org/NAEP2002/StatebyState/Detail_CCD.cfm?recordID=Puertopercent20Rico.

8. U.S. Census Bureau, *2000 U.S. Census of Population*, 2001.

9. World Bank Group, Gender Stats, http://genderstats.worldbank.org/.

10. U.S. Census Bureau, *2000 U.S. Census of Population*, 2001.

11. Central Intelligence Agency, 2002.

12. World Bank Group, Gender Stats, http://genderstats.worldbank.org/.

13. Palmira N. Rios, "Export-Oriented Industrialization and the Demand for Female Labor: Puerto Rican Women in the Manufacturing Sector, 1952–1980," *Gender and Society* 4(3) (September 1990): 321–337.

14. Cristina Echevarria, review of *Puerto Rican Women and Work*, by Altagracia Ortiz, *Feminist Economist* 5(1) (1999): 114–118.

15. Helen I. Safa, "Female Employment and the Social Reproduction of the Puerto Rican Working Class," *International Migration Review* 18(4); Barbara A. Zsembik and Chuck W. Peek, "The Effect of Economic Restructuring on Puerto Rican Women's Labor Force Participation in the Formal Sector," *Gender and Society* 8(4) (December 1984): 1168–1187.

16. Caribbean/Latin American Action, *2001 Caribbean/Latin America Profile*. Grand Cayman, BWI: Caribbean Publishing, 2002.

17. Puerto Rico Department of Labor and Human Resources, *Empleo y Desempleo en Puerto Rico, 2000 and 1999*; and *Participación de la Mujer en la Fuerza Laboral 2000*. All subsequent statistics are derived from these sources. San Juan, Puerto Rico: Puerto Rico Department of Labor, 2000.

18. World Bank Group, Gender Stats, http://genderstats.worldbank.org/.

19. Puerto Rican Department of Labor.

20. U.S. Census Bureau, *2001 Statistical Abstract of the United States*, www.census.gov/prod/2002pubs/01statab/stat-ab01.html.

21. Ibid.

22. U.S. Census Bureau, *2000 U.S. Census of Population*, 2001.

23. Ibid.

24. Hilery Z. Simpson, "How Do Wages in San Juan Compare to Wages on the Mainland," *Compensation and Working Conditions* 3(4) (winter 1998), www.bls.gov/opub/cwc/1998/winter/art4exec.htm.

25. U.S. Census Bureau, *1990 U.S. Census of Population*, www.census.gov/main/www.cen1990.html; *Small Area Income and Poverty Estimates: Puerto Rico Estimates, 1997*, www.census.gov/hhes/www.saipe.prtoc.html; *2000 U.S. Census of Population*, 2001; *Hispanic Population in the United States, 2000 March CPS*, www.census.gov/population/www.socdemo/hispanic/h000.html. All subsequent census statistics come from these sources unless noted.

26. U.S. Census Bureau, *Profile of Selected Economic Characteristics: Puerto Rico, 2000*, Table DP-3, http://factfinder.census.gov.

27. Preamble to Law 331 of 2000, www.lexjuris.com.

28. U.S. Department of Labor, OSHA, www.osha.gov.

29. Pan-American Health Organization (PAHO).

30. The text of these Puerto Rican laws is available at www.lexjuris.com.

31. Data from the National Resource Center for Health and Safety in Child Care, www.nccic.org/statepro/puertorico.html.

32. U.S. Census Bureau, *Profile of Selected Social Characteristics: Puerto Rico, 2000*, Table DP-2-PR, at http://factfinder.census.gov.

33. Ineke Cunningham, "An Innovative HIV/AIDS Research and Education Program in Puerto Rico," *Sexual Information of the U.S. (SIECUS) Report* 26(3): 18–20.

34. Ibid.

35. Bron B. Ingoldsby, "A Theory for the Development of Machismo," paper presented at the Annual Meeting of the National Council on Family Relations, Dallas, Texas, November 4–8, 1985.

36. U.S. Census Bureau, *Profile of Selected Social Characteristics: 2000 (Format for Puerto Rico)*, http://factfinder.census.gov/servlet/QTTable?_ts=53419958136.

37. U.S. Census Bureau, 2000.

38. Ibid.

39. U.S. Centers for Disease Control, *Puerto Rico Health Facts, 2002*, www.cdc.gov/nchs/fastats/puerto.htm.

40. Canabal, 1990.

41. Nancy S. Landale and Ninfa B. Ogena, "Migration and Union Dissolution among Puerto Rican Women," *International Migration Review* 29 (fall 1995): 67–92.

42. Nancy S. Landale, "Migration and the Latino Family: The Union Formation Behavior of Puerto Rican Women," *Demography* 31 (February 1994): 133–157.

43. Landale and Ogena, 1995.

44. International Planned Parenthood Federation, Country Fact Sheets: Family Planning in Western Hemisphere (International Planned Parenthood corp. 1996.)

45. World Bank Group, Gender Stats, http://genderstats.worldbank.org/.

46. Ibid.

47. L. Remez, 1999.

48. Religious Coalition for Reproductive Choice, *Puertorriqueñas: Reproductive Health and Sociodemographics among Puerto Rican Women in the United States*, 1992, Gayle Group, 9–19.

49. Ibid.

50. Ibid.

51. Florita Z. Louis de Malavé, *Sterilization of Puerto Rican Women: A Selected Partially Annotated Bibliography*, www.library.wisc.edu/libraries/womensstudies/bibliogs/puerwom.htm.

52. Jenny Rivera, "Puerto Rico's Domestic Violence Prevention and Intervention Law and the United States Violence Against Women Act of 1994: The Limitations of Legislative Responses," *Columbia Journal of Gender and Law* 5(1) (January 1995): 76–126.

53. Ibid.

54. Maria E. Canabal, "An Economic Approach to Marital Dissolution in Puerto Rico," *Journal of Marriage and Family* 53 (May 2, 1990): 515–30.

55. Religious Coalition for Reproductive Choice, 1992.

56. Remez, 1999.

57. International Planned Parenthood Federation, *Country Fact Sheets: Family Planning in the Western Hemisphere* (International Planned Parenthood Federation, 1996).

58. United Nations, *World's Women 2000*, www.un.org/deps/unsd/ww2000.htm.

59. U.S. Centers for Disease Control, *Puerto Rico Health Facts, 2002*, http://www.cdc.gov/hiv/stat.

60. Remez, 1999.

61. Shirley K. Henshaw, Susheela Singh, and Taylor Hass, "The Incidence of Abortion Worldwide," *International Family Planning Perspectives* 25 (January 1999): 530–538.

62. Luis A. Aviles and Yamile Azize-Vargas, "Abortion in Puerto Rico: The Limits of Colonial Legality," *Reproductive Health Matters* 5(9) (1997): 56–65.

63. United Nations, *World's Women 2000*; U.S. Centers for Disease Control, *Puerto Rico Health Facts, 2002*.

64. Lourdes Pieve, "An Ethnographic Study of the Perceptions of Puerto Rican Pregnant Teenagers," *Dissertation Abstracts International: The Humanities and Social Sciences* 62(3), (September 2001): 1226-A–1227-A.

65. International Planned Parenthood Federation, "Responsible for the Future," *Forum* 13(2) (1998): 20–21.

66. Ineke Cunningham, 1998.

67. Remez, 1999.

68. Central Intelligence Agency, *2002 World Factbook*, 2002.

69. International Planned Parenthood Federation, 1996.

70. *Puerto Rico: Country Health Profile*, data updated to 2001, www.paho.org/english/sha/prflpur.htm.

71. U.S. Department of Health and Human Services, Office on Women's Health, *Overview of Region II*, 2002, www.4woman.gov.

72. Yarira Feliciano Torres, Laura Colón, Irma Serrano Garcia, and Evelyn Badillo Cordero, *Women, Vulnerability, and HIV/AIDS: A Human Rights Perspective* (Latin American and Caribbean Women's Health Network: 1998); "What Happens in Puerto Rico Could Happen Anywhere," *Women's Health Journal* 1997, 60–61.

73. U.S. Centers for Disease Control, *HIV/AIDS Statistics*, 2002, www.cdc.gov/hiv/stats.htm#area.

74. Women's Watch, "Health and Family Planning: Puerto Rican Women," *Women's Watch Newsletter* 8(4) (1995): 5; "What Happens in Puerto Rico Could Happen Anywhere," 1997, 6.

75. Cunningham,

76. María Isabel Baez, "Negociación sexual: Un asunto de poder," *La Cara Socio-Económica del SIDA. Serie Aportes para el Debate*, no. 5 (ALAI, Latin America in Movement, 1997). Ecuador: http://alainet.org/mujeres/debates5/m_isabel_baez.html.

77. Laura Colón, "What Happens in Puerto Rico Could Happen Anywhere," *Women's Health Journal*, 1997, 60–62.

78. Karen Glanz, ed., *Cancer in Women of Color Monograph* (Bethesda, MD: Department of Health and Human Service, National Cancer Institute, 2003). Cited March 24, 2003, http://dccps.nci.nih.gov/womenofcolor/index.html.

79. Nilda M. Burgos, Mary Clare Lennon, Milagros Bravo, and Josue Guzman, "Depressive Symptomatology in Single Women Heads of Households in Puerto Rico: A Comparative Analysis," *Women and Health* 23(3) (1995): 1–18.

80. J.D. Koss-Chioino, "Depression among Puerto Rican Women: Culture, Etiology, and Diagnosis," *Hispanic Journal of Behavioral Sciences* 21 (August 1999): 330–50.

81. Burgos, 1995, 1–18.

82. Marangeli Velazquez Columba et al., "Coping Strategies and Depression in Puerto Rican Adolescents: An Exploratory Study," *Cultural Diversity and Ethnic Minority Psychology* 5 (February 1999): 65–75.

83. María de Fátima Barceló Miller, *La lucha por el sufragio femenino en Puerto Rico, 1896–1935* (Río Piedras, PR: Centro de Investigaciones Sociales, Universidad de Puerto Rico, Ediciones Huracán, 1997).

84. Ronald Fernandez, Serafin Mendez, Gail Gueto, *Puerto Rico Past and Present: An Encyclopedia* (Westport, CT: Greenwood Press, 1998).

85. Elizabeth Crespo Kebler and Ana Irma Rivera Lassen, *Documentos del Feminismo en Puerto Rico: Facsimiles de la Historia*, vol. I, *1970–1979* (San Juan, PR: Editorial de la Universidad de Puerto Rico, 2001), 470.

86. www.aclu.org/LesbianGayRights/LesbianGayRights.cfm?ID=8068&c=100&SubsiteID=43.

87. www.lexjuris.com/lexjuris/tspr2002/lexj2002098.htm. Decision of Puerto Rican Supreme Court, July 22, 2002.

88. www.womensmemorial.org/statsWIM.

89. http://www.atsdr.cdc.gov/NEWS/viequesheartreport.html.

90. Rivera, 1995, 78–79.

91. Carla Lehman, "How Religious Are We Chileans? A Map of Religiosity in 31 Countries," *Estudios Publicos* 25 (Summer 2002): 21–40.

92. Central Intelligence Agency, *2001 World Factbook*, 2001.

93. Alan Harwood, "Puerto Rican Spiritism: Part 1: Description and Analysis of an Alternative Psychotherapeutic Approach," *Culture, Medicine, and Psychiatry* 1(1) (April 1977): 69–95.

94. María Isabel Màrtinó Villanueva, "The Social Construction of Sexuality: Personal Meanings, Perceptions of Sexual Experience, and Females' Sexuality in Puerto Rico," Ph.D. diss., Virginia Polytechnic Institute and State University, 1997, http://scholar.lib.vt.edu/theses/available/etd-13514459731541/.

95. Mercedes Rodriguez, "Latest Victim," in *The Right to Live without Violence: Women's Proposals and Action* (Latin American and Caribbean Women's Health Network, 1996), 129–132.

96. Inter Press Services, http://www.ips.fi/koulut/199750/8.htm.

97. Maria Dolore Fernós, "Multicultural Forum on Violence against Women," as reported by Caryn Nesmith for *Women's eNews*, August 3, 2001, http://64.81.195.15/article.cfm/dyn/aid/188/context/archive.

98. Law 233 of 1999, www.lexjuris.com.

99. United Nations, *The World's Women 2000*.

100. Preamble to Puerto Rican Laws of 1998, number 46 of February 28, 1998.

101. Melissa B. Gonzalez Valentin, "Rape Victims on the Island Less Willing to Report to Police," *Puerto Rico Herald*, March 9, 2002.

102. Richard J. Estes and Neil Alan Weiner, *The Commercial Sexual Exploitation of Children in the U.S., Canada, and Mexico* (Philadelphia: University of Pennsylvania School of Social Work, 2001).

103. *Factbook on Global Sexual Exploitation*, www.uri.edu/artsci/wms/hughes/domrep.htm.

RESOURCE GUIDE

Suggested Reading

Aviles, Luis A., and Yamile Azize-Vargas. "Abortion in Puerto Rico: The Limits of Colonial Legality." *Reproductive Health Matters* 5(9) (1997): 56–65.

Briggs, Laura. "Discourses of 'Forced Sterilization' in Puerto Rico: The Problem with the Speaking Subaltern." *Journal of Feminist Cultural Studies* 10 (July 1998).

Browne, Irene, ed. *Latinas and African American Women at Work: Race, Gender, and Economic Inequality.* New York: Russell Sage Foundation, 1999.

Colón-Warren, A.E., and I. Alegría-Ortega. "Shattering the Illusion of Development: The Changing Status of Women and Challenges for the Feminist Movement in Puerto Rico." *Feminist Review* 59 (Summer 1998): 101–17.

Echevarría, Cristina. Review of *Puerto Rican Women and Work*, by Altagracia Ortiz. *Feminist Economics* 5(1) (1999): 114–18.

Matos Rodríguez, Félix V., and Linda C. Delgado, eds. *Puerto Rican Women's History: New Perspectives.* Armonk, NY: M.E. Sharpe, 1998.

Meléndez, Edwin, Clara Rodríguez, and Janis Barry Figueroa, eds. *Hispanics in the Labor Force: Issues and Policies.* New York: Plenum Press, 1991.

Ortiz, Altagracia. *Puerto Rican Women and Work: Bridges in Transnational Labor.* Philadelphia: Temple University Press, 1996.

Safa, Helen Icken. *The Myth of the Male Breadwinner: Women and Industrialization in the Caribbean.* Boulder, CO: Westview Press, 1995.

Votaw, Carmen Delgado. *Puerto Rican Women.* Washington, DC: National Conference of Puerto Rican Women, 1995.

Videos/Films

AIDS in the Barrio: Eso no me pasa a mi. 1990. Produced by Frances Negron Montaner and Alba Martines. Cinema Guild.

Nuyrican Dream. 2000. Produced by Big Mouth Productions in association with John Leguizamo and Jellybean Benitez. Producers: Laurie Collier, Julia Pimsleur and Katy Chevigny. California Newsreel.

Puerto Rico: Paradise Invaded. 1998. Produced by Carmen Sarmiento. Films for the Humanities.

Web Sites

ASPIRA of Puerto Rico, http://pr.aspira.org.
A national nonprofit organization devoted solely to the education and leadership development of Puerto Rican and other Latino youth.

FEMPRESS, www.fempress.cl.
Created in 1981 as a unit of the Latin American Institute for Transnational Studies, FEMPRESS offers information on issues affecting Latin American women, including Puerto Rico. The contact person in Puerto Rico is Norma Valle, nvalle@caribe.net.

National Conference of Puerto Rico Women, www.gvelazco.com/sites/nacoprw/index2.htm.
Organization dedicated to promoting the full participation of Puerto Rican women in various aspects of life.

PROFAMILIA (International Planned Parenthood Federation), www.ippfw.org.

Puerto Rico AIDS Education and Training Center, www.rcm.upr.edu/2K1-PueRicAidEduAndTraCen.html.

Women of the Third World, http://women3rdworld.about.com/cs/latinamerica1/index.htm.
Presents a collection of web sites about women's rights and women's issues in the third world, including Puerto Rico.

Organizations

Coordinadora Paz Para la Mujer
PO Box 193008
San Juan, PR 00919-3008
Email: pazparalamujer@yunque.net

A nonprofit organization providing help to women victims of domestic violence.

Fundación SIDA de Puerto Rico
PO Box 364842
Calle 15 SE Caparra Terrace
San Juan, PR 00921
Phone: 787-782-8888

A nonprofit organization providing help to women with HIV/AIDS.

Oficina de la Procuradora de las Mujeres
PO Box 11382
San Juan, PR 00910-1382
Phone: 787-722-2977, 787-722-2907

Hot line for victims of domestic violence, available twenty-four hours a day, seven days a week.

PROFAMILIA (Asociación Puertorriqueña Pro-Bienestar de la Familia)
Carmen Rivera, Executive Director
PO Box 192221
San Juan, PR 00919-2221
Phone: 787-765-7373

This association, founded in 1954, pioneered family-planning services in Puerto Rico as well as in the Western Hemisphere.

Puerto Rico AIDS Education and Training Center
Daisy Gely, Project Director
Medical Science Campus
University of Puerto Rico
PO Box 365067
San Juan, PR 00936-5067

Email: dgely@rcm.upr.edu

A program of the Ryan White Care Act.

Puerto Rico Coalition against Domestic Violence and Sexual Assault
PO Box 23136,
Rio Piedras, PR 00931
Phone: 787-281-7579
Fax: 787-767-6843
National Hotline: 1-800-799-SAFE or 1-800-787-3224 (TTY).

Taller Salud
Laura Colón Martínez
PO Box 192172
San Juan, PR 00919-2172
Phone: 787-764-9639

A nonprofit organization working with women and HIV/AIDS.

SELECTED BIBLIOGRAPHY

Alan Guttmacher Institute. "The Incidence of Abortion Worldwide." *International Family Planning Perspectives* 25 (January 1999).

International Planned Parenthood Federation. "Responsible for the Future." *Forum*, 13(2) (1998): 20–21.

Rodriguez, Mercedes. "Latest Victim." In *The Right to Live without Violence: Women's Proposals and Action*, 129–32. Santiago, Chile: Latin American and Caribbean Women's Health Network, 1996.

13

TRINIDAD AND TOBAGO

Rhoda Reddock

PROFILE OF TRINIDAD AND TOBAGO

The Republic of Trinidad and Tobago is the southernmost state in the Caribbean archipelago, located between the Caribbean Sea and the North Atlantic Ocean. Tobago lies a few miles northeast of Trinidad and is more similar in topography to the other islands north of it than it is to Trinidad. In 1989, Trinidad was administratively linked to Tobago, creating the two-island state of Trinidad and Tobago. Trinidad, the larger of the two islands, covers an area of 4,828 square kilometers (1,864 square miles) and lies 11 kilometers (7 miles) northeast of Venezuela. The two main urban centers in Trinidad and Tobago are Port of Spain, the capital city, in the northwest of Trinidad, and San Fernando in the south. The capital of Tobago is Scarborough.

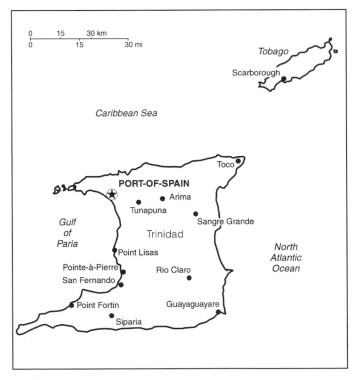

After decades of colonialism by various European powers, Trinidad and Tobago became independent from Britain in 1962 and acquired republican status in 1974. Under the 1976 constitution, Trinidad and Tobago became a parliamentary democracy with a Senate and House of Representatives. Legislation passed in 1980 gave Tobago considerable

Table 13.1
Ethnic Origin in Trinidad and Tobago, 1990

Ethnic Origin	Trinidad	Tobago	Trinidad & Tobago
African	37.41%	91.93%	39.9%
Indian	37.5%	2.4%	40.4%
Chinese	.4%	.1%	.38%
Syrian/Lebanese	.09%	.03%	.08%
White/Caucasian	.66%	.36%	.6%
Mixed	19.01%	4.48%	18.4%
Other	.15%	.24%	.15%
Not Stated	.42%	.70%	.43%
TOTAL	96.0%	4.0%	100.00%

Source: *Trinidad and Tobago, 1990 Population and Housing Census, Demographic Report*, Port of Spain: Central Statistical Office, 1990.

autonomy with the establishment of a separate Tobago House of Assembly with fifteen members. In 1987, Tobago was granted internal self-government. Much of Tobago's earlier history is more closely linked to the other islands of the Eastern Caribbean than it is to Trinidad.

The differences in historical development are most obvious in the contrast between the demographic composition of the two islands, Trinidad's ethnic diversity, on one hand, and Tobago's predominantly African population, on the other. Trinidad and increasingly Tobago are also multireligious. All of these factors are significant in understanding the complexities and specificities of gender relations in this country. Economically as well, Trinidad's dependence on its energy sector contrasts with Tobago's dependence on tourism. In both islands, traditional export agriculture has been declining.

The population of Trinidad and Tobago according to the 1990 census was 1,169,682. Life expectancy at birth was 70.92 years for women and 65.74 years for men. The infant mortality rate was 24.98 deaths per 1,000 births. By 1998, estimates of life expectancy were 76.5 years for females and 71.7 years for males.[1] People who for census purposes define themselves as Afro-Trinidadians and Indo-Trinidadians make up the majority of the population, around 40 percent each (table 13.1). The "mixed" group appeared to have increased significantly since the previous census to 18.4 percent, while other minorities—white/Caucasians, Chinese, Syrians, and Lebanese—though small in number, are highly represented in the social and economic elite. Small numbers of mixed descendants of indigenous people also exist, mainly in the northeastern town of Arima. The vast majority of the people are Roman Catholics and Hindus, and the remainder are Muslims or members of other Christian denominations, including Afro-Christian groups, or have no religious affiliation.

Table 13.2
Age/Sex Distribution in Trinidad and Tobago, 1990

Age Group	Male	Female	Both Sexes
0–14	32.6%	31.9%	32.2%
15–29	26.3%	25.9%	26.1%
30–44	19.3%	19.1%	19.2%
45–59	10.2%	10.4%	10.3%
60 or over	7.9%	8.9%	8.4%
Not stated	3.7%	3.6%	3.7%
TOTAL	584,445	585,127	1,169,572

Source: Trinidad and Tobago Population and Housing Census, Demographic Report (Port of Spain: Central Statistical Office, 1990).

The sex ratio is relatively even (table 13.2), but fertility levels have undergone a transition. Before the 1960s, the crude birth rates were generally in excess of 30 live births per 1,000 estimated midyear population. This rate declined until the 1980s, when there was an increase, but from 1985, it declined once more from 28.6 in 1985 to 18.60 in 1992. Total fertility rates were estimated to be 5.4 in 1960, 3.6 in 1970, 3.3 in 1980, and 2.4 in 1990. In the 1990s, these declined even further, from 1.9 in 1994 to 1.7 in 1997.[2]

Rates of maternal mortality also declined during the 1990s, from 65 per 100,000 in 1995 to 35 per 100,000 in 2000. Unsafe abortion is one of the main causes of maternal mortality, but data on abortions are incomplete because abortion is legal only under certain conditions. Official data suggest a figure of 25.29 per 100,000 maternities, but this cannot be considered a total figure.[3]

OVERVIEW OF WOMEN'S ISSUES

Women in Trinidad and Tobago have a fairly high level of quality of life (life expectancy, education, maternal mortality) compared with that of others in developing countries with a similar economic outlook. The human development index (HDI) ranking for 2000 was 50 out of 174 countries, with a gender-related development index (GDI) of 48 and a gender empowerment measure (GEM) of 22.[4] The status of women varies with age, geographic location (urban or rural), and religious and ethnic factors. Still, women in Trinidad and Tobago struggle with sexism.

EDUCATION

As an ex-slave colony, where bonded labor replaced enslaved labor in the mid-nineteenth century, Trinidad and Tobago has considered education an important mechanism of social mobility. The citizens' commitment to education has always been significant, and for the colonial powers, education in the English language was one way of establishing British values. In 1921, therefore, a Compulsory Education Ordinance was passed for Port of Spain and St. James, although it was not implemented until 1935.[5] By the 1940s, compulsory primary-school attendance for both sexes was in force, although not always observed in practice, and by 2000, universal secondary enrollment was put in place.

Opportunities

The Education Code of 1935 was an important factor in changing the design of the school curricula. It facilitated the implementation of the systematic sex stereotyping in educational opportunity for girls and boys in a much clearer way. For example, increased attention was paid to "provision for instruction in domestic science for primary school girls at special approved centres,"[6] while boys were prepared for a wider range of technical and academic pursuits. Additionally, married women were excluded from permanent employment as teachers. This sex stereotyping became an essential feature in shaping girls' education and, by extension, career goals and opportunities for employment, although to a lesser extent than in some societies.

The 1940s saw little change in the ideology of the state regarding the education of women. In 1945, the West India Royal Commission constituted to investigate the causes of social and labor unrest in the British colonial Caribbean in the 1930s called for equal opportunity in education for both sexes and recommended that "if there are to be happy marriages, girls must be able to be companions to their husbands and therefore need every opportunity for as wide a cultural education as possible."[7] This education, however, was to direct girls to specific women's careers and to be good wives and mothers.[8]

Today, Trinidad and Tobago has a relatively high level of education. By 2000, 99.9 percent of the population had enrolled at primary level,[9] and secondary-level enrollment was 71.5 percent in 1997. By 2000, this latter figure had changed to 100 percent. In both cases, the rate of female enrollment as a percentage of male enrollment was higher for both primary and secondary education. These figures for school enrollment contrast somewhat with studies done in 1995 of functional literacy that suggest that in spite of higher rates of school enrollment and to a lesser extent school attendance, illiteracy still persists in some circumstances.[10] As a result, whereas official data using the criteria "years of schooling" give Trinidad and Tobago high literacy rates, smaller surveys based on literacy tests have had different results.

According to census figures, the levels of educational attainment are relatively similar between the sexes (table 13.3). There has been much stated concern, however, within the English-speaking Caribbean generally over

Table 13.3
Highest Level of Educational Attainment in Trinidad and Tobago, 1990

Education Level	Male	Female	Both Sexes
NONE	10.5%	11.5%	11.0%
Nursery/kindergarten	3.0%	2.9%	2.9%
Primary	48.8%	46.9%	47.9%
Secondary	33.4%	34.9%	34.2%
University	2.2%	1.6%	1.9%
Other	0.8%	1.0%	0.9%
Not Stated	1.3%	1.1%	1.1%
TOTAL	560,934	564,194	1,125,128

Source: *Trinidad and Tobago Population and Housing Census, Demographic Report* (Port of Spain: Central Statistical Office, 1990).

the perception of male underachievement in education. Although this is not evident in these figures, more detailed figures are seen as reasons for concern.

In 1990, there were still more females who had received no education, but they were primarily in the higher age groups. Males exceeded females among the university-educated population (2.2 percent and 1.6 percent, respectively), which overall was an extremely small proportion of the population. However, since that time, the number of females registered and graduating from the University of the West Indies (UWI) has come to exceed that of males. In 1996–1997, for example, females made up 68.8 percent of the undergraduate population, 73.3 percent of those enrolled in diploma programs, 66.8 percent in certificate programs, 65 percent in advanced (postgraduate) diplomas, and 45.6 percent of those enrolled for higher degrees. Females overall made up 56.8 percent of the total UWI population.[11] Girls are making inroads into previously male-dominated fields such as the physical and natural sciences and now are equal to or exceed them in number in these faculties. One exception is engineering, but female enrollment has also increased in this area. As females extend their options, those of males appear to be shrinking. Numbers of males have been declining in the humanities, education, the social sciences, agriculture, and other areas. This has become a major concern.

The number of females enrolled part-time in undergraduate programs is more than double that of males. However, men still exceed women in part-time registration for higher degrees, which is the larger category of registration, although the numbers are fairly equal overall for all registrations. Much attention has been given to this fact, and there have been calls for research into the reasons for this trend. As already noted, however, the university-educated population is an extremely small proportion of the na-

Table 13.4

Enrollment in Technical and Vocational (Craft) Schools by Broad Area of Study and Sex, 1994/1995 and 1995/1996

Subject Area	MALE		FEMALE		TOTAL	
	1994/ 1995	1995/ 1996	1994/ 1995	1995/ 1996	1994/ 1995	1995/ 1996
Fine and applied arts	18	8	26	5	44	13
Commercial subjects (typing, etc.)	-	n.a.	45	n.a.	45	n.a.
Trade, craft, & industrial programs	946	1,359	99	211	1,045	1,390
Engineering	128	178	2	2	130	180
Service trades	40	28	127	60	167	88
TOTAL	1,171	1,681	468	216	167	88

Source: Trinidad and Tobago, Central Statistical Office, *Annual Statistical Digest, 1996* (Port of Spain, 1996), 80–81.

tional population, and the situation of the majority of women in the country leaves much to be desired.

This is especially so because other forms of tertiary education, for example, technical/vocational education, are still largely limited to males. This is particularly important because of the energy and industrial base of the economy. Young girls in secondary schools are not encouraged and often are not allowed to study technical and applied science subjects such as woodwork, metalwork, and technical drawing. Similarly, course enrollment at trade schools, technical institutes, and the new community college, the College of Science, Technology, and Applied Arts of Trinidad and Tobago, are largely gender differentiated, and girls and boys are directed into sex-stereotyped occupations.

For young women who do not complete formal education, therefore, employment opportunities are limited because they are excluded from most of the skilled trades except dressmaking and catering. Data on vocational and technical education reflect this disparity (table 13.4). Overall, female tertiary students were enrolled at a rate of 659 per 100,000 females in 2000. The ratio of female to male tertiary students was 72 percent, and female tertiary science students made up 38.2 percent of all female tertiary students.[12]

Literacy

Trinidad and Tobago is credited with a literacy rate of 97 percent of the female population over fifteen years old, as opposed to 99 percent of the male population over fifteen years old.[13] Literacy is measured by years of primary schooling and the administration of written tests in Trinidad and Tobago. In assessing the literacy situation in Trinidad and Tobago in 1994, however, the Adult Literacy Tutors Association conducted a national survey that revealed that 77 percent of the population was functionally literate, 15 percent was functionally illiterate, and 8 percent was illiterate.[14] This was corroborated by a 1995 study on literacy funded by the Trinidad and Tobago Commission for UNESCO and executed by the Institute of Social and Economic Research of the UWI, St. Augustine campus. It was found that overall, an estimated 12.6 percent of the population fifteen years of age or over was illiterate, while a further 8.7 percent was seen to be "peripherally illiterate," and 16.2 percent of persons currently working were found to be illiterate.

The sample of the 1995 study consisted of 986 female and 836 male respondents. From this survey, 14.2 percent of all males were estimated to be illiterate, as compared to 11.2 percent of females. Among younger persons aged fifteen to twenty-four years and twenty-five to thirty-nine years, the findings point toward higher levels of illiteracy among men than among women. With respect to older persons aged forty to fifty-four years and fifty-five years or older, the situation is reversed, with women having higher levels of illiteracy than men. Levels of adult literacy were highest among the youthful population aged fifteen to twenty-four years. These findings clearly reflect the changes in female education over the years.[15]

It was found that there were no significant variations in the literacy rate between the sexes, but that the majority of those who had gone to any schools were females. With respect to the function of both literates and illiterates in the work environment, it was found that approximately 60 percent of those employed were male, 83 percent of whom were literate, while 40 percent were female workers of whom those recorded as "keeping house" had the highest illiteracy rate at 22 percent.

Those who were unemployed (and wanted to work) were slightly less literate than those who were working (76 percent), but more were classified as functionally illiterate (14.3 percent). There was less disparity in the illiteracy rates between Afro-Trinidadian men (8.8 percent) and women (9.0 percent), while for Indo-Trinidadian men (19.8 percent) and women (16.3 percent), the sex disparity was greater. The data suggest that illiteracy impacts negatively on female employment much more than it does on male employment, and that for poor women, being a housewife is not simply a matter of choice. The ethnic differences for the most part are seen as the result of rural poverty, as Indo-Trinidadians tend to predominate in rural areas, but more importantly as a legacy of the early twentieth century when young Indian girls tended to be removed from school at puberty or not to have been sent to school at all.

EMPLOYMENT AND ECONOMICS

Trinidad and Tobago can be described as a country with a medium level of economic growth.[16] In 1998, its gross domestic product (GDP) per capita was U.S.$7,485 with industry and services contributing 50.7 percent and 47.5 percent, respectively, to the GDP. The main economic sector is the capital-intensive energy sector, of which petroleum and natural gas production are the major components. Derivative energy-related industries such as petrochemicals, iron and steel, and others have been developed.

Income disparity in Trinidad and Tobago is high. Some groups enjoy an economically comfortable lifestyle, but there is still relative poverty among significant sectors, leading to feelings of alienation and deprivation. The ethnic tensions that exist among the country's two major ethnic groups, Afro- and Indo-Trinidadians, can often be interpreted in economic terms and mobilized by political movements, with potentially dangerous repercussions for the society in general and women in particular.

Job/Career Opportunities

Women's participation rate in the labor force in 2000 stood at 38 percent, compared with 61 percent for men.[17] This finding should be tempered by two factors. One is that unemployed women are often hidden in the categories "not in the labor force" or "economically inactive—home duties" and so do not appear in unemployment figures. Unemployed women have the option of defining themselves as housewives or as unemployed. Increasingly, many women are doing the latter, but it is often noted that as female unemployment figures increase, so too do figures of those "not in the labor force."

A second factor is migration. The 1992 *Survey of Living Conditions* noted that long-term unemployment was a greater problem for women than for men. For example, it was found that whereas youth unemployment was serious for both sexes, for males this persisted until age thirty, while for females it continued until ages thirty-one to forty. The survey also noted that older women tend to have higher unemployment rates.[18]

One solution used by women, especially since the economic downturn of the 1980s and the introduction of structural adjustment policies, has been migration, especially to the United States and to a lesser extent Canada, in the former case often illegally. Many women accept employment below their academic qualification in order to facilitate the transition. Many women emigrants leave children behind with relatives or friends. A number of negative social and psychological implications have been identified, as many mothers may be unable to see their children for extended periods, sometimes as long as seven years. Reliable statistics on migration are not easily available. The World Bank in 1983 identified the Caribbean as the region with the highest rates of migration in the world.[19]

Occupational data continue to show that fewer women than men are employed as senior officials, managers, and professionals. Relative to their proportion in the population, women are also overrepresented in the clerical category. However, there was an increase in the proportion of females in the senior professional and professional categories between 1994 and

1995. The percentage of females in the clerical category has remained the same.[20]

The majority of women tend to be employed in the lower professional categories—teachers, nurses, administrative, secretarial, and financial services, manufacturing, and other areas of personal service such as sales, shop and store clerks, and workers in catering establishments or in private homes. Women's employment in agriculture, once the largest area of female employment, has consistently declined. Self-employment or own-account work for women has also been important, especially in the area of personal service and sales and in the so-called informal sector. Sex work, usually associated with urban centers and the tourist industry, is also a factor but is not easily measured.

Pay

In spite of the relative increases in women's participation at all levels in the labor force, and in spite of their high levels of educational attainment and increased participation in various professional fields, women continue to be at the lower end of the socioeconomic ladder and face discrimination in the level of wages that are paid to them, compared to men. No equal-pay legislation exists.

Provisions for minimum wages are made in the Minimum Wage Act No. 35 of 1976 and several national Minimum Wages Orders in relation to sectors of low-wage workers, including domestic/household assistants, store clerks, and shop assistants, who are mainly female. In 1991, the Minimum Wage (Household Assistants) Order provided maternity leave and an increased minimum wage. In 1998, a new Minimum Wages Order established a new minimum wage of $7.00 per hour and minimum terms and conditions for all workers, including an eight-hour working day.

Average monthly wages for males and females in sectors of employment and occupations are shown in tables 13.5 and 13.6. An analysis of individual labor-market participants across wage quintiles shows that 60.6 percent of senior male professionals, compared to 56 percent of females in the same category, are in the fifth quintile or highest level. On the other hand, in the clerical category, which includes 72 percent females, only 39.5 percent of females are in the fifth quintile, compared to 50 percent of males. In the professional category, where women made up 42 percent in 1995, 76 percent of females compared to 67.4 percent of males were in the fifth quintile.[21] Women earned less than men at almost every level of education in 1995.[22] Throughout the world, women have greater opportunity for career advancement in the public sector.[23] This is also true in Trinidad and Tobago. The thrust toward privatization of state-sector activities, therefore, must be seen as not simply a neutral macroeconomic policy but an extremely gendered one.

Table 13.5

Monthly Wages on Primary Job by Sectors of Employment and by Sex in Trinidad and Tobago, 1995

Sector of Employment	AVERAGE MONTHLY WAGE			
	Both	Male	Female	% Difference
FORMAL SECTOR				
Public Sector				
Statutory boards	2,486	2,531	2,444	3
Parastatals	2,507	2,528	2,429	4
Central/state gov.	2,137	2,120	2,166	−2
Private Formal Sector	1,446	1,655	1,129	32
INFORMAL SECTOR				
Unpaid worker	—	—	—	—
Learner apprentice	211	215	120	44
Own account	1,005	1,089	772	29
Informal-sector employer	2,210	2,584	2,066	20

Source: Trinidad and Tobago, Central Statistical Office, Continuous Sample Survey of Population, *Labour Force Report*, 1996 (Port of Spain).

Table 13.6

Monthly Wages on Primary Job by Occupation and Sex in Trinidad and Tobago, 1996

Occupation	AVERAGE MONTHLY WAGE $TT			
	Total	Male	Female	% Difference
Legislators, senior officials, and managers	3,100	3,800	2,400	37
Professionals	5,200	5,500	4,700	15
Technicians and associate professionals	3,100	3,500	2,800	20
Clerks	2,000	2,200	1,900	14
Service workers	1,600	2,000	1,100	45
Agricultural workers	900	1,000	700	30
Craft and related workers	1,500	1,600	800	50
Plant machine operators and assemblers	1,800	2,000	1,000	50
Elementary occupations	1,100	1,200	700	42

Source: Trinidad and Tobago Central Statistical Office, Continuous Sample Survey of Population, *Labour Force Report*, 1996 (Port of Spain).

Working Conditions

Conditions of work vary across sectors and within sectors. Wage differentials exist and are especially sharp in the private sector. Trade-union organization is legal but varies across sectors. Data on the proportion of unionized workers are not easily available, but many female-dominated occupations, for example, teachers, nurses, public servants, and bank employees, are unionized. A 1999 survey carried out by the Ministry of Labour and Cooperatives found that women made up 26,770 or 44 percent of the 61,345 members of twenty-eight trade unions. However, women are not well represented in the leadership of these organizations: the 1999 survey found that women held 7.5 percent of executive positions in eight trade unions.[24] One woman currently heads the Public Services Association, the only woman in such a position.

Sexual Harassment

No sexual harassment legislation exists in Trinidad and Tobago. Draft legislation was prepared more than ten years ago but was never implemented. Some companies have sexual harassment policies in place, and cases have been successfully adjudicated by the Industrial Court using the Industrial Relations Act, but this continues to be an area of much concern and unclarity.

In 1998, the Tobago House of Assembly passed a motion adopting a sexual harassment policy for all its employees. In the debate supporting the motion, Secretary for Health and Social Services Judy Bobb identified it as a gender issue that should be expanded beyond the workplace to schools and other areas.

Support for Mothers/Caretakers

Maternal Leave

Before 1998, maternity leave was only available through collective agreements or individual contracts of employment. However, the Maternity Protection Act of 1998 was passed as the result of years of lobbying by women's organizations. This law covers all women except female members of Parliament in Trinidad and Tobago and provides for paid leave for thirteen weeks every two years. The initial period of leave can be extended for up to twelve weeks for medical reasons, the first six weeks with half the monthly salary and the last six weeks with no salary. Payments are to be covered by the employer and the national insurance scheme such that there is no loss of earnings. Collective agreements with individual employers may not provide less than these provisions. This law, however, like others, may not be uniformly implemented. Cases of women, especially temporary and casual workers, being fired when pregnant still surface, as well as cases of workers not being paid full benefits, especially in small establishments and private homes. In some cases, provisions may be made for two to four days of paternity leave for fathers on the birth of a child.

Daycare

Daycare centers or nurseries are available mainly through private providers and community-based organizations, but a great need still exists.

Family members, especially female relatives, normally provide this support. Preschools for children three to five years old are much more easily available through state-supported schools in community centers and through a network run by the Child Welfare League, a voluntary organization, and SERVOL, a major nongovernmental organization (NGO). Privately run facilities are also available. There is also a demand for homework centers for older children for the period between the end of the school day and the end of the parents' workday. Availability of such facilities is still limited.

Inheritance and Property Rights

A Succession Act was passed in 1981 but has not yet been implemented. This replaced the 1972 Wills and Probate Act and allows wives to contest wills if they are excluded and to apply to the court for maintenance. The 1998 Cohabitational Relations Act, which made legal provisions for common-law spouses, does not allow for inheritance.

Social/Government Programs

Social and government programs are delivered by a number of government departments, for example, the Family Services Division and the Community Development Division. The former provides counseling for victims and survivors of domestic violence, especially in cases related to the implementation of the Domestic Violence Act. The SHARE program of this ministry provides food hampers to needy families, many of which are female headed and managed. Some assistance is given to facilitate microenterprise development in order to generate self-sufficiency among the poor, especially poor women.

Social development programs still require much more support. Recent neoliberal economic policies have encouraged a reduction of state-supported social programs for microenterprise development in favor of poverty alleviation through NGOs staffed mainly by women, the majority of whom are volunteers.

Sustainable Development

Women have been in the forefront of the environmental movement in Trinidad and Tobago, lobbying actively on issues related to wildlife preservation, forest protection, and the protection of endangered wetlands. Examples include the Pointe a Pierre Wildlife Trust, headed by Molly Gaskin and Karlyn Shepherd, and the Caribbean Forest Conservation Association, headed by Sylvia Kacal. Biologist Carol James worked for the establishment of Nature Seekers, a community-based organization committed to protecting the leatherback turtle. Through their organizations, women have also been in the forefront of actions for more sustainable economic and development policies.

Welfare and Welfare Reform

The Social Welfare Department of the government provides social support to the elderly and the extremely indigent through public assistance, including old-age pensions, public assistance to families in need, disability grants, and emergency care fund grants. These are all minimal and seldom raise the level above the poverty line. Poor female heads of households and their children often have difficulty in accessing welfare benefits because the status of the male is the determining factor. In 1997, the Public Assistance Act was amended to provide the assistance to the person "who in the opinion of the Local Board is head of a family."[25] This improved somewhat women's ability to access this fund.[26]

A compulsory contributory National Insurance Scheme is in operation. It provides very minimal sickness benefits, invalid benefits, death benefits, survivor benefits, and disability benefits. In most cases, women inherit equally based on their contributions. Their survivors, however, may not benefit in the same way due to assumptions based on the male breadwinner concept.

FAMILY AND SEXUALITY

Gender Roles and Marriage

It has been noted that in the Caribbean, "the family is a social institution that assumes an elusive character, [which] is primarily due to the individuals' myriad interpretations of structures and inherent social relations that characterise the family."[27] The range and diversity of family arrangements have generated a significant body of research studies and have led to the identification of the household and not the family as the main unit of analysis. In addition to individual choice, Caribbean family forms are the result of ancestral traditions in Africa, Asia, and Europe, the impact of slavery and indentured labor systems, and the influence of patriarchal Christian, Islamic, and Hindu religious traditions.

Among Trinidadians of mixed and African descent, family forms tend to be informally matrilineal and include visiting unions, common-law or free unions, and legal marriage. Marriage tends to take place later rather than earlier, and in many instances one or more of the partners may already have had a child. Motherhood and fatherhood are important signs of adulthood. Marriage often takes second place to parenthood. The informal matrilinearity in these households means that blood ties to one's family of origin tend to be much closer than the conjugal ties of marriage. In many instances, for example, women's and men's family responsibilities often extend to matrilineal kin, and men's loyalty to their mothers is important.

For this reason, Afro-Caribbean families have often been characterized as mother centered, and female-headed households are seen as characteristic of this region. The existence of these households has been variously attributed to cultural persistence of African family patterns, specific experiences of plantation life, male migration that yielded a higher proportion of females than males, and poverty and socioeconomic adversity.

Among Indo-Trinidadians, the opposite is the case, although to some degree trends are becoming more similar. Marriage is an important rite of passage into adulthood, and children normally follow marriage among this group. In the past, very early marriage characterized this group. This is no longer the case, but marriage is still an important symbol. Patrilinearity and patrilocality (less frequent now than formerly) characterize this group, so family and household dynamics and relationships differ in significant ways.

Overall, of the population fifteen years of age or over in 1990, 44 percent of men and 37.6 percent of women were never married. Similar proportions of both sexes were married, 43.3 percent. More females (8.4 percent) were widowed than males (2.6 percent), and this was especially the case for older women. Very small numbers were divorced or legally separated.[28]

An examination of data for union status of women fifteen years of age or over gives a more meaningful picture of women's intimate relationships. Data on marital status reflect a legal status and not the actual situation in which women are living. Data on union status, however, are not collected for men, as they were originally seen as a mechanism for gaining fertility-related information. In 1990, 43 percent of women were identified as in a married union, while 22.6 percent had never been in a union, 10.8 percent were living in a free union, locally referred to as a common-law union, and only 1.5 percent were identified as being in visiting unions. Eight percent were no longer living with their spouse, and 3.8 percent were no longer living with their common-law partner.[29]

In addition to ethnic differences in family forms, class and religious differences also occur. Legal marriages tend to predominate among the upper and middle classes, while diversity exists among all economic groups. Formal and informal polygamy is practiced by a minority of Muslims.

A 1994 study of the family in Trinidad and Tobago found that of a total of 1,973 households, 34 percent were nuclear families—husband, wife, and children. This was the largest grouping, followed by 15.7 percent other extended households and 13.9 percent single-person households. Grandmother extended households were 5.7 percent of the sample. Thus all extended households were 21.4 percent of the sample.[30]

In predominantly African-descended Tobago, the situation is much more stark. Nuclear families—husband, wife, and children—were only 22.5 percent of the sample, while extended families, 13.8 percent grandmother extended and 21.3 percent other extended, were the most significant other grouping, together making up 35.1 percent of the sample. Generally, single-mother and grandmother families tended to be in dire economic circumstances, so extended families may be a response to economic need. A 1997 study found that 52 percent of single-mother families and 44.1 percent of grandmother families were estimated to have no one working on a full-time basis, although extrahousehold assistance may be available.[31]

Female single-parent households were less significant in Tobago, making up only 5.0 percent of the sample, most likely because single mothers continue to reside in extended family households. This contrasts greatly with the predominantly African-descended areas of Trinidad. Tobago was the only area where the proportion of male single-parent households (6.3 percent) exceeded that of female single-parent households (5.0), although only slightly. These differences could be due to a number of factors, including migration of mothers to Trinidad to work, poverty, and problems of economic scarcity in addition to the cultural factors.

The proportions of nuclear families are highest in predominantly Indian communities, but in all cases these were still less than 50 percent. Next most frequent were extended households and single-person households. Extended households, although most likely with differing structures and internal dynamics, were significant for all parts of the country.

Since the 1980s, a spate of legislation such as the Matrimonial Proceedings Act of 1972, the Status of Children's Act, the Family Law of 1983, and the Cohabitational Relationships Act of 1998 has been implemented that reflects significant attitudinal changes toward the status of women and children in the family. The concept of illegitimacy has been abolished; persons enjoy relatively easy access to divorce and judicial separation based on no-fault grounds; common-law unions of more than three years' duration have been granted legal recognition; and the law provides for equality of treatment between mothers and fathers with reference to rights and responsibilities toward children, particularly in relation to custody and maintenance. The judiciary has also established the machinery for intervention into the realm of family justice. In spite of numerous calls, however, a family court has not been established, although a Family Court Bill has been drafted but not passed in Parliament.

The women's movement has also had an impact on women's consciousness and gender relations. Its activism has influenced the introduction and subsequent revision of legislation on, for example, sexual offenses (1986), domestic violence (1991, 1999) and the attachment of earnings (1988, 1995) for workplace deductions of court-mandated child-support payments. The improvement of resources to facilitate the full education on and implementation of this legislation is still required. The nongovernmental women's movement has been very important in providing support services in these areas. Trinidad and Tobago has eight shelters for battered women, two rape crisis centers, and other support and referral centers. In addition, the government's Gender Affairs Division runs a Domestic Violence Unit and a hot line with a toll-free number.

Reproduction

Sex Education

There is no national program on sex education in schools. Some teaching on sex and sexuality has taken place through family-life education, which has been introduced into some schools but is not universal. Teenage sexual activity is a cause of much concern, but young people are not provided with formal sex education. The national Family Planning Association has been involved in community and school outreach programs on sex education, but these again have not reached all young people. Special programs have been established for young women and men visiting the offices of the Family Planning Association.

Contraception and Abortion

Contraception is widely available through local clinics of the Family Planning Association, at government health centers, and through the private sector. Contraceptive use among married women was 58 percent between 1985 and 1990, but in the age group fifteen to nineteen, 22 births occurred per 1,000 women.[32] According to data for 2000 from the Family Planning Association, oral contraceptives were the main method used (49.5 percent of cases).[33]

Abortion is legally available only to preserve the physical and/or mental health of the mother. However, illegal abortions are widespread and sometimes fatal. Women often end up in the hospital for abortion-related problems. In one hospital, the dilation and cutterage procedure for the evacuation of the retained products of conception was performed 1,177 times in 1999 and 615 times between June and September 2000. An active campaign for the decriminalization of abortion began in 2002, led by the organization Advocates for Safe Parenthood.[34]

Teen Pregnancy

Urbanized areas have high teen pregnancy rates, and 13.5 percent of all births are by teenagers.[35]

HEALTH

Health Care Access

Children and women living in the seven Caribbean countries have generally experienced good health status. These countries have managed to eliminate many of the basic health problems normally associated with the developing world. Improvements in nutrition, sanitation, access to immunization, and family planning since the 1970s have contributed to lower mortality rates and increased life expectancy.[36]

Reports on infant and maternal health usually report that women and children in Trinidad and Tobago are in relatively good health. The availability of basic health and social services, such as access to clean water, has improved consistently since 1945. Im-

Hospital emergency department, Scarborough, Tobago. Photo © TRIP/ H. Rogers.

munizations and access to prenatal care have improved infant and maternal health. In 1996, according to some sources, 98 percent of women received prenatal care, and a similar proportion were attended by a skilled attendant at childbirth.[37] Between 1970 and 1990, the crude death rate declined from 7.7 to 6.6, and life expectancy has increased from 65.7 to 70.1 years.[38] Women's life expectancy in 1998 was 76.4 years.[39] However, a 1995 World Bank study suggests that in spite of these gains, "the health status of the population still falls below that of many middle income countries, largely due to limited preventative care and the low quality of services offered in both the public and private sector. Nearly 50 percent of the population still dies before they have reached the age of 65 with many of these deaths avoidable."[40]

Until recently, women's health was seen mainly as a reproduction issue. Today, issues of general health, for example, cancer and heart disease, lifestyle, diet, physical fitness, and sexual health, are also receiving attention. Because of the neoliberal economic adjustments of the 1980s and 1990s, under which state spending on health and social service delivery has been substantially reduced and food subsidies have been removed or reduced, problems of health have been heightened by problems of poverty.

Diseases and Disorders

The main causes of death in women are heart disease, cancer, diabetes, cerebrovascular disease, and injuries, which may include injuries from accidents as well as criminal and sexual violence (table 13.7). There is also

Table 13.7
Main Causes of Mortality among Women 24–44 and 45–64 Years Old in Trinidad and Tobago, 1994

Cause of Death	25–44	45–64
Diseases of the circulatory system	20.1%	39.5%
Cancer	19.1%	20.5%
External causes—accidents, suicides, homicides, and so on	13.2%	2.2%
Diabetes	—	21.2%

Source: "Trinidad and Tobago," in *Health in the Americas* 2 (1998): 486.

increasing concern about the rising incidence of old and new communicable diseases, such as tuberculosis and HIV/AIDS.

Additionally, Trinidad and Tobago was mentioned in a Pan-American Health Organization/World Health Organization Report as being among the countries of the region where abortion and its complications were the leading cause of maternal death.[41] Because abortion is illegal in Trinidad and Tobago except in certain circumstances, information on its prevalence is not easily available.

A national survey of health carried out in 1994–1995 found that more males (41.8 percent) rated their health as excellent or very good than females (31.4 percent); more females (25.2 percent) reported being affected by long-standing illness, disability, or infirmity than males (18.7 percent); and males reported a higher prevalence of injury (14.3 percent) than females (7.4 percent). In Tobago, this disparity was even greater, 24.5 percent for males and 7.5 percent for females. The prevalence of angina pectoris, a high indicator of the risk of heart disease, varied with ethnicity and gender. The overall prevalence was 4.6 percent for males and 7.6 percent for females. The incidence was higher for persons of Indian origin than for persons of African origin. Afro-Trinidadian males in general had a low incidence of 3 percent, while Indo-Trinidadian males had an incidence of 6.7 percent. For females, the rates were 6.7 percent and 8.5 percent, respectively.[42] The prevalence of diabetes mellitus was 9.6 percent for males and 12.6 percent for females thirty-five years of age or over. The highest prevalence was among Indo-Trinidadian females, 17.0 percent. The rate of hypertension was generally high in the population but especially among females, who had a rate of 28.1 percent, compared to 18.2 percent for males. This difference remained consistent across all ages and among all ethnic groups. One-third of all males and one-half of all females reported high blood pressure.[43] Smoking is a predominantly male activity; 28.8 percent of males and 5.1 percent of females reported current smoking. As many as 10.5 percent of male drinkers had consumed more than twenty-one drinks in the previous week, while 3.6 percent of females had consumed fourteen drinks during the same time period. More males were involved in leisure-type exercise, 16.6 percent, than females, 5.9 percent.[44]

In conclusion, the report stated that "the association of gender with health status is seen throughout. . . . Males have higher risks of injury but for almost all categories of morbidity explored more women report morbidity, disability and perceived ill health. In many cases this was apparently linked to lifestyle. Women have higher rates of obesity and do not exercise regularly. They tend to have lower indices of socio-economic status."[45]

AIDS

Since the 1980s, HIV/AIDS has become a major cause of death in Trinidad and Tobago. Between 1983 and 1996, there was a steady increase from 8 cases in 1983 to approximately 350 cases in 1996. While initially prevalent among men, the "incidence of HIV/AIDS among women aged 15 through 19 has doubled between 1989 and 1990." In 1996, the female-to-male infection ratio was 5:1. Data also suggest that females are infected at earlier ages than males and are at greater risk of infection,[46] as well as death, as women comprised 33 percent of adults who had died by the end of 1997.[47]

There is particular concern over the disturbing projection for women in Trinidad and Tobago that the number of women at risk of transferring HIV to a child is expected to increase from 33,766 in 1997 to 49,970 in 2005, an increase of 48 percent.[48] A survey carried out in 1999 under the auspices of the Caribbean Epidemiology Centre noted that in calculating the costs of HIV/AIDS care, the unpaid services of women as housewives who care for AIDS patients when hospitalization is not available are not directly measurable because they are not included in the accounting practices of most countries of the region and the world.[49]

POLITICS AND LAW

Suffrage

In 1946, the declaration of universal adult suffrage granted the vote to women in Trinidad and Tobago, and in 1950, barriers to women's nomination as candidates in national elections were removed.

Political Participation

Women have been active members of political parties since their inception, but have not been represented in Parliament in corresponding proportion. After the 2001 general elections, of thirty-six elected representatives, five were women. However, women were appointed to a number of ministerial positions, including that of attorney general, and to the nominated Senate. The major obstacles for participation in parliamentary politics have been the male-dominated adversarial political culture, women's domestic responsibilities, and other institutional mechanisms. Many women find the verbal violence of election campaigns and day-to-day politics uncomfortable.

Since the 1990s, women's organizations in Trinidad and Tobago have begun to influence the political process in a number of ways. For example, before the 1995 general election, a Women's Political Platform was organized with representatives from a range of women's organizations. This platform developed a list of demands titled *10 Points to Power* that was addressed to all political parties, usually through a meeting with political leaders. Additionally, a coffee morning of all women candidates was organized to give solidarity and support regardless of political affiliation. In general, the women's movement has sought to develop a nonpartisan approach toward women in politics. However, the extremely partisan political tradition, sharpened by ethnic tensions, has worked against these efforts. In 1999, the Network for the Advancement of Women of Trinidad and Tobago, an NGO, developed a strategy for the 1999 local government elections. Activities of the nonpartisan initiative included training programs, joint publicity focusing on women candidates, lobbying political leaders to name women as candidates, and provision of small financial grants to assist with campaigning. While the number of women candidates has been increasing, their races tend to be for "unsafe seats," and thus the majority are unsuccessful. This has been redressed to some extent with nominations to the Senate, which in recent years has had more women than the elected House of Representatives.

There is currently much dissatisfaction with the existing "first past the post" (the winning candidate is the person who wins the most votes) electoral system inherited and adapted from the British Westminster system (Parliamentary Democracy). In Trinidad and Tobago, in particular, it has been blamed for entrenching an ethnically divided, extremely partisan system where winners and losers are ethnically defined. Women's organizations have been critical of this system and are involved in current efforts aimed at facilitating progressive constitutional change.

Women's Rights

The women's movement has a rich history in Trinidad and Tobago dating back to the nineteenth century. From very early in the movement, links with women's organizations in other parts of the region have been important, but discrimination and status considerations based on class, color, and race have influenced the approach and positions taken by these organizations. Charity and economic self-sufficiency were the main concerns of the earliest, predominantly white organizations, while issues of women's employment, education, "upliftment of the race," and economic and political rights were paramount for the early-twentieth-century black and colored organizations. Since the mid-1970s, women's groups have been fighting to end legal discrimination against women.

Feminist Movements

By the mid-twentieth century, nationalist women's organizations were providing much of the support in the field to the early nationalist political parties, but they seldom assumed national political leadership or challenged the sexual division of labor. The 1960s and 1970s witnessed the emergence of a new women's movement and a revitalization of the old one. The newer, more radical women's groups created a climate that facilitated a new consciousness of women's rights, supported by international efforts in this regard.

Lesbian Rights

In January 2001, Trinidad and Tobago made its report to the United Nations Commission on Human Rights, and a number of issues were raised by the commission, including the need for a national gender policy and the continued discrimination against persons involved in same-sex relations. Lesbians and gays have no rights in Trinidad and Tobago. Immigration law forbids entrance to the country by homosexuals, and the 1986 Sexual Offenses Act allows for up to twenty years of imprisonment for same-sex sexual acts by men and women.[50] Amnesty International notes that lesbians and gays have been "regularly subjected to discrimination and intimidation."[51]

Military Service

Trinidad and Tobago is a non-conscripting nation that only accepts males into its armed service.

RELIGION AND SPIRITUALITY

Trinidad and Tobago is a multireligious society. Although the largest proportion of the population claims Christianity as its religious affiliation, other traditions, mainly Hinduism and Islam, are important. The multireligious and multiethnic nature of society results in great diversity. In addition to tolerance and competition among groups, there is a great deal of collaboration and participation in the rituals and festivals of different traditions.

Rituals and Religious Practices

Religion and spirituality are especially important to women, and women comprise the majority of religious practitioners. Religion provides a legitimate space for women's participation outside of the home.

In addition to formal religion, the expression of alternative spiritualities is also important to some women, both within and outside these formal traditions. Grassroots syncretic traditions derived from Africa and India such as the Shouters/Spiritual Baptists and Orisha practitioners as well as Kali Puja affiliates are becoming more visible, accepted, and recognized. Recently Orisha (Shango) religious leaders were granted the legal right to perform marriages. This is significant because women tend to have more opportunity for leadership in these nonhegemonic traditions, although many of the practices and values are still patriarchal in character.

The emergence of Rastafarianism, which began in early-twentieth-century Jamaica, has had an important impact on the entire region. It has been described as emerging in cultural opposition to neocolonial social and economic conditions and political developments and as having an anticapitalist stance.[52] In Rastafarianism, women as spouses

Corpus Christi procession, Trinidad and Tobago. Photo © TRIP/H. Rogers.

(daughters) and queens have important, although subordinate, positions, a situation many Rastafarian women are seeking to redefine.

The main religions, however, tend to have a male-dominated leadership, and in recent times, the influences of competing religious fundamentalisms have had important impacts on women. For example, the introduction of veiling of Islamic women is a late-twentieth-century development, while U.S.-derived Christian fundamentalisms have found fertile ground in Trinidad and Tobago, taking members away from the more traditional Christian denominations. Hindu fundamentalism is closely associated with movements for Indian identity, some of which tend to be linked to Indian-based nationalist movements. Thus formal religions of various types have great influence on education and political decisions, especially with the decline of more secular solidarity traditions such as the trade-union movement.

VIOLENCE

Gender-based violence has emerged as a public political issue in the Caribbean, largely due to the tireless efforts of women's organizations throughout the 1970s, 1980s, and 1990s. It is recognized that violence against women is a crime and a violation of fundamental human rights. Trinidad and Tobago has ratified various international conventions such as the Inter-American Convention on the Prevention, Punishment, and Eradication of Violence against Women (Belem Convention) and the Convention on the Elimination of All Forms of Discrimination against women (CEDAW). Trinidad is also a signatory to the World Conference on Human Rights (WCHR) Programme of Action and the Declaration and Programme of Action adopted by the Fourth World Conference of Women in Beijing. In recent years, shifts in the traditional human rights discourse to embrace an analysis of gender-based violence as a human rights issue have made possible appeals for state protection of women and the provision of legal remedies for violations to their persons.

Domestic Violence

Between January and October 1995, twelve women and seven children were the victims of reported instances of domestic violence.[53] A Domestic Violence Act was passed in 1999. However, the continued invisibility and increased incidence of domestic violence have forced women's advocates to rethink the potential of legal approaches in eliminating the problem.

Rape/Sexual Assault

Between 1991 and 1993, violence against women and children continued to rise. Charges of rape and serious indecency rose from 185 to 250 between September and November 1995, while between January and October 1994, 23 women were murdered.[54]

Trafficking in Women and Children

There is no evidence that trafficking in women and children exists in Trinidad and Tobago.[55]

OUTLOOK FOR THE TWENTY-FIRST CENTURY

In some respects, the outlook for women in Trinidad and Tobago in the twenty-first century is positive. Women continue to work hard at personal self-development as well as career advancement. Women seek opportunities for further education in spite of domestic and family responsibilities. Women's advancement in education and subsequent visibility in positions of management, especially in the public sector, have been causes of great concern among men. This has resulted in a "male marginalization thesis" that depicts women's advancement as the cause of male underperformance in education and other areas. These gains have not been universal, and many poor women still have limited opportunities for economic and social autonomy, hence the large-scale migration of women to North America. Nevertheless, this perceived shift in the balance of power between women and men has been suggested as one reason for the persistent violence against women and efforts to delegitimize the actions of women's organizations. At the same time, the women's organizations and activists of the 1970s are growing older and are less able to continue the struggle in the same way. The issue of the generational transfer to young women is important for the movement, and its degree of success will in many ways dictate the future outlook.

NOTES

1. United Nations Development Programme, *Human Development Report, 2000* (Oxford: Oxford University Press, 2000), 161.

2. Trinidad and Tobago, *Population and Vital Statistics Report* 1996, 31, www. caricom.org/archives/26sccs=bs.htm.

3. Ibid.; World Health Organization, www.who.int/reproductive=health/ publications/RHR.

4. The HDI is a composite index constructed by the UNDP since 1990 that measures average achievement in basic human development using life expectancy at birth, adult literacy rates, combined educational enrollment ratios, and adjusted per capita income in U.S. dollars (United Nations Development Programme, *Human Development Report, 2000*, 147). The GDI is a composite measure of achievements in the same variables as the HDI, but taking into account the inequality in achievement between women and men.

5. Campbell, 1996, 253.

6. Rhoda Reddock, *Women, Labor, and Politics in Trinidad and Tobago* (London: Zed Books, 1994), 49.

7. West Indian Royal Commission, 1945, 130; as quoted in Reddock, 1998, 229.

8. Campbell, 1985.

9. United Nations Development Programme, *Human Development Report, 2000*.

10. National Literacy Survey 1995, www.uwi.tt/socasci/ises/curr_ac.html.

11. University of the West Indies, *Statistics, 1996/1997* (Mona: Office of Planning, the Vice-Chancellery).

12. United Nations Development Programme, *Human Development Report, 2000*, 255.

13. United Nations Development Programme, *Human Development Report, 2001* (Oxford: Oxford University Press, 2001).

14. ALTA, 1994.

15. Godfrey St. Bernard and Carol Salim, *Adult Literacy in Trinidad and Tobago: A Study of the Findings of the National Literacy Survey* (Trinidad and Tobago: University of the West Indies, 1995).

16. United Nations Development Programme, *Human Development Report, 2001.*

17. World Bank 2000, www.worldbank.org/data/wdi2000/pdfs/table%201-5.pdf.

18. Ibid.

19. World Bank Group: Trinidad-Tobago, www.worldbank.org/tt.

20. Ministry of Labor Reports, www.labour.gov.tt/mlchome.htm.

21. World Bank, *Trinidad and Tobago: Poverty and Unemployment in an Oil-Based Economy*, Report No. 14382-TR (October 27, 1995), using information from the 1992 *Survey of Living Conditions.*

22. Trinidad and Tobago, Central Statistical Office, Continuous Sample Survey of Population, *Labour Force Report, 1995.*

23. *The World's Women, 1990*, www.skk.uit.no/ww99/ww02FANN.html.

24. Decline of Women in Trade Union Management: Trinidad-Tobago, www.bgwu.bizland.com/decline_of_women.htm.

25. Report to CEDAW, 2000, 111–112, www.un.org/womenwatch/daw/cedaw/committ.htm.

26. Initial, Second and Third Report to CEDAW, December 2000.

27. St. Bernard, 2001, 92.

28. United Nations Statistics Division, http://unstats.un.org/unsd/demographic/ww2000/table2a.htm.

29. Caribbean Community Secretariat, Regional Census Office, *1990–1991 Population Census of the Commonwealth Caribbean: Volume of Basic Tables of Sixteen CARICOM Countries.*

30. St. Bernard, 2001, 108.

31. Ibid., 111.

32. United Nations, Department of Economic and Social Affairs, *The World's Women, 2000* (New York, 2000), 48.

33. Family Planning Association of Trinidad-Tobago, www.ttfpa.org.

34. Report on CEDAW, 2000, 97.

35. International Planned Parenthood Federation, "Country Profiles: Trinidad and Tobago," http://ippfnet.ippf.org.

36. UNICEF, 1997, 51, www.unicef.org/sowc97.

37. United Nations, *The World's Women 2000*, 81.

38. World Bank, 1995, 49.

39. United Nations Development Programme, *Human Development Report, 2000*, 161.

40. World Bank, 1995, 49.

41. World Health Organization and Pan-American Health Organization document to mark World Health Day, 1998, *Trinidad Guardian*, 1999, 24.

42. Trinidad and Tobago National Health Survey, 1994–95, 108–9, www.childinfo.org/eddb/TrinidadTobago_EP1.12.01.pdf.

43. Ibid., 110.

44. Pan-American Health Organization, Special Program for Health Analysis, *Third Evaluation of Health for the Year 2000: Trinidad and Tobago*, www.carec.org.

45. Trinidad and Tobago National Health Survey, 115.

46. Brathwaite, 1998, 1.

47. United Nations, *The World's Women 2000*, 81.

48. Biali Camara, Shelton Nicholls, and Roger McLean, *The Epidemiological Situation in Trinidad and Tobago, and Jamaica*, 1998, www.sidalac.org.mx/spanish/publicaciones/s_epidemiologica/s_epidemiologica.pdf.

49. Ibid., 24.

50. International Lesbian and Gay Association, "World Legal Survey: Trinidad and Tobago," www.ilga.org.

51. Amnesty International, "Amnesty International Report 2001: Trinidad and Tobago," http://web.amnesty.org.

52. Alicia Mondesire and Leith Dunn, *Towards Equity in Development: A Report on the Status of Women in Sixteen Commonwealth Caribbean Countries* (Georgetown: Caribbean Community Secretariat, 1995), 14.

53. Domestic Violence Act of 1999, www.ttparliament.org/bills/acts/1999/a1999_27.pdf.

54. Central Statistical Office, www.cso.gov.tt/statistics/psvs/default.asp.

55. United Nations, Committee on Elimination of Discrimination against Women, "Committee on Elimination of Discrimination against Women Concludes Consideration of Trinidad and Tobago Report," Press Release WOM/1316, November 1, 2002, www.un.org.

RESOURCE GUIDE

Suggested Reading

Mondesire, Alicia, and Leith Dunn. *Towards Equity in Development: A Report on the Status of Women in Sixteen Commonwealth Caribbean Countries*. Georgetown: Caribbean Community Secretariat, 1995.

Prince, Rosa Christine. *Social Change: Women and Health Care in Trinidad and Tobago, An Executive Summary*. York University, Environmental Studies Department, 1998.

Reddock, Rhoda, and Elsa Leo-Rhynie. *Report on Women and the Family in the Caribbean: Historical and Contemporary Considerations: With Special Reference to Jamaica and Trinidad and Tobago*. Georgetown: CARICOM Secretariat, 1999.

Reddock, Rhoda, Rosalie Barclay, and Roberta Clarke. *United Nations Inter-agency Campaign on Gender Violence against Women and Girls: National Report: Trinidad and Tobago*. United Nations Development Programme, February 2000.

St. Bernard, Godfrey. *The Family and Society in Trinidad and Tobago: The Findings of the National Survey of Family Life*. Ministry of Social Development/Institute of Social and Economic Research, University of the West Indies, 1999.

Videos/Films

A Match for Life. 1990. Directed by Roland K. Pirker. MATCH International Film. Provides an overview of MATCH International's work with women's groups on five projects in Trinidad and Tobago.

My Mother's Place. 1983. Directed by Richard Fung. Video Data Bank. A forty-nine-minute film that explores race, class, and gender under colonial rule in Trinidad and Tobago through the eyes of the granddaughter of a Chinese indentured servant.

Tacarigua: A Village in Trinidad and Tobago. 1990. Directed by Daniel Booth and Selwyn Reginald Cudjoe. Educational Television Center, Cornell University, and Calaloux Research Associates. A Cornell University film that depicts normal village life.

Organizations

Canadian Women's Club
PO Box 3351
Maraval
Trinidad

Caribbean Association for Feminist Research and Action
PO Bag 442
Tunapuna Post Office
Tunapuna
Trinidad and Tobago

Feminist communication network.

Caribbean Women's Association
PO Box 49
Basseterre, St. Kitts

Represents thirteen Caribbean women's organizations.

Centre for Gender and Development Studies
University of the West Indies
St. Augustine, Trinidad
Trinidad and Tobago

SELECTED BIBLIOGRAPHY

Antoine, Marlene. "Enhancing the Participation of Women in the Rural Development Process in Trinidad and Tobago." Ph.D. diss., University of the West Indies, St. Augustine, Trinidad, 2000.

Caribbean Community Secretariat. Regional Census Office. *1990–1991 Population Census of the Commonwealth Caribbean, Volume of Basic Tables of Sixteen CARICOM Countries.*

Daly, Stephanie. *The Developing Legal Status of Women in Trinidad and Tobago.* Port of Spain, Trinidad: National Commission on the Status of Women, 1982.

Economic Intelligence Unit. *Country Report: Trinidad and Tobago, 2000.*

Kuboni, Olabisi. "An Assessment of Some Functional Literacy Requirements of Disadvantaged Youth of a Small Developing State." In *Literacy in the Modern World: Proceedings of the Symposium.* Faculty of Education, University of West Indies, St. Augustine: 1992.

Ministry of Health of Trinidad and Tobago and the Pan-American Health Organization/World Health Organization. *Adolescent Health Survey 1998.*

Mohammed, Patricia. *Gender Negotiations among Indians in Trinidad, 1917–1949.* New York: Palgrave Publishing, 2002.

———. *The Women's Movement in Trinidad and Tobago since the 1960s.* Barbados: University of the West Indies, 1995.

Reddock, Rhoda. *Women and Poverty in Trinidad and Tobago.* St. Michael, Barbados: University of the West Indies, 1995.

————. *Women, Labor, and Politics in Trinidad and Tobago*. London: Zed Books, 1994.

Report on the Trinidad and Tobago National Health Survey, 1994–1995. Ministry of Health of Trinidad and Tobago/Central Statistical Office, 1996.

Trinidad and Tobago. Central Statistical Office. Continuous Sample Survey of Population. *Labour Force Report, 1966*. Port of Spain.

————. Central Statistical Office. *Population and Housing Census, 1990*. Vol. ii, *Demographic Report*. Port of Spain.

————. Gender Affairs Division. *National Report on the Status of Women in Trinidad and Tobago*. Prepared for the Fourth World Conference on Women, September 4–15, 1995.

Trinidad and Tobago. Office of the Attorney-General. *Initial, Second, and Third Periodic Report of the Republic of Trinidad and Tobago on the International Convention on the Elimination of All Forms of Discrimination against Women*. December 2000.

United Nations. Department of Economic and Social Affairs. *The World's Women 2000*. New York: 2000.

United Nations Development Programme. *Human Development Report, 2000*. Oxford: Oxford University Press, 2000.

————. *Human Development Report, 2001*. Oxford: Oxford University Press, 2001.

University of the West Indies. *Statistics, 1996/1997*. Mona, Office of Planning, the Vice-Chancellery.

14

THE UNITED STATES

Cheryl Toronto Kalny

PROFILE OF THE UNITED STATES

The United States is a highly technologized, modern society widely considered the dominant economic and military power in the world today. It has a representative form of government with a bicameral legislature. The population is 285,627,004, three-quarters of which lives in urban areas. It is an ethnically diverse nation composed of whites (77.1 percent), blacks (12.9 percent), Asians (4.3 percent), Hispanics (12.5 percent), and Amerindians (1.5 percent). The high life expectancy (averaging seventy-six years), the 97 percent literacy rate, an infant mortality rate of 6.44 deaths per 1,000 live births, and an unemployment rate of 4 percent are indications of a high quality of life enjoyed by Americans.[1]

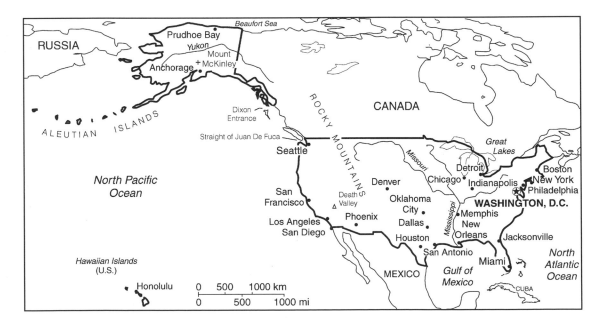

The United States has a diverse and technologically advanced economy that, since World War II, has contributed to the creation of a two-tier labor market. Workers on the bottom tier, many of whom are women and minorities, often fail to receive pay increases, health insurance, and other benefits. While per capita income in the United States is among the highest in the world, averaging $31,500, approximately 13 percent of Americans live below the poverty level.[2]

OVERVIEW OF WOMEN'S ISSUES

As American women entered the twenty-first century, they could reflect upon tremendous advances made in rights and opportunities throughout the twentieth century while also looking forward to more struggles in obtaining full participation and representation in all areas of life. While women had won the right to vote with the passage of the Nineteenth Amendment in 1920, by the end of the twentieth century they made up less than 5 percent of the members of Congress or of state legislatures. After World War II, the numbers and percentage of women participating in the workforce continued to grow, yet a wage gap and glass ceiling remain to deny women full equality in the economic life of the nation. Similarly, by the 1980s, women began to outnumber men in attending institutions of higher learning. More than twenty years later, however, women make up only 27 percent of faculties in the United States, and a woman with a four-year degree can expect to earn roughly the wage of a male with a high-school diploma.[3] These political, economic, and educational inequalities are further magnified for women of color in American society, who earn less than women in general and have lower life expectancy rates and higher infant mortality rates.

EDUCATION

Opportunities

Education for women in the United States has always been race and class based. Oberlin College in Ohio became the first to admit females in the 1830s, but only the daughters of the wealthy could afford to attend it, the coeducational land-grant colleges opened to women by the Morrill Act of 1862, or the elite, private women's colleges such as Radcliffe, Vassar, Smith, and Bryn Mawr founded in the 1860s, 1870s, and 1880s. By 1900, despite the fact that more than 15 percent of all college alumni in the country were female, the traditional professions of the ministry, law, and medicine remained largely closed to women.[4]

Following World War II, despite women's service to the country during the war, they were not eligible for GI benefits. Returning male veterans received tuition grants from the federal government and crowded into colleges throughout the 1950s, while the number of women in college dropped sharply. Although their numbers began to improve in the 1960s, most women students continued to major in "women's" fields such as teaching, social work, and nursing. Not until the 1980s did women outnumber men in institutions of higher learning, and even then, college-educated women continued to swell the ranks of the typically female professions.[5]

Since World War II, greater percentages of the American population have graduated from high school and completed bachelor's degrees. In 1970, 78 percent of Americans finished four years of high school, and 22 percent received a college diploma. By 2000, those percentages had risen to 88 percent and 33 percent, respectively, driven mostly by increases in female enrollments.[6]

Today, while women make up 57 percent of those awarded college diplomas and 35 percent of Ph.D. degrees, this increase in education has not translated into full equality for women either within or outside academia. More than 70 percent of male faculty members in the United States are tenured, compared to 52 percent of female faculty, and women full professors continue to earn approximately 88 percent of what their male colleagues earn. Similarly, outside academia, working women with bachelor's degrees can expect to earn approximately $36,559, while comparable males will earn $51,405.[7]

For minorities, as well, there have been educational gains that have fallen short of full equality. High-school completion rates for minorities in the United States have traditionally lagged considerably behind those for whites by more than 23 percentage points. By 2000, the gap had narrowed to a difference of 7 percentage points.[8]

Literacy

Although the United States enjoys one of the highest literacy rates in the world (97 percent), recent studies have revealed that more than 90 million Americans are functionally illiterate, lacking skills and proficiency in reading, writing, and speaking English. As the volume and variety of written information continue to rapidly increase in the technologically advanced American society, National Adult Literacy Surveys conducted in 1992 and again in 2002 reveal that growing numbers of Americans are unable to integrate and synthesize information from a variety of sources, compare and contrast ideas, or apply sequential arithmetic operations.[9] More than 25 percent of these adults were immigrants still learning the language, another 60 percent had never graduated from high school, and more than 30 percent suffered from physical and mental difficulties that limited their abilities to fully participate in school, work, and society. The association between skills and opportunities is increasingly evident in today's society, where those who scored in the lowest levels on literacy and proficiency tests are far more likely to be part-time, low-wage workers receiving food stamps and living in poverty. The U.S. Department of Labor estimates that more than 50 percent of the unemployed in the United States are functionally illiterate, while the U.S. Department of Education reports that functionally illiterate Americans earn 42 percent less than high-school graduates.[10]

EMPLOYMENT AND ECONOMICS

Job/Career Opportunities

In the twentieth century, women workers in the United States grew steadily in number and as a proportion of the workforce. In 1900, 5.3 million women made up 18 percent of the workforce. By 1950, 18.4 million women made up 30 percent of the workforce. In 2000, 63 million women made up 47 percent of the labor force in the United States.

Telemarketer, United States. Photo © TRIP/J. Greenberg.

Changes in the labor market since World War II, which have steadily shifted the American economy from a manufacturing to a service-industry economy, appear to have favored women workers. In 1960, 30 percent of jobs were in manufacturing, an industry that has traditionally discriminated against women. By 2000, only 14 percent of jobs were in manufacturing. Service-industry jobs today make up four-fifths of all jobs in the United States and account for tremendous job growth for women. Between 1960 and 2000, 4 million jobs for women were added in education, and 6.6 million jobs in health services.[11]

The top ten jobs for women today, according to numbers employed, remain traditional, service-oriented occupations: retail trade, personal services, secretaries, cashiers, nurses, elementary-school teachers, nurses' aides and orderlies, bookkeepers and accountants, receptionists, and cooks. All are heavily female-dominated jobs with wage gaps ranging from 60 percent to 88 percent of what male workers in these jobs earn.[12]

Despite educational advances, women have made little progress breaking into nontraditional "male" jobs. Women today make up only 2.3 percent of construction workers, 3.9 percent of airline pilots, 12 percent of physicists and astronomers, 13 percent of clergy, 16.5 percent of police, and 20 percent of professional athletes in the country.[13]

Pay

One of the enduring characteristics of the labor market in the United States has been the persistent wage gap between men's and women's earnings. In 1980, women workers earned 60 percent of what their male counterparts earned. In 1990, that figure was 71.6 percent, and by 2000 it still hovered around 75 percent. Even at a 25 percent differential, however, it has been estimated that over a lifetime of full-time work, a woman will earn $523,000 less than the average working man.[14] Equal pay remains a consistent demand among working women.

For women of color, this wage gap is even wider. Asian American women earn 67 cents for every dollar earned by men, African American women earn 58 cents, and Hispanic women 48 cents.[15] The Glass Ceiling Commission reported in 1995 that the top leadership positions in American companies remain overwhelmingly male and white. Approximately 95 percent of senior-level managers of Fortune 500 companies are men, and 97 percent are white.[16]

The Equal Pay Act of 1963 was the first legislative recognition of the wage gap that had existed between men and women workers since the nineteenth century. Because of the limitations of that act, which required only equal pay for exactly equal work and failed to include professional and administrative workers, efforts to close the wage gap persisted throughout the remainder of the twentieth century. The concept of "comparable wages" for work that is comparable in skill, effort, and responsibility was recognized in the 1981 Supreme Court case *County of Washington v. Gunther*. The most recent government legislation to address this inequity in wages, the Fair Pay Act, was enacted by Congress in 1994 to prohibit wage discrimination in "equivalent" jobs.

Working Conditions

In 1998, 70 percent of all part-time employees in the United States were women, 55 percent of all workers hired by temporary agencies were women, and 47 percent of multiple-job holders were women. Many of these women were also the sole or primary maintainers of families, earning considerably less than their male coworkers. Approximately 70 percent of working women in 1998 earned less than $25,000.[17] Not coincidentally, female union membership more than doubled in the last decades of the twentieth century. While women represented only 19 percent of membership in the AFL-CIO in 1960, by 1998, 40 percent of that union's rank and file were women. With more than 5.5 million female members, the AFL-CIO is the largest organization of women in the United States, as well as the best chance working women have to address priority issues such as retirement security (28 percent of working women have none); affordable employer-provided health insurance (25 percent of women workers have none); paid family leave (one-third of women do not have paid sick leave); child care (74 percent of women have no child-care benefits from their employers); and equal pay.[18]

Sexual Harassment

A form of aggressive discrimination against women in the workplace, sexual harassment was addressed by the Supreme Court in 1986 in a widely publicized case, *Meritor Savings Bank v. Vinson*. With the *Meritor* decision, conduct that made submission to sex a condition for employment or advancement or that created an "intimidating, hostile, or offensive working environment" was found criminal.[19] What constituted illegal conduct was based on the "reasonable woman" standard set in 1991 by the Ninth Circuit Court of Appeals in *Ellison v. Brady*.

The Equal Employment Opportunity Commission (EEOC) defines sexual harassment as "unwelcome sexual advances, requests for sexual favors, and other verbal or physical conduct of a sexual nature . . . when submission to or rejection of this conduct explicitly or implicitly affects an individual's employment, unreasonably interferes with an individual's work performance, or creates an intimidating, hostile or offensive work environment."[20] In 2000, 15,836 cases of sexual harassment were filed with the EEOC, 86 percent of which were initiated by women. The total costs in monetary benefits from these claims were approximately 55 million dollars.[21] Sexual harassment, its definition, and its prevalence continue to be controversial issues not only in the workplace and on the streets, but also in American schools, where the same types of harassment are found, quid pro quo demands and hostile environment.[22]

Support for Mothers/Caretakers

Much attention and public lip service have been devoted in recent years to the needs of working mothers for flexible schedules to accommodate unexpected emergencies such as sickness, snow days, and absent babysitters that commonly arise in family life. A 2002 study conducted by the Economic Policy Institute suggests that despite such public recognition of this need, gender and racial differences in job flexibility continue to exist in the American workforce.[23] Job flexibility is defined as the ability of workers to determine their arrival and departure times, as well as the ability to decide when to take a day off work. Under this definition, working mothers are actually less likely to experience job flexibility than men, and single mothers have even more rigid work schedules. Black workers are much less likely to exercise any autonomy over their work schedules than white workers.

Furthermore, the study's data on pay and flexibility do not support the prevailing theory of compensating differentials, that is, the belief that workers with more rigid schedules are compensated with higher wages for their sacrifices, and vice versa. Women and minority workers with less flexible schedules also experience lower wages than white males. The study recommends legislative policy changes to redress this discrimination against working mothers, such as statutory numbers of sick days, personal days, and vacation time. The United States is the only Western country that does not require a minimum number of sick days and vacation days. Since blacks and women are less likely to have flexible jobs or equal pay, stricter enforcement of equal-opportunity and affirmative-action laws is also recommended in this study.[24]

Maternal Leave

There are approximately 38 million women between the ages of sixteen and forty in the American workforce. With the passage of the Pregnancy Discrimination Act of 1978, which considered childbirth a "temporary disability," women were typically granted a six-week maternity leave without pay. Studies published in the 1990s, however, raised concerns about the standard six-week leave. While full recovery and resumption of activities commonly required a leave of up to six months, many women returned to work well before then, due mostly to money concerns.[25]

Daycare

Women's groups lobbied the government throughout the 1980s for federal legislation to make daycare more accessible to working mothers. As a result of these efforts, in 1990, Congress created the Childcare and Development Block Grant Program to provide money to the states for childcare programs. These funds were earmarked particularly for those low-income parents who most need assistance. Despite this program, affordable, high-quality daycare remains one of the most pressing problems facing working women today. More than 88 percent of children whose mothers work full-time were enrolled in some form of child-care situation, whether in-home or center based. By 1999, six out of every ten American children under age five—almost 15 million—experienced either full-day or partial-day care on a regular basis each week.[26] Working mothers commonly pay an average of $85 per week for child care, with lower-income earners spending as much as 35 percent of their incomes on child care.[27]

Family and Medical Leave

In 1985, Representative Patricia Schroeder, a Democrat from Colorado, introduced the Family and Medical Leave Act. This proposal guaranteed family and medical leaves for working mothers, as well as paternity leaves for fathers. The bill was passed by Congress in 1990, only to be vetoed by

President George H.W. Bush. President Bill Clinton eventually signed the Family and Medical Leave Act into law in 1993, giving workers up to twelve weeks of unpaid leave to care for a newborn or to assist a family member with a serious health problem. These workers are guaranteed their old job or its equivalent upon return to the workplace.

Inheritance and Property Rights

Throughout most of the eighteenth and nineteenth centuries, American women exercised no control over either the real or personal property they inherited or the children they bore. English common law, as outlined in Blackstone's *Commentaries*, defined a married woman as a femme covert, having no legal identity apart from her husband "under whose wing, protection, and cover she performs everything."[28] Even widows were subject to these laws of coverture. While they were commonly entitled to their "widow's third," their share of property could not be sold or bequeathed without permission of the courts. Coverture began to give way only late in the nineteenth century with the state-by-state passage of married women's property laws, gradually extending women's rights over their property, their earnings, and their own children.

Social/Government Programs

Sustainable Development

In September 2002, the United States participated in the World Summit on Sustainable Development in Johannesburg, South Africa. This summit marked the tenth anniversary of the 1992 Earth Summit held in Rio de Janeiro, Brazil. The United States, through the participation of the Environmental Protection Agency, strongly reaffirmed the Rio principles outlined in the document Agenda 21, referring to the twenty-first century. These principles, identified as priority actions, include safe drinking water, air-pollution control, clean energy, and chemical information exchange. The United States is also a member of the United Nations Commission on Sustainable Development established in 1992 to implement Agenda 21 at local, regional, and international levels. As an industrialized, economically privileged nation, the United States must continue to integrate and prioritize both goals: sustaining economic growth and development along with environmental protection and conservation. Global environmental issues must remain a vital part of U.S. national and foreign policy.[29]

Welfare and Welfare Reform

In 1996, the Personal Responsibility and Work Opportunity Reconciliation Act, commonly called the welfare reform act, imposed a five-year limit on receiving federal welfare benefits and permitted individual states to impose even shorter terms. Studies show that in an economy where 31 million Americans—11.3 percent of the population—are living below the government poverty threshold, most women who have left the welfare rolls since 1996 are working in service jobs in the low end of the labor market, and more than one-third report struggles in providing food for their families and/or paying rent.[30] As of May 2001, more than 3 million families were still registered on the welfare rolls. By the end of 2002, families began reaching the five-year limit imposed in 1996.[31]

FAMILY AND SEXUALITY

Gender Roles

The United States has had a long history of patriarchy, and ample evidence suggests that America today remains a resolutely gendered society. Women exercise little real power or leadership in the arenas of business, politics, law, religion, or the military and continue to be the primary caretakers of the young and the elderly and to spend larger proportions of their time than do men in unpaid domestic work. The persistence of gender stereotypes is a contributing factor in the undervaluing of work done by women and the devaluing of women's achievements. While women have increasingly moved into the paid workforce since World War II, a comparable and complementary shift has not happened in men's participation in domestic work. Women continue to pull a "double shift," coming home from paid work each night to do more than 75 percent of the domestic work, including meal preparation, cleaning, laundry, and child care. It is estimated that mothers average ten hours per day in child care, while fathers average one hour per day of solo child care.[32]

Marriage

Marriage rates in the United States have fallen nearly 30 percent since 1970, while the median age at first marriage, twenty-five years, has increased by one year every decade since 1960. Divorce rates, however, have increased by 40 percent over that same period of time. Between 1970 and 2000, the number of first divorces quadrupled from 4.3 million to 18.5 million. By the millennium's beginning, almost 10 percent of Americans had been divorced at least once. Most will eventually remarry.[33]

The number of people who have never married has also increased since 1970. Today, 22 percent of women between the ages of thirty and thirty-four have never been married, contributing to the increase in the number of single mothers from 3 million in 1960 to 10 million by 2000. One in four American families is headed by a single mother.

Reproduction

Birthrates in the United States have been falling since the baby-boom period following World War II. In the 1950s, the fertility rate was approximately 3.5 births per woman of childbearing age in the population. Today the rate is 1.8 in the general population and 2.5 for minority women. Out-of-wedlock births have continued to increase; by 2000, 33 percent of all births in the nation were out of wedlock.[34]

Sex Education

While sex education classes are taught in virtually every public school in the United States, studies conducted in 2002 by the Kaiser Foundation found that the material presented in these classes varies widely from district to district. Concerning the prevention of teen pregnancy, for example, a third of schools teach that abstinence is the only appropriate behavior for teenagers. Fewer than half the states supply their students with information about obtaining contraceptives, and while HIV/AIDS is mentioned in 95 percent of sex education classes throughout the country, only 37 percent mention abortion, and 36 percent discuss sexual orientation. Schools in southern Bible Belt regions are more reluctant than those in the North to provide a comprehensive sex education curriculum. An abstinence-only policy is adhered to in 55 percent of southern schools, while such a curriculum is featured in about 20 percent of northern schools.[35]

Contraception and Abortion

Women in the United States have struggled for control over their own bodies and reproductive rights since the beginning of the twentieth century. From the Comstock Laws of the 1870s, which classified information about contraception as obscenity, and the formation of Margaret Sanger's Birth Control League in the 1920s to the opening of Planned Parenthood clinics in the 1960s, American women challenged federal and state laws designed to block access to contraception. It took two Supreme Court cases, one in 1965 and another in 1972, to affirm that the constitutional right to privacy included the right of access to birth control.

The fight for abortion rights parallels that of the birth-control movement, but has been even more controversial and bitterly contested since 1900. Throughout the first half of the twentieth century, abortion remained illegal except to save the life of the mother. Women's groups such as the National Organization for Women and the National Association for the Repeal of Abortion Laws lobbied throughout the 1960s to repeal state abortion laws.

As with the birth-control movement, it took a landmark Supreme Court case in 1973, *Roe v. Wade*, to affirm that a woman's right to privacy takes precedence over a state's right to regulate abortions. This ruling invalidated nearly all existing state laws, but it has not stopped state legislatures from continuing to place restrictions on a woman's right to an abortion. In response to an escalation in violence by right-to-life groups in the 1990s, including bombings of clinics and shootings of physicians, Attorney General Janet Reno called for federal legislation to protect women and health-care providers. The Freedom of Access to Clinic Entrances Act passed in 1994, made it a federal crime to block entrances to, or harass employees of, reproductive health clinics. Today birth control and abortion remain among the most controversial topics in the field of women's rights, and are seen to be at risk under the current administration.

Teen Pregnancy

Despite a 22 percent decline in the teen birth rate since 1991, teenage pregnancy remains a serious problem in the United States. A peak rate of 117 pregnancies per 1,000 women aged fifteen to nineteen was recorded in 1991. By 2000, that figure was reduced to 48.5 births per 1,000 among this age group. Despite this, the National Campaign to Prevent Teen Pregnancy reported in 2000 that four out of every ten women—1 million each year—get pregnant before age twenty.[36] This has disastrous consequences for many of these young women and for their children, according to recent findings. Less than one-third of teen mothers complete high school, three-fourths show up on welfare rolls within the first year of motherhood, and 25 percent have another child within twenty-four months of the first birth. Infants of teen mothers have a greater than average chance of being born prematurely and with lower birth weights.[37]

HEALTH

Health Care Access

It is widely believed that the health-care system in the United States is the best in the world. Access to that system, however, has often been determined by race, class, and, to some extent, gender. Historically, infant and maternal mortality rates were highest in minority and immigrant neighborhoods. Even today, Native American life expectancy rates (66 years for men and 74 for women) are lower than national averages (73 and 79.4 years, respectively). Infant mortality rates among black communities in the United States (28 per 1,000 births) are significantly higher than the national average (7.2).[38] Much of this is tied directly to unequal access to, and quality of, health care, which are, in turn, tied to income discrepancies. A woman with a family income of more than $50,000 is twice as likely to get a mammogram as one with an income under $10,000.[39]

Diseases and Disorders

Alcoholism and drug abuse ruin the lives of more than 4 million women in the United States. Death rates are higher among women alcoholics than among men due to increased risks for suicide, accidents, cirrhosis, and hepatitis. Alcohol and drug use by women also make them more vulnerable to violence. Almost 55 percent of rape victims and 50 percent of domestic assault victims report alcohol or drug involvement in their assaults.

Maternal mortality rates have hovered around 8 per 100,000 births since 1980. In the United States, approximately one woman per day dies from a pregnancy-related cause. African American women are four times more likely to die from a pregnancy-related cause even at comparable economic levels.[40]

Perhaps one of the most serious health problems for women in the United States today, however, is not a disease or an illness, but the lack of health insurance. Almost 15 percent of white women have no health insurance, and the numbers for minority women are even higher. More than 23 percent of African American women, 25 percent of Asian American women, and 42 percent of Latino women have no health insurance.[41]

AIDS

By 2002, the Centers for Disease Control estimated that more than 470,000 Americans had died from AIDS and another 800,000 to 900,000 were living with the infection. Today, women represent one in four reported new AIDS cases, resulting in the births of an estimated 1,500 to 2,000 HIV-infected infants each year. More than 47 percent of all reported AIDS cases in the United States are African American, and AIDS is now the second-largest killer of African American women between the ages of twenty-five and forty-four.[42]

Eating Disorders

Anorexia nervosa is a chronic psychiatric condition that affects between 2 and 3 percent of American women, or approximately 7 million girls and young women. Between 10 and 20 percent of these individuals struggling with anorexia will die, making anorexia one of the most lethal mental health conditions. Today, 45 percent of girls as young as age nine report being on diets, and Americans spend more than $40 billion each year on diet products.[43] Excessively thin images of women in media and advertising continue to promote and exacerbate eating disorders such as bulimia and anorexia, already serious social and health problems in the United States today.

Cancer

Breast cancer remains the most common form of cancer among women in the United States, but lung cancer has become the leading killer. In 2000, 41,943 women died from breast cancer, while 63,210 lost their lives to lung cancer. The mortality rate for lung cancer among women has risen 600 percent since 1950, with women accounting for 40 percent of all smoking-related deaths in the United States. The U.S. Surgeon General's Office issued a report in 2001 that since 1981, approximately 3 million American women have died from a smoking-related illness.[44] Studies have suggested that women may, in fact, be genetically at greater risk than men for tobacco-related cancers.[45]

Heart Disease

While the number of cancer-related deaths remains high, heart disease is the number one killer of women in the United States today. The American Medical Association has reported that 43.3 percent of all female deaths occur from cardiovascular disease (CVD), which includes strokes and coronary disease. In 2000, CVD claimed the lives of 502,938 females, while all forms of cancer caused 258,467 female deaths.[46] Risks of developing CVD increase with such factors as age, obesity, and tobacco use. In 2000, more than 40 million women were aged fifty or over, and many of them exceed safe and healthy weight limits, according to the U.S. Centers for Disease Control.[47] More than 50 percent of all women over the age of twenty, approximately 47 million women, are classified as overweight. Another 25 percent, or 23 million women, are considered obese. Among minority groups, percentages are even higher. More than 65 percent of African American women and 66 percent of Mexican American women have health-threatening weight problems.[48]

Despite the fact that cardiovascular disease is the single greatest threat to women's health and lives, it remains largely a hidden threat. Symptoms commonly associated with heart attacks and strokes, such as tightness of chest and arm pain, are male norms of symptomatology. Women may present atypical symptoms that even their physicians often do not recognize. Recent surveys of American women discovered that 90 percent did not recognize nausea, fatigue, dizziness, shortness of breath, jaw, neck, and shoulder pain, or vomiting as symptoms of CVD.[49] This often results in delayed treatment or less vigilant and aggressive treatment.[50] Each year, 40,000 more women than men die from strokes and coronary disease.

Depression

More than 12 percent of American women, compared to 6 percent of men, suffer from clinical depression sometime during their lives. Reasons for this significant gender difference are being researched, and early findings point to such factors as differences in stress levels in the lives of modern men and women, and in serotonin synthesis levels in the brains of men and women.[51] The advent of antidepressants, coupled with psychotherapy, provides relief for approximately 80 percent of sufferers today.

POLITICS AND LAW

The fight for women's political and legal rights in the United States began early in the nineteenth century and was rooted in the evangelical and volunteer associations of middle- and upper-class women. Bound by the strictures of the "domestic code" that barred women from paid labor and restricted them to hearth and home, women of means formed benevolent societies to combat a host of social and moral ills confronting an increasingly urban, industrial America. Several decades of moral and public crusades waged by organizations of women on behalf of orphans, prostitutes, and the poor culminated in women's active participation in the abolitionist movement that took shape in the 1830s. Abolitionist women honed their public-speaking skills and their courage, stumping the country for more than twenty years, addressing often hostile crowds. They forged under fire an absolute dedication to cause, and equally as important, they also learned the political necessity of bridge building. All of these lessons proved invaluable when women in the United States began to organize for their own rights in the middle of the nineteenth century.[52]

Suffrage

The first women's rights convention was called in 1848 at Seneca Falls, New York. It was organized by a coalition of women who were already experienced in the abolitionist, temperance, and property-law-reform movements. Their initial meeting produced a Declaration of Sentiments that outlined the major initiatives that would occupy activist women into the next century: higher education for women, entrance into the trades and professions, custody and property rights, and suffrage. Many came to believe, in the decades after Seneca Falls, that winning the vote was the key to rectifying the whole complex of social and institutional oppressions that limited women's lives. It took seventy years of ceaseless struggle, and a world war, to produce a federal constitutional amendment, the Nineteenth, which granted women the right to vote in 1920.

Political Participation

Throughout most of the twentieth century, women made up less than 5 percent of the members of Congress or of state legislatures. Publicized as the Year of the Woman, 1992 galvanized female candidates, who won an unprecedented 108 seats in the House and 11 Senate positions. By the end of the century, women made up 11 percent of the U.S. Congress and held 25 percent of elective state offices. To encourage and assist women candidates, female political action committees formed in the late 1980s. EMILY's List was formed in 1985 as a political network for pro-choice Democratic women candidates. EMILY stands for "Early Money Is Like Yeast." In the 2000 elections, EMILY's List supplied early seed money in $100 amounts to women's campaigns, totaling about $9.3 million. Since 1985, EMILY's List has helped elect eleven Democratic women senators, fifty-four congresswomen, and seven governors.[53] The National Organization for Women's Political Action Committee draws on the support and resources of the largest grassroots feminist organization in the country and endorses candidates at every level of government based on a broad feminist agenda including reproductive rights, support for lesbian and gay rights, affirmative action, and ending violence against women.[54] Women in the Senate and House (WISH) List, the Republican counterpart to EMILY's List, is a national political network created in 1992 to raise funds for Republican pro-choice women candidates. Since 1992, it has directed more than $2 million in contributions toward a threefold increase in the number of pro-choice Republican women in the U.S. Senate and more than a 50 percent increase in the House.[55] The Republican Network to Elect Women also contributes seed monies to help finance the campaigns of women on the local, state, and national levels. The success of women and family-friendly legislation will depend on increasing the proportion of women in elective offices at every level.

Gender differences have been noted between men and women voters on such issues as war, the environment, gun control, national health care, and racial discrimination, with women consistently supporting more liberal positions.[56] Moreover, in the last decades of the twentieth century, women voters in the United States were twice as likely as men to vote for Democratic candidates, except in cases where female Republican candidates were supportive of social programs or women's issues.

Women's Rights

By definition, women's rights are human rights. The rights enunciated in the Declaration of Sentiments adopted in 1848 at the first U.S. women's rights convention, namely, women's right to a political voice, to an equal marriage, to own property, and to equal educational and economic opportunities, are the same rights proclaimed exactly 100 years later in the Universal Declaration of Human Rights adopted by the United Nations General Assembly in 1948. Generations of American women in the past have fought to advance these rights and have accomplished tremendous gains for the women of today, many of whom erroneously believe that the battle is long over. Glass ceilings continue to exist, however, throughout the workplace, women's images in the print and electronic media continue to be distorted and objectified, growing levels of violence threaten and limit women's public and private lives, and many minority women remain on the bottom rungs of nearly every ladder of opportunity in U.S. society. Ultimately, the future of the women's rights movement in the United States will depend on its ability to unite a movement historically divided along race and class lines and to redefine the movement to appeal to a new generation of women.

Feminist Movements

The first women's rights movements formed as a result of the first women's rights convention in 1848 at Seneca Falls, New York. Two feminist movements, the American Woman Suffrage Movement and the National Woman Suffrage Association, differed substantially over methodology and ideology. The American favored state-by-state referendums on woman suffrage, retained ties with Republican supporters, and invited male board membership. The smaller, more radical National worked for a federal suffrage amendment and would not allow males to hold leadership positions in the organization. The suffrage movement remained divided and unsuccessful until the two organizations merged in 1890 and formed the National American Woman Suffrage Association (NAWSA). This new organization intensified state campaigns and forged critical links with other women's groups, most notably with the larger Woman's Christian Temperance Union.[57]

Once the female suffrage amendment was ratified, however, with the passage of the Nineteenth Amendment in 1920, the women's rights movement again split into opposing factions. The NAWSA was reborn as the League of Women Voters, whose goals to educate voters on issues and candidates and to support legislation friendly to women and children have remained constant since 1920. A smaller group, the National Woman's Party, proposed an Equal Rights Amendment (ERA) to the Constitution in 1923. Its brief document asserting that "men and women shall have equal rights throughout the United States" was designed to combat discriminatory state laws and to erase sex as a legal classification.[58] To date, despite intensive efforts by feminist groups, the ERA has not been ratified.

The birth-control movement in the United States was almost single-handedly founded by a public health nurse in New York City in 1914, Margaret Sanger. Sanger and her Birth Control League disseminated birth-control information through the postal system in a monthly magazine, the *Woman Rebel*. In 1916, Sanger opened the first birth-control clinic in a working-class neighborhood in Brooklyn, and by the 1920s, Sanger's American Birth Control League had forged an alliance with physicians, who were the sole dispensers of birth control, and with the American Medical Association, which endorsed contraception to "cure or prevent disease."[59]

Today's Planned Parenthood is a direct descendant of Sanger's early birth-control movement.

The National Organization for Women (NOW) was founded in 1967 after almost a decade of women's participation in various other civil rights and student organizations. The immediate spur to the creation of a new women's movement, however, was the passage of the Civil Rights Act of 1964. Title VII of this historic act contained a provision against sex discrimination in employment and established the Equal Employment Opportunity Commission (EEOC) to handle sex-discrimination grievances. By 1966, however, the EEOC had become inundated with cases and favored race-discrimination and class-action complaints over the cases of individual women. NOW was formed as a political pressure group to press for "a fully equal partnership of the sexes" at home and in the workplace.[60] Today, NOW is the largest feminist organization in the United States, with national headquarters in Washington, D.C., and state and local chapters throughout the country.

Lesbian Rights

Lesbians have figured prominently in the second wave of the women's rights movement since the 1960s, actively working to gain legal recognition of same-sex marriages, for the passage of domestic partnership laws, and for changes in adoption rights. In 1998, President Clinton issued Executive Order 13087 reaffirming government policy that prohibits discrimination in the hiring and promotion of federal employees and adding sexual orientation to the list of protected categories that already included race, color, religion, sex, national origin, handicap, and age. As of January 1, 2002, a California state law allows same-sex couples to register with the state as domestic partners. Such registration provides a couple with legal rights such as access to family health, dental, and life insurance.

Marriage and Parenthood. Only Vermont has recognized the legality of same-sex civil unions. The lack of legal recognition of same-sex unions in any form in most states poses significant problems for couples who want to bear children through artificial insemination or to adopt children. Many states prohibit the placement of children in lesbian homes, and many physicians continue to deny them in vitro services.[61]

Military Service

In 1973, the male military draft ended and the all-volunteer force began. Female participation in the military rose from 1.6 percent in 1973 to more than 10 percent by the end of the 1990s. The air force has the greatest number of women in the U.S. military, with almost 80,000 women serving as enlisted personnel. The army and navy have similar female participation rates, with women making up approximately 15 percent of enlistments in both branches of the service. The U.S. Marines, however, seem still to be looking for "a few good men," with the result that only about 10,000 women currently serve in that branch of the armed forces. Today, almost 49 percent of all women in the military are minority women.[62]

Discrimination against and harassment of females in the military have remained concerns since the Tailhook Convention scandal became public in 1991. The navy pilots' thirty-fifth annual convention that year resulted in 83 women reporting sexual assaults and harassment, implicating 117 naval officers, and faulting navy leaders for failing to stop such conduct. The fallout from these charges ended or damaged the careers of 14 admirals and almost 300 aviators. Thereafter, the secretary of the navy announced a zero-tolerance policy regarding harassment and intimidation in the U.S. Navy.[63]

RELIGION AND SPIRITUALITY

From the beginning, the United States has guaranteed not only freedom of religion as one of the basic rights of every American, but freedom from religion as well. While religious diversity remains a fundamental aspect of American society, with virtually every world religion finding a following in America, more than a million Americans feel free to profess atheism. The United States is a largely Christian nation, with Roman Catholics making up 25 percent of the population and Protestants 28 percent. In addition, more than 6 million Americans are Jewish, about an equal number are Muslims, and 3 million are Buddhists.[64]

Historically, tension has always existed in the United States over the doctrine of the separation of church and state. Issues of interpretation of this doctrine continue to be hotly debated in a number of churches. The practice of mandatory closing of businesses on Sunday/Sabbath dates back to the Virginia colony in the 1600s, but the legality of this practice was still being considered by the U.S. Supreme Court in the late twentieth century as in the case of the *Estate of Thornton v. Calder* in 1985. In the *Estate of Thornton v. Calder*, the U.S. Supreme Court declared Sunday closing laws unconstitutional on the grounds that the laws had the direct effect of advancing a particular religious practice. Fundamentalist Mormons continue to practice polygamy, believing this legacy of Joseph Smith to be above and beyond the purview of the law. Perhaps the most hotly contested issue surrounding separation of church and state, however, is that of prayer in public schools. Despite fundamentalist challenges, the Supreme Court has ruled from the first case, *Engel v. Vitale* in 1962, to the most recent case in 2000, *Santa Fe School District v. Doe*, that including prayer as a part of school functions and activities is an unconstitutional breach of the separation of church and state.[65]

Women's Roles

Women have always made up the majority of congregations and the largest group of participants and volunteers in mainstream churches in the United States. Until late in the twentieth century, however, women were barred from leadership roles in American churches. Not until the 1980s (United Methodist) and 1990s (Anglican and Episcopal) did Protestant churches begin ordaining women. At the start of the twenty-first century, more than 1,000 women were serving as ordained ministers in the Southern Baptist Convention, and more than a dozen women as bishops in the Methodist Church. Today, women make up 5 percent of Protestant senior pastors (United Methodist Church).[66]

Despite these advances, however, women clergy continue to face discrimination within the very churches they serve. A 2000 study reported significant salary discrepancies between male and female clergy within the Methodist Church and an exodus of ordained women from the ministry due to "the pettiness, the patriarchy, and the pressures of ministry."[67] Similarly, the 2001 Profile of Protestant Pastors reveals not only compensation differences between male and female pastors, but differences in educational levels (86 percent of female pastors were seminary trained, compared to 60 percent of male pastors), in theological orientation (40 percent of females described themselves as theologically liberal, compared to 10 percent of male pastors), and in divorce rates (twice as many female pastors were divorced, 31 percent, as male, 12 percent).[68] The Roman Catholic Church continues to bar women from ordination.

By the late twentieth century, women had found diverse and informal ways of exercising leadership roles in American churches. The most visible and publicized example of this was the proliferation of female televangelists. Some of these television preachers were in public ministries with their husbands, playing supportive roles. Jim and Tammy Faye Bakker were early forerunners of this type with their enormously popular and financially rewarding televised Praise the Lord Club. Other women, however, have since established themselves at the head of ministerial empires reaching out weekly through televised programs to large audiences around the country. In the tradition of itinerant preachers of earlier centuries, these female preachers also regularly stump the country, packing convention halls and amphitheaters—the contemporary equivalent of the old tent revival meetings.

VIOLENCE

During the last decades of the twentieth century, Americans became increasingly aware of and concerned about the rising level of physical and sexual violence that threatened women in their private as well as public lives. Feminists began to draw direct correlations between the violence against women depicted throughout the culture in magazines, movies, and advertising and the epidemic of rapes and domestic battering perpetrated in society.[69] Particularly targeted was the billion-dollar pornography industry, which continues to be protected under freedom of speech, despite the growing belief that "pornography is the theory; rape is the practice."[70]

Violence against women in American society reached such a crescendo in the 1990s that the FBI declared it at epidemic proportions. More than 600,000 assaults are reported each year, with approximately 200,000 of them serious enough to require hospitalization.[71] Low-income and minority women are disproportionately the victims of assault and rape.

Domestic Violence

Approximately 1,500 women each year are killed by husbands and boyfriends. Almost 20 percent of pregnant women report being battered. Domestic violence rates are more than five times higher among families living below poverty levels. One in four women can expect to be beaten by their partners at some point in their relationships. More than 35 percent of women who are treated each year in emergency rooms across America are there as victims of domestic violence. Women today are more than twice as likely to be murdered by a spouse as by a stranger.[72]

Because of statistics such as these, the Violence against Women Act (VAWA) was passed by Congress in 1994. This law instituted mandatory arrest policies and allocated $1.8 billion to address issues of violence against women. Individual states can apply for federal grant money to fund shelters, hot lines, and community education programs. The U.S. Justice Department created the Violence against Women Office in 1995 to fully implement the act. The 2000 VAWA continues the commitment of the government to end the violence, strengthens federal laws against domestic violence, stalking, and sexual assault, and administers more than $270 million annually in grants to states and communities.

Rape/Sexual Assault

Each year an estimated 2 million rapes and 6 million physical assaults against women are reported in the United States, but the Justice Department estimates that 70 percent of sexual assaults are never reported. To address this serious issue of societal violence aimed at women of all ages, races, and income levels, Services, Training, Officers, and Prosecutors (STOP) grants were instituted in the 1990s to provide these resources to communities across the country. STOP grants are federal funds available to states to develop and improve law-enforcement efforts, prosecution success rates, and services to help women victims of abuse and assault. Despite initial difficulties in distributing funds equally and in expanding services to all underserved communities in the country, by the end of the 1990s, it appeared that the STOP program was having measurable success in helping to stem the tide of violence against women.[73]

Further headway was made in 1996, when gender was added as a category to hate-crimes legislation. Now, crimes that are racially or religiously motivated or that specifically target women or the disabled may qualify offenders for penalty enhancements due to the special nature of their crimes. Violence against women remains a pervasive and deeply troubling issue in American society today.

Trafficking in Women and Children

The U.S. Attorney General's Office estimates that more than 50,000 women and children are trafficked into the United States from other parts of the world each year. Both the George W. Bush administration and the former Clinton administrations have taken strong steps to address this issue and to stop the trafficking in female bodies. The Anti-Trafficking in Persons Act of 1999 attacked the problem with a three-part strategy: stepping up the prosecution of traffickers, protecting and supporting victims, and working to prevent trafficking. The United States also introduced and supported a United Nations protocol that would require countries everywhere to criminalize trafficking.

The Trafficking Victims Protection Act, introduced by the Clinton administration and passed by Congress in 2000, launched a new visa system for victims of trafficking. The new T visa would enable victims to apply for permanent residency in the United States. They and their families would also qualify for nonimmigrant status.[74]

OUTLOOK FOR THE TWENTY-FIRST CENTURY

During the twentieth century, women in the United States were successful in their fight to win the vote, participate in a wage economy, receive an education, and create legal identities with rights of their own. In no arena, however, whether legal, political, economic, or social, do women enjoy full equality today. It remains for the next generations of American women to close the gaps that still exist between men's and women's opportunities and rewards, to claim a more equal representation and voice not only in their own local communities, but in the power circles of the nation as well, to confront and deconstruct the damaging stereotypes and publicized images that continue to harm women, and to do all of this while retaining the distinctive values and perspectives that have defined women everywhere at every time. Women in the United States in the twenty-first century will continue to build on the efforts and successes of all those who have participated before them in the longest-lasting and most far-reaching civil and human rights movement in U.S. history.

NOTES

1. U.S. Census Bureau, "Demographics," 2000, www.census.gov.

2. U.S. Census Bureau, "Demographics," 2000, www.census.gov.

3. Hilary M. Lips, "Women, Education, and Economic Participation," 1999, 9, www.runet.edu/gstudies/sources/nz/keyecon.htm.

4. Miriam Chamberlain, ed., *Women in Academe: Progress and Prospects* (New York: Russell Sage Foundation, 1988), 3–6.

5. Barbara Miller Solomon, *In the Company of Educated Women* (New Haven, CT: Yale University Press, 1985).

6. U.S. Census Bureau, 2000.

7. American Association of University Women, 2001, www.aauw.org/.

8. U.S. Census Bureau, 2000, www.census.gov.

9. National Adult Literacy Surveys, www.nces.ed.gov.

10. U.S. Department of Labor, www.dol.gov.

11. Ibid.

12. Ibid.

13. U.S. Department of Labor, Women's Bureau, 2001, www.dol.gov.

14. Ibid.

15. Lips, 1999, 2.

16. Ibid., 4–5.

17. AFL-CIO, 2000, http://www.aflcio.org/search/index.htm.

18. Ibid.

19. Nancy Woloch, *Women and the American Experience* (New York: McGraw-Hill, 1996), 366.

20. Equal Employment Opportunity Commission, www.eeoc.gov.

21. U.S. Department of Labor, www.dol.gov/wb.

22. U.S. Department of Education, www.ed.gov.

23. Elaine McCrate, "Working Mothers in a Double Bind," May 2002, www.epinet.org/briefingpapers.

24. Ibid., 1–20.

25. Jillian Dickert, "Making Family Leave More Affordable in Massachusetts," Research conducted at the University of Massachusetts, August 1999, www.umb.edu/research.

26. National Center for Education Statistics, 2002, www.nces.ed.gov.

27. U.S. Department of Health and Human Services, 2001, www.os.dhhs.gov.

28. Woloch, 1996, 46.

29. U.S. Environmental Protection Agency, International Affairs, World Summit on Sustainable Development, www.epa.gov/international/WSSD.

30. Brauner and Loprest, "Where Are They Now? What State's Studies of People Who Left Welfare Tell Us," May 1999, www.urban.org/url.cfm?ID-309065.

31. U.S. Department of Health and Human Services, 2001, www.os.dhhs.gov.

32. Lips, 1999, 5–6.

33. U.S. Census Bureau, 2000.

34. Ibid.

35. "Sex Education in America: A View from Inside the Nation's Classrooms," Henry J. Kaiser Family Foundation Study, September 2002, http://www.kff.org.

36. National Campaign to Prevent Teen Pregnancy, 2001, http://campaign@teenpregnancy.org.

37. U.S. Department of Health and Human Services, 2001, www.os.dhhs.gov.

38. U.S. Census Bureau, 2000.

39. National Cancer Institute, 2001, http://cancernet.nci.nhi.gov/pdg.htm.

40. UN Development Fund for Women, 2001, www.unifem.undp.org.

41. National Black Women's Health Project, www.blackwomenshealth.org/.

42. Centers for Disease Control, www.cdc.gov/hiv/pubs/faq/faq13.html.

43. National Association of Anorexia Nervosa and Associated Disorders, www.anad.org.

44. United States Surgeon General's Office, *Women and Smoking Report*, 2001, www.ussgo.gov.

45. National Cancer Institute, 2000, www.nci.org.

46. *Journal of the American Medical Association*, 1999, www.jama-assn.org.

47. Zheng Zhi-Jie, Women and Heart Disease Study, Centers for Disease Control and Prevention, 1996, http://cdc.gov.

48. *Journal of the American Medical Association*, 1999.

49. "Cardiovascular Disease in Women," www.pathoplus.com/cvdwomen/html.

50. Centers for Disease Control, www.cdc.gov.

51. Bhatia and Bhatia, "Depression in Women: Diagnostic Treatment Considerations," *American Family Physician*, July 1999, www.findarticles.com/cf-dis/M3225/pl/article.html.

52. Cheryl Toronto Kalny, "United States: The Great Work before Us," in *Women's Rights: A Global View*, ed. Lynn Walter, 184–85 (Westport, CT: Greenwood Press, 2001).

53. EMILY's List (Early Money Is Like Yeast), www.emilyslist.org.

54. National Organization for Women Political Action Committee, www.nowpacs.org.

55. Women in the Senate and House (WISH), www.thewishlist.org.

56. Nancy E. McGlen and Karen O'Connor, *Women, Politics and American Society*, 2nd ed. (Upper Saddle River, NJ: Prentice Hall, 1998), 68–71.

57. Kalny, 2001, 192.

58. Christine Lunardini, *From Equal Suffrage to Equal Rights: Alice Paul and the National Woman's Party, 1910–1928* (New York: New York University Press, 1986).

59. Sara M. Evans, *Born for Liberty* (New York: Free Press, 1989), 227.

60. Kalny, 2001, 190.

61. McGlen and O'Connor, 1998, 219–220.

62. U.S. Department of Defense.

63. "U.S. Navy Sexual Harassment Policy Statement," www.navy.mil/policy1.html.

64. U.S. Religious Affiliation Pew Research Council, 2000, www.adherents.com/rel_USA.html.

65. www.religioustolerance.org/constitution.

66. "The Status of Female Ordination in America," www.religioustolerance.org/femelroy.html.

67. General Commission on the Status and Role of Women, 2000, http://gcsrw.org.

68. Ibid.

69. Catherine A. MacKinnon, *Only Words* (Cambridge, MA: Harvard University Press, 1994).

70. Ibid.

71. Intimate Partner Violence, 1993–2001, www.sip.usdoj.gov.vawo/statistic.html.

72. McGlen and O'Connor, 1998, 250–253.
73. U.S. Department of Justice.
74. Ibid.

RESOURCE GUIDE

Suggested Reading

Baxandall, Rosalyn, and Linda Gordon, eds. *America's Working Women: A Documentary History, 1600 to the Present*. New York: W.W. Norton, 1995.

Collins, Patricia Hill. *Black Feminist Thought: Knowledge, Consciousness, and the Politics of Empowerment*. Rev. ed. New York: Routledge, 2000.

Cott, Nancy F. *The Grounding of Modern Feminism*. New Haven, CT: Yale University Press, 1987.

Evans, Sara M. *Born for Liberty*. New York: Free Press, 1989.

Flexner, Eleanor. *Century of Struggle: The Woman's Rights Movement in the United States*. Rev. ed. Cambridge, MA: Belknap Press of Harvard University Press, 1975.

Hochschild, Arlie. *The Second Shift*. New York: Viking Press, 1989.

Kessler-Harris, Alice. *Out to Work: A History of Wage-Earning Women in the United States*. New York: Oxford University Press, 1982.

———. *Women Have Always Worked*. Old Westbury, NY: Feminist Press, 1981.

MacKinnon, Catharine A. *Only Words*. Cambridge, MA: Harvard University Press, 1994.

McGlen, Nancy E., and Karen O'Connor. *Women, Politics, and American Society*. 2nd ed. Upper Saddle River, NJ: Prentice Hall, 1998.

Norton, Mary Beth, ed. *Major Problems in American Women's History*. Lexington, MA: D.C. Heath, 1989.

Takaki, Ronald T. *Strangers from a Different Shore: A History of Asian Americans*. Rev. ed. Boston: Little, Brown and Company, 1998.

Walter, Lynn, ed. *Women's Rights: A Global View*. Westport, CT: Greenwood Press, 2001.

Videos/Films

Between the Lines. 2001. Directed by Yunah Hong. Women Make Movies. Documentary that examines the lives of Asian American women.

Not for Ourselves Alone: The Story of Elizabeth Cady Stanton and Susan B. Anthony. 1999. PBS. Examines the lives of America's leading suffrage organizers.

Ribbons of the Osage. 1999. Full Circle Videos. Highlights three generations of Osage history and traditions.

Shattering the Silences: The Case for Minority Faculty. 1997. California Newsreel. Interviews with eight pioneering scholars who narrate their experiences on college campuses today.

Still Killing Us Softly: Advertising Images of Women. 1990. Cambridge Documentary Films. Examines the images of women used by advertisers to sell products, as well as the potential impact of these images on young women.

Web Sites

Feminist Majority Foundation Online, www.feminist.org/.
Provides feminist news on a variety of topics nationally and internationally.

Lesbian.Org, www.lesbian.org/.
Provides links to a variety of sites, including Lesbian Mothers Support Groups, Lesbian History Project, and Matrices Newsletter.

National Organization for Women, www.now.org.

National Women's Health Information Center, www.4woman.gov/.
A branch of the U.S. Department of Health and Human Services that provides a gateway to federal and private-sector health information resources.

Women's Bureau of the Department of Labor, www.dol.gov/dol/wb.
The federal government agency that provides local, regional, and national information about women in the U.S. workforce.

Women's Health Interactive, http://womens-health.com.
Provides health information and resources for women on key health concerns from nutrition to breast cancer.

Women's Resources on the Net, www.wic.org/misc/resource.htm.
An alphabetical listing of links encompassing a diverse range of topics and issues.

Women's Studies Database, www.womensstudies.umd.edu/.
Maintained by the University of Maryland, the database provides links on a variety of women's studies programs and issues.

Organizations

American Association of University Women
1111 Sixteenth Street NW
Washington, DC 20036
Phone: 800-326-AAUW
Fax: 200-872-1425
Email: info@aauw.org
Web site: www.aauw.org/

A national organization that promotes education and equity for all women and girls. Its Education Foundation funds pioneering research, while its Legal Advocacy Fund provides funds for women seeking legal redress for sex discrimination in higher education.

American Medical Women's Association
801 N. Fairfax Street Suite 400
Alexandria, VA 22314
Phone: 703-838-0500
Fax: 703-549-3864

Email: info@amwa_doc.org
Web site: www.amwa-doc.org/

An organization founded in 1915 and today made up of more than 10,000 women physicians and medical students dedicated to the advancement of women's health and of women in medicine.

League of Women Voters
1730 M. Street NW
Suite 1000
Washington, DC 20036
Phone: 202-429-1965
Fax: 202-429-0854
Email: lwv@lwv.org
Web site: www.lwv.org/

A nonpartisan political organization formed out of the suffrage movement in 1920 that encourages informed and active participation of citizens in government and seeks to influence public policy through education and advocacy.

National Black Women's Health Project
600 Pennsylvania Ave. SE
Suite 310
Washington, DC 20003
Phone: 202-548-4000
Fax: 202-543-9743
Email: nbwhp@nbwhp.org
Web site: www.blackwomenshealth.org/

An advocacy group founded in 1983 and devoted to improvement in the health of black women and girls through research, education, and empowerment.

National Organization for Women
733 15th Street NW
Second Floor
Washington, DC 20005
Phone: 202-628-8669
Fax: 202-785-8576
Email: now@now.org
Web site: www.now.org/

The largest organization of feminist activists in the United States, with more than 550 chapters in all fifty states. Founded in 1966 to take action to bring about equality for women.

National Women's Political Caucus
1634 Eye Street NW
Suite 310
Washington, DC 20006
Phone: 202-785-1100
Fax: 202-785-3605
Email: info@nwpc.org
Web site: www.nwpc.org/

Founded in 1971 as a grassroots organization whose goal is to increase the number of pro-choice women in elected office regardless of political affiliation.

United Nations Development Fund for Women
304 E. 45th Street
15th Floor
New York, NY 10017
Phone: 212-906-6400
Fax: 212-906-6705
Email: unifem@undp.org
Web site: www.unifem.undp.org/

Provides financial and technical assistance to programs that promote women's human rights.

SELECTED BIBLIOGRAPHY

Chamberlain, Miriam, ed. *Women in Academe: Progress and Prospects*. New York: Russell Sage Foundation, 1988.

Cott, Nancy F. *The Bonds of Womanhood*. New Haven, CT: Yale University Press, 1977.

Crow Dog, Mary, and Richard Erdoes. *Lakota Woman*. New York: Harper, 1991.

Goldberg, Gertrude Schaffner, and Eleanor Kremen. *The Feminization of Poverty*. New York: Praeger, 1990.

Kalny, Cheryl Toronto. "United States: The Great Work before Us." In *Women's Rights: A Global View*, ed. Lynn Walter, 183–97. Westport, CT: Greenwood Press, 2001.

Langley, Winston E., and Vivian C. Fox. *Women's Rights in the United States: A Documentary History*. Westport, CT: Greenwood Press, 1994.

Lips, Hilary M. "Women, Education, and Economic Participation," 1999, www.runet.edu/gstudies/sources/nz/keyecon.htm.

MacKinnon, Catharine A. *Sexual Harassment of Working Women*. New Haven, CT: Yale University Press, 1979.

Sidel, Ruth. *Keeping Women and Children Last*. New York: Penguin Books, 1996.

Weddington, Sarah. *A Question of Choice*. New York: Penguin Books, 1993.

INDEX